# Reversing Urban Decline

Why and How Sports, Entertainment,
and Culture Turn Cities
into Major League Winners

Second Edition

# Reversing Urban Decline

Why and How Sports, Entertainment,
and Culture Turn Cities
into Major League Winners

## Second Edition

## Mark S. Rosentraub

**CRC Press**
Taylor & Francis Group
Boca Raton  London  New York

CRC Press is an imprint of the
Taylor & Francis Group, an **informa** business

CRC Press
Taylor & Francis Group
6000 Broken Sound Parkway NW, Suite 300
Boca Raton, FL 33487-2742

© 2014 by Mark S. Rosentraub
CRC Press is an imprint of Taylor & Francis Group, an Informa business

No claim to original U.S. Government works

Printed on acid-free paper
Version Date: 20140609

International Standard Book Number-13: 978-1-4822-0621-0 (Hardback)

---

**Library of Congress Cataloging-in-Publication Data**

---

Rosentraub, Mark S., 1950-
 Reversing urban decline : why and how sports, entertainment, and culture turn cities into major league winners / Mark S. Rosentraub.
  pages cm.
 Includes bibliographical references and index.
 ISBN 978-1-4822-0621-0
 1. Sports--Economic aspects. 2. Amusements--Economic aspects. 3. Urban policy. I. Title.

GV217.R67 2015
338.47796--dc23                                                             2014005664

---

**Visit the Taylor & Francis Web site at**
**http://www.taylorandfrancis.com**

**and the CRC Press Web site at**
**http://www.crcpress.com**

# Contents

# Preface

The "coin of the realm" for decades among independent and academic policy analysts, myself included, was that public sector investments in arenas, ballparks, and stadia, to attract and retain professional sports teams, were very poor decisions. We concluded that when mayors, county officials, or governors chased professional sports teams, they were either poorly informed or focused on advancing the interests of local economic elites and team owners. Independent policy analysts could find no empirical evidence that teams and the venues they used improved regional economies.

The guidance we offered to communities seems to have been underscored again by the financial problems and issues involved with a publicly financed arena in Glendale, Arizona—which celebrated its 10th anniversary as home to the Arizona (née Phoenix) Coyotes in early 2014. Jobing.Com Arena in Glendale and the nearby real estate development have failed to produce the tax revenues needed to repay the bonds sold by Glendale to finance the city's investment in the venue. But the shortfall in needed funds for the bond payments does not begin to identify Glendale's financial risks and losses.

The Coyotes had to seek bankruptcy protection, and for several years the National Hockey League operated the franchise. The team and the arena's finances were so dismal that it took almost 3 years to find investors willing to purchase the team and operate the venue. The group of investors that finally bought the team did so only after Glendale agreed to provide $15 million of additional financial support *each year* through 2028. The team could pay as much as $9 million in fees to Glendale from arena operations, reducing the city's new investment to, perhaps, an estimated $6 million. That annual investment, of course, is in addition to the payments that still remain on the bonds sold to build the arena. This outcome and the dozens of articles and books published in the 1990s seem to be stern and reoccurring warnings against public subsidies for sports venues.

This stark reality raises obvious questions with the need, value, and contribution this book could make. First, is a second and substantially revised version of a book that claimed cities could *financially* benefit from sports venues (and cultural centers) needed and unbiased? Second, is it not a tad audacious to put forward an idea (and title) that suggests sports venues could revitalize cities? Third, are public–private partnerships for the building and maintenance of sports venues still code words for subsidies to team owners, a city's economic elite, and even highly paid professional athletes?

My students and academic colleagues often ask me these questions. And many want to know why I changed my mind about how sports venues can be valuable and what sort of public–private partnerships make financial sense for cities 14 or 15 years since the publication of *Major League Losers: The Real Cost of Sports and Who's Paying for It?* In that book I argued public sector investments in sports venues were *poor public policy decisions* that were, at best, efforts to placate urban elites.

Have I sold out or gone over to the "dark side"? I think not.

In response to the first question, I remind colleagues and students that the decentralization of economic activity in every urban region has so dramatically accelerated across the past few decades that the financial viability of most central cities is currently threatened. As higher-income people and businesses locate away from central cities and live and work in suburban and exurban communities, what results is a form of economic segregation that can cripple the financial ability of central cities to deliver needed public services to the remaining residents and businesses. Simply put, and as noted by many, the increasing decentralization of economic activity into suburban areas had led to high levels of economic segregation and the concentration of lower-income households in central cities. In addition, those central cities that are suffering the loss of businesses and wealthier households to suburban areas cannot change their boundaries to capture the taxes paid by higher-income suburbanites and businesses. As a result, declining central cities have insufficient tax revenues to pay for the public services needed by their remaining residents (who cannot afford to pay higher taxes). The weakening of central cities' tax bases would not be a problem if suburban cities, nearby counties, the state, or the federal government agreed to share more of their revenues with central cities. But they don't.

So, how does a city attract or deflect regional economic activity back into its taxing borders? What activity attracts a large number of visitors each and every year and is also an activity that suburban cities cannot duplicate or also offer? The answer to that question is professional sports. Let me explain.

Cities tried festival marketplaces as a way to bring economic activity back into central cities long after the classical downtown department stores had closed their doors. But those efforts were easily duplicated by suburban cities. Some central cities tried to popularize their downtown areas without changing the mix of amenities, but those efforts were also duplicated as suburban cities built or renovated their own town centers or developers built lifestyle retail centers that offered an antiseptic if "faux downtown," replicating the childhood memories of what going downtown meant to families. Now it was possible for younger families to give their children a feeling of a trip downtown in their suburban communities and disconnect themselves from central cities that were increasingly home to lower-income households.

In the midst of all of these dynamic changes, what asset continues to attract people and cannot be duplicated? The answer is professional sports.

If one builds a ballpark there will be (in most instances) more than 2 million visits to the area, and possibly 3 million. An arena can be expected to generate more than 1.5 million visits if it is home to either a National Basketball Association or National Hockey League team (or both).* The challenge for cities, my students, and my colleagues is then summarized by this task. If I could guarantee you more than a million visits each year to a specific part of a downtown area, how would you redevelop the surrounding real estate to benefit (1) the team, (2) the facility's owner and operator, and (3) the city? As I will explain and explore in the first and second chapters of this new volume, I have reached the conclusion (based on deductions built from the research of others) that sports is an extremely valuable tool, and if a city uses it properly, sports can indeed lead to urban revitalization and the relocation of regional economic activity.

And to the second question I respond, no, I am not being audacious.

Major league sports are very popular and have the ability to reposition regional economic activity. The four (or five if you include soccer) major sports leagues will ensure that in the vast majority of markets there will be only one team from each sport. The exceptions are anomalies linked to the amalgamation of competing leagues, and that means that in most metropolitan areas there will be but one basketball, baseball, football, hockey, or soccer team. What is unacceptable is for leadership in cities to fail to appreciate how to use the popularity of sports to recentralize economic activity.

This book is designed to explain why and how to use sports for revitalization efforts and to illustrate the lessons learned by those cities that have not subsidized facilities and teams, but instead made successful strategic investments. As investments, the tax dollars expended for venues have generated positive net financial returns. Cities can and do win in the sense that the financial returns the public sector receives are more than the funds expended, and that makes them *major league winners*, discarding the label of *major league losers*.

This book is also designed to underscore that those cities and teams that have profited from the relocation of economic activity to downtown areas have warmly and extensively embraced cherished principles of urban planning and design. Those new real estate development projects that are anchored by sports venues and have benefited cities and teams are those that adhere to ideas and concepts carefully

---

* Reaching that attendance level is a function of the number of venues in an area and the ability to host a number of entertainment events. The location of the venue can also impact attendance. In the case of Jobing.Com, there are two other arenas in the Phoenix metropolitan area creating a very competitive environment for the hosting of concerts and shows. In addition, Glendale is rather distant (west side of the region) from the concentration of wealthier households (e.g., Scottsdale and Maricopa County's east side) and the location of the region's largest firms.

articulated by Jane Jacobs and other pillars of the art, practice, and science of urban planning and design.

What those of us who look to sports facilities as anchors for urban revitalization have rejected is that instead of a slow and evolutionary perspective on changing a downtown area or neighborhood, rapid redevelopment is needed. Why will slower evolutionary planning processes cherished by many urban experts not succeed? Decentralization rates are accelerating and suburban areas are racing to establish themselves as the economic centers of each region. Central cities need to be aggressive in responding to this new dynamic challenge to their role in regional economies. The successful revitalization efforts anchored by sports venues are those that have involved a rapid building of a new neighborhood and the designation of a single master developer. That, in my view, is not a repudiation of ideas advanced by many of the best thinkers about cities and their design. It is rather a fine-tuning and an adjustment of principles to respond to an accelerating rate of decentralization. This extraordinary rate of decentralization is rapidly destabilizing the finances of central cities. Without equally rapid responses that capitalize on market forces, central cities will not have the revenues needed to offer residents the services they deserve and need.

Regarding the third question and a "sell-out" to the forces of capital, it has been too often argued that any city that endorses the use of public funds for sports venues is in effect abandoning any other community revitalization strategies and ignoring activities designed to improve neighborhoods in other parts of the city. As will be demonstrated in several case studies, it was the downtown business interests that often wanted new sports facilities while also leading efforts to improve inner city schools and neighborhoods. Another contribution made by this book is to ask students and leaders to look at the full range of activities undertaken by a community's business elite when the issue of revitalization is discussed.

Finally, this book is about engaging capital. Cities cannot be revitalized without private investment. Therefore, a city's leadership has to figure out how to engage with the private sector and its investment capital to ensure that revitalization occurs and that regional economic activity is repositioned into a central city. Such a task is not easy, but few ever thought changing the economy of deteriorating central cities would be simple work. Deindustrialization and the decline of the eras of mass manufacturing jobs was a gradual process that became a tidal wave that engulfed central cities. In some small way it is hoped this book shows how some cities found a way to rebuild, and from those experiences hopefully others can understand the theory and practice that has made several cities major league winners.

# Acknowledgments

This book and its initial incarnation grew from presentations I made at the University of Pennsylvania's Institute for Urban Research.

My first presentation discussed how some cities had or could turn subsidies for arenas, ballparks, and stadia—linked to well-designed plans for new neighborhoods—into strategic investments. In a second conference years later, that included leaders from the professional sports industry, Professor Genie Birch let me discuss the ability of teams to relocate regional economic activity from suburban areas to central cities. Those presentations allowed me to develop the conceptual framework that is the heart of this book. My discussion at that second conference also illustrated how urban revitalization could be very profitable for teams while also benefitting cities. My view now is that teams can "do well by doing good," if that good is a well-designed neighborhood that includes substantial levels of private sector investments for real estate development. Genie, thank you for your encouragement and for the opportunities to expound on new ideas, or ideas that were new to me, in front of students, industry leaders, and my friends at the University of Pennsylvania.

For the past several years I have had the privilege of discussing the linkage between sports facilities, real estate development, and the repositioning of regional economic activity with several extraordinary professionals. Jeff Wilpon and Fred Wilpon (New York Mets) and Paul Dolan (Cleveland Indians) gave freely of their time and gave me the opportunity to discuss sports management and development issues with them. Their insights helped improve this work. The conversations I have had with other professionals have also been very meaningful to me and for my work. Matt Rossetti, Janet Marie Smith, Richard Browne, and Eric Larson spent countless hours talking with me about sports facilities, urban design, real estate development and financing, facility construction and design, and team finances. They made it possible for me to refine my understandings and improve on the ideas that I have incorporated into this volume, in my professional work and teaching, and in my other books.

I have been very fortunate to have had and continue to have the opportunity to discuss elements of the sports business and sports economics with three of the world's finest minds and colleagues on the issues of economics, finance, and market behavior. Professors Rodney Fort, Stephen Szymanski, and Jason Winfree (real economists in every sense of the term) were and are always there to debate issues with me and point out my foibles, errors, and occasionally, things that I had right. Even when they disagreed with my logic or ideas, they always made me see other perspectives and potential flaws in my logic and model. In several ways they made this book far better, and in numerous ways have helped make me a better scholar and student. I cherish their insights and their friendship. Dan Mason, my great friend and colleague at the University of Alberta, has created numerous opportunities for me to expand my understanding of the business of sports in Canada. I am in his debt too, as the insights gained from our work together in Edmonton helped shape parts of Chapters 1, 2, and 10.

For the past several years I have taught undergraduate and graduate classes focused on the relationship between sports, economic development, urban economics, urban planning and design, and team operations at the University of Michigan. Teaching classes with and for dedicated and motivated students allowed me to improve my ideas and concepts. Many of the students questioned materials included in the first incarnation of this book; their suggestions have made this newer book far better.

In every city people provided me with more help than I deserved. Charles Isgar in Los Angeles helped me more than he knows by his probing questions, insights, and biting sense of humor. His jokes pushed me to make this book a far better product. I am very lucky to have been able to call Steve Soboroff a friend. He is a leader, a part of Los Angeles's economic leadership who lives the meaning of community development each and every day. In San Diego, Mike Aguirre is the driving critic and community leader who forces every city to consider how to avoid subsidies. Eric Judson was also a great help. In Indianapolis—a city I still call home—Susan Williams and a score of public and community leaders have been a great help. Anthony Schoettle of the *Indianapolis Business Journal* was also willing to help chase down even the smallest details of Indianapolis' revitalization efforts. In Cleveland, special thanks is owed to the Greater Cleveland Partnership and its staff for providing access to their records and history. Mike Ehlerman and Al Boscov in Reading were not only invaluable sources, but their commitment to the city's future is an extraordinary inspiration. I have been partially infected by their love of Reading and now find myself hoping that goggleWorks leads an unprecedented revitalization.

Last, in 2008 the University of Michigan offered me the Bruce and Joan Bickner Endowed Professorship in Sport Management. This extraordinary position and the resources it has made available to me made this book possible. The financial support of the Bickner family through their generosity to the University of Michigan helped me in numerous ways, including the ability to hire the two students who assisted me on the research and editing tasks associated with this volume. A last thank you goes to those students, Stephanie Gerretsen and Madelaine Moeke. Stephanie and

Maddie, I hope this book helps you understand the dreams and goals I have for each of you and, of course, what I expect from both of you. The time is approaching for both of you to be leaders of our research team and in those roles blaze new paths and themes that make this book, in time, pedestrian and dated.

There are, to be sure, mistakes that these fine people did not convince me to eliminate. All those errors that remain are my responsibility.

**Mark S. Rosentraub, PhD**
*Bruce and Joan Bickner Endowed Professor of Sport Management*
*University of Michigan*

# About the Author

**Mark S. Rosentraub** has been studying and writing about the economics of sports teams, events, and facilities and the linkage between sports, amenities, and urban and economic development for more than 30 years. *Sports Finance and Management: Real Estate, Entertainment and the Remaking of the Business* (CRC Press/Taylor & Francis, 2011, coauthored with Jason Winfree) explores the dramatic changes in the sports business landscape and the implications and opportunities for cities, teams, and the sports business professionals.

Dr. Rosentraub's *Major League Winners: Using Sports and Cultural Centers as Tools for Economic Development* was published in 2010 and explains the theory behind the efforts of several communities to use amenities in the competition to attract and retain human capital for economic development. The case study communities have been able to turn public investments in sports and cultural facilities into strategic investments. *Major League Losers: The Real Cost of Sports and Who's Paying for It* appeared in 1997 (revised edition, 1999), and *The Economics of Sports: An International Perspective*, with two other colleagues, was published in 2004.

Dr. Rosentraub's professional work has not been limited to publications. He has helped numerous cities across North America frame redevelopment strategies involving sports and culture. He worked with the San Diego Padres and the City of San Diego in designing the Ballpark District that resulted in more than $2 billion of new real estate development. Dr. Rosentraub also worked with the City of Los Angeles in its work that led to the building of Staples Center and L.A. LIVE. Staples Center and L.A. LIVE became the backbone for the resurgence of downtown Los Angeles.

Dr. Rosentraub has advised two different mayors of Indianapolis across more than a decade on downtown redevelopment strategies linked to sport facilities and teams. He has or is working with the Baltimore Orioles, Detroit Pistons, Detroit Red Wings (a new arena for downtown Detroit and associated real estate development), Green Bay Packers (new real estate development surrounding Lambeau Field), Indianapolis Colts (Lucas Oil Stadium), New York Mets (Willets Point/Citi Field Real Estate Development), San Francisco Giants, the City of Edmonton (in its successful efforts to build a new arena with the Edmonton Oilers and redesign its downtown area), the City of Hamilton, Ontario (on participatory sport strategies and the use of sport facilities for downtown redevelopment), and Bedrock Management on economic development projects involving Dan Gilbert's assets in downtown Cleveland (the Cleveland Cavaliers and a casino) and in downtown Detroit.

Dr. Rosentraub has also worked with the University of Nevada, Las Vegas on its plans for a mega-event stadium on its campus, together with the building of a mixed-use university village, and has projected the economic value of that venue for the Las Vegas economy. Dr. Rosentraub is part of the team led by Forest City Ratner/Barclays Center and Blumenfeld Development Group in the effort to renovate the Nassau Coliseum, reposition the facility as a center for entertainment and sports, and develop the adjacent real estate.

In 2003 the Cuyahoga County Commissioners appointed Dr. Rosentraub to the board of the Gateway Economic Redevelopment Corporation. Gateway is the public corporation responsible for Progressive Field, home to the Cleveland Indians baseball team, and Quicken Loans Arena, home to the Cleveland Cavaliers basketball team. This is one of the largest public–private partnerships for sports in the United States. Dr. Rosentraub helped rewrite the leases for both teams that avoided substantial financial problems for Cleveland and Cuyahoga County, saving taxpayers more than $4 million each year.

In 2009 Dr. Rosentraub became the University of Michigan's first holder of the Bruce and Joan Bickner Endowed Chair in Sport Management in the School of Kinesiology. Dr. Rosentraub has been a Lady Davis Fellow at the Hebrew University of Jerusalem and a visiting scholar at Humboldt University and the Free University in Berlin, Germany. He has given guest lectures at numerous universities across the United States, Canada, Germany, Jordan, and Israel. In August 2012 he was a distinguished visiting scholar at the School of Business, Griffith University in Gold Coast, Australia, and at La Trobe University in Melbourne, Australia.

## Chapter 1

# Urban Change, a Loss of Centrality, and New Destinies for Downtowns

## 1.1 Introduction

On March 14, 2013, Michigan's governor, Richard Snyder, announced the appointment of Kevyn Orr—an accomplished bankruptcy attorney—as the emergency financial manager for Detroit. Governor Snyder's appointment of an emergency financial manager meant Detroit's elected officials were no longer responsible for the city's financial affairs and policies. The emergency financial manager could consult with the mayor and council and keep each informed of his decisions, but Detroit's elected leaders had lost their authority to lead the city's business affairs.

The governor's appointee has the authority to take any and all actions he deems necessary to fix the city's finances. Those actions include the power to annul contracts and terminate operating and employment agreements with labor unions and any municipal employees. The emergency financial manager can also suspend and cancel any previous financial or management policies and decisions made by the mayor or the city council. Motown—a city that gave America affordable automobiles and an enduring sound that helped define popular music for decades—became the largest city in American history to be stripped of its fiscal powers and independence. As 2013 came to an end, Detroit had the ignominious honor of being the largest city in American history to seek bankruptcy protection.

Other large cities have endured periods of extraordinary financial stress. In 1978, Cleveland became the first city since the Great Depression to almost default on its debt (approximately $16 million; $53.7 million in 2013 dollars).[1] Three years earlier New York City faced a financial crisis, and without help from New York State and the federal government, it might have defaulted on approximately $14 billion in debt ($57.4 billion in 2013 dollars). Detroit's debt had been estimated to be approximately $20 billion (2013 dollars) when the emergency financial manager was appointed. That figure was far smaller than the debt problems that plagued New York City. However, with a 2013 population of approximately 707,000, however, Detroit's debt relative to the number of people who call the city home dwarfs the financial challenges that confronted New York City (and Cleveland), or for that matter any city in American history. Several cities have extensive unfunded pension liabilities, but no other municipality is facing the scale of financial challenges that must be addressed by Detroit.

What caused these substantial fiscal problems? To be sure, there have been excesses related to (1) management inefficiencies (failure to collect taxes), (2) poorly financed pension funds, (3) corrupt business and political processes, and (4) politically advantageous labor agreements that might have been negotiated to ensure that city workers voted for the reelection of city councilors and mayors.[2] Many of these labor contracts may have also offered city employees compensation and benefit packages that exceeded what private sector employees earned.

It would seem easy to ascribe all of Detroit's financial problems to excessively generous labor agreements, patronage, incompetence, and malfeasance. To do so, however, would obscure and ignore longer-term trends that have changed the financial climate for every central city. Politics, policies, and malfeasance may have exacerbated Detroit's financial situation, but those bad decisions did not cause the extraordinary set of fundamental economic and social changes that led to a loss of wealth for many older central cities. Simply put, the movement of people and businesses to suburban and exurban areas has meant that former central cities and their downtown areas are far less important to a region's economy. New town centers or mini-downtowns have been built in suburban areas from coast to coast reducing the need for and importance of central cities. The core cities of most regions are now the home to larger and larger proportions of an area's lower-income households and in a struggle to collect the tax revenues required to deliver the needed public services.

### 1.1.1 Population Change

A quick trip through any metropolitan area illustrates dimensions of the change. What is often not understood, however, is that with cities dependent on local property, sales, and income taxes (often referred to as own-source revenues), and as people, jobs, and flagship department stores leave central cities for the suburbs, the financial health of these communities declines. By 1960, 31 percent of the U.S.

population lived in suburban cities, a proportion virtually equal to the 32 percent living in central cities. Within a decade the vast majority of the population growth taking place in America was concentrated in suburban cities. Some of these communities had so many workers (and job centers) and had grown so large that they became known as a second central city (or third central cities in larger areas) within their regions. By 1980, 44.8 percent of American residents lived in the suburbs and by 2000 half of America's residents called suburban cities their home.[3]

Complacency with the growth of suburban areas turned to concern as it became clear that the central cities were increasingly characterized by growing concentrations of a region's lower-income households. Wealthier households began to prefer suburban cities, and in many regions, higher-income households completely abandoned neighborhoods that for decades were well maintained and stable. A new form of segregation emerged, with higher-income households isolating themselves in suburban areas. Some central cities were losing so many middle- and upper-class families that the average income of families in center cities was less than half of the average income of families in the suburbs. Within one generation, the movement of large numbers of wealthier households meant a substantial portion of a central city's tax base had relocated to suburban towns and cities. Those communities were now able to offer higher levels of public services unburdened by the responsibility of providing education, parks, or recreation services to lower-income households.

These changes meant the economic and social leadership of many regions passed in a decade or two from central cities that had dominated regions for centuries to newer suburban communities. These new cities and towns were laced with business parks adjacent to beltways that isolated these communities from decaying core cities. Even the largest and most robust central cities, such as Boston, Chicago, and New York, were not immune to some or all of these changes; some even lost residents. The percentage declines, however, were far more substantial for cities like Baltimore, Cincinnati, Cleveland, Detroit, and Kansas City. Each of those lost more than a third of its 1950 population base by the end of the 20th century despite the growth of the United States. More importantly, *every* central city in Table 1.1 had become home to a far smaller portion of their region's population. This pattern of becoming a smaller portion of their region also involved the consolidated city/county of Denver and Indianapolis.

The City of Denver and Denver County were consolidated in 1902. The merged municipality was able to unilaterally annex land from adjacent counties through 1974. Denver's authority to add land was curtailed by the state legislature in 1974. Since 1975, annexations were permitted only if agreed upon by a boundary commission that included representatives from surrounding counties. Consolidation and the ability to annex land through 1974 did not protect Denver from being home to a smaller proportion of its region's population. In 1950, more than two-thirds of the region's population lived in Denver. By 2010, Denver was home to only 23.6 percent of its region's population. City-county consolidation in Indianapolis created an image of a growing city, but the number of residents in the city's older boundaries declined. Despite the consolidation of Indianapolis with most of the

Table 1.1 The Declining Centrality of Selected American Cities: 1950–2010

| Central City/ MSA/City As Share of MSA | 1950 | 1960 | 1970 | 1980 | Percent Change 1950–1980 | 1990 | 2000 | 2010 | Percent Change 1990–2010 |
|---|---|---|---|---|---|---|---|---|---|
| Baltimore | 949,708 | 939,024 | 905,759 | 786,775 | -17.2 | 736,014 | 651,154 | 620,961 | -15.6 |
| MSA | 1,337,373 | 1,727,023 | 2,089,438 | 2,199,497 | 64.5 | 2,382,172 | 2,552,994 | 2,710,489 | 13.8 |
| City Share | 71.0 | 54.4 | 43.3 | 35.8 | | 30.9 | 25.5 | 22.9 | |
| Boston | 801,444 | 697,197 | 641,071 | 562,994 | -29.8 | 574,283 | 589,141 | 617,594 | 7.5 |
| MSA | 2,369,986 | 2,589,301 | 2,753,800 | 2,805,911 | 18.4 | 4,133,895 | 4,391,344 | 4,552,402 | 10.1 |
| City Share | 33.8 | 26.9 | 23.3 | 20.1 | | 13.9 | 13.4 | 13.6 | |
| Chicago | 3,620,962 | 3,550,404 | 3,366,957 | 3,005,072 | -17.0 | 2,783,726 | 2,896,016 | 2,695,598 | -3.2 |
| MSA | 5,495,364 | 6,220,913 | 6,093,287 | 6,060,401 | 10.3 | 8,182,076 | 9,098,316 | 9,461,015 | 15.6 |
| City Share | 65.9 | 57.1 | 55.3 | 49.6 | | 34.0 | 31.8 | 28.5 | |
| Cincinnati | 503,998 | 502,550 | 452,524 | 385,457 | -23.5 | 364,040 | 331,285 | 296,943 | -18.4 |
| MSA | 904,502 | 1,268,479 | 1,384,851 | 1,401,491 | 54.9 | 1,844,915 | 2,009,632 | 2,130,151 | 15.5 |
| City Share | 55.7 | 39.6 | 32.7 | 27.5 | | 19.7 | 16.5 | 13.9 | |
| Cleveland | 914,808 | 876,050 | 750,903 | 573,822 | -37.3 | 505,616 | 478,403 | 396,815 | -21.5 |
| MSA | 1,465,511 | 1,909,483 | 2,063,729 | 1,898,825 | 29.6 | 2,202,069 | 2,148,143 | 2,077,240 | -5.7 |
| City Share | 62.4 | 45.9 | 36.4 | 30.2 | | 23.0 | 22.3 | 19.1 | |

| | | | | | | | | | |
|---|---|---|---|---|---|---|---|---|---|
| Detroit | 1,849,568 | 1,670,144 | 1,511,482 | 1,203,339 | −34.9 | 1,027,974 | 951,270 | 713,777 | −30.6 |
| MSA | 3,016,197 | 4,050,840 | 4,554,266 | 4,488,072 | 48.8 | 4,470,315 | 4,452,557 | 4,296,250 | −3.9 |
| City Share | 61.3 | 41.2 | 33.2 | 26.8 | | 23.0 | 21.4 | 16.6 | |
| Denver | 415,786 | 493,887 | 514,678 | 492,365 | 18.4 | 467,610 | 554,636 | 600,158 | 28.3 |
| MSA | 612,128 | 859,945 | 1,106,384 | 1,428,836 | 133.4 | 1,980,140 | 2,109,282 | 2,543,482 | 28.4 |
| City Share | 67.9 | 57.4 | 46.5 | 34.5 | | 23.6 | 26.3 | 23.6 | |
| Indianapolis[a] | 427,173 | 476,258 | 744,624 | 700,807 | 64.1 | 731,278 | 781,870 | 820,445 | 12.2 |
| MSA | 551,777 | 944,475 | 1,111,352 | 1,166,575 | 111.4 | 1,380,491 | 1,607,486 | 1,726,241 | 25.0 |
| City Share | 77.4 | 50.4 | 67.0 | 60.1 | | 53.0 | 48.6 | 47.5 | |
| Kansas City | 456,622 | 475,539 | 507,087 | 448,159 | −1.9 | 435,146 | 441,545 | 459,787 | 5.7 |
| MSA | 814,357 | 1,266,447 | 1,437,204 | 1,504,209 | 84.7 | 1,636,527 | 1,836,038 | 2,035,334 | 24.4 |
| City Share | 56.1 | 37.5 | 35.3 | 29.8 | | 26.6 | 24.0 | 22.6 | |
| Minneapolis | 521,718 | 482,872 | 434,400 | 370,951 | −28.9 | 368,383 | 382,618 | 382,578 | 3.9 |
| MSA | 1,151,053 | 1,482,030 | 1,981,951 | 2,137,133 | 85.7 | 2,538,776 | 2,968,806 | 3,279,833 | 29.2 |
| City Share | 45.3 | 32.6 | 21.9 | 17.4 | | 14.5 | 12.9 | 11.7 | |

*(Continued)*

**Table 1.1 The Declining Centrality of Selected American Cities: 1950–2010 (Continued)**

| Central City/ MSA/City As Share of MSA | 1950 | 1960 | 1970 | 1980 | Percent Change 1950–1980 | 1990 | 2000 | 2010 | Percent Change 1990–2010 |
|---|---|---|---|---|---|---|---|---|---|
| New York | 7,891,957 | 7,781,984 | 7,894,862 | 7,071,639 | –10.4 | 7,332,564 | 8,008,278 | 8,175,133 | 11.5 |
| MSA | 14,018,852 | 14,437,000 | 17,068,000 | 16,363,000 | 16.7 | 16,846,046 | 18,323,002 | 18,897,109 | 12.2 |
| City Share | 56.3 | 53.9 | 46.3 | 43.2 | | 43.5 | 43.7 | 43.3 | |
| Phoenix | 106,818 | 439,170 | 581,562 | 789,704 | 639.3 | 983,403 | 1,321,045 | 1,445,632 | 47.0 |
| MSA | 374,961 | 726,183 | 1,319,189 | 2,040,495 | 444.2 | 2,238,498 | 3,252,876 | 4,192,887 | 87.3 |
| City Share | 28.5 | 60.5 | 44.1 | 38.7 | | 43.9 | 40.6 | 34.5 | |
| San Diego | 334,387 | 573,224 | 696,769 | 875,538 | 161.8 | 1,110,549 | 1,223,400 | 1,307,402 | 17.7 |
| MSA | 556,808 | 1,033,011 | 1,357,854 | 1,861,846 | 234.4 | 2,498,016 | 2,813,833 | 3,095,313 | 23.9 |
| City Share | 60.1 | 55.5 | 51.3 | 47.0 | | 44.5 | 43.5 | 42.2 | |
| St. Louis | 856,796 | 750,026 | 622,236 | 453,085 | –47.1 | 396,685 | 348,189 | 319,294 | –19.5 |
| MSA | 1,719,288 | 2,060,103 | 2,363,017 | 2,376,998 | 38.3 | 2,492,525 | 2,603,607 | 2,830,355 | 13.6 |
| City Share | 49.8 | 36.4 | 26.3 | 19.1 | | 15.9 | 13.4 | 11.3 | |

*Source:* U.S. Bureau of the Census, various years.

*Note:* MSA = metropolitan statistical area.

[a] Indianapolis consolidated with Marion County, and that accounts for the large population increase from 1960 to 1970. However, even the consolidation could not stem the outflow of residents to surrounding counties from 1970 to 1980.

county surrounding it, outmigration from the center part of the city continued. By the end of the 20th century, growth in the region was concentrated in suburban counties. In 1950, three-quarters of the region's residents lived in Indianapolis; however, that proportion had declined to 47.5 percent by 2000.

When a city, county, or state loses residents, it does not necessarily mean that wealth or centrality is also lost. It is possible, for example, for a community to gentrify. What that means is that older multifamily homes are replaced with residences that are far more expensive. Such a process raises important public and social policy issues and may be unethical and unfair as it reduces access to improving neighborhoods for lower-income households. Yet, where gentrification occurs, wealth levels could rise and more local taxes might be produced for local governments. The challenge for every city is to have a sufficient number of higher-income households living in its neighborhoods to ensure that sufficient tax revenues are generated to finance the urban services needed by all residents. In most instances, however, declining population numbers usually mean there is a level of economic contraction resulting in longer-term declines in tax revenues and, eventually, a loss of jobs as businesses follow people to the suburbs.

The overall pattern of change taking place in the United States is illustrated in Table 1.1. These data also highlight the emerging competition between central cities and suburban areas for residents. Notice that in 1950 each of the central cities (except for Phoenix) accounted for more than 50 percent of its region's population. Phoenix would meet that standard in 1960. By 2010 *none* of the central cities would be home to half of their region's residents. In each region, the suburban areas were growing at a faster rate than the central cities, and the pattern was consistent regardless of the section of the United States in which a region was located. In other words, rust- and sunbelt central cities had each lost a degree of centrality measured by the proportion of their region's population bases that lived in the core urban community. Even the consolidated cities of Denver and Indianapolis were home to less than half of their region's residents in the 21st century.

## 1.1.2 Changing Geography of Jobs and Escalating Decentralization of Regional Economies

With so many households relocating to the suburbs, retail centers soon followed. Several center cities could do little more than watch as numerous grand department stores that defined the holiday season and were part of the vibrancy of downtown areas closed their doors. With the development of shopping malls and then town centers in the suburbs (that re-created the imagery of downtown retail centers) hundreds of thousands of retail jobs moved from central cities to the suburbs. The exodus of entry-level and valuable part-time jobs meant longer commutes for inner city residents needing those positions. By 2006, just 13 percent of all retail jobs were located within 3 miles of older central business districts and half were located in suburban areas (Kneebone, 2009).

## TOWN CENTERS AND LIFESTYLE CENTERS

The first retail centers in suburban locations were bulky box-like structures anchored by department stores. Larger malls might have four or more flagship department stores. Connecting the department stores were long corridors lined with scores of smaller retail outlets. Several malls included entertainment venues, and larger ones had amusement centers with thrill rides for children. As the retail market scene changed as a result of people's use of the Internet and consumers had a desire for a more outdoor/downtown feel for shopping centers, as opposed to enclosed malls with little architectural distinction, developers tried to create more varied and exciting experiences to encourage people to visit malls. Lifestyle centers similar to the one located in suburban Denver (see Figure 1.1) sprouted across the country in the 1990s and into the 21st century. The Eaton Centre in suburban Columbus, Ohio— one of the nation's largest lifestyle centers—effectively contributed to the obsolescence of a new traditional mall built in downtown Columbus. The Capitol Centre Mall closed within 10 years of opening its doors.

**Figure 1.1** **Lifestyle center in suburban Denver: A downtown feel complete with public art. (Courtesy of Mark S. Rosentraub.)**

Changing transportation and communication costs have made it possible for employers to choose business locations closer to where their employees want to live. The movement of businesses to the suburbs also defined the second half of the 20th century. By 1996, across the 100 largest metropolitan areas, just 21 percent of the region's jobs were located within 3 miles of the center city's core area. Kneebone (2009: 1) found that 45 percent of the jobs in these regions were at least 10 miles from the center of the core city. Further, her analysis showed that "from 1998 to 2006, 95 of 98 metropolitan areas saw a decrease in the share of jobs located within three miles of downtown."

At the century's turn, Glaeser and Kahn (2001: 7) noted that the "monocentric model [had become] a poor approximation of the reality of American cities." Their conclusion was a stern reminder that the reality of metropolitan areas was that they were now comprised of multiple job centers. This intraregional competition for businesses and residents made it critically important for the leaders of central cities to focus on policies and initiatives to ensure that their older central business districts could attract businesses to produce a reliable stream of tax revenues to support the urban services needed by residents. As jobs vanished from what were *central* business districts, older core cities had less revenue to pay for the urban services the remaining residents needed. Central cities also had to compete for residents who could now easily live in suburban areas that provided higher levels of public services, including better schools. In addition, those suburban areas provided a sense of safety, as most also offered a high degree of economic segregation.

It might seem that with fewer residents, a declining revenue base would be sufficient to meet the public service needs of the remaining households. Lower-income households, however, are more dependent on the services provided by local governments. For example, fewer lower-income families can afford private schools or access to private recreation centers and camps for their children. As a result, while tax revenues declined, the demand or reliance on the public sector for services actually increased with the expanding concentration of lower-income households and reduced tax collections. Baltimore, Cleveland, Chicago, Dallas, Denver, Detroit, Houston, Indianapolis, and New York were among those cities that needed to enhance tax revenue streams to ensure that the needed levels of public services would exist. Public leaders and community leaders in central cities were suddenly confronted with the reality that higher-income households, when they lived in their communities, paid local taxes while not consuming the services provided by local governments. This created an environment where the public services needed by lower-income households could be delivered without substantially elevating tax levels. Simply put, the presence of wealthier residents who needed fewer services made it financially viable to meet the needs of lower-income families. When higher-income households relocated to the suburbs, the demand for public services in central cities was relatively unchanged, but central cities now had fewer wealthy taxpayers. In addition, when the quality of services declined, higher-income families had an additional incentive (or in their minds, a justification) to relocate. As a result, America's metropolitan areas in the late 20th and early 21st centuries had become polycentric, comprised of competing centers each trying to attract business and residents. To reduce the likelihood that lower-income households would move into the economically segregated suburban areas, building codes were adopted that ensured that homes and multifamily complexes were also more expensive. This was achieved by requiring homes to be sufficiently large (high square footage requirements, making them more expensive), and multifamily complexes had to also have fewer units, making each more expensive too.

Underscoring the implications of this economic segregation for central cities, Glaeser and Kahn (2001: 5) also noted that "worker residential preferences appear to be extremely important" when businesses select locations. "If spatial patterns in the past [where businesses chose to locate] were dictated mainly by productivity advantages of particular locales for firms, spatial patterns now seem to be driven as much by consumption advantages" desired by workers. Simply put, firms in the 21st century have chosen to locate *where workers* want to live, and increasingly that has meant suburban and exurban communities that were economically segregated from older communities. As the value of highly educated workers has become more important to the success of every business, locating where that talent wants to live is more cost efficient than the advantages offered by access to natural resources. Access to natural resources (and large pools of labor) predicted the economic success of cities in the 19th and 20th centuries. Financial success for any city now is more dependent on the creation of the amenities that well-educated workers want and the urban services and neighborhoods they prefer for their families.

## 1.2 The Real Fiscal Implications of Decentralization

Deka (1998) warned that the decentralization of jobs was having a detrimental effect on the income earned by central city residents and the rising poverty rate in the older employment centers. Joassart-Marcelli et al. (2005) noted that the concentration of a region's lower-income households in central cities as a result of the loss of jobs and economic segregation created substantial fiscal stress for older central cities. One way to offset the concentration of lower-income households in central cities—and the movement of jobs to suburban areas—would be for a state government or neighboring cities and towns in a metropolitan area to share revenues with central cities with a growing concentration of lower-income households. Indeed, one way for older central cities to get some degree of relief from increasing levels of economic segregation and avoid a focus on policies to attract and retain higher-income households as well as better-trained workers would be for suburban communities to share tax revenue produced by their residents.

Very few tax-sharing programs exist to ensure that wherever growth occurs in a metropolitan area, a central city is also likely to enjoy additional revenue. In the Minneapolis–St. Paul region, a portion of the growth in property tax revenues is shared regardless of the city in which growth occurs. In some states local governments are granted the authority to collect a local income tax based on where people work (which is known as an earnings tax). This was introduced as a way for a central city to tax commuters, but its success, of course, depends on the extent to which jobs are retained by a central city. Elsewhere some communities have agreed to help pay for certain amenities that are located in central cities (arenas, ballparks, and stadiums). The central cities are then allowed to retain the taxes produced by spending that takes place at the amenity or by the redevelopment of real estate adjacent to the venue. Each of these revenue-sharing programs is valuable, but none is sufficient to offset the loss of wealth suffered by central cities. There is, as would be expected, little political support from residents of suburban cities to provide substantial levels of financial help to central cities. Some of that reluctance could be tied to prejudices, but more is related to a demand for lower taxes and more self-reliance by cities (as opposed to a central city or any city becoming dependent on revenue transfers from state, provincial, or other local governments to pay for the services needed by its residents).

State and provincial governments have also faced their own fiscal challenges since 2001; as a result, the allocation of general revenue-sharing revenues to central cities has declined. Those rising costs are associated with expenses for prisons, higher education, state support for public education at the primary and secondary levels (K–12), and the need for extensive investments in infrastructure (e.g., roadways, bridges, etc.). While the exact circumstances and level of the reduced support vary state by state, a look at changes that Cleveland had to adjust to between 2001 and 2010 are representative. The lower level of state support has increased the pressure on central cities to attract and retain jobs and higher-income residents. Table 1.2 shows the revenues received by Cleveland from Ohio's local government fund. In 2010, for example, Cleveland received 34.6 percent less revenue from Ohio through the state's local government fund than it did in 2001. At a time when the city's population was declining and the proportion of lower-income households making up the city's residential base was rising, less revenue sharing from Ohio was available.

Factors related to recessions or the contraction of a state's (or the national) economy is not the only reason interest in revenue sharing has declined. There is even evidence that revenue sharing that helps a central city provide enhanced urban services produces benefits for suburban economies (Haughwout and Inman, 2002). The Gallup Organization, while not asking specific questions regarding tax-base sharing among local governments, has been asking Americans if they believe "governments should or should not redistribute wealth by levying higher taxes on the rich?" The country has been split on this issue since 1939, with approximately half of respondents supporting and opposing redistribution by raising taxes on the wealthy.[4] In addition, more than a third of respondents believe the property tax

**Table 1.2 Annual Revenues Received by Cleveland from the State of Ohio's Local Government Fund, 2001–2010 (in thousands of dollars)**

| Year | Actual Allocation | Adjusted (2010) | Percent Change from 2001 | Real Decline in Annual Revenues from Ohio |
|---|---|---|---|---|
| 2010 | 47,992 | 47,992 | −34.6 | −25,439 |
| 2009 | 45,590 | 46,886 | −36.1 | −26,544 |
| 2008 | 52,269 | 53,730 | −26.8 | −19,701 |
| 2007 | 53,506 | 57,366 | −21.9 | −16,065 |
| 2006 | 55,908 | 61,180 | −16.7 | −12,250 |
| 2005 | 55,899 | 63,608 | −13.4 | −9,822 |
| 2004 | 55,808 | 65,391 | −10.9 | −8,040 |
| 2003 | 55,462 | 66,237 | −9.8 | −7,194 |
| 2002 | 56,436 | 69,151 | −5.8 | −4,280 |
| 2001 | 59,252 | 73,431 | — | — |

is the least fair, suggesting that using revenue from that tax to adjust differences between local governments might also be less popular.[5] With all governments seeking to reduce taxes, transferring scarce resources to other communities is a difficult, if not impossible, political risk for any politician.

Finally, the National League of Cities reports that there are only 34 city-county consolidated governments among the 3,069 counties across the United States.[6] Some of these involve rural counties where there is no declining central city. As noted, the last city-county consolidation of a central city with its suburban communities involved Louisville in 2003, and few, if any others, are being seriously considered. Consolidating Detroit with its surrounding county, Wayne, is not politically viable even though the central city asked for bankruptcy protection. To provide the services urban residents need, central cities have to focus on strategies to generate higher levels of revenue. What options exist given these political realities and the pace of decentralization?

## 1.3 The Responses to Decentralization

There may have been some sense that even as suburban cities began to boom in the post-World War II decades, central cities would retain each region's business, entertainment, culture, and retail centers. With the U.S. population booming, there might well have been enough growth to ensure that central and suburban cities would both grow and prosper. When decentralization trends escalated, it became clear that central cities would need to compete with suburban areas to protect their fiscal stability. The initial focus of this competition involved a reinvigoration of retail trade based on the festival marketplace concept and designs of James W. Rouse. Redesigning historical buildings or venues—what is known as repurposing—became a trademark of what seemed like a viable approach to reintegrate historical buildings into a city's life and offer a retail experience that was different from that at a suburban mall. Those initial retail centers had little architectural significance. A common criticism was that these buildings were bland and were separated from the surrounding community by an "ocean of asphalt" (parking lots). Mr. Rouse's legendary designs tried to create unique retail experiences in historical buildings, classical meeting places, or in any other larger-scale civic facilities that had been abandoned. Retail and then retail centers with different mixes of entertainment and eating places soon appeared in meeting halls, train stations, post offices, and market areas that were no longer needed.

Why use retail centers to reclaim past glory?

Central cities, after all, had always been the location of glamorous shopping experiences. Mr. Rouse and others were attracted to the potential for remodeling historical buildings that were unique civic assets that still dominated the physical space of downtown areas. These buildings and railway stations often had intriguing architectural charms that could not be easily replicated in the suburbs. In short order, however, many of these valiant efforts failed. Why? These retail centers actually could offer a shopper little that was different from what was available at suburban malls. In addition, while vast oceans of asphalt isolated most suburban malls from surrounding communities, they did offer abundant and easily accessible parking spots. Convenient, safe, and relatively inexpensive parking adjacent to clusters of hundreds of stores located near their homes was more important to shoppers than architecturally significant buildings located in dense downtown areas. Suburban shopping malls with hundreds of stores—even with bland architecture and surrounded by parking lots—prospered and many festival or urban marketplaces failed.

The possibility of any restoration of legendary downtown retail centers and the glorious department stores suffered a second and fatal blow in the 1990s as town centers or lifestyle retail malls became quite popular and ubiquitous (see Figure 1.1). As noted, these centers artificially re-created the feeling of a downtown retail experience featuring small streets of stores with individual entrances. The key difference, however, was that these faux streets or mock downtowns were built in former vacant lots or agricultural fields. As each provided smaller cities with their own "mini downtown areas," there was less need for a central city.

Some cities escaped the complete collapse of their downtown retail centers. Chicago, New York, Pittsburgh, and San Francisco were exceptions to what took place in cities such as Atlanta, Baltimore, Cleveland, Dallas, Detroit, and Los

Angeles (to name a few) and in numerous Canadian cities. That does not mean that unique and boutique shops (especially those that feature goods that are locally designed or manufactured) could not establish niche markets in some shrinking downtowns. Instead, if centrality were to be restored, another commercial vehicle would be needed to encourage people to live in downtown areas.

Two practices emerged in the 1980s and 1990s in response to this observation or conclusion. The first focused on investments in expensive facilities—dubbed "big ticket" items—such as an arena (for basketball, hockey, and other entertainment events), a ballpark (baseball), new centers for music, dance, and theatrical presentations, museums, or a stadium (football or soccer). These large capital projects were often located in downtown areas in an effort to return a sense of vibrancy to areas abandoned by businesses and residents. Across more than three decades there were an unprecedented number of taxpayer-financed sports facilities built in downtown areas from Baltimore to San Diego and from Charlotte, North Carolina to Seattle. (Miami would join in the effort in the 21st century in a controversial project for the Miami Marlins.) New or renovated theatres and museums were often joined to these sports facilities, and the public sector often paid most or all of the costs for these new entertainment centers too. More sports facilities also had some level of investment by teams and responsibilities for short- and long-term maintenance that were shared between teams and the public sector.

Why did the public sector invest in these facilities?

It was hoped that the billions of dollars invested in these amenities by the public sector would make central cities more attractive and encourage people to live and work in central cities. Elected leaders also hoped these new venues would make downtown "the place to be," bringing in tourists and visitors from suburban areas. Those visits could transform images of decline with crowds of people of all ages eager to live, work, and play in the "comeback" cities and their revitalized downtown areas. The presence of crowds would also generate new tax revenues through the sale of food, beverages, and souvenirs. By making real estate more valuable, property tax revenues would also increase.

The second strategy involved an effort to protect and enhance older residential neighborhoods. This strategy included new investments by the public sector in schools, roads, curbs, and other forms of infrastructure to make neighborhoods more attractive. The abatement of some property taxes was also provided to encourage people to build new homes or make substantial improvements to their existing houses. In many ways this strategy was similar to the one used for downtown areas. Public funds were used to build new infrastructure, and property tax abatements encouraged private sector investments. In the downtown area the infrastructure built took the form of big-ticket amenities. Property tax abatements were used to lure tenants to new commercial office complexes and to attract people to residences. In many, if not most, cities, both strategies were pursued. Often arguments or debates ensued questioning if one approach, the big-ticket strategy, received more or too much support at the expense of neighborhood redevelopment efforts.

Some urban theorists and community leaders argued that a focus on neighborhood revitalization was the best policy to revitalize older central cities and attract and retain higher-income households. As confidence in urban school districts declined, there were also initiatives launched to improve public education. Many advocates for central city revitalization argued that without quality educational options that matched those available in suburban areas, older cities would never succeed in attracting higher-income households. Some critics of the inclusion of big-ticket facilities in a central city's revitalization strategy worried that those projects reduced the focus on schools and neighborhoods. As will be discussed in the chapters that follow, most, if not all, of the cities that made investments in big-ticket assets also focused on community or neighborhood development activities, and no state or city ignored the needs of its public schools. Corporate associations that pushed for the building of sports facilities were sometimes the strongest advocates for increasing the property taxes paid for by their members to improve inner city schools. The case study of the redevelopment of Cleveland provides insight into the work of one of the growth regimes and the city's corporate elite in building public support for sports facilities while also leading programs that led to higher taxes for local companies and a higher commitment from local corporations to provide volunteers to help improve inner city schools.

Was there a diversion of resources from neighborhoods or from community development activities to pay for sports facilities? That possibility will also be considered in the chapters that follow. A point that will be made, however, is that the formation of a coalition to support an overall revitalization strategy often required that both strategies—community/neighborhood development and big-ticket investments to revitalize downtown areas—were political complements of each other in an effort to ensure that businesses and their economic and social capital remained vibrant supporters of revitalization efforts. The insights from each of the case studies will afford an opportunity to decide if different cities made the right policy choices, and if strategies focused on both neighborhood-level and big-ticket items are compatible and complementary.

## 1.4 Can Sports and Big-Ticket Investments Relocate Economic Activity?

The very reason that retail centers would not work for revitalization efforts *underscores* the value of sports and museums. While it is possible to replicate retail options anywhere in a region, and stores and merchants can locate anywhere they wish, the number of sports teams that can exist is controlled by the four major sports leagues. Each league has worked hard to ensure that there can only be one team in each market area. Rarely and only in the largest markets are multiple teams allowed (after permission from existing teams in that market is received).

As a result, if games are played in the central city, and if the facility and the land around it can be designed to capitalize on the movement of economic activity, there will *likely be no other economically similar attraction* in the region. Shopping centers can easily be duplicated and faux downtown (lifestyle centers) areas can be built anywhere. There will not be a second Major League Baseball (MLB) team in each region, and in regions with multiple teams in the same sport, their size permits each franchise to be successful. There are two basketball teams in Los Angeles and New York, for example, but they share markets with more than 14 million people. The three hockey teams in the metropolitan New York region—if the population of that region were divided so that each gets one-third—would each serve a population base larger than that available to any team in the NHL except for the Toronto

## A CARTEL AS AN ASSET FOR REDEVELOPMENT STRATEGIES

When people think that the four leagues have sometimes approved the location of more than one team in the same city or market area, they forget the history that led to the presence of a second team in the same area. The New York Giants (now the San Francisco Giants) and the Brooklyn (Trolley) Dodgers (Los Angeles) were part of the National League. When both teams were formed, Brooklyn was an independent city. Travel between Brooklyn and New York was inconvenient and relied on ferry service. To serve what were at that time the two largest cities in the United States, one team was placed in each city. The Yankees did emerge as a third team in the City of New York, but just as the Boston Red Sox (Stockings) and St. Louis Browns (now the Baltimore Orioles), they were initially members of the competing American League. The American and National Leagues would merge, and for several years there were multiple teams in a few cities. The Boston Braves of the National League moved to Milwaukee in the 1950s and then to Atlanta; the St. Louis Browns also moved to Baltimore (Orioles), and the Philadelphia A's relocated first to Kansas City and then to Oakland. The American Basketball Association merged with the National Basketball Association (NBA), resulting in two teams in the New York region. When the World Hockey League tried to enter the New York market in its efforts to compete with the National Hockey League (NHL), the older league placed its own second team in the region. The New York Jets were part of the American Football League, which competed with the National Football League (NFL) for several years before the two leagues merged as today's NFL.

The essential point is that the leagues rarely allow a second team to enter a region, meaning that central cities can consider revitalization plans that include professional sports a unique amenity that will not exist elsewhere in the region.

Maple Leafs and Chicago Blackhawks. Quibbling over the actual market sizes available, however, obscures the essential point. The limited number of franchises makes it possible to build a development strategy around a unique asset. That creates an opportunity to recentralize a level of economic activity that can enhance the fiscal outlook for central cities.

While there can be benefits for central cities from the cartel status of the professional leagues, the restriction on supply has led to bargaining tactics by team owners for public subsidies that have produced some egregious outcomes. Much can be learned from the deals that turned cities and regions into major league losers (Rosentraub, 1997a). Understanding how to change cities from losers to winners in the effort to revitalize downtown areas is a primary goal of this book.

## 1.4.1 The Era of Subsidies and Hope

The 1980s and 1990s—an era defined by large-scale investments by the public sector in dozens of sport facilities across North America—was not the first time governments had paid for sports facilities. What made this new wave of public investments unique was that state, provincial, and local governments agreed to pay for all or part of the cost to build and maintain new facilities while permitting team owners, event promoters, and other investors to retain most, if not all, the revenue streams created by these state-of-the-art facilities. What would make several of these leases with teams particularly egregious was that many franchises paid little or nothing while retaining most, if not all, of the revenues. These new facilities included luxury seating and numerous new advertising opportunities, including the right to sell a name for the facility to the highest bidder. Airlines, high-tech firms, and banks frequently placed their names on sports facilities, and some of these long-term deals produced millions of dollars for teams. (In some instances the public sector received some of the income from the sale of naming rights or luxury seating to offset the cost of building the facility. When that was done, those revenues were identified as an owner's investment in the facility.)

The new facilities and their innovative designs offered fans improved sight lines, meeting areas to socialize with business guests, family members, or friends, and expansive retail centers for the sale of memorabilia. Food and beverage services and choices were expanded, generating more profits. Performing arts centers followed the lead with regard to naming rights, and soon facilities from Austin to Estes Park, Colorado, to Durham, North Carolina, and to Los Angeles were adorned with the names of corporations and other benefactors.

In those instances where the public sector's leadership failed to ensure that sufficient financial benefits were received by taxpayers, teams typically received all of the revenues generated by fans at the new facilities, and in many instances shifted the cost for all or some of the facility to taxpayers. When that took place, the value of teams soared as profits increased (as a result of lower capital expenses and more

## WHEN ARE TAXES FOR A SPORTS FACILITY A SUBSIDY? WHEN ARE TAXES SPENT ON A FACILITY A STRATEGIC INVESTMENT?

For more than three decades local and state governments made large investments in venues in efforts to attract and retain teams. Property, sales (which include food and beverage taxes, taxes on alcohol and tobacco products, and taxes on hotel rooms and car rentals), income, and gaming taxes have been used to pay for part or all of the costs associated with the building and operations of new arenas, ballparks, and stadiums. The use of the public's money to pay for the building or maintenance of these facilities has sometimes been labeled as subsidies for billionaire team owners and millionaire players. It is clear that the sports industry generates sufficient revenue to pay for the complete cost of building and maintaining needed facilities. Does the spending of tax dollars on facilities mean taxpayers are subsidizing billionaires and millionaires?

If tax dollars are spent and there is no appropriate (market rate) financial return for taxpayers and the public sector, then indeed it might be appropriate to classify the use of taxes as a subsidy. What is meant by a market rate of return? If the public sector invests funds and those revenues produce an annual rate of return that exceeds 6 percent (given 2013 interest rates), then it is not appropriate to consider that a subsidy exists. If both a team and taxpayers earn a fair rate of return, then an advantageous partnership exists. If there is no increase in revenues to the public sector from new spending by fans or from the development of adjacent real estate, then the taxes expended are a subsidy. It is important to note that the public sector's investment in a sports facility does not by itself denote a subsidy. *A subsidy exists when market rate levels of financial returns are not earned by the public sector for its investment.*

How can the public sector secure a market rate return on its investment? Returns can be defined by growth in the amount of property, sales, or income taxes received as a result of the building of the facility. There have also been instances where particular revenue streams produced by a facility are assigned to the public sector. Regardless of the source, what separates a subsidy from an investment is some form of a financial return at prevailing market rates. Those returns separate major league losers from major league winners.

Some suggest that part of the value of a team's presence lies in the intangible benefits of image, quality of life, or the creation of a feeling that a city is "major league." There are ways to quantify those benefits too, and if the return were positive, then it would be appropriate to include those in any assessment of the public sector's gains. My bias, however, is to focus on the financial gains to ensure that taxpayers are made better off financially for having been involved in a commercial enterprise.

income generated by the facility). Some owners who benefitted from these overly profitable deals were able to sell their teams and earn 200- or 300-percent returns on the money they invested in the franchise. Outcomes of that nature produced a set of major league losers when independent analysts looked at the outcomes for governments and the teams. The actual increment in the value of franchises will be discussed later in this chapter. It is sufficient to note at this point that new facilities contributed to a substantial increase in the value of teams.

Team owners, however, were not the only ones to benefit when substantial subsidies were provided. Some of the higher-revenue streams found their way to the players, and many more of them became millionaires. But it must also be noted that during the time of major investments by governments in sports facilities there was little, if any, objection from fans. Attendance levels also soared. Indeed, when subsidies were the largest, protests only came from a minority of all taxpayers, some community activists, and some independent analysts.

The criticisms of these subsidies highlighted not just the scale of the returns to team owners and athletes, but the higher levels of debt assumed by cities. Other cities were frustrated by unrealized dreams of a revitalized downtown area. When focusing on the financial returns to the public sector, what separates winners from losers? How is it that some cities had better negotiators than others? The answers to these questions lie in understanding why and how sports and other special forms of entertainment can relocate regional economic activity. That understanding separates the winners from the losers.

The combination of sports, entertainment, and culture was the three-pronged approach used to rebuild downtown areas and create new images for a city and its center. Sports facilities and entertainment and cultural centers by themselves, however, are unlikely to change a region's economy.[7] Most of the spending that takes place at these venues would occur elsewhere in the region if the new facilities were not located in downtown areas. In the absence of attending games, shows, or other live performances, people spend money on other things.[8] As a result, sports facilities and cultural centers generate little or no new regional economic development even if a region attracts more tourists.[9]

## 1.4.2 What Can New Facilities Do for a Region and City?

New sports and cultural facilities can be anchors for the redevelopment of nearby real estate. The facilities themselves are catalysts or engines of real estate development strategies. In addition, by their physical size these facilities have the potential to become iconic assets that replace dilapidated and deteriorating buildings.

What defines a mixed-use entertainment district?

It is one that includes residential and office space and neighborhood retail outlets (e.g., food markets, restaurants, parks, and coffee shops) as well as unique entertainment assets. A sport venue has to be both an anchor for a new

By itself, however, a big-ticket asset does not change economic patterns within a region. Those are only changed when adjacent real estate is redeveloped to produce a new neighborhood and a mixed-use entertainment district. If related real estate development does not occur, it is unlikely that real economic benefits will be produced for a host city. **If there are no real economic benefits or financial returns for a city that hosts a professional sports team, then there is no reason for the public sector to invest in a venue.**

neighborhood and an integral part of the area integrated with the other uses. A facility must fit with the other uses and properties that are built as the same time as the facility. When this planned development occurs, an area is created where people want to live, work, play, and spend money. That spending creates new tax revenues for central cities by moving discretionary spending from suburban to downtown areas. In the areas with the most sophisticated development plans new neighborhoods are developed.[10] When that happens, even more tax revenues are generated. Sports facilities as a result of the large crowds that attend games produce a volume of economic activity that creates the potential to redistribute spending patterns within a metropolitan area. When that occurs, the central city gains revenues, as the spending by fans and visitors produces taxes that would have likely been collected in suburban areas. But to change revenue flows in a region, the appropriate mix of real estate projects needs to be built adjacent to the facility. Cities become major league winners when the right mix of real estate is built adjacent to the facility that, in turn, increases tax flows for the city. When that occurs, the money spent by the public sector is a strategic investment. When the appropriate mix of real estate is not built, the public sector's dollars for building and maintaining a facility becomes a subsidy.

Many communities in the 1980s and 1990s invested tax money in sports, entertainment, and cultural facilities hoping mixed-use neighborhoods or districts would then be built, as investors would be attracted to the area. Strategies like that rarely work. What is needed is a detailed master plan that is prepared when the sports facility is designed. That plan must also include private sector investments or commitments to build related real estate projects *at the same time* as the sports facility is built. Private investments have to be coordinated with those made by the public sector. Both partners have to accept risk at the same point in time. What usually fails as a process is anticipated or hoped for future investments *after* the public sector has made its investment. Simply put, too many cities did more hoping than they did planning and insisting on establishing partnerships with private capital to achieve success.[12]

**WHAT MAKES A CITY A MAJOR LEAGUE WINNER
WHEN INVESTING IN SPORTS? THERE IS ONLY
ONE ANSWER TO THAT QUESTION**

The building of entertainment, residential, and commercial properties anchored by sports and cultural facilities establishes for community leaders an opportunity to capitalize on the attraction of large crowds and the relocation of economic activity. That is the real value of sports and cultural amenities for cities. When that development does not occur, the taxes spent to build facilities become subsidies. Sports facilities, entertainment complexes, and cultural facilities that are part of large-scale redevelopment efforts involving substantial levels of private investment can renew downtown areas and generate real economic development. But outcomes like that require plans and a substantial investment of private capital.[11]

## 1.5 The Beginning of an End for the Need for Central Cities: Human Capital and Economic Development

Why did voters, elected officials, and community leaders continue to raise taxes to subsidize sports and other cultural facilities when the initial warnings claimed that there would be no economic benefits?[13] The reasons vary, but the themes in every instance were similar. When it comes to sports, many argue that large cities or regions without teams do not have a "major league image." It is believed that second-rate images mean businesses and highly skilled workers will choose to locate elsewhere.[14] One St. Louis leader, when asked why he favored a subsidy to convince the NFL's Rams to move from California to Missouri, replied that too many people thought the city's best days were behind it (because it had lost its football team to the Phoenix metropolitan region). Some believed the Rams would make St. Louis "big league" in ways the St. Louis Cardinals (baseball team) or Washington University could not. That is difficult to understand given the success of the baseball team (won 11 World Series, second only to the New York Yankees) and the stature of Washington University (ranked 31st in the world).[15]

To be sure, sports teams are treasured assets; it is also clear that sports are important to people when tens of millions of fans will pay billions of dollars for tickets. That importance would not lead to tax subsidies if the major sports leagues were not given the ability to control the supply and location of teams. Antitrust exemptions and special laws allow the leagues to create auctions where cities compete to host teams.[16] If any city does not meet an owner's demands, teams have the ability to move elsewhere and the leagues—more often than not—would only replace the team if an even larger subsidy were provided in later years. But to understand why cities turned to sports and entertainment to change economic development patterns, a bit more history is needed.

## 1.5.1 Human Capital and Amenities

The changing structure of the U.S. and world economy—and the breakthroughs in communication and transportation—means that companies can now locate where the best and brightest workers want to live. As people's incomes rise, they also want to live in areas that offer a greater number of varied and interesting tourism experiences that can be enjoyed on weekends. So the new middle and upper classes want high-quality urban services and a high quality of life in what Pine and Gilmore (1999)[17] describe as the "experience economy." It is not only that work and presentations have become wedded to experiences. Consumers have shifted their consumption preferences to include a desire to be able to enjoy experiences through the unique entertainment produced by sports, arts, culture, and other amenities. Cities that offer more experiences are more desirable, and businesses want locations that appeal to talented workers. That frequently means that the most desirable cities are those with the best quality of life, the best mix of amenities, and a set of large-scale and neighborhood-based entertainment assets. People need to live where the jobs are, but the companies that create jobs want to locate where they are confident there will be the right mix of amenities that appeal to the idea generators needed to increase profits. Economic development is driven by human capital, and corporations choose to locate where employees want to live.

Professional sports remain an integral part of the mix of amenities valued by employees, and ignoring them is not a viable option. Communities need to make public safety and education their highest priorities. Cities can offer a very high quality of life without being home to a professional sports team or a major collegiate sports program. Yet virtually all of the towns and cities on the myriad of "best places to live lists" are located in close proximity to facilities that are home to one or more professional sports teams, entertainment and performing arts centers, or universities and colleges with major sports programs.[18] The real opportunity for a city's leadership is not to choose between sports and public safety or education, but to understand how some community leaders were able to use sports, entertainment, and cultural facilities to advance the quality of life while producing tax revenue that could be used for public safety or any other needed services. As Eisinger observed:

> Few people would argue with the proposition that facilities that bring high or even mass culture, sports, and recreational opportunities to a city may enhance the quality of life. Stadiums and performing arts centers and festival malls help to transform places that would otherwise simply be markets or dormitories.... The issue, then, is not whether to spend public money [for sports or entertainment facilities]; rather the issue is a matter of balance and proportionality.[19]

This book is about the balance achieved by successful leadership in several different cities and the positive economic development outcomes that took place. In each of the case studies the risks taken by the cities, the commitment by the private sector, and the specific plans developed will be discussed. The outcomes in each situation for the downtown areas, for the cities and their financial capabilities, and other impacts will also be identified. Through these analyses the opportunities available to other cities will be identified.

## 1.5.2  Are Sports (Entertainment and Culture) a City's Fool's Gold?

If numerous festival marketplaces failed to relocate economic activity and advance central city revitalization, why should anyone have any faith that the outcome from sports (entertainment and culture) will be any different? Their value lies in their timeless importance. While some disdain the importance of sports or simply ignore it, sports have been an integral part of most, if not all, societies. Some might think the mass popularity of sports is a product of the modern media age, ESPN, and fantasy leagues. Sports, however, have had a similar level of importance for past civilizations that probably matches the zeal produced by fantasy teams and those willing to pay premium prices for the best seats to important games. To be sure, at no other time in history have athletes earned the financial rewards now available, and never before have prices for tickets to some events been as expensive while the demand for more experiences continues to exceed supply. But that does not minimize the timeless appeal of sports.

For example, ancient Rome used sports to showcase its technological achievements as well as its wealth through the building of a facility replete with luxury seating, the ability to host both aquatic and land-based spectacles, and room for 50,000 spectators. The Colosseum, built more than 1,900 years ago, was larger in terms of spectator capacity than the home fields of every MLB team except the New York Yankees and the Los Angeles Dodgers.[20] Its incorporation of luxury seating with colorful cloth coverings to protect the elite from the sweltering sun was said to be part of the inspiration for the building of America's first indoor stadium, Houston's Astrodome, and the offering of luxury seating options to fans. For Western societies, written records from as early as 776 BCE document the importance placed on sports; those records are the earliest reports of organized athletic competitions. Potter (2012) suggests the Olympics might have begun in 600 BCE. The games continued for more than nine centuries by Potter's estimate and were only ended in 393 CE. With the acceptance of Christianity by the Roman Empire, the Olympics, with their association with Greek deities, might have seemed to be an inappropriate fit. More importantly, the games had also become quite expensive, and some leaders questioned their value. That is a sentiment that is reflected today by some critics of the Olympics and the World Cup.

The Roman contribution to sports—some credit the empire with the creation of professional sports, or at least making sports a profession—begins in 310 BCE with the onset of gladiatorial games and the establishment of training centers for combatants. By 183 BCE major gladiatorial contests involved as many as 60 pairs of fighters with far larger spectacles to follow in later years. The apex of sports in the Roman Empire involved the building of the Colosseum and the staging of events involving boats, animals, and gladiators. Beyond the brutality of gladiatorial games and the construction of facilities throughout the empire to underscore the empire's prowess, the Romans also used facilities as a central component of the design of cities from Rome through the Decapolis (the 10 cities on the eastern edge of the empire) to Pula (Croatia). Roman cities had sports facilities or performing arts venues at their center, a pattern American cities would follow in the 1980s and 1990s when many tried to rebuild deteriorating downtown areas.

The Romans' credit for professionalizing sports is a result of their establishment of training centers (schools) for gladiators and a system where "rookies," or gladiators with lower or untested skills, were sent to contests in smaller cities (or markets). As gladiators won matches in these "minor league" markets, they were promoted to matches in larger cities. Those who eventually made it to Rome could actually win their freedom if they survived. The technological mastery of flooding the lowest levels of the Colosseum to permit water games established the prowess of the empire's engineering skills and was an early forerunner of the design of facilities to handle many different types of events. In the modern era, arenas are designed for basketball and other platform-type events, ice hockey and shows, and events involving dirt racing and "monster trucks."

Sports events also have a long history of being part of religious or holiday celebrations. The Great Ball Court at Mexico's Chichen-Itza is more than 1,000 years old and was the site of games tied to religious rites, including human sacrifices that took place at the conclusion of the matches. The Hippodrome of Constantinople was the sporting and social center built in the second century (CE) and then expanded by Constantine in 324. The races held at this location began at least 1,700 years ago, making sports a central part of urban life in the Byzantine period and extending through the years of the Ottoman Empire. The city's largest religious center faces the Hippodrome.[21]

Sports' cross-cultural significance or role is also underscored by the game of lacrosse. Invented by Native Americans, it received its modern name from French missionaries, and became adopted by many settlers in the New World. Although it is unclear when the playing of lacrosse began, what is apparent is that the native population of North, Central, and South America played sports long before the Europeans arrived. Sports have been part of numerous societies and assuming central religious, political, and social roles for at least 2,500 years. Today, sports remain an integral part of holiday celebrations, with featured games on Christmas Day and the celebration of the New Year dominated by college football's bowl games.

The long-standing role of culture and entertainment in society is easily under-scored by the inclusion of the performing arts and plays in ancient Greece; plays were also performed as part of the Olympic Games or festivals. The emergence and importance of English theatre dates back at least 500 years. Music's role in defining a city's identity and its cultural standing shares a similar, if not a longer, history. The continuing and long-standing nature of these assets suggests the prudence of their incorporation in revitalization strategies.

While some might dislike sports, their enduring importance and the physical value placed on the facilities used for games are what make them a part of soci-ety's social capital. Social capital has been defined as institutions that facilitate "the development of relationships of mutual reciprocity embedded in social net-works that enable action— ... generate trust, establish expectations, and create norms. Social capital's value centres upon the fact that it identifies certain impor-tant aspects of community social structure and the significance of social organiza-tion."[22] Sports are also part of the social capital of society, and through their role as socializing institutions increase stability and underscore the political values of a society.[23] Lefebvre has concluded that places within a city that encourage identifi-cation with a group facilitate the ability of individuals to build relationships that enhance identities and reduce the stress of isolation that can be endemic in large urban societies.[24]

How do sports and the facilities they use create this type of social capital? Any community can point to celebrations when teams win major games or champion-ships and the "electricity" that seems to change daily life.[25] The power or strength of a society is underscored by games. The Roman gladiatorial games held in the large structures built by the engineering expertise of the Roman Empire were designed to visibly demonstrate the expertise of Rome. When different governments and regimes seek to stage major athletic events, they sometimes do so to underscore the superiority and accomplishments of their society. Numerous other examples of the use of sports and sport venues to highlight a society's accomplishments could include the Greeks' staging of the original Olympics to proclaim the virtues of their civilization to the modern era, international events held by the Nazi regime in Berlin, and messaging regarding China's new role in the world as a result of host-ing the Summer Olympics in Beijing. America's return to some level of normalcy after the 9/11 attacks was inexorably tied to the resumption of MLB games and the staging of the World Series.[26] The outpouring of emotion at these sporting events is probably the most poignant example of the role of sports as social capital. Baseball also assumed a role in socializing immigrants to the American way of life, whereas soccer assumed a role in relieving the drudgery of industrial life in England and maintaining stability.[27]

Some might still note that there were ancient retail centers that attracted large crowds, and these too dominated in the center parts of cities across numerous empires. Are downtown sports facilities destined to fail, as have many downtown retail centers? Here the issue of unique activity within a region and its availability at one location is critical. Professional sports teams, and to a similar extent live performances by leading entertainers and museums, cannot be easily replicated elsewhere in a region. While retail was able to decentralize to suburban areas, the vast majority of metropolitan regions will only have one team in each of the four major sports leagues, one set of museums, and one or two arenas for first-run concerts.[28] Where these teams play creates unique experiences for that region.

## 1.6 Sports, Entertainment, and Culture: The Trinity for Redevelopment

While sports facilities have received the most attention in assessments of redevelopment efforts, in virtually every instance entertainment, arts, and cultural centers were integral parts of the overall development plan. Baltimore's harbor front was expanded to include a ballpark and stadium, but it is also home to the National Aquarium. Indianapolis wanted to become the amateur sports capital, but its extensive downtown redevelopment plan also included refurbished performance halls for the Indianapolis Symphony and the Indiana Repertory Theatre and several museums. Cleveland's redevelopment effort included five theatres for the performing arts and two museums. Reading, Little Rock, and Louisville each also included the performing arts as anchors in their redevelopment, and L.A. LIVE may well establish a new standard for a downtown entertainment zone with several theatres for movies and the performing arts joined to residential space and a hotel. Denver started its focus on LODO (lower downtown) before the Colorado Rockies were part of the revitalization effort. There too arts and cultural centers were part of the city. How cities successfully used sports for redevelopment is a formula laden with examples of the use of performing arts centers.

### 1.6.1 An Uneven Negotiating Table

The importance of the principles for ensuring that taxes expended for sports and entertainment venues become investments and not subsidies is underscored by the distinct advantages team owners and others have when seeking support from cities.

Across three decades, taxpayers across North America spent billions of dollars for dozens of sports facilities.[29] Why did they do this? They and their elected officials were driven by a fear that if they failed to give a team or a sports league what they demanded, some other city would "pay the piper" and an integral part of the losing city's image and quality of life would decline. That decline was seen as a threat to the ability to attract and retain corporations. Cities that lost teams were afraid they would be seen as less desirable places to live and places avoided by successful firms. The fear led to a failure to protect taxpayers.

Some thought owners were to blame for the lack of financial return for the public sector and taxpayers. Nothing could be further from the truth. Owners, league officials, or those who operate entertainment venues are not responsible to protect or advance the interests of taxpayers. That responsibility rests with elected and appointed officials. This book is for them and for students who want to lead their communities. There are ways to forge real public–private partnerships that benefit teams and taxpayers. It is the responsibility of public officials to lead those partnerships. This book is designed to give those who will lead the tools and understandings to make their cities major league winners.

Team owners were quick to capitalize on the fears that some city leaders had, and bidding wars ensued where the city that often paid the most became home to the franchise. Cities did not analyze returns, and most did not develop strategies that ensured taxpayers received sufficient value for their investment. Too many public officials were driven by the fear that if their city failed to meet a team's demand, the community would lose the franchise. In the 1980s and 1990s, the Baltimore Colts, Los Angeles Rams, Cleveland Browns, and Houston Oilers moved to other cities, each in response to a better offer for a new stadium, respectively from Indianapolis, St. Louis, Baltimore, and Nashville. The Chicago White Sox and Cleveland Indians announced they too would move if a tax-supported facility was not built, and rather than calling their bluff, both communities raised taxes. New facilities with tax subsidies were also provided by several cities to secure expansion franchises. Cleveland (Browns), Denver (Rockies), Houston (Texans), and Phoenix (Diamondbacks) promised MLB and the NFL they would build new stadiums or ballparks if awarded a new franchise, and each was successful in getting the team it wanted.

Fear of a loss of a franchise, however, does not warrant failing to ensure that tax dollars do not become subsidies. Tax dollars should be prudently invested. Fear leads to poor decision making, and too often those ill-advised actions lead to unwarranted and unnecessary subsidies. There are partnerships that can be formed that benefit both team owners and cities. There are win-win scenarios, and finding those outcomes is the responsibility of elected and appointed officials.

Every partnership with a sports team must be guided by seven rules. First, at the regional level, facilities and teams have slight marginal effects on economic development. Second, facilities developed for large-scale events that attract a large number of tourists on a one-time basis do not generate longer-term economic returns to a host city or country. Indeed, research suggests that after the Olympics or World Cup, annual tourism levels cannot sustain the use of the facilities built or hotels and other amenities created for the event.[30] Third, if a set of amenities can attract a large number of events every year (such as entire seasons of games and other entertainment events), regional economic activity can be *relocated* to the benefit of the host city.[31] Fourth, it does matter *where* facilities are built in that downtown locations are able to (1) concentrate other amenities into a package that enhances local spending in the area of a facility and (2) it is indeed possible to move recreational spending through a facility's placement that can enhance a central city's finances.[32] Fifth, it is possible to use sports facilities to anchor redevelopment efforts that relocate spending and economic activity within a region.[33] Sixth, where development occurs within a region may well be as important as whether it even occurs. Sports facilities can change the location of development.[34] Seventh, if there is no real estate development adjacent to a facility, there will be no real fiscal economic benefits for the public sector.

## THE BENEFITS FROM NEW FACILITIES FOR OWNERS AND PLAYERS

Taxpayer-supported subsidies are just one of the factors that can lead to increases in the values of teams and higher salaries for players. Television contracts and ticket revenues can be equally or more important in terms of increasing a team's value or the salaries paid to players. When teams do not have to pay the full cost for building facilities, this too improves their bottom line. How well did the owners and players do?

Table 1.3 illustrates the changing value of MLB teams (in 5-year intervals) from 1995 through 2010. *Forbes* annually estimates the value of every major sports franchise. While some question the accuracy of these estimates, the sale prices of teams has usually exceeded *Forbes'* projections. For example, in 2012, *Forbes* estimated the value of the Los Angeles Dodgers at $1.4 billion. The team was sold for more than $2 billion. In 2012, the Sacramento Kings were thought to be worth approximately $300 million. A year later, the team was sold for more than $525 million. As a result, the *Forbes'* estimates could be considered conservative.

These increasing values of franchises are a function of several factors, including the revenue streams generated by ballparks. In recent years it would be prudent to note that the rising value of media rights has made all teams more valuable. The revenue streams from facilities, however, also contribute to a team's valuation. In real terms, the value of MLB franchises increased 65.7 percent. The changes for each individual team and the estimated market value for all franchises (in 2013 dollars) are shown in Table 1.3.

The players have also done very well as a result of the new revenue streams produced by new facilities and rising media contracts. Focusing on MLB players, in real terms aggregate salaries increased by 28 percent from 2000 to 2010 (see Table 1.4). The benefits enjoyed by owners and players underscore the need for public officials to ensure that cities also benefit and enjoy market rate returns on the investment of tax dollars.

**Table 1.3 The Increasing Value of Major League Baseball Teams, 1995–2010, Selected Years (in 2013 millions of dollars)**

| Team | 1995 | Team | 2000 | Team | 2005 | Team | 2010 |
|---|---|---|---|---|---|---|---|
| All teams | 4,734 | All teams | 9,523 | All teams | 11,952 | All teams | 15,772 |
| New York Yankees | 283 | New York Yankees | 745 | New York Yankees | 1,140 | New York Yankees | 1,712 |
| Atlanta Braves | 251 | Boston Red Sox | 528 | Boston Red Sox | 676 | Boston Red Sox | 931 |
| Cleveland Indians | 240 | New York Mets | 495 | New York Mets | 606 | New York Mets | 918 |
| Baltimore Orioles | 233 | Los Angeles Dodgers | 472 | Los Angeles Dodgers | 509 | Los Angeles Dodgers | 778 |
| Los Angeles Dodgers | 223 | Seattle Mariners | 442 | Seattle Mariners | 498 | Chicago Cubs | 777 |
| New York Mets | 219 | Chicago Cubs | 427 | Chicago Cubs | 478 | Philadelphia Phillies | 575 |
| Colorado Rockies | 219 | Philadelphia Phillies | 415 | Philadelphia Phillies | 470 | Los Angeles Angels | 557 |
| Texas Rangers | 207 | Atlanta Braves | 400 | Atlanta Braves | 458 | St. Louis Cardinals | 522 |
| Seattle Mariners | 205 | San Francisco Giants | 394 | San Francisco Giants | 457 | San Francisco Giants | 517 |
| Boston Red Sox | 184 | St. Louis Cardinals | 386 | St. Louis Cardinals | 444 | Chicago White Sox | 499 |
| Houston Astros | 179 | Houston Astros | 381 | Houston Astros | 428 | Houston Astros | 485 |
| Arizona Diamondbacks | 168 | Baltimore Orioles | 364 | Baltimore Orioles | 409 | Texas Rangers | 483 |
| Chicago Cubs | 158 | San Diego Padres | 329 | San Diego Padres | 395 | Atlanta Braves | 482 |

*(Continued)*

**Table 1.3 The Increasing Value of Major League Baseball Teams, 1995–2010, Selected Years (in 2013 millions of dollars) (Continued)**

| Team | 1995 | Team | 2000 | Team | 2005 | Team | 2010 |
|---|---|---|---|---|---|---|---|
| San Francisco Giants | 156 | San Francisco Giants | 322 | Texas Rangers | 391 | Seattle Mariners | 470 |
| Oakland Athletics | 155 | St. Louis Cardinals | 298 | Cleveland Indians | 383 | San Diego Padres | 437 |
| Kansas City Royals | 147 | Detroit Tigers | 272 | Washington Nationals | 372 | Minnesota Twins | 433 |
| Philadelphia Phillies | 147 | San Diego Padres | 268 | Los Angeles Angels | 353 | Cleveland Indians | 418 |
| Florida Marlins | 141 | Anaheim Angels | 265 | Colorado Rockies | 348 | Washington Nationals | 414 |
| Houston Astros | 141 | Cincinnati Reds | 238 | Arizona Diamondbacks | 343 | Colorado Rockies | 411 |
| California Angels | 135 | Milwaukee Brewers | 227 | Chicago White Sox | 314 | Arizona Diamondbacks | 406 |
| Cincinnati Reds | 129 | Chicago White Sox | 226 | Cincinnati Reds | 306 | Baltimore Orioles | 402 |
| Detroit Tigers | 127 | Tampa Bay Devil Rays | 222 | Detroit Tigers | 287 | Detroit Tigers | 401 |
| Minnesota Twins | 122 | Toronto Blue Jays | 220 | Pittsburgh Pirates | 262 | Milwaukee Brewers | 376 |
| Montreal Expos | 116 | Pittsburgh Pirates | 219 | Toronto Blue Jays | 257 | Kansas City Royals | 365 |
| Seattle Mariners | 116 | Philadelphia Phillies | 204 | Milwaukee Brewers | 250 | Cincinnati Reds | 354 |

| Milwaukee Brewers | 115 | Oakland Athletics | 182 | Florida Marlins | 247 | Toronto Blue Jays | 349 |
|---|---|---|---|---|---|---|---|
| San Diego Padres | 113 | Florida Marlins | 170 | Kansas City Royals | 224 | Florida Marlins | 339 |
| Pittsburgh Pirates | 107 | Kansas City Royals | 166 | Oakland Athletics | 222 | Tampa Bay Rays | 338 |
| | | Minnesota Twins | 124 | Minnesota Twins | 214 | Oakland Athletics | 316 |
| | | Montreal Expos | 121 | Tampa Bay Devil Rays | 211 | Pittsburgh Pirates | 309 |

*Source: Forbes, various years.*

*Note:* Major League Baseball expanded and the values for the Arizona Diamondbacks and Florida Marlins are included beginning in 2000. Since there were more teams in 2000, the aggregate value of all teams would have been expected to increase from 1995 to 2000, but not by 101.2 percent. The rising value was related to new and higher-revenue streams enjoyed by teams. The real increase between 2000 and 2010 reflects the full complement of 30 franchises. The Montreal Expos became the Washington Nationals in 2005.

**Table 1.4  The Increasing Salaries of Major League Baseball Players, 1995–2010, Selected Years (in 2013 millions of dollars)**

| Team | 1995 | Team | 2000 | Team | 2005 | Team | 2010 |
|---|---|---|---|---|---|---|---|
| All teams | 1,323 | All teams | 2,229 | All teams | 2,554 | All teams | 2,854 |
| Toronto Blue Jays | 74.7 | New York Yankees | 123.6 | New York Yankees | 243.7 | New York Yankees | 216.7 |
| New York Yankees | 70.0 | Los Angeles Dodgers | 120.2 | Boston Red Sox | 144.5 | Boston Red Sox | 170.6 |
| Atlanta Braves | 67.8 | Baltimore Orioles | 110.6 | New York Mets | 118.5 | Chicago Cubs | 154.0 |
| Baltimore Orioles | 61.3 | Atlanta Braves | 110.0 | Philadelphia Phillies | 111.8 | Philadelphia Phillies | 149.0 |
| Chicago White Sox | 60.0 | Boston Red Sox | 108.0 | St. Louis Cardinals | 107.8 | New York Mets | 141.1 |
| Cincinnati Reds | 55.9 | New York Mets | 106.1 | San Francisco Giants | 105.5 | Detroit Tigers | 129.0 |
| Oakland Athletics | 54.0 | Arizona Diamondbacks | 105.4 | Seattle Mariners | 102.7 | Chicago White Sox | 110.8 |
| Detroit Tigers | 54.0 | Cleveland Indians | 101.8 | Los Angeles Angels | 102.5 | Los Angeles Angels | 110.2 |
| Cleveland Indians | 52.8 | Texas Rangers | 94.1 | Chicago Cubs | 101.8 | San Francisco Giants | 103.6 |
| San Francisco Giants | 52.4 | Tampa Bay Rays | 85.7 | Atlanta Braves | 101.2 | Minnesota Twins | 102.4 |
| Seattle Mariners | 51.4 | St. Louis Cardinals | 83.9 | Los Angeles Dodgers | 97.2 | Los Angeles Dodgers | 100.1 |
| Chicago Cubs | 48.7 | Houston Astros | 82.6 | Chicago Cubs | 89.8 | St. Louis Cardinals | 98.2 |

| | | | | | | | |
|---|---|---|---|---|---|---|---|
| Texas Rangers | 48.6 | Detroit Tigers | 82.1 | Chicago White Sox | 88.0 | Houston Astros | 97.0 |
| Houston Astros | 47.5 | Colorado Rockies | 81.6 | Baltimore Orioles | 86.5 | Seattle Mariners | 90.8 |
| Colorado Rockies | 46.7 | Seattle Mariners | 78.8 | Detroit Tigers | 80.8 | Atlanta Braves | 88.6 |
| St. Louis Cardinals | 46.4 | San Diego Padres | 73.1 | Arizona Diamondbacks | 74.1 | Colorado Rockies | 88.4 |
| Los Angeles Dodgers | 45.7 | San Francisco Giants | 71.2 | San Diego Padres | 74.1 | Baltimore Orioles | 85.7 |
| Los Angeles Angels | 43.5 | Houston Astros | 69.3 | Cincinnati Reds | 72.4 | Milwaukee Brewers | 85.2 |
| Boston Red Sox | 43.0 | Los Angeles Angels | 68.2 | Miami Marlins | 70.8 | Tampa Bay Rays | 75.5 |
| Philadelphia Phillies | 42.9 | Philadelphia Phillies | 62.4 | Minnesota Twins | 65.7 | Cincinnati Reds | 75.4 |
| Kansas City Royals | 41.4 | Toronto Blue Jays | 61.7 | Texas Rangers | 65.3 | Kansas City Royals | 75.0 |
| San Diego Padres | 38.9 | Cincinnati Reds | 58.8 | Oakland Athletics | 64.9 | Toronto Blue Jays | 65.4 |
| Minnesota Twins | 36.8 | Milwaukee Brewers | 47.6 | Washington Nationals | 56.8 | Washington Nationals | 64.5 |
| New York Mets | 36.5 | Montreal Expos | 44.6 | Colorado Rockies | 56.3 | Cleveland Indians | 64.3 |
| Miami Marlins | 35.5 | Oakland Athletics | 42.7 | Toronto Blue Jays | 53.5 | Arizona Diamondbacks | 63.8 |
| Pittsburgh Pirates | 25.6 | Chicago White Sox | 41.4 | Cleveland Indians | 48.6 | Miami Marlins | 60.0 |

*(Continued)*

**Table 1.4  The Increasing Salaries of Major League Baseball Players, 1995–2010, Selected Years (in 2013 millions of dollars) (Continued)**

| Team | 1995 | Team | 2000 | Team | 2005 | Team | 2010 |
|---|---|---|---|---|---|---|---|
| Milwaukee Brewers | 24.3 | Pittsburgh Pirates | 35.3 | Milwaukee Brewers | 46.7 | Texas Rangers | 58.0 |
| Montreal Expos | 18.1 | Kansas City Royals | 30.8 | Pittsburgh Pirates | 44.6 | Oakland Athletics | 54.2 |
|  |  | Miami Marlins | 26.4 | Kansas City Royals | 43.2 | San Diego Padres | 40.0 |
|  |  | Minnesota Twins | 20.8 | Tampa Bay Rays | 34.7 | Pittsburgh Pirates | 36.7 |

*Note:* Major League Baseball expanded and the salaries for players for the Arizona Diamondbacks and Florida Marlins are included beginning in 2000. Since there were more teams in 2000, the aggregate value of all teams would have been expected to increase from 1995 to 2000. The real increase between 2000 and 2010 reflects the full complement of 30 franchises. The Montreal Expos became the Washington Nationals in 2005.

## 1.6.2 Rising Prices, Rising Values, and Rising Salaries: Any Fan Protests?

Have fans been disenchanted with higher taxes for sports facilities, higher salaries for players, higher ticket prices, higher prices for food and souvenirs, and the escalating value of team franchises? The answer is no. Even after paying higher sales, parking, property, car rental, and other taxes to support the ability of state and local governments to help build arenas, ballparks, and stadiums, fans continued to buy tens of millions of higher priced tickets. Even through the severe recession that began in 2008, fans continued to buy tickets to games.

In 2010, NFL teams sold 17,007,172 tickets to their regular season games. In 2011, 17,124,389 tickets were sold, and in 2012, 17,178,573 were sold. There has been no substantial change in the overall demand for tickets even though some teams did suffer a decline in attendance. In 2010, MLB teams sold 73.1 million tickets; in 2012, 74.9 million were sold. Both the NBA and NHL suffered through work stoppages, but neither saw a loss in popularity, and there were numerous reports that the 2013 Stanley Cup play-offs were the most watched in league history. The NBA Finals in 2013 also enjoyed robust television ratings. Fans are clearly not disaffected by taxes for sports facilities or by being required to pay higher prices for tickets or for food, beverages, and merchandise sold at sports facilities.

With fans buying tickets (or watching games in large numbers), it might seem there would be little interest from players, owners, or even public officials to change the system. If there is no resentment or push-back from fans, why worry if there are cities that subsidize sports facilities and fail to receive market rate returns on the funds expended for arenas, ballparks, and stadiums? Despite record attendance, there is substantial dissatisfaction with the failure of the public sector to benefit from the building of sports facilities from voters. For example, in many communities large proportions of voters have been opposed to new taxes for a sports facility even when a team threatened to move. MLB's commissioner told Clevelanders he would support the team's relocation if they did not approve a tax hike to build a new ballpark, but 48 percent of the voters and a majority of those who lived and voted in Cleveland cast their ballots against a new ballpark.[35] The suburban residents who would pay more than two-thirds of the taxes to build the new facility were the margin of victory. Columbus, Ohio's voters rejected a subsidy for a new arena to secure an expansion franchise in the NHL, and had the facility not been privately financed, the Blue Jackets would not have been created.

Timmons[36] found that slightly more than half, 54 percent, of 35 referenda for tax-subsidized sports facilities across the last 27 years were passed; with 46 percent failing, there is clearly substantial discontent with the structure of many sports facility development proposals. While some proposals did enjoy very strong support—81 percent of the voters supported the building of a new ballpark and stadium in Detroit for the Tigers and Lions—in Arlington, Texas, even after an extensive and well-financed campaign by the Dallas Cowboys, the plan for $325 million in taxpayer support for a new stadium was supported by only 55 percent of the voters. There was virtually no financial support behind the antistadium forces, but a small group of opponents was able to convince 45 percent of the voters to oppose the use of a sales tax increase to pay for part of a new home for the Cowboys. In Houston a proposal for a new ballpark received support from just 51.1 percent of the voters, and a referendum placed before Milwaukee's voters for a new home for the Brewers was rejected. The ballpark was eventually built when the state legislature approved a subsidy. The Minnesota Vikings and the Minnesota Twins saw several of their proposals for new facilities fail to receive legislative support before success was finally secured. The Florida state legislature in 2013 refused to consider a plan from the Miami Dolphins for renovations to their stadium that would have involved the commitment of public money matched by funds from the team. That action was inexorably linked to voters' dissatisfaction with the substantial subsidy provided for a new ballpark for the Miami Marlins. After providing substantial support for a new ballpark, Floridians were forced to watch as the owner reduced the team's payroll, making the franchise far less competitive. With little new real estate development surrounding the new ballpark, public leaders and voters were left to ask what the value was of their investment. That question plagued the discussion of an investment for improvements to the stadium used by the Miami Dolphins despite the NFL's promise of another Super Bowl. In summary, while fans are still buying tickets and watching games in record numbers, voters and legislators still question the value of the public sector's investment in facilities. This book is designed to help avoid the negative outcomes suffered in Florida and elsewhere.

Electoral discontent is not the only measure of the resentment over the subsidies provided to teams. When the Colts left Baltimore for Indianapolis, they narrowly avoided seizure through an eminent domain action. The effort failed as the legal process took a few days, and when the Colts' owner heard about the effort, he arranged to move the team in the middle of the night. While Baltimore's effort was unsuccessful, in a resulting court action, the right of a city to seize the tangible and intangible assets represented by a team was upheld. Baltimore's claim was only denied because the team had left a few hours before the papers could be legally served. Years later, Indiana's legislature held hearings on the issue of eminent domain and sports franchises when there was fear the Colts might leave. The city attorney of San Diego has ensnared the Chargers in numerous legal battles while also considering the use of eminent domain to prohibit a move. The Chargers have still not resolved their need for a new stadium, as a public–private partnership acceptable to all parties has not been forged. Building partnerships that avoid confrontations and build the needed facilities is in everyone's interests. And it is possible for teams, players, fans, and taxpayers to each benefit when a new facility is built.

If teams were not important to communities, this conflict could just be shrugged off and classified as being far less critical than many of the other issues that mayors, county leaders, and communities must address. But sports and teams enjoy a level of importance, and the ability to capitalize on that importance to secure subsidies calls for a very different approach to the building of sports facilities. Teams and the facilities they use generate a great deal of economic activity and attract a great deal of attention. Those assets create the opportunity for cities and teams to fashion new approaches to the development of facilities that substantially enhance the financial benefits received by cities. If that can be achieved, citizens' dissatisfaction with many of the deals that led to the building of new ballparks, stadiums, and arenas can be minimized.

## 1.7 Misplaced Revenues, Misplaced Values

Any assessment of the role of sports, entertainment, and cultural facilities in urban revitalization occurs against the backdrop of the supposed, anticipated, or actual linkage between amenities and economic development. There are many social scientists and policy experts who argue that any public money spent on amenities—sports or otherwise—will not change economic development patterns.[37] From their perspective, this book might appear to be unnecessary or, at best, misguided and offer no real policy guidance for communities.

As will be more fully explored in Chapter 2, there should be no debate over the importance of human capital, and therefore education for economic development. Skilled labor is what drives an economy. The failure to produce and attract the educated workers that firms need will lead to economic decline. Areas that grow are those with higher concentrations of educated workers. In that regard, then, there should be no confusion that what is discussed in this book does not contradict the central view of the dominant and determining role of human capital in economic development and for any revitalization or rebuilding strategy. No one should doubt that any amenity is as important as programs to educate workers. It would be foolish to build sports or entertainment facilities while ignoring or underfunding human capital development activities.

Yet the value of human capital and lower transportation and communication costs means that corporations and people are less bound to specific geographic areas. As other needed resources (energy, capital, etc.) also become available regardless of a corporation's location, a key question becomes: Where do or where would skilled workers prefer to live? If labor is the driving force in a corporation's profitability, then it follows that firms will seek to locate where they are assured of a steady flow of productive workers. Businesses will locate where people want to live.

A collateral question on the minds of many community leaders is that with North America's colleges and universities producing high numbers of trained workers, how does a city like Cleveland, Detroit, Edmonton, Hamilton (Ontario), Indianapolis, or Louisville, or a smaller area such as Fort Wayne, Green Bay, or Reading, convince well-educated individuals to live in their communities? How does a city with a deteriorating downtown area compete with suburban cities? For these communities, the issue is not should investments be made in human capital. State and provincial governments are making investments in education and human capital development. These communities face the challenge of convincing educated workers to live in their neighborhoods. Climate assumes a role in attracting and retaining people. But some cold weather areas such as Boston, Chicago, or Minneapolis–St. Paul are growing as fast as some warmer regions. What amenities do these areas have that attract and retain human capital? Can other cities build similar amenity packages? At the outset, then, this book is based on the understanding that human capital does indeed drive economic development.[38] What is also relevant and will be more fully discussed in Chapter 2 is that as comparative geographical advantages decline in importance (as a result of declining transportation and communication costs), and as workers and firms have more locational choices, areas with higher levels of amenities will more likely be attractive to highly skilled labor. As a result, all businesses that must strive to be as efficient and profitable as possible will also be attracted to these areas.[39]

In noting that amenities assume an important role, recognition must also be made that there are community- or neighborhood-level amenities that may be as important or far more valuable than big-ticket items, such as sports facilities, museums, and cultural centers.[40] The recognition that amenities are an asset or tool in the attraction and retention of skilled labor for economic development underscores the importance of strategies that leverage private sector resources for neighborhood-level as well as big-ticket amenities.

## 1.8 Goals and Organization of This Book

This book is about how cities can earn market-appropriate returns on their investments in big-ticket amenities and build amenity packages that create an opportunity to compete for highly educated workers. The path to this strategy begins with a review of several different ideas that have been at the center of the discussion and debates over the role of sports, entertainment, the arts, and cultural amenities in the redevelopment of downtown areas. Understanding how the relationship between cities and teams became unbalanced highlights the need for civic leaders to find nonconfrontational strategies to ensure that when tax dollars are used for sports facilities, these dollars are turned from subsidies into investments.

Chapter 2 provides the second part of this volume's conceptual framework. In this first chapter, I tried to explain that the decentralization of economic activity has placed every central city in a new competitive environment to attract and retain human capital. Educated human capital will ultimately produce the tax revenues required by cities to deliver needed urban services to their residents. In the competition for human capital, central cities are disadvantaged by neighboring suburban cities that can create economically segregated communities that minimize the use of taxes paid by higher-income households to pay for the services needed by lower-income families. In this political-economic environment sports become a vital amenity because of their popularity and their cartel structure that prohibits replication within a metropolitan area.

If a central city can attract and retain a professional sports team, it has the potential to change the location of regional economic activity if properly planned new neighborhoods are anchored to the venue. Chapter 2 explores policy options to successfully achieve the objective of building a new neighborhood anchored by a sports facility.

Chapters 3 through 9 are case studies of cities that have tried to use sports and other amenities to change regional economic patterns. Each case study— Indianapolis, San Diego, Los Angeles, Columbus, Denver, Cleveland, and the smaller cities of Reading and Fort Wayne—was developed and included to provide insight into what works and what does not. Chapter 10 summarizes the lessons learned and the strategies that seem to make some cities major league winners when it comes to using sports to change regional economic activities.

# Endnotes

1. Cleveland did not have sufficient money available to meet its scheduled payments for several bonds. No bondholder, however, demanded immediate payment. As a result, Cleveland did not technically default and was able to present a plan that permitted satisfaction of its obligations.
2. While not focusing on Detroit, Erie, S.P., V. Kogan, and S.A. Mackenzie. (2011). *Paradise plundered: Fiscal crisis and governance failures in San Diego.* Stanford, CA: Stanford University Press discussed the ways in which San Diego's city council and mayor used favorable pension plans to secure electoral support from city workers.
3. Hobbs, F., and N. Stoops, *Demographic trends in the 20th century: Census 2000 special reports* (Washington, DC: U.S. Department of Commerce, Bureau of the Census, 2002).
4. http://www.gallup.com/poll/1714/Taxes.aspx (accessed April 29, 2013).
5. http://www.gallup.com/poll/15937/Which-Unfairest-Tax-Them-All.aspx (accessed April 29, 2013).
6. http://www.nlc.org/build-skills-and-networks/resources/cities-101/city-structures/ city-county-consolidations (accessed April 30, 2013).
7. See, for example, Baade, R.A., Professional sports as catalysts for metropolitan economic development, *Journal of Urban Affairs* 18(1): 1–17, 1996. Also, Humphrey, B., and D.R. Howard, eds., *The business of sports: Economic perspectives* (New York: Praeger Publishers, 2008).
8. Sandy, R., P.J. Sloane, and M.S. Rosentraub, *The economics of sports: An international perspective* (New York: Palgrave McMillan, 2004).
9. Judd, D.R., and S.S. Fainstein, eds., *The tourist city* (New Haven: Yale University Press, 1999).
10. See, for example, Rosentraub, M.S., Stadiums and urban space, in *Sports, jobs, and taxes: The economic impact of sports teams and stadiums*, ed. R.G. Noll and A. Zimbalist (Washington, DC: Brookings Institution, 1997), 178–207. Also, Nelson, A.C.,

Locating major league stadiums where they can make a difference, *Public Works Management and Policy* 7(2): 98–114, 2002. Both works illustrate the impact the movement of economic activity can have relative to public policy goals. Within metropolitan areas, insuring that levels of recreational spending takes place in central cities can relocate tax dollars to enhance the fiscal capacity of central cities that have large concentrations of lower-income households.

11. Zimbalist, A., *The bottom line: Observations and arguments on the sports business* (Philadelphia: Temple University Press, 2006).

12. See, for example, Baade, R.A., and R. Dye, Sports stadiums and area development: Assessing the reality, *Heartland Policy Study* 68, 1988. Also, Danielson, M.N., *Home team: Professional sports and the American metropolis* (Princeton, NJ: Princeton University Press, 1997). Both works illustrate the hopes cities have for their investment in the facilities used by professional sports teams. My earlier book highlights the lack of planning by cities to capitalize on these investments: Rosentraub, M.S., *Major league losers: The real cost of sports and who's paying for it* (New York: Basic Books, 1997).

13. Pierce, N.R., Ohio looks hard at what's lost through business subsidies, in *Readings in urban economic issues and public policy*, ed. R.W. Wassner (Malden, MA: Blackwell Publishers, 2000), 151–153.

14. See, for example, Euchner, C.C., *Playing the field: Why sports teams move and cities fight to keep them* (Baltimore: Johns Hopkins University Press, 1994). Also, Noll, R.G., and A. Zimbalist, Build the stadium—Create the jobs! in *Sports, jobs, and taxes: The economic impact of sports teams and stadiums*, ed. R.G. Noll and A. Zimbalist (Washington, DC: The Brookings Institution, 1997), 1–54.

15. In some of the case studies done for my earlier book, public leaders repeatedly underscored the need for a team to produce a major league image. Leaders in Columbus, Ohio, as will be discussed in Chapter 6, also wanted a professional team to enhance its image despite the presence of the Ohio State University and its prominent sports teams. See Rosentraub, M.S., *Major league losers: The real cost of sports and who's paying for it* (New York: Basic Books, 1997), http://www.shanghairanking.com/Institution.jsp?param=Washington%20University%20in%20St.%20Louis.

16. Kennedy, S., and M.S. Rosentraub, Public–private partnerships, professional sports teams, and the protection of the public's interests, *American Review of Public Administration* 30(4): 436–459, 2000.

17. Pine, J., and J.H. Gilmore, *The experience economy: Work is theatre and every business a stage* (Cambridge, MA: Harvard Business Press, 1999).

18. Money Magazine, 100 best places to live and launch, 2008, http://money.cnn.com/galleries/2008/fsb/0803/gallery.best_places_to_launch.fsb/index.html (accessed September 9, 2008).

19. Eisinger, P., The politics of bread and circuses, *Urban Affairs Review* 35(3): 316–333 (330–331), 2000.

20. While Shea Stadium, home to the New York Mets from 1964 to 2008, had more seats than Rome's Colosseum, its new home, Citi Field, has a planned seating capacity of 45,000.

21. Wilson, J., *Playing by the rules: Sport, society, and the state* (Detroit: Wayne State University Press, 1994).

22. Misener, L., and D.S. Mason, Creating community networks: Can sporting events offer meaningful sources of social capital, *Managing Leisure* 11: 39–56, 2006.

23. Andrews, D., Sports in the late capitalist movement, in *The commercialization of sport*, ed. T. Slack (London: Routledge, 2004), 3–28.

24. See Lefebvre, H., *Writings on cities* (Maiden, MA: Blackwell Publishers, 1996). Earlier assessments by Lefebvre are also important amplifications of this relationship: Lefebvre, H., *The production of space* (Maiden, MA: Blackwell Publishers, 1991).

25. For a practicing professional's perspective see Chema, T., When professional sports justify the subsidy: A reply to Robert A. Baade, *Journal of Urban Affairs* 18(1): 19–22, 1996. Mr. Chema was a leader in the development of Cleveland's new ballpark and arena. Another professional (and an academic) has important insights into this point too: Euchner, C.C., *Playing the field: Why sports teams move and cities fight to keep them* (Baltimore: Johns Hopkins University Press, 1994).

26. Home Box Office (HBO), *Nine innings from ground zero: The healing of a nation began with the swing of a bat*, 2008, http://www.hbo.com/sports/nineinnings/ (accessed October 8, 2008).

27. See, for example, Levine, P., *From Ellis Island to Ebbets Field: Sport and the American Jewish experience* (Cary, NC: Oxford University Press, 1993). Also, V. Duke and L. Crolley place this point in an international perspective in *Football, nationality, and the state* (London: Addison Wesley Longman, 1996).

28. It has become increasingly common for metropolitan areas to have one large arena (seating for approximately 20,000 people) and a second smaller one for acts that attract 15,000 or fewer fans. In the largest markets it is possible for a region to have more than one large-scale arena. In addition, for cities that are also home to major universities, a second large arena could exist to serve the needs of the university. Some markets such as Phoenix and the Minneapolis–St. Paul areas have two large-scale arenas. Whether or not these areas can attract enough events to financially sustain both facilities remains unclear.

29. Zimbalist, A., and J.G. Long, Facility finance: Measurement, trends and analysis, *International Journal of Sport Finance* 1: 201–211, 2006.

30. See, for example, Searle, G., Uncertain legacy: Sydney's Olympic stadiums, *European Planning Studies* 10(7): 845–860, 2002; also, Kang, Y.S., and R. Perdue, Long-term impact of a mega-event on international tourism to the host country: A conceptual model and the case of the 1988 Seoul Olympics, in *Global tourist behavior*, ed. M. Uysal (New York: Haworth Press, 1994), 205–226; Kurtzman, J., Economic impact: Sport tourism and the city, *Journal of Sport Tourism* 10(1): 47–71, 2005; Chalip, L., *Using the Olympics to optimise tourism benefits: University lecture on the Olympics* (Barcelona: Centre d'Estudis Olympics), http://olympicstudies.uab.es/lectures/web/pdf/chalip.pdf (accessed December 21, 2008).

31. Austrian, Z., and M.S. Rosentraub, Cities, sports and economic change: A retrospective assessment, *Journal of Urban Affairs* 24(5): 549–565, 2002.

32. Nelson, A.C., Locating major league stadiums where they can make a difference, *Public Works Management and Policy* 7(2): 98–114, 2002.

33. Rosentraub, M.S., Sports facilities, redevelopment, and the centrality of downtown areas: Observations and lessons from experiences in a rustbelt and sunbelt city, *Marquette University Sports Law Journal* 10(2): 219–236, 2000.

34. Rosentraub, M.S., The local context of a sports strategy for economic development, *Economic Development Quarterly* 20(3): 278–291, 2006.

35. Rosentraub, M.S., *Major league losers: The real cost of sports and who's paying for it* (New York: Basic Books, 1997).

36. Timmons, A., Winning on the field and at the ballot box: The effect of the fan base on stadium subsidies, unpublished public policy thesis, Stanford University, Department of Economics, 2006.

37. See, for example, Coates, D., and B.R. Humphreys, The growth effects of sports franchises, stadia, and arenas, *Journal of Policy Analysis and Management* 14(4): 601–624, 1999.

38. See, for example, Garmise, S., *People and the competitive advantage of place: Building a workplace for the 21st century* (Armonk, NY: M.E. Sharpe, 2006).

39. Rosentraub, M.S., and M. Joo, Tourism and economic development: Which investments produce gains for regions? *Tourism Management* 30(5): 759–770, 2009.

40. See, for example, Clark, T.N., ed., *The city as an entertainment machine* (Amsterdam, The Netherlands: Elsevier-JAI Press, 2004). Also, Professor H. Sanders has consistently documented the persistent overestimation of the positive effects of some big-ticket amenities and their ability to actually operate at levels sufficient to produce jobs and generate substantial economic returns: Sanders, H., *Space available: The realities of convention centers as economic development strategy* (Washington, DC: Brookings Institution, 2005).

*Chapter 2*

# Planned Development vs. Organic Change: Tools in the Effort to Revitalize Central Cities and Downtown Areas

## 2.1 Introduction

For more than 50 years some national, state (provincial), and local officials, philanthropic organizations (e.g., Cleveland Foundation, Ford Foundation, Lilly Endowment, Kresge Foundation, etc.), community leaders, and academicians have focused on strategies to revitalize central cities. These efforts have been needed to respond to the effects of *social* and *economic* changes that have redefined the use of land in metropolitan areas. In most regions, central cities have lost residents and jobs. With fewer people and firms, property values declined, leading to budget shortfalls.

That loss of financial strength has made it increasingly difficult for numerous cities to provide the public services (e.g., safety, education, infrastructure) residents need. Declining service levels make cities less attractive as a place to live. A greater understanding of the economic and social changes that have created the fiscal challenge confronting cities is necessary to chart corrective policies. Needed policies must shift or realign the demand for residential, commercial, and retail space from a focus on suburban locations to one that makes central cities desirable places to live and work. Can central cities offer individuals, families, and corporations attractive places for their homes and businesses? How does a central city shift the demand for homes and business locations? The answers lie in an understanding of the forces that have tilted the demand for locations to suburban areas. A central thesis of this book is that big-ticket assets dominated by sports facilities can change the demand for residential and commercial space toward downtown areas. To sustain this policy orientation—and before examining the success and lessons learned by the investments made by numerous cities using sports to anchor revitalization efforts—a more detailed description of the forces that initially shifted demand toward suburban areas is needed.

# 2.2 The Social and Economic Forces Changing Urban Space

## 2.2.1 Segregation and Hegemonic Actions

Ethnic, income, and racial segregation remain pervasive determinants of the use of urban space (and land) despite some changing attitudes. One of the factors changing societal attitudes toward racial segregation is related to higher levels of intermarriage and the number of biracial and biethnic children that are a part of every major North America city. Despite this important progress, however, people still choose areas to live where there are large numbers of others from the same ethnic or racial group. More importantly for the ideas in this book, where there is a level of integration along racial or ethnic lines, there is a preference for areas that are economically segregated. Economic segregation minimizes the transfer of taxes paid by higher-income households to fund the services needed by lower-income families. That transfer has always been required. In many ways, however, it was invisible to people in the past because high-, middle-, and lower-income families lived in different neighborhoods that were located in the same city.

As changing transportation and communication costs made it feasible for higher-income people to choose residences that isolated them from central cities that contained larger proportions of a region's lower-income households, an economic incentive was created that allowed higher-income individuals to reduce the transfers of the taxes they paid to fund services provided to lower-income households. Urban planners, public administrators, and urban policy specialists have been wrestling with this reality for the past several decades in an effort to ensure that quality schools and other urban services necessary for economic mobility continue to be available to lower-income families.

In the 19th and for more than half of the 20th century, central cities had segregated neighborhoods, but different income cohorts or groups of people still lived in the same single central city. Now groups have been able to segregate themselves into independent suburban cities, and thus insulate themselves from income transfers to less wealthy individuals. There is, as a result, a profound level of *economic* segregation between central and suburban cities. This form of segregation does not mean that ethnic and racial segregation are of less importance. But economic segregation short-circuits opportunities for job and economic mobility for people with lower incomes and reduces the financial resources available to central cities to respond to social and infrastructure needs.

Ethnic and racial segregation is troubling and problematic on numerous levels, and combating it requires vigilant action. What makes attention to economic segregation now more important, however, is that domestic policy in the United States is characterized by a lack of revenue sharing between more and less wealthy cities. There has also been a loss of political support for expanded levels of financial support for central cities from the federal and state governments. Central cities must respond to the growing concentration of lower-income households with their own initiatives. This is why central cities must be focused on changing the demand for land within their boundaries.

There has been a level of debate as to the causes of all forms of segregation. Some have argued that people's preferences for living in close proximity to other members of an individual's ethnic or racial community has been a defining characteristic of life and people across North America. Without challenging the observation that many people prefer living in more homogenous communities dominated by single-family homes, other public policy analysts have noted that lower-density suburbs were also a product of decisions made by businesses. Why would some companies prefer urban regions dominated by low-density suburbs?

The benefits enjoyed by those companies involve the increasing preference by many employees to use personal automobiles for their journey to work; there are some cities where mass transit is popular and used by all income groups. Yet in many other areas, there is a preference for the use of private automobiles. The lower land costs in suburban areas make it feasible for businesses to offer inexpensive parking options for their employees. In addition, lower densities make public transit less profitable, and its elimination from a market means a greater demand for cars and buses (built by the automobile corporations). If automobile manufacturers actually eliminated mass transit options, then the development of lower-density suburbs may not have been driven by the demands of consumers but by the lack of transit options. If that did take place, then the manipulation of the market or consumers' preferences is referred to as a hegemonic control of urban development. It is hegemonic (the control over some group's ideas, behavior, or choices by another group) in that a corporate elite tried to shape people's attitudes to maximize their wealth. How is this possible?

There were actions taken by corporations that encouraged or biased consumers' choices toward suburban areas with lower population densities. Those corporate decisions led to the elimination of some public transit systems. The collapse of those systems forced or led people to want automobiles. Lower levels of public transportation meant it became more efficient for people to purchase cars. Having more cars in turn reduced the densities required to make mass transit more cost-effective, making those systems more costly to operate. As the systems were shuttered, people purchased more cars, causing mass transit to become less reliable (aging infrastructure needing more repairs, which were more difficult to finance given lower usage) and less convenient (and reduced schedules as a result of declining demand). The availability of more cars made it more convenient for people to explore the cost advantages of living where land and houses were less expensive. Spending more for transportation (costs of owning a car generally exceed what people would have to pay for mass transit, but automobiles offer far more convenience) attracted people to areas where land and homes were less expensive. Less expensive houses were generally found in suburban areas. The availability of low-interest loans—especially for U.S. military personnel in the years after World War II and the Korean War—accelerated the movement of people from central cities to the suburbs. Whether or not there were aggressive actions made by General Motors or other automobile companies to destroy public transit and bias lending patterns, people relocated from central cities to suburban communities.

Why is it important to understand these interactions? Whether driven by individual preferences or preferences shaped by corporate decisions, as transportation and communication costs shifted, it became possible for new levels of economic segregation to exist. This segregation is what has led to the financial challenges that require the leaders of central cities to devise policies to deflect regional economic activity back into the taxing boundaries or jurisdictions of central cities. If those leaders fail to achieve this goal, it becomes impossible to deliver the public services needed by lower-income households to facilitate economic mobility. Every central city mayor is in a search for tax dollars, and sports have emerged as a tool to reallocate or reposition regional economic activity. If that activity can then be appropriately taxed, central cities could have the needed revenue streams to deliver the services their constituents deserve.

## 2.2.2 American Folklore, Rural Tranquility, and Suburbs

American culture has also had a long-standing bias against cities and urban life. Thomas Jefferson in the 18th century helped establish the antiurbanism that has been part of American life. In thinking about the fate of a new country, he concluded in a note to James Madison, "I think our governments will remain virtuous for many centuries as long as they are chiefly agricultural."[1] Glaab observed that antiurbanism in the United States was a product of the rising economic importance of cities. That negative view of cities helped frame an idyllic view of rural and suburban areas as being more gentile and tranquil, and therefore superior to urban life, even as cities began to dominate the fiscal affairs of the new country.

Bolstering this image of discordant cities was the rampant corruption that defined urban politics in the late 19th and early 20th centuries. The rise of political machines and their trading of economic favors for votes from the waves of arriving immigrant groups created an image in conflict with the ideal of an American way of life.

Immigrants, many of whom had never voted, were more than willing to trade their new right for economic rewards. As long as groups of elected and community leaders who were soon defined as political machines delivered economic benefits (jobs and services) to immigrants, they were supported at the ballot box. It was often argued or fantasized that this sort of political corruption would not exist in more rural areas. Rural and then suburban lifestyles were presented as being far less corrupt, and therefore the real identity of America. In 1896, William Jennings Bryan refocused the antiurbanism argument by reminding his followers that farmers and their rural lifestyle sustained the growth of cities and of America. As Glaab concluded, Bryan captured the prevailing sentiments of the pristine value of rural life contrasted with the chaos and squalor of cities when he noted that if cities were destroyed, they would be rebuilt. But if farms were destroyed, cities would fall into decay, presumably because of a loss of food and the superior American values that were part of nonurban lifestyles. In later years, religious aspects were joined to the antiurban sentiments as cities were described as being focused on materialism as opposed to the spiritual side of life.[2] Ignored in this rhetoric that was robustly received by willing supporters was the violence that existed in rural areas and the discrimination in those communities that deprived certain groups of the right to vote and due process. Neither cities nor rural or suburban areas were immune from corruption and political machines or regimes that controlled political decisions that excluded some people from the democratic principles established by the U.S. Constitution.

The spectacular increase in the population size of cities in the post-Civil War period did not necessarily create political machines and corruption, but each did become a staple of municipal politics as cities grew at unprecedented rates. For example, in 1900 New York had 3.43 million residents. By 1920 its population was 5.62 million. The city was adding almost 110,000 residents each year, leading to a perpetual housing shortage and overcrowding; social services were also in short supply, as no level of government took responsibility for enhancing the life of immigrants. In 1900 Detroit had 285,704 residents. Twenty years later there were 993,078 residents, and there would be 1.6 million residents by 1940. Chicago also added 1 million residents from 1900 to 1920. Public services could not expand fast enough to meet the rising demand from immigrants and the families being formed each year. With overcrowded tenements and building practices that were not sufficiently focused on the safety standards demanded by the overcrowding that was taking place, the attraction to a vision of a more idyllic space surrounded by parks and less density in suburban areas is easy to understand. The American dream became a detached single-family house in a suburb where there were no tenements, less crowded streets, and safer schools (no urban gangs), with fewer students in each class. The seeds for an infatuation with suburban life were planted by the rapid growth of cities.

If overcrowding was not enough to steer people to the suburbs, the social conflict between immigrant groups kept people's focus on moving to more segregated enclaves. The mistrust between waves of immigrants from Ireland (Catholics),

Italy (Catholics), and Eastern Europe (Catholics, Protestants, and Jews) did not necessarily mean economic and social conflict was necessary, but it was probably inevitable. Groups segregated in part to provide related newcomers with a degree of familiarity and an introduction to life in America. This socialization process often led to bloc voting and support of political machines, as those with more experience navigating life in America influenced newcomers. More importantly, in the late 19th and early 20th centuries expansive roles for the public sector in the provision of services to immigrants did not exist. Assistance was forthcoming mostly from self-help organizations that often restricted their services to co-religionists or people with the same ethnic backgrounds. This began a process of segregation in the sense that there were more services and information available in areas where there were concentrations of Jews, Italians, Irish, etc. Once established, regardless of the root causes, segregated residential patterns emerged. These patterns were then transferred into suburban areas that may or may not have been advanced or accelerated by actions taken by automobile manufacturers or lending practices associated with home mortgages.

The rapid growth of cities was often accompanied by a shortfall between the demand for and the supply of homes and apartments. Often that gap could only be met by building on less costly land that was readily available in suburban areas. The rapid growth of North American cities was frequently defined by the hundreds of thousands of people living in overcrowded tenements in the center parts of the largest cites, followed by the expansion of housing opportunities in suburban areas. In addition, overcrowded living areas predictably led to unsanitary living conditions and catastrophic events. The expansion of factories to capitalize on the vast supply of cheap labor flooding into urban centers also meant workplaces were overcrowded and dangerous. Catastrophic events were to be expected. Underscoring the long-standing suffering of millions of residents and workers was the legendary Triangle Shirtwaist Factory fire in New York that killed 146 people. The scale of the tragedy led to public intervention into business affairs through regulations related to safe work places and worker safety. Unions were organized to protect workers, and these new organizations took responsibility for ensuring that employees were protected from unsafe work environments. The growing strength and role of unions underscored for others the chaotic nature of cities, even though there were employment-related deaths in rural areas. All of these factors contributed to the popularity of suburban areas.

Racial and ethnic conflicts and violence were never limited to urban areas, but some riots became more infamous and continued to underscore the chaotic nature of urban life. One such legendary conflict was Chicago's 1919 race riot that was instigated by the murder of an African-American who had crossed into a section of Lake Michigan's waters informally reserved for whites. After 8 days of rioting, approximately 40 people were dead and a substantial number of homes where African-Americans lived were destroyed. Cleveland suffered through a riot in 1946 involving the beating of African-Americans and it was also one of the cities shaken by race-related riots in the mid-1960s. Detroit also had a severe race riot in 1943 involving an amusement park, and it too would be decimated by race-related violence in the mid-1960s. The severity of conflicts between people of different racial groups in urban centers again focused people's desire on moving to a more peaceful and safe part of a metropolitan area.

Riots or fights between racial and ethnic groups were not limited to physical space. Economic segregation was also underscored by different ethnic groups staking out claims to parts of America's private and public sector economies. The Irish immigrants, for example, had a leading role in the first urban police departments, which led to discriminatory actions against other ethnic groups. Different trade associations were established to assume domination of different industries, and some ethnic groups were able to control unions that in turn excluded limited employment opportunities to members of the group. Excluded groups sought economic success in emerging industries, which explains the early domination of the movie industry by Jews. All of this conflict over physical and economic space led to a focus on moving to suburban areas, where it was hoped there would be less conflict.

Finally, the racially related riots of the 1960s shattered any pretense of economic or any other form of integration. Large numbers of whites moved to suburban areas. While the proportional loss of residents was most notable in places such as Cleveland and Detroit, there was a large movement of people in cities across the United States. This led to separate schools and school districts, and when federal courts ordered an end to segregation in public education, private and parochial schools became even more popular as many families tried to avoid integrated schools. There were then also levels of class, racial, and religious discrimination in admission to colleges or universities. There was a high level of segregation in all aspects of American life that was part of the antiurbanism framework. All of these factors fueled the interest in a suburban lifestyle.

Whether intentional or by design, the mass media also proclaimed the value of lower density and suburban lifestyles. The infatuation with automobiles was advanced by advertising and product placement in movies and television shows. The order to be found in the households of *Father Knows Best*, the *Donna Reed Show*, and the *Adventures of Ozzie and Harriet* was contrasted by the stresses in the urban life portrayed by Jackie Gleason and his troupe in the *Honeymooners*. Did those shows mean there was some level of hegemonic control over consumers' preferences for cars, the suburbs, and lower-density living arrangements? While certainly contributing to the popularity of the suburbs, it has to be acknowledged that through the media, American society was already imbued by a predilection toward less crowded environments, physical separation from what was seen as overcrowded urban centers, and segregation related to economic class, ethnicity, and race.

Despite its separate culture and value system, high levels of suburbanization also define several of Canada's large urban centers. The point here is not to compare or contrast suburbanization trends, but to identify the factors that for more than two centuries have framed the use of urban space. A better understanding of those long-term trends and the elements that shape the contemporary efforts of revitalization is essential before focusing on programs, policies, and outcomes with regard to revitalization efforts in several cities. This book focuses on the best ways to undertake revitalization efforts that are anchored by big-ticket investment in sports, entertainment, and cultural facilities. Such a focus for a revitalization strategy rests on the expectation that sports and a big-ticket investment can help reposition regional economic activity when it has shifted to suburban areas. Success for any revitalization strategy emphasizing an investment in a big-ticket amenity is defined by (1) a deflection of regional economic activity into central cities, (2) an improved attractiveness of the downtown area as a place where people and businesses want to locate, and (3) an enhanced fiscal position for the central city. If those factors are the measures of success before judging whether or not a policy approach is successful, it is necessary to better understand the dimensions of the problem being confronted.

## 2.2.3 Economic Changes

Economic success for cities, regions, or countries was usually defined by comparative advantages. A comparative advantage results from the ability of a person or a region (city, town, etc.) to unify proximity to natural resources and sufficiently skilled labor to efficiently produce a good or service. A region or person achieves the most efficiency from its labor and proximity to natural resources by producing more of the goods or services that require the least amount of inputs. If a good or service is in high demand and no other region or person can produce it as cheaply, the wealth of the area increases.

It is probably easier to understand the concept of comparative advantage and why it fades or dissipates when considering the economic rise and decline of Detroit. Because of its proximity to water (and the resulting lower transportation costs of securing raw materials and transporting finished automobiles to numerous market areas) and the concentration of labor with the skills to build and repairs ships and their engines (workers who could use those skills for automobiles), Detroit became the "motor city" by building and selling more cars more cheaply than any other region in the world. Once the skills and techniques associated with the building of cars could be easily replicated, assembly plants were built in other large market areas to reduce the cost of transporting completed cars. In time, competing companies mastered the techniques pioneered by Ford, General Motors, and the Chrysler Corporation, resulting in even less need to produce cars in Detroit. This led to the loss of jobs, a decline in wages and benefits, and the resulting depletion of wealth for a segment of the population.

The value of all comparative advantages dissipates (or declines) when other areas are able to match or exceed the efficiencies that previously existed only in another area. No comparative advantage will be sustained forever. Technology has the potential to minimize any area's comparative advantage. In relation to the given example of the manufacturing of cars, once cargo ships were able to efficiently transport thousands of automobiles from Asia to North America, the comparative advantage of manufacturing vehicles in the United States or Canada deteriorated. Subsequently, wealth declined where there was a concentration of workers focused only on the assembly of cars.

One way for an area to avoid losing its comparative advantages is to be able to produce numerous products or services. That is one strategy; another is to focus on competitive advantages. While there is a level of ambiguity with regards to its definition, the initial way to think about a competitive advantage is that it is a specialization that cannot be easily replicated by or in another area or region. In many instances, the specialization cannot be duplicated at all. How is that possible when few, if any, comparative advantages cannot be sustained?

The roots of the concept of competitive advantage can be found in the work of Joseph Schumpeter and his definition of creative destruction.[3] Schumpeter presented his concept in the context of explaining that new ideas destroy existing products to better serve markets and their needs. Social systems that encourage creative destruction (capitalism in his view) were far more likely to produce more wealth than any other. What is required to drive new ideas for production and products? What drives innovation? It is educated labor.[4] Pools or clusters of well-educated workers constantly advancing ideas with other educated people leads to more creative destruction. If an innovate thinker knows that there will be a pool of similarly motivated and creative thinkers in a certain area, he or she gravitates to that location and is often reluctant to relocate elsewhere. Other areas might try to lure one creative person or a pool of people, but the separation from clusters of creative people can be quite costly. Those costs are related to the observation that ideas become better and more refined when they are discussed within larger pools of educated people. In addition, where there are larger pools of talented people, it is easier to start a new business since there are a large number of potential employees who can be easily recruited to join the new venture.

This abstract concept can be better understood with a few examples.

Silicon Valley (including Stanford University and the University of California), Hollywood (including the University of Southern California, Cal Tech, and UCLA), the financial center that is New York (including Columbia, NYU, and several other universities), Harvard University and MIT in the Boston area, Yale University, and the University of Michigan are each clusters or at the centers of clusters of competitive excellence. Each has its own environment that is difficult to replicate, and the easy access to large numbers of talented people makes it valuable as entrepreneurs can easily find employees for new businesses. These areas or institutions create competitive advantages that are involved with creative destruction each day. The evidence of their competitive advantage is to be found in the patents produced or the networks of idea generators that continue to work with each other.

The goal for any economic development policy—including the renovation of a downtown area—is to build spaces that attract and retain innovators or people who are creative destroyers. Long before Michael Porter correctly focused attention on competitive advantages for all revitalization and economic development plans and policies,[5] Alfred Marshall, in his 19th-century treatise on economics, explained that wealth was created from "ideas in the air." What he meant, of course, is that where creative thinkers congregate and put ideas in the air (and debate with each other), new products and processes develop.[6] Those areas with more ideas in the air become wealthier; those with fewer ideas in the air decline.[7]

Attracting and retaining human capital to ensure that economic development takes place in cities and regions, then, has been a focus for theorists since at least the 1890s. It began, perhaps, with Alfred Marshall and his concept that wealth was a function of the ways in which people combine ideas to create new products and processes. His concept of "ideas in the air" meant that the location of economic wealth was a result of cities that created spaces in which people's ideas collided to advance innovation. This theme was recently underscored by Edward Glaeser's *Triumph of the City* (2011) in which he proclaims that cities are the greatest of human inventions since they have made societies richer, smarter, greener, healthier, and happier. His concept is valid, but as will be noted below, it is not the city but "urban areas" comprised of numerous cities that, unfortunately, do not share tax revenues with less fortunate communities in the same region.

In the 1930s Joseph Schumpeter advanced understandings of the formation and distribution of wealth when he noted that economies advance only when innovation creates new products or more efficient means of production. Cities or economies that are home to companies that engage in "creative destruction" advance; those cities or regions where innovation is stagnant decline. When that decline becomes endemic middle class jobs are destroyed, as are opportunities for people to advance along any sort of ladder of economic opportunity. For Marshall and Schumpeter what was or is essential for economic development is human capital. For them, wealth or growth is explained by the attraction and retention of human capital. Without the best minds, if their theories were valid, economies, cities, and regions fall into economic decline, workers lose jobs, and families lose the ability to advance along any job ladders that enhances their wealth.

Jane Jacobs in the 1950s and 1960s added to Marshall and Schumpeter's ideas noting for cities to be successful in attracting innovators or creative destroyers, areas with declining real estate values were essential. It was in these diverse areas that entrepreneurs could find low cost locations to live and work as they pursued invention and innovation. From those declining or dying areas of a city would be borne new products and processes. If those areas were also diverse there was even a greater likelihood that there would be more ideas in the air. Once the firms were successful, in her view, the firms would locate to more prosperous areas in the city and create new jobs.

Michael Porter, in the 1980s, through his concepts of competitive clusters actually sounded a provocative warning for central cities. Noting that competitive clusters of human capital could or would spread within metropolitan areas, it became possible for a region to be quite economically successful while a particular city declined. A careful reading of his ideas would make it clear that it was quite possible for a region to build competitive clusters or human capital in its suburban areas and in effect completely bypass a central city. While Jane Jacobs was right that regions needed lower cost areas for innovation to thrive, she did not see an epoch of declining communication and transportation costs that would make it profitable for successful firms to align in clusters outside of the boundaries of central cities. Thinking through the work of each of these scholars it becomes clear that it is possible for the Cleveland, Detroit, or St. Louis regions (among many others) to recover and thrive at the same time that former central cities decline or lose their ability to attract and retain human capital. And, if the surrounding successful cities decide not to share tax revenues, then older central cities can even lose the ability to provide the urban services their growing concentration of lower income households need. When that happens, central cities become synonymous with declining schools, inadequate police and fire departments, and deteriorating streets and infrastructure.

Revitalizing a city or a downtown area means that a community has to be focused on designs and activities that attract and retain creative minds. How do sports, entertainment centers, and cultural amenities fit into that strategy? They fit because each attracts large crowds, and through that attraction, it becomes possible to offer creative destroyers what they want. What creative destroyers need are entertaining living places where they are able to engage with other creative destroyers or where clusters of ideas in the air are likely to occur. The ways in which sports, other big-ticket amenities, and neighborhoods can contribute to the building of competitive advantages, and reduce the reliance on comparative advantages, is detailed in the next section.

## 2.3 Why Invest in Any Amenities? Why Invest in Big-Ticket Amenities?

There are some natural amenities that are clearly valuable in attracting and retaining educated human capital. It is hardly surprising that Southern California and Northern California are desirable locations. Both areas offer temperate climates, spectacular vistas, and easy access to attractive beaches. It is hardly surprising that clusters of highly skilled workers engaged in creative destruction have formed in those areas.

But there are other areas without similar environmental amenities that developed a similar level of clusters or competitive advantages. Why? The answer is found in other assets found in California that could be duplicated. First, in both Southern and Northern California there are clusters of extraordinary research universities. Second, each region also has a large set of extraordinary entertainment amenities, and this combination of assets makes it easier to understand why numerous clusters of different industries and sectors of the economy emerged. Looking at the clusters in California, one might be tempted to argue that no other area could have similar levels of success. This is not the case.

Chicago, for example, does have proximity to an extremely attractive coastal area (Lake Michigan), but its climate offers extremes not found in California. Snowstorms and extreme cold are part of Chicago's environment as well as sweltering summer days. Yet, it is also home to a set of extraordinary competitive clusters that are supported by three premier research universities (Chicago, Northwestern, and the University of Illinois–Chicago). Chicago's urban architecture is world-class, equal to that found in any other city, and an amenity by itself. Tourists flock to the Chicago River for tours of the city's architecture. In addition, Chicago's mix of sports and other cultural amenities offers residents a calendar of events that matches what exists anywhere in the world. Boston, Minneapolis–St. Paul, and New York are also examples of cities that have climatic disadvantages compared to what is available to residents of Southern and Northern California, yet none of those areas suffers from a dearth of highly skilled workers or competitive clusters that lead aspects of the world's economy. If areas can use a mix of education, amenities, and urban design to make even less temperate climates centers with competitive advantages, what set of amenities, educational resources, and urban design principles can be incorporated into a policy to advance revitalization and economic development?

This is where sports facilities can become anchors for new neighborhoods to assume a role in revitalizing areas. How do sports facilities and other cultural amenities fit in with an orientation focused on attracting and retaining the talent that is engaged in creative destruction that can lead to the formation of clusters of competitive advantage? Several different components have to be woven together to achieve a level of success.

## 2.3.1 The Popularity of Sports

As already noted, sports events repeatedly attract large crowds. Detroit—in the midst of the worst financial crisis that any city has ever endured—benefitted from the presence of more than 4 million visits to its downtown area by fans attending Lions', Red Wings', and Tigers' games. In addition, a few hundred thousand visits to the area were associated with other entertainment and athletic events held at the same venues and at the renovated Fox Theatre. If a city's leadership understands that more than 4 million visits predictably occur each year in a small part of the community, how can that level of activity be used to revitalize the area in ways that lead to the building of clusters for competitive advantages? Teams and the facilities they use do not change regions and their economic destinies. What does, however, is the incorporation of iconic sports facilities into a neighborhood or entertainment district. From that success emerges a set of principles that communities need to follow when contemplating an investment in an arena, ballpark, or stadium.

### 2.3.1.1 Build Iconic Facilities

Sports facilities that attract millions of visits create an opportunity to develop a new iconic image for a city and its downtown areas. Facilities that are built without sufficient attention to their outside appearance and fit with a neighborhood or an entertainment district minimizes the value of the venue for enhancing a city's image. An iconic anchor for a neighborhood or an entertainment district contributes to economic development and revitalization because it creates a space in which people want to congregate. Those spaces create an environment for ideas in the air to be exchanged by those involved with creative destruction. Exciting architecture stimulates minds and overcomes other environmental shortcomings for a region.

Scholars and architects have long discussed the importance of iconic architecture for creativity and in making a city a desirable place to live, work, and visit. Kotler et al. (1993) translated these concepts into marketing strategies for cities in their classic, *Marketing Places*. Its subtitle helped explain the allure for big-ticket items—*Attracting Investment, Industry, and Tourism to Cities, States, and Nations*—and focused the attention of countless leaders on what they could or should do to advance the image of their city through the building of physical facilities that make a statement.

In the post-*Marketing Places* years, even large cities, or those classified as "world cities," continue to build new iconic structures. For example, Chicago built Millennium Park that includes extraordinary public art to add to its long list of iconic structures. Downtown Los Angeles was reimaged and reimagined with Frank Gehry's design of the home of the Los Angeles Philharmonic Orchestra, Disney Hall, and the new entertainment center, L.A. LIVE. In rebuilding Ground Zero in New York City, not only were a set of iconic buildings and a memorial created that allow people to honor the memories of those who perished, but the new buildings also create a new skyline for Lower New York that will inspire people for generations (see Figure 2.1).

Smaller cities have followed the lead of larger communities in an effort to put themselves on the economic radar screens of companies. These cities also want to provide the amenities that are seen as capable of attracting and retaining the human capital needed by expanding businesses. Indianapolis boasts new museums, the Bankers Life Fieldhouse, and Lucas Oil Stadium (home to the 2012 Super Bowl) as part of its new image and skyline. Cleveland is home to I.M. Pei's designed Rock and Roll Hall of Fame and Museum, and new downtown sports facilities were built to reconstruct its rust-belt image. Nashville's Sommet Center was designed to extend and enhance the city's music-based image (the home of broadcasted country music, if not country music itself), and Arlington (Texas) has made investments in sports facilities to give it a Texas-sized image through the Ballpark in Arlington (Texas Rangers) and the mega-stadium (AT&T Stadium) that is home to the Dallas Cowboys.

Obviously sports facilities are not the only tools used to help create iconic architecture. Examples of parks, buildings, and memorials each produce images that attract people to a city and offer spaces that appeal to those who engage in creative destruction. Sports, however, as a result of their sustaining popularity, offer an opportunity to recreate space that through iconic architecture attracts and retains the human capital needed for competitive clusters, unlike most other tools.

Freedom Tower, New York City

(a)

**Figure 2.1   Attention to iconic architecture: (a) Freedom Tower, New York City. (Courtesy of Mark S. Rosentraub.) (Continued)**

## 2.3.1.2 Integrate Facilities into New Neighborhoods

The changing environment for older central cities became quite clear by 1960. The 1960 Census revealed that for the first time in U.S. history, the proportion of people living in suburban areas was similar to the proportion living in central cities. This was a profound change in the distribution of people and economic activity from central cities to newly created suburban areas. Within another decade central cities that used to define their regions would account for less than one-third of the nation's residents, while suburban areas had become home to 37.6 percent of the nation's population. The gap continued to grow, and suburban cities accounted for 44.8 percent of the U.S. population in 1980, 46.2 percent in 1990, and half of the nation's population by 2000. Although America's population was now more urbanized, and a larger proportion of Americans were living in cities, most people were living in suburban cities. The wealthiest residents of most metropolitan areas were living in suburban areas far away from contracting

The 9/11 Memorial Fountain, Ground Zero, New York City

(b)

**Figure 2.1 (Continued)  Attention to iconic architecture: (b) 9/11 Memorial Fountain, Ground Zero, New York City. (Courtesy of Mark S. Rosentraub.) (Continued)**

central cities that were now becoming home to the largest proportion of a region's lower-income households.

Central cities were initially located on bodies of water where transportation costs were minimized. Those lower costs allowed raw materials to be efficiently brought to central locations to be transformed into finished products (or materials that contributed to the production of finished goods). Those products could then be efficiently distributed to markets for final sale. Since numerous legal, financial, and real estate services were needed for all of these tasks to be completed, there was a corresponding growth in the legal, finance, and real estate businesses that had to be located close to one another in order to reduce communication costs. These growing needs led to the dominance of central cities in all economies and economic systems. Large numbers of workers, many with limited skills and education, were attracted to these areas and their comparative advantages, as numerous jobs requiring few skills were available.

The Hi Line Park Built on a Former Elevated Train Line,
West Side of Manhattan

(c)

**Figure 2.1 (Continued)    Attention to iconic architecture: (c) High Line Park built on a former elevated train line, West Side of Manhattan. (Courtesy of Mark S. Rosentraub.)**

Enhanced train service and the interstate highway system, as well as the declining cost of air travel and freight service, decreased the value of locations adjacent to bodies of water. The Internet, email, and other forms of technological communication advances (text messaging, photo distribution, document distribution, and video communication) created another incentive for businesses to locate in suburban areas. Firms could now locate anywhere in a metropolitan area, giving rise to larger suburban and exurban cities. Decreasing transportation and communications created new competitive areas, reducing the need for many businesses to locate in central cities.

Highly skilled workers are able to travel between suburban and exurban locations where land prices made luxurious homes more affordable. Businesses located in central cities soon found it economically advantageous to locate closer to where their most valuable employees wanted to live and where land prices were lower. Loops or interstate rings were soon built around central cities, and along these roadways office parks and later assembly and manufacturing centers could be found. The need for central cities dissipated, and what was often left behind in these core communities were abandoned buildings and homes, a growing concentration of lower-income households, and fewer and fewer job opportunities.

Cities that were located in areas without geographic impediments were among the first to become centers of decline. The Detroit metropolitan area is one in which there are no geographic "choke points" that make travel inconvenient. While

## WHAT IS ICONIC ARCHITECTURE AND HOW
## DO YOU KNOW IT WHEN YOU SEE IT?

Just as "beauty is in the eye of the beholder," what defines iconic architecture can be a matter of taste. To some extent that is true, but in planning a revitalization strategy, and in thinking about what attracts and retains those people who are "creative destroyers," it is best to describe iconic architecture as something that excites and engages people and their minds. In some instances their engagement could take the form of disdain. In other instances a building might create a smile or even surprise. What one seeks in iconic architecture is an emotional reaction that engages the mind of every person that sees the building. Some examples are presented in Figure 2.2. For a few readers, one or two buildings might be ugly, while others will find each attractive. Still even others will have a favorite or will find one or two that appeals to them. Each has a level of controversy, *but none is bland.*

Two views of Brooklyn's Barclays Center are presented; the rust-colored skin mixed with glass was to represent Brooklyn's gritty past as a manufacturing center or a stepchild to the glitz of Manhattan, a short ride away across the Brooklyn and Manhattan Bridges. The sweeping entrance with its very modern video board (teardrop format) is a symbol of Brooklyn's high-technology future and its leading role in reimagining urban space.

The Jackie Robinson Rotunda at Citi Field (New York Mets) celebrates the legendary home of the Brooklyn Dodgers and the extraordinary contribution of Jackie Robinson to American society through sports. Lucas Oil Stadium, the home of the Indianapolis Colts, has a sliding glass window as wide as a football field through which fans can see the entire downtown area. Frank Geary's design of Disney Hall—home of the Los Angeles Philharmonic Orchestra—was designed to create an entirely new image for a deteriorating downtown area. Years later it was joined by the futuristic designs of L.A. LIVE. AT&T Stadium in Arlington, Texas, while not integrated into a community or urban setting, is defined by two iconic atriums, a sliding panel that opens the roof, seating for 100,000 people, and the world's largest video board suspended above the field. The video monitor is more than 50 yards long and has become a tourist attraction for visitors to North Texas (see Figure 2.2).

Manhattan is an island, raising commutation costs (and increasing the value of living on the island), numerous roadways can easily access almost every part of the metropolitan Detroit region. As a result, people and businesses can locate almost anywhere and enjoy easy connections to other parts of the region. The lack of congestion accelerated the formation of a polycentric form of urbanism with numerous business centers, leaving central cities economically segregated.

(a)

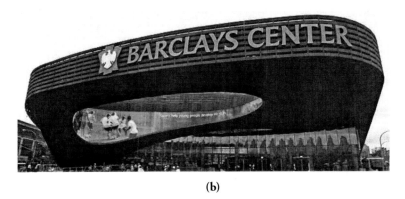

(b)

**Figure 2.2   Examples of iconic architecture: (a, b) Barclays Center, Brooklyn: An iconic "skin" reflecting Brooklyn's past and a video board representing Brooklyn's future. (Photographs courtesy of Mark S. Rosentraub.) (Continued)**

The decentralization trends will continue to make more dispersed patterns of development possible as a result of decreasing communication and transportation costs. There was some degree of optimism that the rising cost of fossil fuels would encourage a recentralization of economic activity. Theory, however, would not sustain this expectation. Each change in the cost of raw materials creates incentives for realizing more technological efficiencies in transportation. Those efficiencies

(c)

(d)

**Figure 2.2 (Continued)** Examples of iconic architecture: (c) Citi Field, Flushing, New York: The Jackie Robinson Rotunda reflecting the architecture of Ebbets Field, the history of National League Baseball in New York, and the legacy of Jackie Robinson. (d) Lucas Oil Stadium, Indianapolis. (Courtesy of Mark S. Rosentraub.) (Continued)

(e)

(f)

**Figure 2.2 (Continued)    Examples of iconic architecture: (e) Disney Hall, Los Angeles. (f) Cowboys Stadium, Arlington, Texas. (Courtesy of Mark S. Rosentraub.) (Continued)**

include engines *less* dependent on fossil fuels, the greater use of composite (lower-weight) materials, and the application of computer technology to reduce other operating costs (fewer accidents, etc.). As communication and transportation costs continue to make it possible for people to live farther and farther from aging central cities, new town centers emerge in polynucleated urban areas.

(g)

**Figure 2.2 (Continued)** **Example of iconic architecture: (g) L.A. LIVE, Los Angeles. (Courtesy of Mark S. Rosentraub.)**

Within this reality, what becomes the destiny of downtown areas? Four factors have to be at the forefront of strategies to revive central cities and their downtown areas.

First, the very nature of a downtown area or neighborhood has to be changed. Downtown areas have to be changed into residential communities with entertainment amenities, live-work space, and some level of commercial activity. This combination of activities has to reconcentrate a level of economic activity and become a driving component of a city's property tax base. This means that governmental functions and buildings have to be redistributed to other communities to help eliminate blight and anchor revitalization efforts in those areas.

Second, the new downtown areas have to be designed to attract and retain higher-income households. No city can balance its financial portfolio without a population mix that includes wealthier families and individuals. It is those individuals and families that generate the tax revenue cities need to revive neighborhoods. A reformatted downtown area is a prudent step in achieving a level of economic integration and eliminating economic segregation.

Third, the design of downtown areas has to emphasize linkages between emerging centers of entertainment and residences that create and integrate a set of mini-neighborhoods in a city's core area. Downtown Denver consists of three or four neighborhood areas anchored by entertainment venues, neighborhood-scale amenities, numerous residences that weave through the venues and areas, and a linkage plan that integrates each area with adjoining sections located within a 3-mile radius of the center. Today more than 62,000 people live in downtown Denver. To guide the construction of new downtown areas, Goldberg et al. note there is a statistically significant higher level of happiness among residents and citizens living in high-density cities that have mixed-use and walkable neighborhoods. That finding demonstrates the need for linked mini-neighborhoods in new downtown areas to eliminate any sense of social isolation. Cities need to incorporate meeting places filled with public art, music, and a diverse selection of restaurants and niche retail outlets.[8] Downtown areas that create this environment succeed, as that is where greater entrepreneurial productivity takes place.[9]

Fourth, no city is revived without a focus on each of its neighborhoods. Governmental offices and operations need to be relocated where there is no demand for residences, and therefore little interest from the private sector to invest its capital. It is those areas in which governmental offices should be located. Existing public buildings need to move from downtown areas and be replaced by big-ticket amenities surrounded by new residential properties and neighborhood retail outlets and restaurants. Once government facilities replace blighted properties in outlying neighborhoods, private capital might return to produce the services those government agencies require. An entirely different design of cities is required. As will be demonstrated in the case studies, big-ticket amenities surrounded by neighborhood retail have attracted private capital. In turn, when government buildings are relocated to blighted neighborhoods, derelict structures and vacant lots are replaced and filled by buildings. Some businesses will also relocate to these areas to provide services that workers in those buildings require during the business day.

How do sports and culture fit into this plan? The venues that host events become the intertwining nodes upon which new residential and commercial cores are built. In a revived downtown, that includes space for highly skilled labor to meet, mill about, and congregate. Figure 2.3 provides a few examples of different design strategies that incorporate a sports facility into downtown neighborhoods.

## 2.3.1.3 Amenities or Neighborhood Development? The Answer Is Both

To implement Alfred Marshall's concept of ideas in the air, cities have to be designed with space or neighborhoods where people can interact and where ideas are put into motion. Ideas are not only exchanged in the workplace. Creative people walk, talk, and interact with one another. It may be a sports facility, entertainment event, a show or play, or an art exhibition that attracts a crowd. But that crowd needs properly designed space for interacting. Lastly, people live in neighborhoods. Revitalization means focusing on amenities and neighborhoods. It is not an either-or proposition. Without either, competitive clusters will not form.

Every city that has been attracted to the idea of iconic architecture either for its image or for the building of sports facilities, museums, or cultural centers could simultaneously point to projects designed to enhance the culture and quality of life in other

(a)

(b)

Figure 2.3 Sports facilities as part of downtown areas: (a) San Diego's PETCO Park (left) and the Ballpark District. (b) Denver's Coors Field (center at end of street) and LODO Denver. (Courtesy of Mark S. Rosentraub.) (Continued)

(c)

(d)

**Figure 2.3 (Continued)** Sports facilities as part of downtown areas: (c) Barclays Center and Flatbush Avenue in Brooklyn. (d) Nationwide Arena and the Arena District, Columbus, Ohio. (Courtesy of Mark S. Rosentraub.)

neighborhoods. Columbus would boast of its success in Germantown, Indianapolis would point to the Fountain Square neighborhood and its theatre, as well as the Bohemian area known as Broad Ripple, and Cleveland would point to its Bohemian West Side and the racially mixed area around Shaker Square. Indeed, all of the case studies will underscore that leaders in those cities believed the big-ticket projects in their downtown areas would help attract and retain human capital. Equally important, in no instance did any city ignore neighborhood development projects. If they did, economic development would be curtailed. In summary, even when big-ticket items are developed, they cannot supplant a simultaneous focus on neighborhoods. While public resources were involved with all of the big-ticket projects, there is also evidence of substantial efforts to advance neighborhood development.

Urban planners, team executives, community leaders, and fans have to understand that the path to mutual gain and higher levels of economic development are rooted in a new downtown neighborhood anchored by sports facilities and cultural centers that are themselves iconic in nature. Each of these elements of a revitalization strategy can and should be achieved. Neither minimizes the possibility of other community development activities in traditional residential neighborhoods. What also has to be understood is that the traditional central business district has to change to focus on the urban residential life that attracts private capital investment to downtown areas.

Indianapolis' balanced approach is illustrated with its new "culture path" being built in downtown amidst several big-ticket assets (see Figure 2.4). This path unites

**Figure 2.4    Uniting big-ticket items and neighborhood amenities: Indianapolis'
downtown bike path. (Courtesy of Mark S. Rosentraub.)**

all of the mini-neighborhoods of downtown Indianapolis with the numerous sports and cultural facilities that turned a blighted, aging core into one of Indianapolis' most vibrant communities. Indianapolis has changed its downtown into one more now known as a residential neighborhood with a smaller downtown business district. Its downtown image is bolstered by the Lilly Corporation's research and administrative complex, but is also defined by a large urban university and a set of hospitals. Linking all of the parts of the new downtown is both a walking path and a bicycle path.

### 2.3.1.4 Build Space for Ideas in the Air and Where Creative Destroyers Meet

Numerous urban planners and designers have created great urban neighborhoods that are based on the pioneering concepts advanced by Jane Jacobs. Those precepts will be discussed in greater detail later in this chapter, but at this juncture it is important to again focus on the ideas of Alfred Marshall. If wealth, competitive advantages, and creative destruction are products of ideas in the air, then the new neighborhoods, entertainment districts, and sports facilities have to be designed with spaces for people to interact and exchange ideas. The popularity of suites and the entertaining spaces within this luxury product and the club areas included in all new sports facilities are examples of providing space for people to network, share ideas, and put, as Marshall would note, ideas into the air. The public spaces included in San Diego's Ballpark District, Eutaw Street in Baltimore's Oriole Park at Camden Yards, and Columbus' Arena District are all examples of including space to facilitate ideas in the air. As will be discussed, Jane Jacobs had critical ideas for urban design that are in many ways aligned with Marshall's theories regarding wealth. She did not foresee the rapid rate of decentralization that would soon define economic development and what role sports can and do play in recentralizing economic activity in the very cities she adored. There are many imaginative ways to build public spaces for people to interact and exchange ideas that are linked to the popularity of sports. The Ballpark District in San Diego includes three: a public park, a miniature baseball diamond for children to play in while their parents watch Padres' games, and a family section that includes a sandbox for children to play in while their parents watch the game or visit with friends.

Nokia Plaza in L.A. LIVE has outdoor seating where people can also watch games or shows that are broadcast on large video screens. Many ballparks now include party decks or suites that accommodate at least 100 people. Each of these elements incorporated into facilities or neighborhoods is an example of creating space for interaction and the circulation of ideas in the air. These spaces allow for people to interact and for young families to feel comfortable, while creating open spaces integrated with iconic structures. Every major facility that has the potential to attract people has to include areas for people to mix. Ironically, facilities that only offer traditional seating reduce the opportunities for interaction. That design feature has to be balanced with places for people to interact (see Figure 2.5).

(a)

(b)

Figure 2.5    Building public spaces adjacent to sports facilities to create the space for ideas in the air: (a) Public park built just beyond the outfield fences in San Diego's Ballpark District, (b) children's ball field just beyond the outfield fences in San Diego's Ballpark District. (Continued)

(c)

(d)

Figure 2.5 (Continued)   Building public spaces adjacent to sports facilities to create the space for ideas in the air: (c) Family seating and the sand box for children beyond the center field fence at PETCO Park, San Diego, and (d) The Nokia Plaza facing the Staples Center and part of L.A. LIVE, Los Angeles.

## 2.3.2 Amenities, Human Capital, and Economic Development

There is little disagreement with the idea that businesses in the 21st century locate where they have the greatest confidence that people with the needed skills and talent will want to live (McGahey and Vey 2008). Where there is disagreement, however, is with the importance of large-scale or big-ticket amenities such as a sports facility or a museum or a theatre district in attracting talented workers (Wojan et al. 2007). Some suggest that regardless of the type of amenity—clubs with live entertainment or sports facilities—it is the presence of wealth that creates a demand and a market that attracts investors interested in providing entertainment and cultural opportunities. Facilities are then built in these areas as entrepreneurs seek to profit from the discretionary income that can be spent as a result of a region's growing wealth (Hannigan 1998; Hoffman et al. 2003). Advocates of this position question or wonder if the reverse relationship is true. If subsidies are used to ensure the presence of sports teams and arts and cultural amenities, will their existence attract human capital and businesses? Will the economic development that results from rising levels of human capital and new business expansion produce the wealth needed to ensure that a sports team, entertainment center, or arts and cultural amenity continues to exist without ongoing subsidies?

The critics who challenge or question whether sports or any other amenity can or will attract human capital suggest that policies focused on education and training should assume a paramount position in any regional economic development strategy. Advocates of the position that cities can change their images and create an attractive environment for entrepreneurs argue that entertainment centers do not minimize the need for education and training systems. They underscore that while all regions are focused on improving and enhancing education and training through investments in primary, secondary, and higher education, amenities must also exist to ensure the presence of desired images and development levels. The human capital or economic development argument that underpins the policies followed in each of the case studies is that central cities can attract the human capital needed to form clusters through the building of amenities.

When mass manufacturing offered millions of jobs, and industries were dependent on the specific physical locations (frequently with access to water) to minimize production costs, people moved to where these businesses needed to locate. As Garmise (2006) notes, success in the 21st century economy is increasingly a function of the competitive advantage of places relative to their ability to attract and retain human capital. With ideas increasingly the currency of innovation and the inputs that drive an economy and a business' future, corporations now locate where people want to live. The age-old axiom that people move to where the jobs are is changing, and the new reality is that corporations locate where they believe (1) people want to live and (2) in areas where they have the greatest confidence that they can attract and retain the human capital required to foster innovation. Communities, cities, and regions that attract idea generators or the people likely to foster innovation are now as important for a corporation's location as a river was in the 19th century. As more and more manufacturing is outsourced or becomes more mechanized (robots), job growth is dependent on innovation. Perhaps innovation and ideas—best enumerated by patents filed—have always driven the economy (Fogarty et al., 2002). But at a time when America was home to both innovation and manufacturing, the focus for many companies was on the physical location where manufacturing could be the most profitable. With ideas, centers of innovation, and research increasingly separated from manufacturing locations, businesses now choose idea centers for their home. Idea centers are the places where people choose to live based on what is important to them in terms of valued amenities—climate, entertainment, recreation, sports, culture, and neighborhoods.

Building on the themes of competitive advantage explained by Porter (1985), Garmise directs community leaders to focus on policies and programs that ensure that their communities are ones that produce, attract, and retain the "creative classes" or idea generators needed by firms. This focus means that regions have to build the urban environments in which people want to live, instead of focusing on ways to reduce costs to encourage businesses to locate in their region. It also means that a region must have educational or training programs that either produce the human capital needed or continuously attract new capital. In practice, a human capital approach to economic development requires a focus on establishing exceptional education and training programs, but it also means ensuring that the right mix of amenities is available to give cities and regions the image and quality of life demanded by high-value human capital (Hannigan 1998).

## 2.3.3 The Supply of Amenities

An investor's decision to be involved in providing an amenity is related to his or her interest in securing a profit and in being associated with a particular asset's presence in a region. Sloane (1971) described these two sets of aspirations or attributes as profit maximization and welfare maximization. Profit maximization involves the actions of an owner of any amenity interested only in securing the greatest return from his or her investment. Welfare maximization refers to the intangible benefits or gains an owner receives as a result of ensuring an amenity's presence in a community (e.g., a team, orchestra, opera, etc.). Many supporters of the Cleveland Orchestra take great satisfaction from its national ranking and international prestige; therefore, their donations are made not to secure any financial return, but to guarantee the orchestra's success and presence in Cleveland.[10]

In communities where a welfare-maximizing benefactor is not present and when private entrepreneurs perceive the risks of earning a profit from the building of sports, entertainment, or arts and cultural facilities to be too high, a new asset will only be built if the public sector also makes an investment. The public sector's investment reduces the risks to the private sector partner and helps ensure the profitability of the project. In some instances the public and nonprofit sector partners are asked to finance the capital costs associated with both the tourist amenity and needed support facilities (hotels, restaurants, etc.). The public sector is also frequently responsible for any improvements needed in transportation, water, or environmental systems (Rosentraub 1997a).

## 2.4 Life from Death for Cities, Organic Urban Change vs. Planned Redevelopment, and Neighborhood Design: Reinterpreting Jane Jacobs' Philosophy in the Age of the Internet and Decentralization

Jane Jacobs was one of the most important voices shaping the intellectual focus of urban planning for much of the second half of the 20th century. Her ideas are still dominant themes guiding the efforts of practicing planners and academics focused on urban revitalization strategies, planning, and design. Three of her extraordinary ideas are important to consider at this juncture: (1) the availability of lower-cost real estate to provide space for new businesses to germinate new economic life from death or the decay of property, (2) a focus on organic or indigenous revitalization as opposed to large-scale planned redevelopment efforts, and (3) a focus on "walkable" blocks and neighborhood-scale designs that integrate building and people into the fabric of urban settings.

### 2.4.1 The Life from Death Cycle of Urban Areas

In the *Death and Life of Great American Cities*, Jane Jacobs pointed attention to the creative destruction that takes place ever year. Today the term that is used to describe this process is *churn*. *Churn* means that each year hundreds of thousands of firms are closed and hundreds of thousands are formed. Churn quantifies Joseph Schumpeter's theoretical perspective of creative destruction. New products and new processes make some firms obsolete while others are created. Firms that cease operations eliminate jobs, and new jobs are created in the newly established businesses. A sense of the scale of churn in the United States is described in Table 2.1. Within the 2009–2010 time frame more than 646,740 businesses were created, but 719,225 were closed. A total of 4.93 million jobs were created by these new businesses, but the firms that ceased operations resulted in the loss of 5.22 million jobs. Across the entire country there was a loss of 2.54 million jobs. The results reported for each state illustrate losses largely attributable to the substantial recession. Note, however, there was a large number of new businesses created in every state. As Joseph Schumpeter noted, since the Great Depression and in the midst of the most substantial contraction of the U.S. economy, creative destruction was taking place every year and in every state.

**Table 2.1   The Life from Death of Business Creation, 2009–2010**

| | Businesses Created | | Businesses Closed | | Net Change | |
|---|---|---|---|---|---|---|
| Area | Number | Jobs | Number | Jobs | Businesses | Jobs |
| United States | 646,740 | 4,926,317 | 719,225 | –5,216,964 | –72,485 | –2,535,142 |
| Alabama | 7,580 | 59,523 | 9,472 | –67,311 | –1,892 | –45,544 |
| Alaska | 1,770 | 10,041 | 1,640 | –8,267 | 130 | 3,214 |
| Arizona | 13,286 | 125,875 | 16,157 | –117,096 | –2,871 | –56,231 |
| Arkansas | 5,328 | 41,308 | 5,665 | –37,929 | –337 | –6,369 |
| California | 79,161 | 568,137 | 91,682 | –660,808 | –12,521 | –306,794 |
| Colorado | 15,148 | 102,519 | 17,164 | –99,170 | –2,016 | –49,653 |
| Connecticut | 6,751 | 52,771 | 8,020 | –53,509 | –1,269 | –29,756 |
| Delaware | 2,062 | 13,852 | 2,383 | –15,727 | –321 | –12,571 |
| D.C. | 2,038 | 17,632 | 1,808 | –14,777 | 230 | –2,735 |
| Florida | 55,315 | 398,284 | 58,701 | –559,259 | –3,386 | –240,837 |
| Georgia | 20,286 | 147,324 | 24,049 | –174,795 | –3,763 | –96,136 |
| Hawaii | 2,403 | 19,894 | 2,930 | –19,715 | –527 | –9,700 |
| Idaho | 4,033 | 20,547 | 4,818 | –21,266 | –785 | –10,767 |
| Illinois | 25,712 | 201,199 | 28,943 | –211,423 | –3,231 | –139,236 |
| Indiana | 10,370 | 86,163 | 12,260 | –91,970 | –1,890 | –48,488 |
| Iowa | 5,453 | 37,328 | 5,825 | –46,293 | –372 | –26,930 |
| Kansas | 5,458 | 44,481 | 6,164 | –42,802 | –706 | –25,391 |
| Kentucky | 6,977 | 56,851 | 7,687 | –54,518 | –710 | –29,295 |
| Louisiana | 8,410 | 67,728 | 8,556 | –58,911 | –146 | –38,537 |
| Maine | 3,200 | 18,604 | 3,411 | –17,742 | –211 | –8,758 |
| Maryland | 11,519 | 85,984 | 12,982 | –89,204 | –1,463 | –44,534 |
| Massachusetts | 13,345 | 104,179 | 14,634 | –101,655 | –1,289 | –37,817 |
| Michigan | 16,369 | 126,250 | 20,523 | –161,237 | –4,154 | –101,276 |

*(Continued)*

**Table 2.1    The Life from Death of Business Creation, 2009–2010 (Continued)**

| Area | Businesses Created | | Businesses Closed | | Net Change | |
|---|---|---|---|---|---|---|
|  | Number | Jobs | Number | Jobs | Businesses | Jobs |
| Minnesota | 11,143 | 86,972 | 12,394 | –96,559 | –1,251 | –60,483 |
| Mississippi | 4,651 | 32,922 | 5,218 | –35,446 | –567 | –22,470 |
| Missouri | 13,552 | 92,525 | 14,699 | –91,384 | –1,147 | –63,496 |
| Montana | 2,993 | 15,570 | 3,354 | –12,851 | –361 | –2,849 |
| Nebraska | 3,829 | 25,995 | 3,772 | –21,832 | 57 | –11,229 |
| Nevada | 6,707 | 66,401 | 7,593 | –55,544 | –886 | –39,729 |
| New Hampshire | 2,966 | 21,500 | 3,344 | –22,594 | –378 | –4,275 |
| New Jersey | 20,089 | 145,016 | 24,024 | –180,221 | –3,935 | –80,319 |
| New Mexico | 3,586 | 23,574 | 4,475 | –25,211 | –889 | –15,484 |
| New York | 49,665 | 329,273 | 48,472 | –318,826 | 1,193 | –63,397 |
| North Carolina | 19,581 | 148,360 | 21,828 | –153,424 | –2,247 | –95,192 |
| North Dakota | 1,630 | 9,853 | 1,415 | –12,904 | 215 | –1,542 |
| Ohio | 17,535 | 153,012 | 21,775 | –163,945 | –4,240 | –110,052 |
| Oklahoma | 7,159 | 54,784 | 7,877 | –56,760 | –718 | –48,852 |
| Oregon | 9,704 | 55,988 | 10,740 | –56,770 | –1,036 | –13,126 |
| Pennsylvania | 21,448 | 185,356 | 24,314 | –182,118 | –2,866 | –66,251 |
| Rhode Island | 2,343 | 18,114 | 2,650 | –15,264 | –307 | –14,304 |
| South Carolina | 8,689 | 72,155 | 10,222 | –65,548 | –1,533 | –40,887 |
| South Dakota | 1,990 | 13,399 | 1,900 | –10,731 | 90 | –1,595 |
| Tennessee | 10,503 | 89,710 | 12,490 | –103,090 | –1,987 | –55,598 |
| Texas | 49,590 | 478,922 | 48,786 | –400,549 | 804 | –143,526 |
| Utah | 7,367 | 53,714 | 8,092 | –51,596 | –725 | –37,491 |
| Vermont | 1,534 | 9,665 | 1,687 | –7,272 | –153 | –612 |

*(Continued)*

**Table 2.1   The Life from Death of Business Creation, 2009–2010 (Continued)**

| Area | Businesses Created | | Businesses Closed | | Net Change | |
|---|---|---|---|---|---|---|
| | Number | Jobs | Number | Jobs | Businesses | Jobs |
| Virginia | 16,538 | 125,938 | 18,384 | −147,245 | −1,846 | −61,069 |
| Washington | 16,286 | 106,462 | 18,020 | −101,303 | −1,734 | −59,140 |
| West Virginia | 2,506 | 21,006 | 3,103 | −19,812 | −597 | −13,873 |
| Wisconsin | 9,626 | 75,851 | 11,174 | −74,335 | −1,548 | −34,492 |
| Wyoming | 1,556 | 7,806 | 1,949 | −8,446 | −393 | −9,668 |

*Source:* U.S. Bureau of the Census, www.census.gov/ces/dataproducts/bds/data_estab.html

What does this have to do with urban planning and the building of new neighborhoods surrounding sports and cultural facilities?

Jane Jacobs noted that the creation of new economic life requires a section of a city or region that has a level of deteriorating or low-cost real estate to serve as the start-up space for new businesses. If a city or region destroys all of its lower-cost commercial space, it short-circuits the economic life from death process. Creative destruction requires the availability of low-cost commercial space. Any plans for the building of a new sports facility and surrounding residences and commercial space cannot be planned in a vacuum. An overall redevelopment and revitalization strategy has to include sufficient space for new start-up businesses. This can be accomplished in many ways. Some communities have preserved warehouses and renovated them to accommodate start-up enterprises. Another strategy has been to build "incubator" space that serves as the short-term home for new enterprises. Older buildings serving as homes to new businesses often include residential space, offering new and young entrepreneurs live-work space to help reduce their start-up costs. These areas also serve as places where young talent can live as they try to develop new technologies, new processes, new companies, and art. If all neighborhoods in a city were redeveloped, the cost of land and space would thwart the creation of new businesses, as there would be no place for those start-up operations to exist (Jacobs 1969, 1993).

Jane Jacobs saw the life from death process—the creative destruction of a city's economy—as a way in which cities were restored and fostered life within declining areas of a community or city. In the 1950s and 1960s, when her arguments were framed, it was reasonable to expect that new businesses that became successful in a city would move from start-up space to more valuable, expansive, and expensive commercial space in the *same* city. The reality of the 21st century, and even of the last decades of the 20th, was that when start-up firms became successful, they were as likely to locate in suburban communities, or even other parts of the country, as they were to stay in central cities. Indeed, what life from death means today is that a city ensures that sufficient space for start-up companies exists while also building the environment in which businesses can grow and flourish. That requires attention to building the new neighborhoods and amenities that attract and retain the skilled labor newly formed businesses need to can grow and succeed.

## 2.4.2 Indigenous Revitalization vs. Large-Scale Planned Redevelopment

Jane Jacobs' work has also been at the forefront of thought championed by many that successful revitalization—defined as long lasting and inclusive of a community's residents—needs to grow from an area's existing assets and resources. This can be thought of as an indigenous revitalization hypothesis and her concept is best defined by understanding its polar opposite strategy, the master-planned new neighborhood. Those efforts are represented by San Diego's Ballpark District that involved more than $2 billion in new development; the building of L.A. LIVE, Staples Center, and the thousands of condominium units in downtown Los Angeles; and Columbus' Arena District with its entirely new neighborhood. Each is an example of a new master-planned neighborhood that is injected into areas that have been characterized by slow growth, abandonment, or no growth for decades. These efforts are not indigenous and they may not grow or capitalize on existing assets. Rather, new assets are built, the new condominiums, apartments, and townhouses that are built attract new residents (even though below-market-rate units are usually built to ensure that new housing opportunities exist for households with a wide range of annual incomes), and of course, there is the presence of at least one big-ticket amenity (usually an arena, ballpark, or stadium). This planning framework is not an evolutionary approach to change. It is a revolution with the imposition of a new neighborhood and new amenities that do not evolve over time, but are injected into an area. Was Jane Jacobs correct in fearing that these efforts cannot be successful and will also destroy long-standing communities? Insights and data are available to respond to both fears, and the individual case studies that follow will provide additional insight. At this juncture, however, several points need to be made that suggest that some of Ms. Jacobs' ideas need to be adjusted given the dynamic aspects of the changing patterns of the use of land and space in urban regions.

### 2.4.2.1 The Rate of Decentralization and Retaining Start-Ups and Human Capital

It would be unfair to suggest that anyone studying cities and revitalization strategies in the 1950s and 1960s would have been able to project the current rate of economic decentralization. As discussed in Chapter 1, the rate of decentralization is increasing as a result of personal preferences and reduced communication and transportation costs. In addition, with less political support for revenue sharing between growing suburban cities and central cities, and with states reducing grants too, central cities with large supplies of lower-cost real estate can lose the opportunity to capture the economic gains when these firms succeed and relocate. Once the businesses that take advantage of the lower real estate prices become successful, the lure of other locations will grow. Staff will prefer reduced commutes, and therefore interest in suburban locations for successful businesses is a likely outcome. A way to compete for the property, sales, and income taxes that could be lost if a successful start-up firm is evaluating alternative locations is to offer new neighborhoods that exceed the amenities available elsewhere in a region.

Given the pace of decentralization, ensuring that there is a master-planned development that abides by Jane Jacobs' design principles, yet includes amenities unavailable elsewhere in the region, may be the best way to capture the development that takes place. When Ms. Jacobs formulated her perspective, the idea that successful firms would leave a central city was a far more remote possibility than it is today. In the 1950s and 1960s, successful firms could be expected to remain in other parts of the central city. Responding to the possibility of firms now choosing to stay in a region, but in another city, core areas have to change their inventory of available space and locations to exceed the convenient options offered by suburban areas. That can only be accomplished with the building of new downtown neighborhoods, as was done in Columbus, Denver, Indianapolis, Los Angeles, and San Diego. That is best done with a master-planned new area built in the downtown area of central cities.

## 2.4.2.2 Success: Sustained New Neighborhoods

Some of the fear of master-planned new neighborhoods for downtown areas is that they would not be sustainable. In other words, newly planned neighborhoods that are not properly linked to other parts of the downtown area would not be successful. If a proper measure of success is the number of residents in the master-planned neighborhoods, available data from several cities would suggest that concern has been eliminated. Downtown Los Angeles, in the aftermath of years of racial strife and conflict, had lost a substantial portion of its residential base. In 2011, the Downtown Center Business Improvement District reported that the area had 45,518 residents. Downtown Denver has more than 62,000 residents, and in the 2010 Census there were 37,095 residents living in or adjacent to San Diego's Ballpark District. Downtown Indianapolis' residential population stands at more than 20,000 since 2010. When redevelopment began in the 1970s, fewer than 5,000 lived in downtown Indianapolis.[11] Columbus' Arena District is an entirely new downtown neighborhood. By 2010 it had 12,790 residents. The available evidence does not sustain the fear that a master-planned neighborhood's mixing of sports, entertainment, commercial space, and residential space could not be successful. Indeed, what is more apparent is that these neighborhoods are stable or growing even when the pressures to decentralize are increasing.

## 2.4.2.3 Economic and Social Integration

There were also legitimate concerns that master-planned developments would become economically and racially segregated. Neither of the master-planned neighborhoods in downtown Los Angeles or San Diego has become income or racially segregated. In 2011, 47.7 percent of the residents of downtown Los Angeles were non-Caucasian. More than one-third of the residents were either Asian or Hispanic. Of the 28,861 residential units in downtown Los Angeles, 38.2 percent were classified as affordable or not market rate. More than one-third of the respondents surveyed lived in households with annual incomes of less than $75,000.[12] Cantor and Rosentraub (2012) noted that San Diego's Ballpark District did indeed attract a larger proportion of higher-income households to live in the downtown area, but more than half of the area's residents lived in households with annual incomes of $75,000 or less (through 2012). Most importantly, however, by 2012, the proportion of residents who had at least a 4-year college degree had increased from 5.6 percent in 2000 to 24.8 percent by the decade's end. The attraction of highly skilled talent back to the central city had been achieved. Finally, during the severe recession, residential property in the Ballpark District was better able to sustain its value compared to most of San Diego's other neighborhoods. These data suggest that a master-planned development that was built in a decade could indeed be sustainable and integrated.[13]

## 2.4.3 Why Do Master-Planned Developments Succeed?

Why did these large-scale master-planned neighborhood projects succeed, create spaces for idea generators to meet, and provide a sort of Bohemian environment from which economic development could emerge? They succeeded by incorporating Jane Jacobs' urban design principles into their plans. Rather than disagreeing with Jacobs' basic concepts, the planners behind projects such as San Diego's Ballpark District, Columbus' Arena District, and Los Angeles' Staples Center and L.A. LIVE would argue that they just accelerated or advanced development to counter decentralization pressures that were diverting economic activity away from central cities and their downtown areas. While Jacobs' preferred an evolutionary approach and a natural evolution of ideas that fostered innovation and the formation of clusters of economic activity, the political and economic elites pushing for redevelopment of aging neighborhoods and downtown areas want to accelerate change. They see their actions as responding to increasingly rapid decentralization trends. What was taken directly from Jane Jacobs' ideas was to create short blocks that could be easily walked. On each block there were numerous retail outlets, places to sit, public parks, and different uses (residences, entertainment venues, and commercial space). Parking garages were placed on the periphery of the areas encouraging more street-level foot traffic and, wherever possible, the inclusion of retail or commercial space on the first floor of parking structures. The more foot traffic that is generated at street level, the greater the sense of personal and collective security.

Master-planned neighborhoods also took advantage of the large footprint of sports facilities to remove blighted buildings and abandoned lots. With that done, areas that had expanses of nonperforming real estate were immediately transformed by a sense of vibrancy. Arenas often host events on 150 to 175 dates; ballparks, however host fewer than 90 events. How can the space be used to encourage activity on nonevent days? That was accomplished by community events, affording the opportunity for the public to watch the players practice, and by surrounding the facilities with residences, parks, and commercial space. The sports facilities were then part of a 365-days-a-year neighborhood. What is crucial in making a new master-planned neighborhood a success is to ensure that no single facility or amenity is the only piece of real estate contributing to the area's sense of vibrancy.

Why were leaders willing to accept a master-planned development? The public and some community leaders in each of the cities studied in this book decided sufficient time had passed, and with development not taking place as quickly as was needed in a section of downtown to enhance the city's vitality, they implicitly asked, "How long does one wait before interceding to change the location of economic activity and improve conditions in a declining part of a city?" Beyond the issues of the creation and attraction of clusters of highly skilled human capital and firms, such a question is particularly relevant for cities trying to ensure that the collected property and income taxes are sufficient to pay for needed public services. When a declining area improves, or when businesses in that area expand, more tax money is realized.

## 2.5 Regimes and Urban Redevelopment

Master-planned developments anchored by sports and large-scale cultural centers also conjure fears of elite domination of decision-making processes. Does an elite or an urban regime dominated by corporate leaders pushing for big-ticket items mean that what is built is not in a central city's best interest? Before focusing on outcomes in each of the case studies, the question of elite decision making and public and private benefits also has to be considered.

Clarence Stone (1989), in his study of Atlanta's political power structure, built upon the research and reasoning initiated by Hunter (1953) assessing the roles that elites from the public and private sectors assume in shaping economic development decisions. An intellectual debate ensued between those who found decision making to be shaped by competing groups—the pluralistic approach to understanding power in American cities—(e.g., Dahl 1961; Jennings 1964) and those who found elites controlled economic development decisions (Molotch 1976, 1979; Logan and

Molotch 1987; Elkin 1987; Davies 2002). Two terms introduced by these lines of research, *growth coalitions* and *regimes*, refer to the roles assumed by elites from the public and private sectors. Growth coalitions refer to business elites that have an "unrivaled position" (Elkins 1995: 583) in dominating the policy agenda pursued by cities. A growth coalition becomes a regime when the same institutions (and individuals) dominate decision making for an extended period of time, creating a virtual private government of leaders steering local development policy. Rosentraub and Helmke (1996) described elite groups forming and reforming to direct economic development programs in a medium-sized city. These growth coalitions were described as a loosely coupled regime uniting to respond to specific opportunities. Each lacked the permanence usually identified with a regime, but when opportunities for economic advancement arose, the needed actors united to ensure that required actions by the public and private sector actors occurred. Their work highlighted that regimes could exist even if they met far less regularly than what Stone and Elkin had found.

Regardless of the extent to which elites led economic development activities, the issue of concern was whether limited participation meant the interests of cities were relegated in favor of those belonging to an elite. What is characteristic of many decision processes when growth coalitions or regimes are involved is that there are very limited opportunities for widespread public debate or opportunities for participation. The public's participation may be limited to votes on a specific referendum to support public money for a facility. The planning and design of facilities as well as their fit into neighborhoods and overall development strategies is rarely characterized by widespread public participation. That work is left to the growth coalitions and elites that assume strong leadership roles and the public sector. There is a distinctly antidemocratic nature to the actions of growth coalitions and regimes. Yet, in communities where no coalitions exist, some talk about a lack of concerted leadership to either advance a region's economic development or lead new initiatives (Rosentraub and Helmke 1996). The provision of excessive subsidies for economic development identified and studied in Squires' collection (1989) pointed to the unbalanced nature of the power exerted by growth coalitions and regimes. This imbalance may have led to excessive subsidies to sustain the development desired by elite groups. Other factors, however, also assume large roles in explaining why subsidies persist when it comes to the building of sports facilities (Kennedy and Rosentraub 2000). Local elites may have assumed a far smaller role in the provision of subsidies than earlier researchers concluded (Swindell and Rosentraub 2009).

What is generally argued is that elites have consistently assumed leading roles in the selection of economic development policies that have led to the building of sports facilities, convention centers, and arts and cultural centers (Delaney and Eckstein 2003; Sanders 2002, 2005). There is legitimate concern that this focus has diverted communities from exploring and implementing alternative economic development strategies (Imbroscio 1998; Levine 2000; Reese and Fasenfest 2004). There is a possibility that large-scale projects consume a community's available financial resources, eliminating other options or simply consuming so much time that leaders cannot entertain other competing strategies for renewal.

In each of the cities studied, elites led the redevelopment efforts. In Los Angeles and Denver, a new mayor and his staff built a coalition that included owners of professional sports teams and other corporate leaders. In San Diego, the team's owner reached out to the city and other elites to create a new plan and initiative. In Cleveland and Indianapolis the redevelopment efforts were led by long-standing regimes. In Columbus, members of the regime who saw their proposal for a tax increase in order to build a new arena defeated by voters put forward a new plan that protected the public's interest. This proposal was approved by elected officials without substantial opportunities for widespread public participation. Yet, even critics of the original plan applauded the creation of the Arena District, a new arena for a professional hockey team paid for by private investors, and the new real estate projects that followed. In Cleveland and Indianapolis, support for and focus upon a big-ticket redevelopment strategy did not preclude active participation in other community development efforts and extensive redevelopment in other parts of the cities. The role of elites is investigated in each case study with attention directed to other projects in other parts of the city.

Recognizing the benefits that can and do accrue to team owners and other business interests, it is essential that the outcomes of each redevelopment effort are analyzed noting what was actually gained by the central city. The benefits could be higher tax revenues, new levels of private investment, a new economically and socially integrated neighborhood, or a new vibrancy to a formerly deteriorating downtown area. In each instance, respecting the possibility of elite control, the returns to the central city are carefully analyzed.

# 2.6 The Value of Urban Space to Teams

Across the past several decades, some of the investments made by cities in sports facilities to attract and retain teams did not take full advantage of the ways in which real estate, the media, and entertainment have changed the business of sports. Anchoring the Ballpark District to PETCO Field advanced the sale of more than $2 billion of real estate. The same businessman who owned the San Diego Padres also owned the development firm that built much, if not all, of the real estate in the Ballpark District. John Moores took the risks associated with the project through a commitment to guarantee almost half a billion dollars of new development. The Ballpark District illustrates to all cities and teams that there is substantial profit potential associated with the building of new real estate adjoining a sports facility. The benefits of that development can be shared between the public and private sector and create returns for governments. Those returns change subsidies into investments, but too many public officials and community leaders failed to learn the lessons from the outcomes in San Diego, Los Angeles, Columbus, and

Indianapolis. These lessons are critical for understanding why urban space, real estate development, and master-planned neighborhoods are valuable to teams and are needed to ensure that any use of tax dollars to build a sports facility creates returns for the public sector.

The value of urban space to teams is not limited to the real estate surrounding a facility. The value of regional markets that have supported large new contracts from broadcast and cable operators underscores why teams are unlikely to leave the largest areas. Several teams own their own cable television systems (Boston Red Sox, New York Mets, and the New York Yankees), and each of the major sports leagues has also created independent networks. The value of those networks is a product of having teams in each of the largest media markets. The NHL, for example, has three teams in the largest media market in North America (New York Islanders, New York Rangers, and New Jersey Devils). The financial value of large media markets with robust fan bases means teams are less likely to leave a larger region for a smaller area. The issue of the size of a market for media sales is less important to individual NFL clubs, as the national television contact is shared by all 32 franchises. Smaller markets, however, raise substantial financial revenue issues related to real estate, ticket prices, and the sale of luxury seating.[14]

The value of a regional market to a team is probably best underscored by the value of the Detroit Red Wings. Despite the city of Detroit's substantial financial problems and bankruptcy, *Forbes* estimates that the Red Wings are the ninth most valuable franchise in the NHL. The team's value illustrates the importance of a regional market's size relative to media contracts. That value needs to be considered in the calculation of returns to the team and the returns the public and private sectors each enjoy from their respective investments in a sports facility.[15]

## THE NEGOTIATING GAME IN PRACTICE: HOW CITIES SOMETIMES MISS THEIR VALUE TO TEAMS

In the late 1980s, the Chicago White Sox threatened to move to Florida, and that prompted major concessions from the Illinois legislature. The public sector agreed to pay almost 100 percent of the cost of the new facility. And where did the White Sox threaten they would move? They were prepared to move to the Tampa–St. Petersburg area where the Tampa Bay Rays now struggle to attract fans. In June 2006, the Chicago metropolitan region had a population of 7.9 million while the Tampa–St. Petersburg area had 2.7 million people. Even if one divides the Chicago market in half, due to the presence of the Cubs, the White Sox were threatening to leave a larger market for a smaller one. In addition, in 2005 the Chicago metropolitan area had a median income level of $68,550, while the comparable figure for the Tampa Bay–St. Petersburg area was $52,150. Would the White Sox have been better off in a smaller market with a lower median income figure, or did Illinois misread the value of its market?

The public sector also decided to assume responsibility for a majority of the cost to renovate Soldier Field. That project cost $587 million, and the public sector paid $387 million, even though there were no realistic relocation options available to the NFL's Bears. The team had looked for a better deal throughout the region. The team first looked at a short move across the border into Indiana, and when that was not feasible, the team examined the possibilities in Chicago's western suburbs. Despite the realization that the Bears could not find a better location in the NFL's second largest market area, the team was still able to secure a substantial public investment to one of the nation's most historic athletic facilities, Soldier Field.

When MLB, which had purchased the Montreal Expos, decided to relocate the franchise, Washington, D.C. was competing with one of its western suburbs and possible locations in southeastern Virginia and Portland, Oregon. The choices were narrowed to Portland or Washington, D.C. Again, from a statistical standpoint, there did not seem to be much real competition. In 2006, the Washington, D.C. region had a population of 5.1 million people, more than twice that of Greater Portland (2.1 million). In 2005, the median household income in Greater Portland was a robust $65,900, but this is $20,000 lower than the $86,200 figure for Washington, D.C. and its suburbs. The team committed $20 million toward construction and accepted an amusement tax on tickets sold and on the sale of memorabilia.[16] The team is also responsible for all routine maintenance throughout the duration of the lease, with its rental payments starting at $3.5 million and then escalating to $5.5 million in the seventh year. In future years, the rent increases by 2 percent (less $10,000) and there is an additional rental fee of $1 for every ticket sold in excess of 2.5 million. Rent increments can only be negated if the Nationals' attendance falls below the median of all MLB teams across any 3-year period. Lastly, necessary capital improvements are the responsibility of the public sector. If the public sector and the team cannot agree on what constitutes a necessary capital improvement, an outside arbitrator reviews the claim and decides whether the team or the public sector must bear the cost. The public sector often undervalues its market for sports.

## 2.7 Summary

The focus on big-ticket amenities for revitalization is rooted in understanding the need to attract and retain human capital. Each expenditure has been made in response to the view that amenities are inexorably linked to human capital, and the regions that will prosper in the future are those that attract and retain more of these idea generators or those that drive each and every economy through creative destruction. The big-ticket investments need to be a part of new neighborhoods that follow Jane Jacobs' design principles while ensuring that after achieving success, start-up companies are convinced to stay in these new neighborhoods. Central cities need to reinvent downtown areas to compete with the amenity packages routinely available in suburban areas.

The reinvention must be focused on turning downtown areas into residential areas surrounded by entertainment districts. These are the packages that will attract private capital to invest again in downtown areas. There will be a continuing commercial presence in downtown areas, but it is likely that it will continue to diminish as firms decide to locate in suburban cities. For those that decide to remain or relocate downtown, they will do so only if there are new residential properties and products and unique entertainment amenities. If those assets do not exist, all commercial activity will relocate to suburban cities.

At the same time, to replace blighted buildings and fill vacant lots in some residential neighborhoods, it is time to relocate government buildings from downtown locations to those communities. With so many abandoned properties in neighborhoods and vacant lots, private capital will not invest in those areas. That is where government centers should now be located.

If central cities do not reinvent their downtown areas and compete with suburban cities, fiscal and economic decline is inevitable. And when that happens, lower-income households that depend on cities for schools, transportation, and economic opportunity will suffer. The cities that have turned subsidies into investments and reinvested in their downtown areas have chosen paths that link teams to development strategies that have increased profits and generated much needed tax revenues for central cities. The results and the lessons learned from reinvented downtown areas and new neighborhoods unfold in the chapters ahead.

# Endnotes

1. Glaab, C.N., *Wisconsin Magazine of History* 47(1): 19, 1963.
2. Glaab, C.N., *Wisconsin Magazine of History* 47(1): 19–20, 1963.
3. Schumpeter, J.A., *Capitalism, socialism, and democracy* (New York: Harper & Brothers, 1942).
4. Educated individuals can have more degrees, better formal education, than others. More educated individuals can also be self-taught or gain knowledge through experience. The point here is that creative destruction occurs where there is a concentration of educated (accomplished) workers who are rewarded from innovations (new processes or upgrades to existing products) they develop, or in the invention of new products.
5. Porter, M.E., *The competitive advantage of nations* (New York: Free Press, 1998).

6. Some of Michael Porter's ideas surrounding the concept of clusters and their creation of competitive advantages can be seen to be part of Alfred Marshall's concept of ideas in the air. Joseph Schumpeter's focus on creative destruction could also be seen to have roots in the concept that all wealth is created from ideas in the air.

7. Marshall, A., *Principles of economics* (Amherst, NY: Prometheus Press, 1997).

8. Hubbard, P., Urban design and city regeneration: Social representations of entrepreneurial landscapes, *Urban Studies* 33(1441): 1–22, 1996; Short, J.R., L.M. Benton, W.B. Luce, and J. Walton, Reconstructing the image of an industrial city, *Annals of the Association of American Geographers* 83(2): 207–224, 1993.

9. Goldberg, A., K. Leyden, and T. Scotto, Untangling what makes cities livable: Happiness in five cities, *Institution of Civil Engineers* 165(DP3): 1–10, 2012.

10. Observations based on interviews with philanthropists in Cleveland in 2007; the identity of the benefactor and the exact date of the interview are withheld based on their request.

11. Rosentraub, M.S., *Major league losers: The real costs of sports and who's paying for it* (New York: Basic Books, 1997).

12. *Downtown Los Angeles demographic study 2011*, http://www.downtownla.com/survey/2011/Downtown-LA-Demographic-Study-2011.pdf (accessed July 16, 2013).

13. Cantor, M.C., and M.S. Rosentraub, A ballpark and neighborhood change: Economic integration, a recession, and the altered demography of San Diego's Ballpark District after eight years, *City, Culture, and Society* 3: 219–226, 2012.

14. People might suggest that the lack of an NFL team in the Los Angeles–Orange County regions is an exception to the importance of having franchises in each of the largest media markets. Each Sunday, however, football fans can watch at least three games broadcast beginning at 10 a.m. and then extending from 1 p.m. to 4 p.m. In addition, fans in the area also receive Sunday, Monday, and Thursday night broadcasts of games. With at least six and often seven games well available to NFL fans, it would be unfair to note that professional football is not telecast to fans in the second largest media market in North America.

15. The ways in which the sports business has changed and the meaning of those changes for team owners and the public sector is detailed in Winfree, J., and M.S. Rosentraub, *Sports finance and management: Real estate, entertainment, and the remaking of the business* (Boca Raton, FL: CRC Press/Taylor & Francis Group, 2012).

16. Those revenues do constitute payments from the team. In the absence of the extra tax there would be no reduction in prices and the team would realize more income.

## Chapter 3

# Indianapolis as the Broker City

## 3.1 Introduction

Special attention should be accorded to Indianapolis when detailing the efforts of central cities that aggressively focused on sports, tourism, culture, and entertainment amenities to revitalize downtown areas. Indiana's capital, known as the Circle City, was probably the first to declare that sports events, venues, and organizations were going to be the primary vehicles to revitalize a declining downtown area. More importantly, however, Indianapolis' leadership put forward their vision for a very different downtown area in a comprehensive plan. That vision created by Indianapolis' civic and corporate leadership, with little opportunity for broad-based public input into it or the accompanying physical plan, was religiously followed for more than five decades by five different mayors (four Republicans and one Democrat). The plan was made possible by financial support from the Lilly Endowment, but was led by the new consolidated City of Indianapolis and Marion County's Department of Metropolitan Development. Across more than 50 years, the State of Indiana, the City of Indianapolis, and numerous private companies and organizations rebuilt a moribund downtown center and kept it vital. In addition, as some of the facilities built in the 1970s and 1980s became economically obsolete, a second wave of capital projects was launched. Indianapolis joined Dallas and Minneapolis as cities that had to replace sports venues to continue downtown revitalization efforts. Indianapolis then offers an opportunity to understand the long-term demands that a focus on sports and culture places on a community as facilities become economically obsolete.

That pressure now exists in several cities. For example, in Minneapolis, where a new ballpark was already built to replace one built for the Minnesota Twins, a new public–private partnership was agreed to that will lead to the building of a new enclosed stadium for the Minnesota Vikings. Their new home replaces the Metrodome built in 1982. Atlanta and Georgia have also recently agreed to join with the Atlanta Falcons to build a new domed stadium to replace the Georgia Dome that opened in 1992.* Other cities—including St. Louis—will also confront the challenge of replacing obsolete facilities across the next 10 to 15 years. Studying what was accomplished in Indianapolis and how the city has dealt with the building of a second generation of facilities is quite instructive.

When Indianapolis planned its revitalization strategy and branded itself the amateur sports capital of the world, it was at a time when no other city was looking to sports as a tool for revitalization. The amateur sports capital strategy or brand, however, was a bit misleading, as professional sports were always an integral part of the overall revitalization effort. The first major sports anchor in the downtown area was a new arena for the Indiana Pacers that brought the team to the downtown area from a midtown location. A covered stadium was affixed to the convention center in the hope that an NFL team could also be lured to the city. In the 1980s the Colts relocated from Baltimore, making Indianapolis the smallest region in the United States with *two* major sports franchises (and an AAA minor league MLB affiliate).

Added to the complexity of the issues that would be addressed for years was that the presence of two major teams exacerbated the balance between the demand for and supply of sports activities. The presence of two major professional teams added to the supply of available tickets, and the advent of luxury seating added another demand component in a relatively small market. In addition to the Colts and Pacers, the region is also home to the Indianapolis Motor Speedway. The Indianapolis 500 is the largest single-day sports event on the continent (measured by paid attendance). The Speedway also hosts another major race, a NASCAR event, the Brickyard 400, and it too attracts a crowd that is equal to one-third of the annual attendance at Pacers' or Colts' games. While a large number of people from other regions attend both races, many residents of Central Indiana are also at these mega-events. In addition, the Central Indiana region is also expected to support the Division I NCAA programs of Indiana University and Purdue University (basketball and football) and the basketball program of Butler University (which has emerged as a nationally competitive basketball team in the 21st century). Indiana University's basketball has been a legendary staple of the state's sports scene, and

---

* In 2013 the Atlanta Braves announced they would relocate to suburban Cobb County. A new ballpark would be built on a site where the team's owners would be able to also build a new mixed-use neighborhood-community (60+ acres). There were no similar real estate development opportunities for the team adjacent to Turner Field. A new ballpark with enhanced amenities and the opportunity to capitalize on a large real estate development opportunity would generate substantial financial benefits for the franchise's owners.

while suffering through a few years when success waned, its return to previous levels of success underscored the competitive market for discretionary spending that exists. Simply put, the supply of sports products (including rabid support for collegiate teams) in a relatively small market produces challenges for every team and for the Indianapolis Speedway. This level of supply in a small market requires the public sector to be focused on each team's and institution's costs and revenues. Across the past decades the Pacers, Colts, Indiana University, Purdue University, and the Indianapolis Motor Speedway have each added luxury seating products to their home venues. There is, then, a very large supply of tickets and luxury seating available in a market area that has fewer than 2 million residents. The Indianapolis metropolitan statistical area (MSA) is home to more than 1.6 million residents, but the professional sports teams market their games to residents of eastern, western, southern, and northeastern parts of the state. The expanded market base exceeds 6 million people, but in those areas more distant from Indianapolis, other teams and universities also market their games. For example, in different parts of northern Indiana the teams from Chicago and Detroit are popular, as are the teams from the University of Notre Dame. The University of Louisville and the teams in Cincinnati also have fans living in Indiana. Simply put, Indiana and Indianapolis have numerous competitors for fans' discretionary dollars. This raises issues for a revitalization effort tied to sports.

There are then two separate components that make the analyses of outcomes in Indianapolis very important. First, it was the city that initiated the policy or practice of using professional and amateur sports and the venues used for games, matches, and other athletic events to redirect regional economic activity in an effort to revitalize its downtown area. Second, Indianapolis also became the first city to initiate a second wave of facilities to replace the original cornerstones of the sports for revitalization policy as the older assets became economically obsolete. Indianapolis also enjoyed a level of attention and success from its revitalization plan anchored by sports. Several nearby central cities decided to imitate the vision and concept. If the Indianapolis plan worked for a small central city with less than 2.5 million residents in its expanded market region, perhaps the same strategy could help revitalize declining downtown areas in larger or similar-sized markets. While imitation is the highest form of flattery, the competing venues built from St. Louis to Pittsburgh and in Columbus, Ohio, Louisville, and Cincinnati soon created new levels of competition that undermined Indianapolis' financial model for its sports revitalization strategy. With so many new facilities being built and each located within a few hours of each other, a competition to host events emerged. As the supply of facilities increased, the ability to earn revenue from entertainment events declined, as promoters could work to receive the best deal from the facilities located relatively close to each other. If all of these challenges were not sufficient, Indianapolis has also had to deal with competition within its own region, as suburban cities began to incorporate elements of its central city's revitalization plan in their own development strategies. Each of these elements and issues are analyzed in this chapter, producing a set of valuable insights for other central cities and regions.

## 3.2 The Indianapolis Downtown Revitalization Plan: Goals, Objectives, and History

In the late 1960s and early 1970s, Indianapolis' leadership thought a consolidated form of local government joining suburban areas with the central city would convince people and businesses to redevelop the city and its downtown area. UniGov—the popular term given to this particular consolidation—established a blueprint for other communities that would consider city-county mergers as the path to link suburban and wealthier neighborhoods to central cities. In an operational sense, consolidation is little different from the annexation of land that central cities had done in the 19th century. In an effort to include wealthier residents of outlying neighborhoods in their tax bases, central cities have always needed to annex nearby land. When political opposition to annexation grew, consolidation was a way to ensure that central cities could expand their property tax base.

Indianapolis was not the first city to consolidate with its surrounding county. Far earlier forms of consolidation had taken place in Jacksonville, Miami, and Charlotte.[1] Across the past 40 years, however, scores of communities have looked at UniGov to see if a consolidated form of local government could advance redevelopment efforts in their area and stabilize a central city's finances.[2] As noted, however, there has been only one major city-county consolidation in the 21st century and since UniGov was established (involving the central City of Louisville and Jefferson County, Kentucky). The residents of most suburban areas have not found any financial incentive to vote for a merger with a central city. Suburban communities in the Denver metropolitan region, another area where a central city had the authority to unilaterally annex land, united to amend state law. The amendment passed in the 1970s required a board comprised of representatives from the suburbs and Denver to approve any annexation of land. As a result, Denver's ability to add land and expand its property tax base was dramatically curtailed.

Over time, UniGov produced a set of positive population trends for Indianapolis. Prior to consolidation, Indianapolis had 476,258 residents (1960 U.S. Census). After consolidation, the city had 746,992 residents. While the population would decline between 1970 and 1990, by 2000 it had grown to 718,870 residents. New residents in the downtown area, in the suburban areas of the county that were consolidated into the city, and the neighborhoods adjoining the renovated downtown area drove population growth. As a result, in 2010 the consolidated city-county had 820,445 residents. It could be argued that consolidation and the downtown redeveloped strategy it supported, encouraged, or addressed concerns about Indianapolis' declining population. At the start of the 21st century, although growing slowly,

**Table 3.1a    Population Counts and Trends in the Metropolitan Indianapolis Region by Year**

| City/County | 1940 | 1950 | 1960 | 1970 | 1980 | 1990 | 2000 | 2010 |
|---|---|---|---|---|---|---|---|---|
| Indianapolis | 386,972 | 427,173 | 476,258 | 746,992 | 711,539 | 741,952 | 781,870 | 820,445 |
| Boone | 22,081 | 23,993 | 27,543 | 30,870 | 36,446 | 38,147 | 46,107 | 56,640 |
| Hamilton | 24,614 | 28,491 | 40,132 | 54,532 | 82,027 | 108,936 | 182,740 | 274,569 |
| Hancock | 17,302 | 20,332 | 26,665 | 35,096 | 43,939 | 45,527 | 55,391 | 70,002 |
| Hendricks | 20,151 | 24,594 | 40,896 | 53,974 | 69,804 | 75,717 | 104,093 | 145,448 |
| Johnson | 22,493 | 26,183 | 43,704 | 61,138 | 77,240 | 88,109 | 115,209 | 139,654 |
| Marion[a] | 460,926 | 551,777 | 697,567 | 793,769 | 765,233 | 797,159 | 860,454 | 903,393 |
| Morgan | 19,801 | 23,726 | 33,875 | 44,176 | 51,999 | 55,920 | 66,689 | 68,894 |
| Shelby | 25,953 | 28,026 | 34,093 | 37,797 | 39,887 | 40,307 | 43,445 | 44,436 |

*Source:* U.S. Bureau of the Census, various years, www.census.gov/popes+/data/index.html

[a] Population counts for Marion County include all independent cities in 1940–1960 and the four cities that did not join the consolidated city-county from 1970 through 2010.

Indianapolis was not a declining city. This growth, however, is in sharp contrast to outcomes in Cleveland and Detroit (see Table 3.1a).

Despite the population growth in Indianapolis leading to a level of population stability, the rapid growth of suburban counties highlights the need to continue the emphasis on development of the downtown area and adjacent communities. During the last decade many of the suburban counties enjoyed growth rates of 20 percent or more, and Hamilton County (located north of Indianapolis) now has 274,000 residents (see Table 3.1b). More importantly, household income levels in several surrounding counties are substantially higher than those in Indianapolis/Marion County. In 2010, the average household income in Indianapolis was $43,145. In Hamilton County the average household income was $81,947 in 2010, and it was above $60,000 in Boone ($68,594), Hendricks, Hancock, and Johnson. Shelby County's average income, the second lowest in the region, was $9,000 higher than that enjoyed by residents of Indianapolis, which demonstrates that economic segregation is still rampant in the region and a policy issue for Indianapolis' future.

The population losses between consolidation and 1980 suggested that more than changing Indianapolis' boundaries was needed to ensure that economic activity levels in the central city and downtown areas were sustained. The continuing loss of residents to the suburbs and the ongoing deterioration of the downtown area encouraged

**Table 3.1b   Population Trends: Percentage Change by Decade**

| City/County | 1940–1950 | 1950–1960 | 1960–1970 | 1970–1980 | 1980–1990 | 1990–2000 | 2000–2010 |
|---|---|---|---|---|---|---|---|
| Indianapolis | 10.4 | 11.5 | 56.8 | –4.7 | 4.3 | 5.4 | 4.9 |
| Boone | 8.7 | 14.8 | 12.1 | 18.1 | 4.7 | 20.9 | 22.8 |
| Hamilton | 15.8 | 40.9 | 35.9 | 50.4 | 32.8 | 67.7 | 50.3 |
| Hancock | 17.5 | 31.1 | 31.6 | 25.2 | 3.6 | 21.7 | 26.4 |
| Hendricks | 22.0 | 66.3 | 32.0 | 29.3 | 8.5 | 37.5 | 39.7 |
| Johnson | 16.4 | 66.9 | 39.9 | 26.3 | 14.1 | 30.8 | 21.2 |
| Marion[a] | 19.7 | 26.4 | 13.8 | –3.6 | 4.2 | 7.9 | 5.0 |
| Morgan | 19.8 | 42.8 | 30.4 | 17.7 | 7.5 | 19.3 | 3.3 |
| Shelby | 8.0 | 21.6 | 10.9 | 5.5 | 1.1 | 7.8 | 2.3 |

*Source:* U.S. Bureau of the Census, various years, www.census.gov/prod/cen2010/briefs/c2010br-01.pdf

[a] Population counts for Marion County include all independent cities in 1940–1960 and the four cities that did not join the consolidated city-county from 1970 through 2010.

elected and community leaders to think about innovative approaches to revive Indianapolis. The catalyst that launched the sports and downtown development strategy, however, was neither population losses nor declining residential property values. In the aftermath of the consolidation that made Indianapolis the 11th largest city in the United States in 1970—an improvement from its 26th-place ranking in 1960 prior to consolidation—local leadership commissioned a national survey to understand the perception of the city by nonresidents of Indiana. The study's results indicated the city suffered from a "nonimage"; the city was simply unknown to many Americans. Indianapolis was virtually a nondescript part of the Midwest, located somewhere east of Chicago and thought to exist at least one day a year—a result of the international publicity surrounding the annual Indianapolis 500 race.[3]

What could give Indianapolis a new image?

Lore and different views of the city's history note that a coalition of local leaders with financial support from the Lilly Endowment chose sports with a special focus on amateur athletics as the route to Indianapolis' new image. The coalition agreed to try to concentrate development in the downtown area, with the Market Square Arena (the future home of the Indiana Pacers) being the cornerstone of the city's revitalization effort. The Pacers were playing their home games at a facility approximately 3 miles from the downtown area. That location was the site of the

Indiana State Fair, and the arena hosted fair-related events each summer and other entertainment acts. The decision to build a new arena downtown was unique as many basketball teams were seeking to relocate to suburban areas. Many owners were deciding to locate their teams closer to where wealthier fans lived. Those teams were following the decentralization trends dominating growth. For example, the Cleveland Cavaliers left Cleveland for Richfield, a suburban city located between Cleveland and Akron; the Washington Senators became the Texas Rangers when they relocated to suburban Arlington, Texas; the Dallas Cowboys moved from the Cotton Bowl, located in an inner city neighborhood, to the suburban City of Irving, east of Dallas; the Detroit Pistons and Lions moved to suburban Pontiac and Auburn Hills; and new facilities for the Kansas City Royals and Chiefs were built in suburban areas of Kansas City. In contrast to those moves, Indianapolis' leadership and the Pacers' owners might have seemed wrong-headed. In reality, however, they were more than a decade ahead of the trend of building downtown sports facilities to anchor revitalization strategies and to attract business clients to luxury suites and club seats. The growth coalition forged a new policy for Indianapolis and took some risks that probably left many scratching their heads.

## A GROWTH COALITION FOR INDIANAPOLIS

A growth coalition is a term used by social scientists to refer to elites in a community joining together to advance regional development. Residents or voters neither elect this group, nor is it appointed by elected officials. Existing members select other members of the group, meaning these coalitions are self-sustaining and self-appointed. Some social scientists have observed or suggested that the profit motives or self-interest of the individuals or institutions that dominate these groups bias the selection of strategies, and projects supported are in turn endorsed by elected officials. Some have also worried that the selection of notoriously big-ticket items such as ballparks, arenas, museums, entertainment complexes, retail centers, office buildings, and convention centers precludes the selection or discussion of other strategies or emphases on other assets and strategies that might create more jobs and improve communities. Critics have argued that the projects selected by growth coalitions are based on antiquated strategies for economic development.

In response to concerns with the undemocratic principles that are fair criticisms of the ways in which growth coalitions operate, it should be noted that these groups still get things accomplished. The projects implemented create jobs and offer a wide range of benefits. In addition, the idea that these groups of elites only support projects and programs that directly enhance real estate values or business prospects for their members is contradicted by the investments made by some of these coalitions. For example, the Lilly Endowment—a clear member of Indianapolis' regime for sports and downtown development—has, at the same time that it supported building big-ticket sport facilities and a convention center, made commitments of hundreds of millions of dollars for community development across neighborhoods throughout Central Indiana. Its extensive support of public education and programs to reward public school teachers has helped to substantially improve Central Indiana, and it has been a major contributor to the building of the region's arts and cultural assets. Cleveland's Greater Cleveland Partnership—another growth coalition comprised of a region's leading corporate leaders—has long supported housing and community development for inner city neighborhoods and has made a substantial financial commitment to the Cleveland public schools. The performance record of urban growth coalitions remains a complex web of different sets of activities that includes substantial support for big-ticket items while also emphasizing activities designed to advance communities across different regions.

The performance of coalitions has led to important improvements, even if skewed toward support for sports facilities, convention centers, and other downtown projects. Those successes do not obscure issues related to representation and participation in these organizations. In addition, the meetings of these organizations are neither open to the public nor a matter of public record. Membership is frequently limited to directors from the largest corporations and foundations in a community. Local university presidents are occasionally involved, as are elected leaders, if their presence does not create a requirement for meetings to be open to the public.

Molotch illustrated how corporate elites and political leaders met in social or business settings to discuss issues of mutual benefit that led to certain projects for redevelopment (while other options were usually not even considered).[4] There is also evidence that growth coalitions skew the allocation of public funds to meet their agenda, often without any public dialogue. The members of most growth coalitions are frequently the same people who are prominent in raising funds to support the political campaigns of city council members, mayors, and governors. That financial link between growth coalition members, political campaigns, and the public sector's support for sports facilities and convention centers, for example, often generates suspicions of the motives elected officials have when they recommend a city or state make an investment in an arena, ballpark, or stadium.

At the same time that these limitations and problems are recognized, there are other communities that suffer from the lack of a leadership group to advance a region's economic future.[5] There is a fine line between ensuring that the public, private, and nonprofit sectors cooperate for regional economic development and doing what is best relative to the public's interests, assuming, of course, that there is clear understanding of what is in the public's best interest or that its interest is singular. In some instances, these growth coalitions—which become regimes when they have extended longevity and membership from the same organizations—pursued narrow agendas that have led to a narrow distribution of benefits for wealthier residents of an area. Research shows that these regimes have multiple goals and a complex agenda that produce benefits for different groups and neighborhoods. Indianapolis' original growth machine—which led the downtown and sports development effort across three decades—did not become more inclusive until later years. And when it did, most of the major decisions had already been made. At the same time, few question the success that resulted from the rebuilding of the downtown area and enhancement to the city's image.[6] In addition, the growth coalition's leading member, the Lilly Endowment, expended a great deal of money to improve neighborhoods across the region. Simply put, growth coalitions and their contributions to a region's growth are far more complex than many have assumed when they learn a city is contributing to the building of sports facilities for professional teams.

The rebuilding of downtown Indianapolis and the implementation of the amateur sports strategy began with a new arena. The anchor tenant was the Indiana Pacers, who were playing their home games at a facility approximately 3 miles north of downtown. While the theme for Indianapolis' new image and the social glue that united the growth coalition was amateur sports, professional teams were an integral part of the strategy. After the arena was built, attention was focused on the expansion of the convention center through the incorporation of an enclosed stadium. The new stadium provided needed exhibition space for some conventions but was actually designed to lure an NFL team to the city.[7] The notion that an NFL team would want to play in a city nicknamed "India-No-Place" was seen by many as unrealistic and as impractical as building sports facilities in downtown areas. If Indianapolis could attract an NFL team, then the sports strategy would have three professional crowns—an NBA franchise, an NFL franchise, and the most famous event in automobile racing (the Indianapolis 500). These assets would help secure the growth coalition's internal unity and create an image of success from its efforts and the participation of its members. The presence of two teams and a national event would also give Indianapolis an image that dwarfed its status as a modest-sized midwestern city. When the Colts relocated from Baltimore, the dream of a revitalized downtown capitalizing on sports no longer seemed to be a fantasy. What some regarded as misguided intentions of a ridiculous folly had turned into fact and reality.

The covered stadium with seating for 60,000 was completed in 1983 and dedicated on September 8, 1984. Less than a year later, the Colts would move to downtown Indianapolis, giving the city another valuable asset for its sports identity and the revitalization of the downtown area. Suddenly Indianapolis—a market at that time with fewer than 2 million residents—had two major league sports teams and was also home to the largest sporting event held in the United States. Everything seemed possible in the wake of the Colts' move from Baltimore, demonstrating that Indianapolis could have a vibrant downtown and could change its image. What remained to be seen was if a revitalized downtown area anchored by two premier sports franchises could change economic development patterns and the flow of economic activity in the region.

To entice amateur sports organizations to locate their championship events in Indianapolis—and to consider moving their headquarters to the self-proclaimed capital of amateur sports—several new facilities were needed. A new track and field stadium, natatorium, and tennis center were built on the Indiana University–Purdue University Indianapolis (IUPUI) campus on the northwest edge of the downtown area. On several occasions, Olympic team trials were held at some of these new facilities. Then in 1982 a bicycle racing facility was opened 6.1 miles northwest of the downtown area. When Chile and Ecuador had to withdraw as hosts for the 1987 Pan American Games, Indianapolis agreed to hold the games and, with the help of thousands of volunteers, turned the event into a great success, enhancing the city's image. In 1997 Indianapolis also succeeded in convincing the NCAA to relocate from suburban Kansas City to the new White River State Park. Dreams were becoming a reality in the midst of the former cornfields and the former declining downtown area of Indianapolis.

Before turning to the issue of what was built—and a detailed discussion of economic changes—it is important to consider the magnitude of the overall accomplishment in terms of special amateur and professional sports events held in Indianapolis. Summarized in Table 3.2 are the special events held since 2002 and those awarded through 2017. It is possible, of course, that additional special events will be held in the city. Readers are reminded that play-off games hosted by the Indianapolis Colts or the Indiana Pacers are not included in this itemization. A total of 54 amateur and 1 professional sports event (the Super Bowl) were or will be held between 2002 and 2017. That is an enviable record for any city (see Table 3.2).

## 3.3 Indianapolis, Sports, and Redevelopment: What Was Built, How Much Was Invested, and Whose Dollars Were Spent?

Indianapolis' growth coalition always described the sports and downtown revitalization strategy as a public–private partnership. This tagline or slogan was also quite in vogue during the 1980s, but this title caused concern that government-assisted

**Table 3.2  Special Athletic Events in Indianapolis, 2002–2017**

| Year | Event | Venue |
|---|---|---|
| 2002 | Big Ten Men's Basketball Tournament | Bankers Life Fieldhouse |
| 2002 | Big Ten Women's Basketball Tournament | Bankers Life Fieldhouse |
| 2002 | NCAA Rowing Championship | Rowing Center (Eagle Creek Park) |
| 2003 | Big Ten Women's Basketball Tournament | Bankers Life Fieldhouse |
| 2003 | NCAA Rowing Championship | Rowing Center (Eagle Creek Park) |
| 2003 | Swimming Spring Nationals | Indiana University Natatorium |
| 2003 | Duel in the Pool | Indiana University Natatorium |
| 2004 | Big Ten Men's Basketball Tournament | Bankers Life Fieldhouse |
| 2005 | Big Ten Women's Basketball Tournament | Bankers Life Fieldhouse |
| 2005 | NCAA Women's Final Four | RCA Dome |
| 2005 | P&G Gymnastics Championship | Bankers Life Fieldhouse |
| 2006 | Big Ten Men's Basketball Tournament | Bankers Life Fieldhouse |
| 2006 | Big Ten Women's Basketball Tournament | Bankers Life Fieldhouse |
| 2006 | Men and Women's NCAA Swimming and Diving Championship | Indiana University Natatorium |
| 2006 | NCAA Men's Final Four | RCA Dome |
| 2006 | Big Ten Men's Basketball Tournament | Bankers Life Fieldhouse |
| 2007 | Big Ten Women's Basketball Tournament | Bankers Life Fieldhouse |

*(Continued)*

**Table 3.2    Special Athletic Events in Indianapolis, 2002–2017 (Continued)**

| Year | Event | Venue |
|------|-------|-------|
| 2008 | Big Ten Men's Basketball Tournament | Bankers Life Fieldhouse |
| 2008 | Big Ten Women's Basketball Tournament | Bankers Life Fieldhouse |
| 2009 | Big Ten Men's Basketball Tournament | Bankers Life Fieldhouse |
| 2009 | Big Ten Women's Basketball Tournament | Bankers Life Fieldhouse |
| 2009 | NCAA Men's Basketball Midwest Regional | Lucas Oil Stadium |
| 2009 | Swimming Summer Nationals | Indiana University Natatorium |
| 2010 | Big Ten Men's Basketball Tournament | Bankers Life Fieldhouse |
| 2010 | Big Ten Women's Basketball Tournament | Bankers Life Fieldhouse |
| 2010 | NCAA Men's Final Four | Lucas Oil Stadium |
| 2010 | Big Ten Football Championship | Lucas Oil Stadium |
| 2011 | Big Ten Men's Basketball Tournament | Bankers Life Fieldhouse |
| 2011 | Big Ten Women's Basketball Tournament | Bankers Life Fieldhouse |
| 2011 | Big Ten Football Championship | Lucas Oil Stadium |
| 2011 | NCAA Women's Final Four | Bankers Life Fieldhouse |
| 2012 | Men and Women's Division III NCAA Swimming and Diving Championship | Indiana University Natatorium |
| 2012 | Big Ten Men's Basketball Tournament | Bankers Life Fieldhouse |
| 2012 | Big Ten Women's Basketball Tournament | Bankers Life Fieldhouse |

*(Continued)*

**Table 3.2  Special Athletic Events in Indianapolis, 2002–2017 (Continued)**

| Year | Event | Venue |
|------|-------|-------|
| 2012 | Big Ten Football Championship | Lucas Oil Stadium |
| 2012 | Super Bowl | Lucas Oil Stadium |
| 2013 | Big Ten Men's Basketball Tournament | Bankers Life Fieldhouse |
| 2013 | Big Ten Women's Basketball Tournament | Bankers Life Fieldhouse |
| 2013 | Big Ten Football Championship | Lucas Oil Stadium |
| 2013 | Swimming Summer Nationals | Indiana University Natatorium |
| 2013 | NCAA Rowing Championship | Rowing Center (Eagle Creek Park) |
| 2013 | Men and Women's Division III NCAA Swimming and Diving Championship | Indiana University Natatorium |
| 2013 | NCAA Men's Basketball Midwest Regional | Lucas Oil Stadium |
| 2013 | NCAA Division I Men's Lacrosse Quarterfinals | Lucas Oil Stadium |
| 2014 | Big Ten Men's Basketball Tournament | Bankers Life Fieldhouse |
| 2014 | Big Ten Women's Basketball Tournament | Bankers Life Fieldhouse |
| 2014 | NCAA Men's Basketball Midwest Regional | Lucas Oil Stadium |
| 2014 | Big Ten Football Championship | Lucas Oil Stadium |
| 2014 | Men and Women's Division III NCAA Swimming and Diving Championship | Indiana University Natatorium |
| 2015 | P&G Gymnastics Championship | Bankers Life Fieldhouse |
| 2015 | Men and Women's Division III NCAA Swimming and Diving Championship | Indiana University Natatorium |

*(Continued)*

**Table 3.2   Special Athletic Events in Indianapolis, 2002–2017 (Continued)**

| Year | Event | Venue |
|------|-------|-------|
| 2015 | Big Ten Football Championship | Lucas Oil Stadium |
| 2015 | NCAA Men's Final Four | Lucas Oil Stadium |
| 2016 | U.S. Olympic Diving Trials | Indiana University Natatorium |
| 2016 | Men and Women's NCAA Swimming and Diving Championship | Indiana University Natatorium |
| 2016 | NCAA Women's Final Four | Bankers Life Fieldhouse |
| 2017 | Men and Women's Division III NCAA Swimming and Diving Championship | Indiana University Natatorium |

development was nothing more than subsidies for the rich and their corporate interests. This perspective was reviewed in several case studies in Squires' *Unequal Partnerships*. In sharp contrast to the praise offered by such groups as the Committee for Economic Development for public–private partnerships, Squires cautioned[8]:

> What has frequently been overlooked, however, is the inherently unequal nature of most [public–private] partnerships. Frequently they exclude altogether the neighborhood residents most affected by development decisions. Public goals often go unmet and democratic processes are undermined…. The principal beneficiaries are often the large corporations, developers, and institutions because the tax burden and other costs are shifted to consumers. And perhaps the most important public benefits—jobs—are either temporary or low paying or, in the case of good jobs, go to suburbanites or other out-of-towners recruited by local businesses.

Porter and Sweet warned that "the linchpins of public–private partnerships are negotiation and cooperation … [and] almost by definition require equitable commitment of capacity and investment."[9] Unfortunately, these preconditions were rarely met as the public sector invested far more than their private sector partners. The public sector also seemed to be overmatched in the negotiations as a result of the ability of private capital to move to the regions providing the largest subsidies.

Observing two decades of tourist and sports development projects in downtown areas, many of which were public–private partnerships, Eisinger noted a skewing of the civic agenda toward the economic interests of downtown elites.[10] He also focused attention on the distribution of benefits from these public–private partnerships for big-ticket items. Inevitably, there were substantial increases in the value of teams and higher salaries for players.[11] These questions and observations make it crucial to understand exactly what was accomplished by Indianapolis' strategy to rebuild its downtown area and image through sports and myriad related public–private real estate development deals. If Indianapolis is the benchmark relative to the use of sports and cultural facilities for redevelopment, then what happened there, how much money was spent and by whom, and who benefited must be addressed. The analysis that follows is designed to understand if the public–private partnerships changed the trajectory of development in Indianapolis or merely enhanced the wealth of team owners, developers, and other land owners.[12] The analysis helps to understand if the growth coalition diverted public resources from community uses, which Harrison and Bluestone[13] argued was endemic to public–private partnerships, or if Indianapolis achieved a balance between big-ticket projects and neighborhood development.[14]

## 3.3.1  What Was Built?

Nine major sports facilities were built between 1974 and 2008 with the last, Lucas Oil Stadium, the new home for the Indianapolis Colts, opening prior to the NFL's 2008 season (see Table 3.3). Two years after the 1999 opening of Conseco Fieldhouse, Market Square Arena was demolished. When Lucas Oil Stadium opened, the planned conversion of the RCA Dome into additional space for the Indiana Convention Center was initiated. Some of the facilities built as part of the sports strategy for downtown revitalization were also intended for the advancement of IUPUI. The large urban campus is also home to the Indiana University School of Medicine, the Indiana University School of Dentistry, the Indiana University School of Nursing, the Indiana University Hospitals, and numerous other schools. As the campus has grown and built student housing to give it a residential component, these new facilities have bolstered the school's image and attractiveness. The facilities may no longer be a direct part of an overall sports strategy for revitalization, but they are an integral part of the expansion of educational resources that have also enhanced the downtown area.

While publicly embracing amateur and professional sports, the redevelopment effort was broadened to include cultural centers in an effort to make downtown a year-round destination for all forms of live entertainment. The Indiana Theatre was renovated in 1980 as the home of the Indiana Repertory Company, the region's largest live performance troupe. In 1984, the Circle Theatre reopened as the home of the Indianapolis Symphony. A turn-of-the-century grand showplace that first opened in 1916, it was abandoned in the 1970s. The Indianapolis Symphony Orchestra was playing at a midtown location—much like the Indiana Pacers— but after the facility was restored to its original grandeur, the orchestra made the

**Table 3.3   The Sports Facilities in Downtown Indianapolis**

| Facility | Description | Opened | Status |
|---|---|---|---|
| Market Square Arena | Indoor arena for Indiana Pacers; capacity, 16,530 | 1974 | Replaced in 1999 and razed |
| Tennis Center | Seating capacity, 10,000 | 1979 | Razed 2010 |
| Track and Field | Seating capacity, 12,111 | 1982 | Renovated and now a facility for IUPUI |
| Natatorium | Championship pools; capacity, 5,000 | 1982 | Maintained by IUPUI and part of the university |
| Hoosier Dome | Indoor stadium for Colts, other events, conventions; capacity, 57,980; several hundred thousand square feet of exhibition space for conventions | 1984 | Closed in 2008 and razed, convention center expanded into the space where the RCA Dome stood |
| Fitness Center | Training and fitness center for all athletes, public | 1988 | Part of IUPUI |
| Victory Field | Minor league baseball park; capacity, 15,000 for the Indianapolis Indians | 1997 | In current use |
| Bankers Life Fieldhouse | Home for Indiana Pacers, other events; capacity, 18,345 (originally the Conseco Fieldhouse) | 1999 | In current use, confronting financial challenges |
| Lucas Oil Stadium | Domed stadium for Indianapolis Colts, NCAA Championships, other amateur sports events, conventions, concerts; capacity, 63,000 (expandable to 70,000) | 2009 | In current use |

theatre its permanent home. The new downtown home of the Indianapolis Zoo and Botanical Gardens opened in 1988, and the Eiteljorg Museum of American Indian and Western Art opened in 1989. An IMAX theatre opened in 1996, followed by the new home for the Indiana Historical Society in 1999, and the Indiana State Museum in 2002. A spectacular renovation of the Marion County public library was also completed in 2006. These facilities made downtown Indianapolis the cultural capital of the state and region, adding crowds and expanding the definition of recreation and tourism activities far beyond sports. The museums, zoo, park, and theatres helped to also remake downtown Indianapolis into a residential neighborhood.

### 3.3.2 How Much Was Spent to Rebuild Downtown Indianapolis?

From 1974 through 2012, $11.62 billion (in constant 2013 dollars) was spent to create Indianapolis' new downtown area. These dollars included the city's own expenditures in foregone property taxes and the investments by the State of Indiana, the Lilly Endowment, and the private sector. Almost 10 percent of the total investment was for new residential development. From 1974 through 2013, a total of $1.1 billion was invested in new residential development by the private sector. At one level it might seem that spending less than 10 percent of the total investment on residences would mean too little was being invested to build new neighborhoods or to transform the downtown area into a place to live, enjoy entertainment, and work. Included in the total investment, however, is the complete cost of Lucas Oil Stadium and Bankers Life Fieldhouse, the original arena (Market Square Arena), the convention center, the RCA dome, a minor league ballpark, a multistory shopping mall, several other retail centers, the restored state capitol building, the new State of Indiana office complex, and two museums. The costs of several of these mega-projects were quite substantial and vital to the successful revitalization of the downtown area. When the scale of these investments across five decades is agglomerated and reported in constant dollars, the dollars expended are quite robust. That does not belittle the building of residential properties that have created homes for more than 20,000 people living in the downtown area.[15]

### 3.3.3 Who Paid How Much for the New Downtown?

Four separate sets of concerns are raised when growth coalitions or regimes steer revitalization strategies. As Squires and other contributors to *Unequal Partnerships* noted, a concern exists that the public sector would be expected to invest far more than either private businesses or the nonprofit sector. Others were concerned that a regime focused on downtown would ignore other development possibilities and focus private sector development on the downtown area to the exclusion of other communities. Finally, there was also a concern that the outcomes from a downtown redevelopment and sports strategy would fail to generate any real economic, demographic, or social changes for the city or region.

Before addressing each of these elements in turn, a scorecard of sorts is presented to identify the money invested in downtown Indianapolis from 1974

## INDIANAPOLIS DOWNTOWN, INC.

To advance downtown's development and lead the effort to broker deals that would bring new companies to the downtown area while also ensuring that their interests and needs were addressed, Indianapolis Downtown, Inc. (IDI) was created. IDI also has to be given credit for helping to protect and enhance the tax base of the downtown area. Its success attracted the attention of other cities, and many created similar organizations that assisted businesses that decided to relocate to redeveloping downtown areas.

The mission of the IDI clearly suggests that while its focus is on the downtown area, it is concerned with the advancement of the entire region. Because Central Indiana needs a strong and vibrant core, IDI exists to continually improve downtown Indianapolis. IDI, in partnerships with the public and private sectors, is action-oriented and empowered to address issues that affect the growth, visibility, appearance, and convenience (safety) of the downtown area. IDI focuses on three areas: development, management, and marketing of the downtown area to attract visitors and businesses.

The board of directors, as listed on its website, includes representatives from the consolidated city-county government and members of the city-county council, representatives of the state government, one union leader, and numerous representatives of leading corporations and educational institutions located in the downtown area. Some other committees do have community representatives, but for the most part, the organization is clearly a regime comprised of representatives of the institutions in downtown Indianapolis.

While some might object to the organization's membership structure, few can raise complaints with its performance, effectiveness, and the impact it has had in terms of the redevelopment of downtown Indianapolis. In 2006 dollars that development had already surpassed $8.3 billion, and there is probably no mayor or city council member in the United States who is not envious of the success. While the IDI cannot take credit for that level of investment, its stewardship and assistance should not be underestimated in terms of the services it provides to institutions that have made large investments in downtown and the confidence it exudes and maintains in the future for downtown Indianapolis. IDI also ensures that all institutions in the downtown area cooperate to enhance the value of the investments made. Additionally, IDI coordinates initiatives and activities to facilitate the attraction of visitors, businesses, and residents to the area.

through 2006.[16] These years were chosen and information for Lucas Oil Stadium is included (even though it did not open until 2008), since detailed information for each of the projects in those years and for Lucas Oil Stadium was available.

Indianapolis was able to use its resources to leverage substantial investments from the private sector, other governments, and nonprofit organizations to rebuild its downtown area. Indianapolis' commitment was less than $2.5 billion. The reason that this is the "high-end estimate" is that it includes all of the local funding for the new domed stadium, Lucas Oil Stadium. Other local governments (from the counties that surround Indianapolis) paid part of the public sector's investment in the $720 million facility. The investment in the new county library, $142.7 million, is also included. Even though the stadium is located in the northern part of the downtown area, it is a substantial asset for residential development and establishing the identity of downtown and adjacent areas as vibrant residential neighborhoods.

The total investment in downtown Indianapolis from 1974 through 2006 (and for Lucas Oil Stadium) was $8.3 billion (constant dollars). For a (high-end) total commitment of $2.52 billion in public money, Indianapolis was able to leverage $5.79 billion from other sources. For every dollar that Indianapolis invested in its downtown area, an additional $2.28 was committed. Using IDI data, the present value of the residential, commercial, and entertainment projects that were built is $441 billion (excluding Indianapolis' investment) (see Table 3.4).

**Table 3.4  The Investments Made in Rebuilding Downtown Indianapolis, 1974–2006, by Sector, and for the Building of Lucas Oil Stadium (in millions of 2006 dollars)**

| Project Type | Public Sector | | Nongovernmental | | Total |
| | Local | Nonlocal | Private | Nonprofit | |
|---|---|---|---|---|---|
| Sports | 998.2 | 188.8 | 329.6 | 191.9 | 1,708.5 |
| Culture/entertainment | 166.7 | 51.5 | 355.1 | 296.9 | 870.2 |
| Commercial | 1,323.3 | 977 | 2,224.9 | 8.8 | 4,534.0 |
| Residential | 49.2 | 112.6 | 380.4 | 3.7 | 545.9 |
| Education | | 663.9 | | | 663.9 |
| Total | 2,537.4 | 1,993.8 | 3,290.0 | 501.3 | 8,322.5 |

*Source:* Department of Metropolitan Development, Indianapolis; www.indy.gov/eGov/City/DMD/Pages/home.aspx; "Downtown Indianapolis, 2012 Economic Indicators," Indianapolis Downtown, Inc., April 2013.

## 3.4 Has Indianapolis Been Changed by the Sports and Downtown Redevelopment Strategy? Spatial, Demographic, Economic, and Intangible Measures of Success

The inevitable question when more than $11 billion has been spent becomes: What did Indianapolis and Central Indiana get for the money? The information presented permits people to assess whether or not the public–private partnerships were true partnerships, and whether what was leveraged was worth the public sector's investment. The specifics of the financing of Bankers Life Fieldhouse (nee Conseco) for the Indiana Pacers and Lucas Oil Field for the Indianapolis Colts will provide additional insight on the challenges small market areas face when dealing with professional sports teams. Before these specifics can be addressed, the most important questions must be answered. Did the sports strategy for the revitalization of the downtown area change or improve Indianapolis? Has a vibrant new urban neighborhood and downtown area been firmly established?

There is no single or simple answer to these questions. Many people wanted Indianapolis to have an image far different from what it had in the early 1970s, while also ensuring that downtown Indianapolis would remain a vital part of the region. While for others, the strategy and investments were linked to expanding the regional economy, ensuring that the region's largest employers remained in Central Indiana and Indianapolis, and in attracting and retaining a highly skilled and educated workforce. It is also important to evaluate whether the investment in downtown Indianapolis negatively impacted other neighborhoods. At a cursory level there have been notable achievements.

First, more than 20,000 people live in the downtown area and in adjacent neighborhoods. Would these people have chosen to live in the downtown area if there were fewer or no investments in big-ticket amenities? There is no clear answer to that, but what is clear is that the residences were built. The big-ticket amenities helped transform downtown Indianapolis from a declining commercial center to the region's leading sports, entertainment, and cultural center bolstered by impressive parks and green spaces throughout the area. This created the building blocks for a new urban neighborhood that grew in size, sustaining an emerging demand for an urban lifestyle and neighborhood retail amenities. The popularity of the residential offerings spilled over to some adjoining neighborhoods. While some neighborhoods north of the downtown area have yet to grow as much as needed or hoped, downtown Indianapolis is a residential community that is self-sustaining and benefits from the entertainment and cultural district.

Second, the attractiveness of the downtown area has been underscored by the city's hosting of a Super Bowl and the positive reaction to the quality of experience for attendees to the related events and the game itself. Would the Super Bowl have been held in Lucas Oil Stadium—the smallest facility to have ever hosted the Super

Bowl—if the downtown area was not revitalized? What is clear is that national events of the largest possible scale are being held in downtown Indianapolis, a city that in the 1970s was hardly thought of as a destination for national events other than the Indianapolis 500. This is not meant to minimize the importance of that race or the Brickyard 400. It is meant only to underscore that downtown Indianapolis was hardly imagined as a setting for the Super Bowl or premier NCAA events in the 1970s. Now it competes with far larger central cities and regions for every premier event.

Third, the revitalized nature of the downtown area has made Indianapolis a repeated destination for NCAA events and championships. The Big Ten Conference chose Indianapolis to host the first several years of its football championship game even though Detroit and Minneapolis both have covered stadiums. Soldier Field in Chicago could also have been a destination for the game. It is not possible to conclude the attractiveness of downtown Indianapolis elevated its bid over those made by other cities for NCAA events, but the value of the downtown area cannot be minimized when it is noted that these events are repeatedly held in downtown Indianapolis.

Leaving aside these casual inferences of success (without minimizing them), there are other factors that must be considered when evaluating whether the investment of $11 billion produced desirable financial returns.

## 3.4.1 Enhancing Indianapolis' Economic Stature

The policies and practices that led to the investment of $11 billion were designed to protect Indianapolis' economic stability (integration), revitalize the downtown area, and enhance the regional economy. In July 2013, Moody's gave Indianapolis an AAA rating above that given to Chicago, San Jose, and several other cities. That bond rating is a measure that can be used to conclude that after public, private, and nonprofit investments, Indianapolis has secured a financial position that surpasses that of several other rust-belt cities, such as Cleveland or Detroit.

Median household incomes in several other Midwest areas were compared to those of Indianapolis from 1960 through 2010. The convergence or the lack of the dispersion suggests that there has been no substantial change in the relative ranking of median income earned by households in the Indianapolis MSA. Each of the regions focused on economic development in the aftermath of the restructuring of the national economy. It could be argued that Indianapolis and its downtown revitalization were no more successful than any of the policies pursued in other regions if success is measured by changes in the median household incomes. While Pittsburgh's residents still have among the lowest median household incomes, by 2010 income levels were converging toward those found in other areas (see Figure 3.1). While it could be suggested that the revitalization strategy protected and maintained the standing of the Indianapolis MSA relative to median income levels in other nearby metropolitan areas, it is also possible that there was

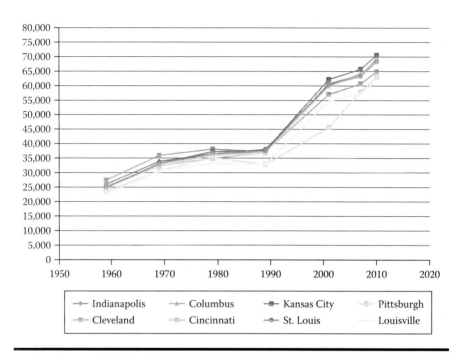

**Figure 3.1   Median household income in selected Midwest cities, 1959–2010.**

no elevation of the region's economy as a result of the sports and downtown revitalization efforts.

There has been a level of success in maintaining the job base in the consolidated city-county of Indianapolis that protects the property tax base of Indianapolis and maintains spending levels as a result of the continued presence of workers in the city. As detailed in Table 3.5, only in the arts and entertainment sector has there been a sizable loss of the proportion of the region's jobs in the consolidated city between 2002 and 2011. The sustained concentration of hospitality sector jobs (hotels and restaurants) also underscores the contribution from the presence of amenities in the city and in the downtown area. Whether consolidation or the downtown revitalization strategy was responsible for the centrality of jobs cannot be determined from these data. The expanded size of Indianapolis meant workers who moved to the suburbs would have convenient and short drives to job centers located in the sections of Indianapolis more distant from the older city boundaries (see Table 3.5).

Outcomes relative to job growth, retention, or stabilization for the downtown area are presented in Table 3.6. While there continues to be a slow decrease in the proportion of the region's jobs located in the downtown area, between 2002 and 2011 the proportion of jobs in many sectors of the economy remained relatively unchanged. As would be expected, manufacturing jobs and jobs in the wholesale sector relocated to areas with lower land prices (further from the center of the area). Retail trade positions were sustained at their prerecession levels, but there was a

**Table 3.5  The Number and Proportion of Jobs, by Sector and Year, in Indianapolis and Indianapolis MSA, 2002–2011**

| Sector/Jobs in MSA and Indianapolis | Number of Jobs, Percent in Indianapolis MSA and City by Year | | | | | | | | | |
|---|---|---|---|---|---|---|---|---|---|---|
| | 2002 | 2003 | 2004 | 2005 | 2006 | 2007 | 2008 | 2009 | 2010 | 2011 |
| Manufacturing | 105,760 | 103,858 | 104,076 | 104,882 | 105,494 | 103,411 | 102,545 | 89,504 | 88,162 | 84,850 |
| Jobs in Indianapolis | 73,720 | 72,387 | 73,055 | 72,941 | 73,566 | 73,162 | 72,761 | 66,089 | 64,334 | 58,312 |
| Percent jobs in city | 69.7 | 69.7 | 70.2 | 69.5 | 69.7 | 70.7 | 71.0 | 73.8 | 73.0 | 68.7 |
| Wholesale trade | 45,694 | 44,689 | 45,043 | 46,329 | 46,127 | 47,580 | 47,577 | 44,753 | 43,667 | 45,911 |
| Jobs in Indianapolis | 33,868 | 31,873 | 31,410 | 31,894 | 31,164 | 31,599 | 31,490 | 29,537 | 28,735 | 29,976 |
| Percent jobs in city | 74.1 | 71.3 | 69.7 | 68.8 | 67.6 | 66.4 | 66.2 | 66.0 | 65.8 | 65.3 |
| Retail trade | 103,506 | 102,440 | 100,620 | 97,283 | 100,960 | 95,958 | 94,766 | 91,216 | 94,061 | 100,216 |
| Jobs in Indianapolis | 67,548 | 66,423 | 64,437 | 60,888 | 62,027 | 57,672 | 56,201 | 52,642 | 54,036 | 56,000 |
| Percent jobs in city | 65.3 | 64.8 | 64.0 | 62.6 | 61.4 | 60.1 | 59.3 | 57.7 | 57.4 | 55.9 |
| Information | 16,136 | 14,647 | 15,533 | 16,469 | 15,610 | 15,981 | 15,775 | 15,727 | 15,907 | 15,387 |
| Jobs in Indianapolis | 10,878 | 9,803 | 11,291 | 11,606 | 11,483 | 11,731 | 11,814 | 11,646 | 11,735 | 11,595 |
| Percent jobs in city | 67.4 | 66.9 | 72.7 | 70.5 | 73.6 | 73.4 | 74.9 | 74.1 | 73.8 | 75.4 |
| Finance and insurance | 45,392 | 48,034 | 46,369 | 43,116 | 43,812 | 44,804 | 41,469 | 38,774 | 42,553 | 43,766 |
| Jobs in Indianapolis | 31,139 | 32,808 | 30,898 | 28,650 | 28,773 | 29,270 | 26,823 | 26,341 | 26,941 | 28,267 |

*(Continued)*

**Table 3.5 The Number and Proportion of Jobs, by Sector and Year, in Indianapolis and Indianapolis MSA, 2002–2011 (Continued)**

| Sector/Jobs in MSA and Indianapolis | Number of Jobs, Percent in Indianapolis MSA and City by Year | | | | | | | | | |
|---|---|---|---|---|---|---|---|---|---|---|
| | *2011* | *2010* | *2009* | *2008* | *2007* | *2006* | *2005* | *2004* | *2003* | *2002* |
| Percent jobs in city | 64.6 | 63.3 | 67.9 | 64.7 | 65.3 | 65.7 | 66.4 | 66.6 | 68.3 | 68.6 |
| Real estate | 14,623 | 14,110 | 14,603 | 15,037 | 15,278 | 15,653 | 15,556 | 14,683 | 14,174 | 14,630 |
| Jobs in Indianapolis | 10,121 | 9,935 | 10,332 | 10,496 | 10,600 | 11,101 | 11,884 | 11,256 | 10,763 | 10,987 |
| Percent jobs in city | 69.2 | 70.4 | 70.8 | 69.8 | 69.4 | 70.9 | 76.4 | 76.7 | 75.9 | 75.1 |
| Professional, scientific | 47,578 | 45,916 | 45,077 | 46,433 | 45,361 | 41,755 | 41,542 | 40,275 | 38,391 | 39,447 |
| Jobs in Indianapolis | 34,189 | 32,932 | 32,511 | 32,676 | 32,160 | 30,049 | 30,146 | 29,715 | 28,402 | 29,943 |
| Percent jobs in city | 71.9 | 71.7 | 72.1 | 70.4 | 70.9 | 72.0 | 72.6 | 73.8 | 74.0 | 75.9 |
| Management | 12,150 | 10,786 | 12,278 | 12,588 | 13,243 | 11,747 | 11,685 | 11,907 | 12,263 | 12,210 |
| Jobs in Indianapolis | 8,640 | 7,781 | 8,679 | 9,126 | 9,129 | 8,097 | 7,838 | 7,234 | 7,226 | 7,345 |
| Percent jobs in city | 71.1 | 72.1 | 70.7 | 72.5 | 68.9 | 68.9 | 67.1 | 60.8 | 58.9 | 60.2 |
| Arts, entertainment | 12,321 | 12,478 | 12,847 | 12,014 | 11,855 | 11,222 | 11,616 | 11,544 | 11,128 | 11,015 |
| Jobs in Indianapolis | 7,404 | 7,654 | 7,984 | 7,940 | 7,920 | 7,379 | 8,184 | 8,297 | 8,003 | 8,454 |
| Percent jobs in city | 60.1 | 61.3 | 62.1 | 66.1 | 66.8 | 65.8 | 70.5 | 71.9 | 71.9 | 76.7 |

| Hospitality | 76,681 | 71,757 | 71,855 | 72,767 | 74,386 | 72,539 | 70,810 | 70,411 | 68,589 | 68,490 |
|---|---|---|---|---|---|---|---|---|---|---|
| Jobs in Indianapolis | 46,207 | 42,857 | 43,160 | 44,455 | 46,160 | 46,249 | 45,791 | 45,168 | 44,829 | 45,221 |
| Percent jobs in city | 60.3 | 59.7 | 60.1 | 61.1 | 62.1 | 63.8 | 64.7 | 64.1 | 65.4 | 66.0 |

*Source:* Bureau of the Census, Department of Commerce. www.census.gov/econ

**Table 3.6 The Location of Jobs in the Indianapolis MSA: Changes in Downtown Indianapolis Compared to Indianapolis and the Region**

| Sector/Jobs in MSA, Indianapolis and Downtown | The Location of Jobs in the Indianapolis MSA, City and Downtown Area by Year | | | | | | | | | |
|---|---|---|---|---|---|---|---|---|---|---|
| | 2011 | 2010 | 2009 | 2008 | 2007 | 2006 | 2005 | 2004 | 2003 | 2002 |
| Manufacturing | 84,850 | 88,162 | 89,504 | 102,545 | 103,411 | 105,494 | 104,882 | 104,076 | 103,858 | 105,760 |
| Jobs in Indianapolis | 58,312 | 64,334 | 66,089 | 72,761 | 73,162 | 73,566 | 72,941 | 73,055 | 72,387 | 73,720 |
| Percent jobs in city | 68.7 | 73.0 | 73.8 | 71.0 | 70.7 | 69.7 | 69.5 | 70.2 | 69.7 | 69.7 |
| Jobs in downtown | 575 | 502 | 943 | 1,111 | 1,193 | 1,265 | 1,457 | 1,430 | 1,468 | 1,698 |
| Percent jobs downtown | 0.7 | 0.6 | 1.1 | 1.1 | 1.2 | 1.2 | 1.4 | 1.4 | 1.4 | 1.6 |
| Wholesale trade | 45,911 | 43,667 | 44,753 | 47,577 | 47,580 | 46,127 | 46,329 | 45,043 | 44,689 | 45,694 |
| Jobs in Indianapolis | 29,976 | 28,735 | 29,537 | 31,490 | 31,599 | 31,164 | 31,894 | 31,410 | 31,873 | 33,868 |
| Percent jobs in city | 65.3 | 65.8 | 66.0 | 66.2 | 66.4 | 67.6 | 68.8 | 69.7 | 71.3 | 74.1 |
| Jobs in downtown | 979 | 1,132 | 1,242 | 1,244 | 1,619 | 1,659 | 1,820 | 1,703 | 2,382 | 2,616 |
| Percent jobs downtown | 2.1 | 2.6 | 2.8 | 2.6 | 3.4 | 3.6 | 3.9 | 3.8 | 5.3 | 5.7 |
| Retail trade | 100,216 | 94,061 | 91,216 | 94,766 | 95,958 | 100,960 | 97,283 | 100,620 | 102,440 | 103,506 |
| Jobs in Indianapolis | 56,000 | 54,036 | 52,642 | 56,201 | 57,672 | 62,027 | 60,888 | 64,437 | 66,423 | 67,548 |
| Percent jobs in city | 55.9 | 57.4 | 57.7 | 59.3 | 60.1 | 61.4 | 62.6 | 64.0 | 64.8 | 65.3 |
| Jobs in downtown | 1,791 | 1,753 | 1,655 | 1,826 | 1,927 | 1,743 | 1,846 | 1,720 | 1,635 | 1,522 |

| | | | | | | | | | | |
|---|---|---|---|---|---|---|---|---|---|---|
| Percent jobs downtown | 1.8 | 1.9 | 1.8 | 1.9 | 2.0 | 1.7 | 1.9 | 1.7 | 1.6 | 1.5 |
| Information | 15,387 | 15,907 | 15,727 | 15,775 | 15,981 | 15,610 | 16,469 | 15,533 | 14,647 | 16,136 |
| Jobs in Indianapolis | 11,595 | 11,735 | 11,646 | 11,814 | 11,731 | 11,483 | 11,606 | 11,291 | 9,803 | 10,878 |
| Percent jobs in city | 75.4 | 73.8 | 74.1 | 74.9 | 73.4 | 73.6 | 70.5 | 72.7 | 66.9 | 67.4 |
| Jobs in downtown | 3,060 | 3,235 | 3,203 | 3,258 | 3,705 | 3,850 | 4,045 | 4,251 | 2,992 | 3,832 |
| Percent jobs downtown | 19.9 | 20.3 | 20.4 | 20.7 | 23.2 | 24.7 | 24.6 | 27.4 | 20.4 | 23.7 |
| Finance and insurance | 43,766 | 42,553 | 38,774 | 41,469 | 44,804 | 43,812 | 43,116 | 46,369 | 48,034 | 45,392 |
| Indianapolis jobs | 28,267 | 26,941 | 26,341 | 26,823 | 29,270 | 28,773 | 28,650 | 30,898 | 32,808 | 31,139 |
| Percent jobs in city | 64.6 | 63.3 | 67.9 | 64.7 | 65.3 | 65.7 | 66.4 | 66.6 | 68.3 | 68.6 |
| Jobs in downtown | 10,676 | 10,213 | 9,182 | 8,836 | 10,402 | 10,890 | 10,630 | 11,034 | 11,729 | 11,218 |
| Percent jobs downtown | 24.4 | 24.0 | 23.7 | 21.3 | 23.2 | 24.9 | 24.7 | 23.8 | 24.4 | 24.7 |
| Real estate | 14,623 | 14,110 | 14,603 | 15,037 | 15,278 | 15,653 | 15,556 | 14,683 | 14,174 | 14,630 |
| Indianapolis jobs | 10,121 | 9,935 | 10,332 | 10,496 | 10,600 | 11,101 | 11,884 | 11,256 | 10,763 | 10,987 |
| Percent jobs in city | 69.2 | 70.4 | 70.8 | 69.8 | 69.4 | 70.9 | 76.4 | 76.7 | 75.9 | 75.1 |
| Jobs in downtown | 1,317 | 1,353 | 1,513 | 1,250 | 1,235 | 1,238 | 1,258 | 1,175 | 1,159 | 1,253 |
| Percent jobs downtown | 9.0 | 9.6 | 10.4 | 8.3 | 8.1 | 7.9 | 8.1 | 8.0 | 8.2 | 8.6 |

*(Continued)*

**Table 3.6 The Location of Jobs in the Indianapolis MSA: Changes in Downtown Indianapolis Compared to Indianapolis and the Region (Continued)**

| Sector/Jobs in MSA, Indianapolis and Downtown | The Location of Jobs in the Indianapolis MSA, City and Downtown Area by Year | | | | | | | | | |
|---|---|---|---|---|---|---|---|---|---|---|
| | 2011 | 2010 | 2009 | 2008 | 2007 | 2006 | 2005 | 2004 | 2003 | 2002 |
| Professional, scientific | 47,578 | 45,916 | 45,077 | 46,433 | 45,361 | 41,755 | 41,542 | 40,275 | 38,391 | 39,447 |
| Indianapolis jobs | 34,189 | 32,932 | 32,511 | 32,676 | 32,160 | 30,049 | 30,146 | 29,715 | 28,402 | 29,943 |
| Percent jobs in city | 71.9 | 71.7 | 72.1 | 70.4 | 70.9 | 72.0 | 72.6 | 73.8 | 74.0 | 75.9 |
| Jobs in downtown | 11,613 | 11,049 | 10,790 | 10,490 | 10,155 | 9,254 | 8,964 | 8,749 | 8,640 | 9,400 |
| Percent jobs downtown | 24.4 | 24.1 | 23.9 | 22.6 | 22.4 | 22.2 | 21.6 | 21.7 | 22.5 | 23.8 |
| Management | 12,150 | 10,786 | 12,278 | 12,588 | 13,243 | 11,747 | 11,685 | 11,907 | 12,263 | 12,210 |
| Indianapolis jobs | 8,640 | 7,781 | 8,679 | 9,126 | 9,129 | 8,097 | 7,838 | 7,234 | 7,226 | 7,345 |
| Percent jobs in city | 71.1 | 72.1 | 70.7 | 72.5 | 68.9 | 68.9 | 67.1 | 60.8 | 58.9 | 60.2 |
| Jobs in downtown | 2,272 | 1,885 | 2,415 | 2,750 | 2,810 | 2,530 | 2,929 | 2,223 | 2,014 | 2,032 |
| Percent jobs downtown | 18.7 | 17.5 | 19.7 | 21.8 | 21.2 | 21.5 | 25.1 | 18.7 | 16.4 | 16.6 |
| Arts, entertainment | 12,321 | 12,478 | 12,847 | 12,014 | 11,855 | 11,222 | 11,616 | 11,544 | 11,128 | 11,015 |
| Indianapolis jobs | 7,404 | 7,654 | 7,984 | 7,940 | 7,920 | 7,379 | 8,184 | 8,297 | 8,003 | 8,454 |
| Percent jobs in city | 60.1 | 61.3 | 62.1 | 66.1 | 66.8 | 65.8 | 70.5 | 71.9 | 71.9 | 76.7 |
| Jobs in downtown | 1,505 | 1,512 | 1,669 | 1,638 | 1,597 | 1,830 | 2,007 | 2,067 | 2,051 | 2,025 |

| Percent jobs downtown | 12.2 | 12.1 | 13.0 | 13.6 | 13.5 | 16.3 | 17.3 | 17.9 | 18.4 | 18.4 |
|---|---|---|---|---|---|---|---|---|---|---|
| Hospitality | 76,681 | 71,757 | 71,855 | 72,767 | 74,386 | 72,539 | 70,810 | 70,411 | 68,589 | 68,490 |
| Indianapolis jobs | 46,207 | 42,857 | 43,160 | 44,455 | 46,160 | 46,249 | 45,791 | 45,168 | 44,829 | 45,221 |
| Percent jobs in city | 60.3 | 59.7 | 60.1 | 61.1 | 62.1 | 63.8 | 64.7 | 64.1 | 65.4 | 66.0 |
| Jobs in downtown | 7,134 | 7,341 | 6,697 | 6,851 | 6,657 | 6,676 | 6,781 | 6,730 | 6,721 | 6,868 |
| Percent jobs downtown | 9.3 | 10.2 | 9.3 | 9.4 | 8.9 | 9.2 | 9.6 | 9.6 | 9.8 | 10.0 |

pronounced loss in the number and proportion of jobs in the information technology sector located downtown. The proportion of the region's jobs in the finance and insurance sector in downtown Indianapolis was unchanged even though the absolute number of positions declined. There was an increase in the number of individuals working in professional and scientific jobs in the downtown area, and the growth of more than 2,000 jobs slightly increased the downtown area's share of the proportion of workers in these fields. The loss of jobs in the arts and entertainment sector indicates that as the region's population continued to move to suburban counties, firms have relocated to provide more services closer to where people live. This is a disappointing outcome given the strategy of focusing on sports, entertainment, and cultural amenities to rebuild the downtown area. The decline in the proportion of hospitality workers in the downtown area illustrates the growth of restaurants in the suburban areas. There was, however, a modest increase in the number of hospitality jobs in the downtown area (increasing by more than 250 jobs from 2002 to 2011) (see Table 3.6).

Table 3.7 shows that there has been an overall loss of concentration of private sector jobs in the downtown area from 2002 to 2011. The small decrement, however, suggests that Indianapolis' development strategy is slowing the loss of jobs, in the downtown area but even the investment of more than $11 billion has not made it possible to entirely deflect decentralization tendencies.

## 3.4.2 Building a New Downtown Neighborhood

Based on the 2010 Census and the information maintained by the Indiana Business Research Center, there were 27,045 residents living in the downtown area.[17] In 1990, there were 14,894 residents of downtown Indianapolis, and this increased to 17,907 in 2000.[18] Relying on U.S. Bureau of the Census information, Birch reported that there were 7,141 housing units in the downtown area in 2000. This means that average occupancy was 2.51 people per unit. Between 2000 and 2006, a total of 3,775 units were built in the downtown area based on information from Indianapolis' Department of Metropolitan Development. Assuming that 95 percent of these units were occupied and using the average number of people per unit that existed in 2000, downtown Indianapolis had 21,682 residents in 2006. This represents an increase of 6,788 people in 16 years. The 2010 Census indicates growth continued and approximately 5,500 more people rented or bought homes in the downtown area.

The investment in new units, the single-family homes and condominiums sold, and the average sales prices for residences in the downtown area from 2000 through 2012 are detailed in Table 3.8. This time period covers the expansion of the housing market in the initial years of the 21st century, the recession, and the recovery. There was an expected decline in investment (new construction) and a loss of value after a steep rise in the early years of the decade. The demand for residences in the downtown area increased as the economy improved in the years after the collapse of real

**Table 3.7  The Proportion of the Indianapolis MSA's Private Sector Employment Opportunities in Indianapolis and in the Downtown Area by Year**

| Private Sector Jobs by Area | Year | | | | | | | | | | |
|---|---|---|---|---|---|---|---|---|---|---|---|
| | 2011 | 2010 | 2009 | 2008 | 2007 | 2006 | 2005 | 2004 | 2003 | 2002 | |
| MSA private jobs | 772,950 | 742,910 | 731,306 | 773,488 | 772,575 | 749,873 | 746,687 | 744,023 | 728,251 | 716,500 | |
| Jobs in Indianapolis | 509,395 | 496,205 | 493,357 | 520,925 | 516,576 | 502,573 | 510,431 | 515,522 | 507,421 | 501,830 | |
| Percent jobs in city | 65.9 | 66.8 | 67.5 | 67.3 | 66.9 | 67.0 | 68.4 | 69.3 | 69.7 | 70.0 | |
| Downtown jobs | 40,922 | 39,975 | 39,309 | 39,254 | 41,300 | 40,935 | 41,737 | 41,082 | 40,791 | 42,464 | |
| Percent jobs downtown | 5.3 | 5.4 | 5.4 | 5.1 | 5.3 | 5.5 | 5.6 | 5.5 | 5.6 | 5.9 | |

**Table 3.8  Residential Construction and Sale Prices in Downtown Indianapolis, 2000–2012**

| Year | Construction Investment[a] | Units Sold | Single-Family Homes[b] | Condominiums[b] |
|------|----------------------------|------------|------------------------|-----------------|
| 2000 | 4.9 | 103 | $174,571 | $143,954 |
| 2001 | 25.1 | 119 | 190,257 | 160,312 |
| 2002 | 37.3 | 139 | 201,948 | 168,852 |
| 2003 | 63.4 | 156 | 204,426 | 191,710 |
| 2004 | 68.7 | 224 | 269,229 | 219,340 |
| 2005 | 15.5 | 224 | 241,837 | 249,278 |
| 2006 | 80.5 | 350 | 239,900 | 272,384 |
| 2007 | 30 | 245 | 286,129 | 322,624 |
| 2008 | 66.5 | 160 | 268,024 | 286,820 |
| 2009 | 6.0 | 147 | 192,867 | 294,963 |
| 2010 | 72.1 | 151 | 230,835 | 284,397 |
| 2011 | 133.4 | 164 | 233,157 | 246,909 |
| 2012 | 176.7 | 220 | 261,327 | 269,124 |

*Source:* "Downtown Indianapolis: 2012 Economic Indicators," Indianapolis Downtown, Inc., April 2013.

[a] In millions of dollars.
[b] Average sale price.

estate markets and the decline in the national economy. That renewed interest in residences in the downtown area suggests a new neighborhood has been established that can prosper even after a severe recession (see Table 3.8).

The downtown sports and revitalization strategy has sustained a level of economic vitality in Indianapolis' older central business district, while the movement of jobs to suburban areas continues. In 2000, one-third of the region's jobs were located between 10 and 35 miles of the central business district. A decade later, the proportion of regional jobs between 10 and 35 miles from the city's center had grown to 40.1 percent (see Table 3.9). Indianapolis did enjoy some success in minimizing job loss in the downtown area (as proportion of jobs in the region). In 2000, 22.3 percent of the region's jobs were within 3 miles of the central business district. By 2010, the proportion of jobs in the region in the downtown area had declined to 19.5 percent. There is then a decentralizing trend that is still taking place, but the central business district is still a major employment center for the region.

**Table 3.9    Job Decentralization in Selected Metropolitan Areas from 2000 to 2010**

| | Proportion of Jobs in the Metropolitan Region Located | | | | | |
|---|---|---|---|---|---|---|
| | 10 to 35 Miles from Central Business District | | | Within 3 Miles of Central Business District | | |
| Metropolitan Region | 2000 | 2007 | 2010 | 2000 | 2007 | 2010 |
| Indianapolis | 33.1 | 39.3 | 40.1 | 22.3 | 19.3 | 19.5 |
| Cincinnati | 49.5 | 53.9 | 52.8 | 19.7 | 16.1 | 17.7 |
| Cleveland | 43.0 | 46.3 | 46.5 | 17.5 | 15.7 | 15.4 |
| Columbus, Ohio | 30.4 | 35.0 | 35.4 | 23.7 | 21.1 | 21.2 |
| Detroit | 76.1 | 77.4 | 77.4 | 7.3 | 7.2 | 7.3 |
| Kansas City | 48.0 | 52.5 | 53.3 | 20.5 | 17.0 | 16.9 |
| Milwaukee | 35.4 | 38.3 | 37.8 | 22.6 | 22.6 | 24.1 |
| Pittsburgh | 44.1 | 45.3 | 45.2 | 26.2 | 25.9 | 25.2 |
| St. Louis | 57.6 | 61.6 | 61.2 | 14.9 | 12.3 | 13.2 |

*Source:* Kneebone, E., *Job Sprawl Stalls: Metropolitan Employment Location* (Washington, DC: Brookings Institutions, 2013), http://www.brookings.edu/research/reports/2013/04/18-job-sprawl-kneebone (accessed July 31, 2013).

Indianapolis' experience with decentralization as it relates to employment opportunities is compared with outcomes from several other rust-belt or Midwest regions. Indianapolis is among a group of several cities that have retained approximately one-fifth of a region's jobs near its central business district. It is also among three cities that have experienced the least dispersion of jobs (see Table 3.9). While it is reasonable to note the attractiveness and vitality of the downtown area—which is a product of the sports and revitalization strategy—there is yet to emerge a clear pattern of job retention that could be attributed to the sports strategy.

In summary, median family income rose, allowing Indianapolis to maintain its ranking among nine other Midwest regions. Downtown employment has increased, but the proportion of the region's jobs in the central business district declined. A robust residential character was established and residential properties have sustained their value through the recession are underscoring the downtown area's vitality. The downtown area has also been successful as a destination, as it has hosted the Super Bowl as well as several NCAA Championships and scores of conventions and other events.

### 3.4.3 The Image of Indianapolis: Intangible Benefits and the Journey from India-No-Place to Super Bowl Host City

Changing Indianapolis' image was a main goal for the redevelopment effort. Not only did a national survey find that Indianapolis had no image, but many also point to favorite son Kurt Vonnegut's remark as a reason for the sports strategy. Appearing on the *Tonight Show*, the author described Indianapolis as a cemetery with lights that came to life one day a year for the Indianapolis 500.[19] Others recall with disdain John Gunther's post-World War II description of the city in his 1947 classic, *Inside U.S.A.*, as dirty and a hotbed of racism.[20] Few would have believed in the early 1970s that Indianapolis could become a favored location for NCAA Championships and a city that would host a Super Bowl (occurring in 2012). Figure 3.2 shows downtown Indianapolis in 1974; the photos in Figure 3.3 show a far different downtown.

Based on numerous surveys of residents and visitors, Indianapolis is repeatedly described as a city with a downtown area with "lots to do" and an abundance of recreation, entertainment, and cultural facilities. The professional sports teams and physical and visual appeal of the downtown are similarly described and ranked as important assets for the region and the state. In ranking the state's leading assets and things that make residents proud to live in Central Indiana, the professional sports teams and downtown events are generally regarded as important as any other asset.[21] When asked to place a value on the intangible benefits of hosting the Indianapolis Colts, respondents to a survey—if projected across the population of Central Indiana—reported benefits that are worth in excess of $25 million per year.[22] The Colts were attracted to Indianapolis because of the new stadium built

**Figure 3.2   Downtown Indianapolis in the early 1970s. (From Indiana Sports Corporation.)**

(a)

(b)

**Figure 3.3**   (a) Downtown Indianapolis today. (From Indiana Sports Corporation.) (b) Bankers Life Fieldhouse, (formerly Conseco Fieldhouse). (From Indiana Sports Corporation.) (Courtesy of Mark S. Rosentraub.) (Continued)

(c)

**Figure 3.3 (Continued)** (c) Indiana Repertory Theatre. (Courtesy of Mark S. Rosentraub.)

in the 1980s and the new look of the downtown area. The team recommitted to Indianapolis for an additional 30 years when the counties in the metropolitan area and the state agreed to build another new home for the Colts that will also host the NCAA Men's and Women's Basketball Championships twice each decade. In 2011, IDI reported that 1.1 million people attended conventions in the city, and that 83 percent of the residents of the region had made at least one trip to the core area for recreation or entertainment.

## 3.5 The Challenges to Sustain the Sports Strategy

There was never any doubt that Indianapolis was going to be challenged to sustain its redevelopment strategy and its sports focus. First, while imitation is the highest form of flattery, as Indianapolis achieved a level of success (a rebuilt downtown area, the retention of an NBA team, the attraction of an NFL team, and the hosting of major NCAA Championships), other cities initiated their own sports strategies. There is now robust competition to host NCAA events from nearby cities—St. Louis, Louisville, Cincinnati, Columbus (Ohio, two arenas), and Fort Wayne—that have built or substantially renovated arenas to anchor redevelopment efforts. Those facilities regularly compete for entertainment and sports events with Indianapolis' new arena (Conseco Fieldhouse, now Bankers Life Fieldhouse).

Second, Central Indiana is one of the nation's smallest markets with two major sports teams. The Indianapolis Motor Speedway hosts two extraordinary events each year (the 500 and the Brickyard 400), and Indiana, Purdue, and Butler Universities sell their tickets for games in the same market. As a result, the supply of events was destined to strain the available household and corporate demand for tickets.

Third, when a new facility was built to be the home of the Indianapolis Colts and the NCAA Men's Basketball Championships, the city created a domed facility that effectively became another competing venue for events with the arena built for the Indiana Pacers. Indianapolis now has two venues for some indoor entertainment events that are also in competition with venues in other nearby cities.

There are currently 10 new venues in the greater Midwest area that includes Indianapolis. Approximately 17 million people live in this Midwest area. Is that too many venues? The New York metropolitan area has 5 million more residents and is served by five arenas (Madison Square Garden, the Barclays Center, the Prudential Center, and two older arenas), but does not have a single domed stadium. In that sense, it has half of the venues of the Midwest markets depicted in Figure 3.4, but approximately 5 million more residents. The Midwest has too many event dates (the capacity of arenas and domed stadiums to host events) compared to the demand or discretionary income that residents and businesses have to buy tickets. As a result, more investment by the public sector is required to offset the lower level of revenue each facility can attract. Without that level of public support, it is not possible to sustain each facility's building and maintenance costs.

Given this overlap, why did Indianapolis agree to build a new domed stadium for the Colts?

In the 1990s the Colts initiated an effort to secure revenue protection from the relatively small size of the Indianapolis market and the competition for dollars from consumers. The RCA Dome, with fewer than 60,000 seats, sparse luxury seating, and too little space for concessions, offered the team few of the revenue options

## THE OVERSUPPLY OF VENUES IN THE MIDWEST

The implications of this competition can be visualized through two different views of the market areas served by these facilities. The first map in Figure 3.4 identifies the arenas and covered stadiums in the Midwest in cities and states adjacent to the Central Indiana market. The second map includes the names and addresses while still displaying the overlapping 2-hour drive times from each facility.[23] The overlapping areas identify where each facility has to compete with another or others to attract spectators to events.[24] When there are two venues in the same city, there is of course even more competition.

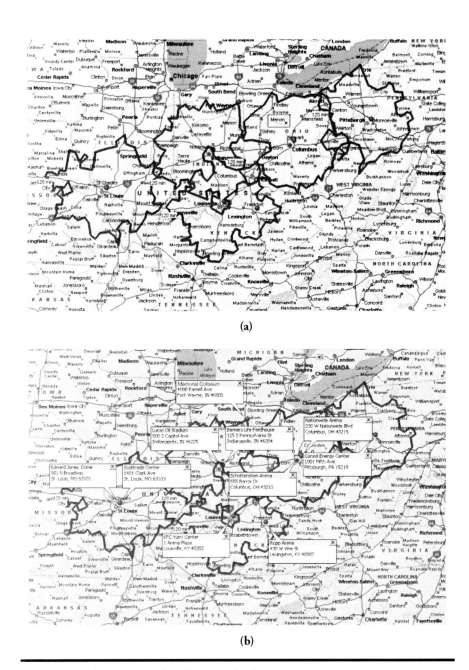

(a)

(b)

Figure 3.4   The oversupply of venues in the Midwest. (a) Map 1: Overlapping 2-hour drive times between arenas and domed stadiums in the Midwest. (b) Map 2: Overlapping 2-hour drive times between arenas and domed stadiums in the Midwest by facility (names included).

existing elsewhere. Indianapolis eventually agreed to make a series of modifications to the RCA Dome to create more luxury seating, but the city also had to agree to guarantee that the Colts' gross revenues would be at the average of all NFL teams. If the Colts' revenues were below the average of all NFL teams, Indianapolis had to make a payment to the team. With several teams playing in new facilities every few years, league revenue averages rose, and each year the payment from Indianapolis became a greater and greater burden for the city. It became clear that it would be less expensive to build a new facility for the Colts and eliminate the required payment from Indianapolis than to continue to make annual payments to the team. A lengthy negotiation process led to an agreement that included a regional tax on meals and beverages consumed at restaurants and pubs and the ending of the annual subsidy to the team from Indianapolis.

The Colts' lease for Lucas Oil Stadium provides no guaranteed revenue levels. In addition, the team agreed to stay in Indianapolis for 30 years with no "escape clause." The team also accepted the provision that any legal dispute regarding the team's location or adherence to the terms of the lease would be adjudicated in an Indianapolis court (which would likely be quite sympathetic to arguments put forward by the city).

What did the Colts get in exchange for these concessions?

The public sector paid $620 million, or 86 percent, of the cost of the $720 million facility. The team's investment was $100 million and the forfeiture of guaranteed revenue from the public sector. Had the new facility not been built, Indianapolis would have been making payments of approximately $20 million each year to subsidize the Colts' operations. The Colts retain all revenue from naming rights, advertising, and the sale of luxury seating. Those seats and suites now offer amenities similar to what is available in many other facilities. The risk is that this luxury seating must still be sold in the league's smallest market and one characterized by slow growth. While the revenue is not guaranteed, the revenue potential elevated the team's value on *Forbes'* list, giving the team the eighth highest value, $1.154 billion.[25] Indianapolis does have the right to use the facility for numerous other events and signed a contract to host the NCAA Men's and Women's Final Four Basketball Tournaments twice each decade for the next 30 years. During conventions, the facility can also be used for additional exhibition space. All events previously held in the RCA Dome, including scores of amateur sports contests, will also be held at Lucas Oil Stadium. Yet, the public subsidy exceeds $600 million, and without another round of substantial private sector investment, the investment is full of risks for both the team and the public sector. For the team, it must now try to generate sufficient revenues in a very small market. For the public sector, it must continue to attract private investments and host numerous events to ensure that its investment does not become a major subsidy producing marginal economic returns.

By the early 1990s, Market Square Arena, which was built for the Indiana Pacers in 1974, was economically obsolete. Its design would not easily accommodate modifications. Further, its elevation (Market Street actually passed under the arena at ground level) made the logistics of staging concerts and other entertainment events impractical and costly, as all equipment had to be moved through a handful of elevators to the floor level that was 20 feet above the street. In 2000, the Fieldhouse opened replete with luxury seating, large concourses, numerous advertising and naming opportunities, and street-level access for spectators and equipment.[26] The public sector was also responsible for the financing of most of the facility and maintenance for any repairs in excess of $50,000. The team handled all other maintenance that was identified as minor, but also retained all revenue from events held at the facility. Its $3.4 million payment for parking and rental fees was tied to a maximum operating loss of $2 million. If in any year the cost of operating the team after all revenue received produced a loss of more than $2 million, the team could move unless the public sector provided a subsidy to reduce the operating deficit. In essence, the lease requires the public sector to ensure that the team's losses do not exceed $2 million even after (1) paying for most of the cost of building the new facility, (2) agreeing to be responsible for all major maintenance costs, and (3) assigning virtually all of the revenues generated by the facility to the team's holding company.

The financial stress for Pacers Sports and Entertainment[27] began with the decline in the Indiana Pacers' performance and the suspensions players received for a brawl with fans of the Detroit Pistons in November 2004. Responding to taunts from Pistons' fans, several Pacers' players entered the seating area and a fight ensued. The team's declining performance and Indiana's fans' reaction to the violence led to declining attendance. The decline for the Pacers was also exacerbated by the recession. Complicating the environment for the Pacers was the success of the Indianapolis Colts and the favorable image of several of their star athletes, including Peyton Manning, Marvin Harrison, Jeff Saturday, and Reggie Wayne. In the midst of the Pacers' decline, the Colts won a Super Bowl and Lucas Oil Stadium opened. The attendance for both teams is illustrated in Table 3.10. The figures in bold represent attendance levels during the first year of operation of each team's new venue. The field house opened for the 1999–2000 season, and Lucas Oil Stadium hosted its first games in 2008. The Pacers are enjoying a slow recovery in attendance as a result of the team's recent success. Notice, however, that attendance levels have not returned to those enjoyed in the early part of the 21st century. The Colts, even with the loss of Peyton Manning and several other popular players, have seen only one season with a substantial decline in attendance. That season was the one in which Peyton Manning could not play because of an injury. Subsequently, the team was able to draft a new star quarterback, and his success has led to an increase in attendance.

At the same time that the Indiana Pacers' on-court performance declined, the onset of the recession and the competition for events with all of the other venues throughout the Midwest reduced the flow of revenues produced at the field house. As a result, the corporation created by the team's owners to operate the arena, Pacers Sports and Entertainment, was losing money. There were even public proclamations by the team's senior managers that Pacers Sports and Entertainment had lost money for almost a decade, and in 25 of the past 27 years. In February 2009

**Table 3.10  Attendance at Indiana Pacers and Indianapolis Colts Games, 1999–2013**

| Year | Pacers Attendance | | | Colts Attendance | | |
|---|---|---|---|---|---|---|
| | Season | Game | Change[a] | Season | Game | Change[a] |
| 2013 | 626,069 | 15,269 | 7.8 | Not available | | |
| 2012 | 467,561 | 14,168 | 4.7 | 521,518 | 65,189 | 0.6 |
| 2011 | 555,077 | 13,538 | –4.7 | 518,627 | 64,828 | –3.2 |
| 2010 | 582,295 | 14,202 | 0.1 | 535,802 | 66,975 | 0.6 |
| 2009 | 581,472 | 14,182 | 16.0 | 532,398 | 66,549 | 0.3 |
| 2008 | 501,092 | 12,221 | –20.4 | **531,026** | **66,378** | **15.8** |
| 2007 | 629,750 | 15,359 | –5.1 | 458,437 | 57,304 | 0.3 |
| 2006 | 663,368 | 16,179 | –4.8 | 457,154 | 57,144 | 0.0 |
| 2005 | 696,764 | 16,994 | 2.7 | 457,373 | 57,172 | 0.1 |
| 2004 | 678,326 | 16,544 | 1.2 | 456,791 | 57,099 | 0.6 |
| 2003 | 670,461 | 16,352 | 2.3 | 454,138 | 56,767 | 0.2 |
| 2002 | 686,537 | 16,744 | 6.4 | 453,357 | 56,670 | 0.6 |
| 2001 | 733,444 | 17,888 | 2.5 | 450,746 | 56,343 | –0.8 |
| 2000 | **752,145** | **18,345** | **85.9** | 454,319 | 56,790 | 0.2 |
| 1999 | 404,536 | 9,866 | | 453,270 | 56,659 | |

*Note:* Statistics in bold are for first year of play in new facility (2000 for the Pacers and 2008 for the Colts).

[a] Percent change.

the team announced that it was anticipating a loss of $15 million. Because of these losses, Pacers Sports and Entertainment wanted to renegotiate the lease it had with the public sector, and it wanted Indianapolis to assume greater financial responsibility for the arena's financial operations.

In 2010 Indianapolis agreed to provide Pacers Sports and Entertainment with $33.5 million of support through the end of 2013. The money was paid in $10 million installments across 3 years, with $3.5 million dedicated to enhancements to the arena.[28]

Negotiations began in late 2013 on a new lease and the ways in which Pacers Sports and Entertainment and Indianapolis can work together to handle any financial shortfalls. The team's success on the court and the economy's gradual improvement will likely translate into higher attendance levels. As a result, the arena will produce more revenue.

There will still be, however, substantial levels of competition with other arenas and stadiums to attract entertainment events, and population growth in the Midwest has not been sufficient to be optimistic regarding the number of entertainment events that can be hosted. While it remains possible for both the Pacers and the Colts to be successful in the same years and attract large numbers of fans, whether there is sufficient wealth to make Pacers Sports and Entertainment financially profitable given the current lease for the field house is the issue the public and private sectors had to discuss. In April 2014, it was agreed that the public sector would provide an annual investment of $10.8 million to offset the operating losses of the arena. The public sector would also invest $33.5 million for facility improvements. The Pacers agreed to renew their lease for 10 years and to offer the city the right find a new buyer if the Simon family decided to sell the team.

Could the Pacers relocate if this deal was not made? While many markets clamor for a new NBA franchise, in terms of regions with larger populations without an NBA team, there are few viable options. There is, however, interest in a team returning to Seattle, and an individual in that area has offered to build a new arena if an NBA team would relocate to the Pacific Northwest. St. Louis and Pittsburgh do not have an NBA team playing in their arenas, but neither region has enough residents or wealth to support an additional team. The size and wealth of the Cincinnati region does not make it a likely home for an NBA franchise. Louisville has at times had leaders who have expressed an interest in being home to an NBA team. That region is also too small to offer a substantial promise of long-term financial success for a team. What lessons emerge from Indianapolis' experience with the Pacers and Colts?

Despite a revived downtown and a total investment of more than $11 billion in a wide-ranging set of entertainment, commercial, residential, and retail facilities, Indianapolis' market size still places the city in a precarious position when negotiating with teams and owners. Furthermore, the investment has not led to a level of population growth and corporate relocations that have propelled the market to a level where extreme confidence can exist with regard to its ability to support two professional sports teams, the events at the Indianapolis Motor Speedway, and the teams fielded by leading universities. As the Colts were able to point out, the intangible benefits of the team's presence were substantial and much larger than the public's investment in the new stadium.[29] The city's leadership in April 2014 decided an investment of an additional $160 million across 10 years was necessary and produced more benefits for downtown's vitality and future.

# 3.6 Indianapolis: The Broker City to Be a Major League Winner

Indianapolis is a paradigm for any city focused on a detailed urban plan for economic development and downtown revitalization utilizing sports and cultural facilities. Three substantial accomplishments stand out as lessons for other cities. First, Indianapolis' leadership put forward a plan that was both an intangible vision of what could be built and a physical blueprint of what was needed for the rebuilding of a deteriorating core area. Partners in the private and nonprofit sectors—as well as state government officials and residents—understood the goals and direction that the city was charting for its future and the future of its downtown area. The focus was initially on sports, but then broadened to include culture and the arts. This three-pronged reliance on sports, the arts, and culture to rebuild a downtown area underscored the value of entertainment and unique regional amenities for both visitors and residents. Those assets generated confidence in a vision for the city. The vision was a bold statement that seemed to many almost impossible to achieve. Leaders, however, were committed to the plan and the effort to make others believe the dreams were possible. The attraction of the Colts to Indianapolis changed many people to believers in the vision of a new downtown area. It is vital for any vision for revitalization to have champions who believe each element can be achieved. It is also important for an early success as evidence that the dream is becoming a reality. Too many plans or programs do not have champions who believe in what can be achieved, and too few plans have successes that can illustrate that what is planned can be achieved. Cities need to have champions and plans that can highlight milestones.

It is also important to point out that Indianapolis' plan was not the product of a review process that incorporated public input or encouraged reviews and comment. The strategy was championed by a regime that made sure benchmarks were achieved. Years later, opportunities for public participation were created, but those chances for public input took place after the overall plan was essentially adopted. Communities would be wise to create more opportunities for broad-based participation and the incorporation of ideas from neighborhood leaders.

Second, Indianapolis succeeded in leveraging substantial financial investments for the revitalization effort from the private and nonprofit sector, as well as the state government. Rebuilding downtown Indianapolis was an effort led by the city's investment, but its success was a function of the billions of dollars invested by other institutions and governments. For every dollar Indianapolis committed to the revitalization effort, almost $2.30 came from other sources. That level of success is not only a model for other cities to emulate, but underscores the point that no rebuilding effort can succeed without private capital. Few would oppose leveraging ratios of more than $2 for every $1 invested by the city. A measure of the success of the planning effort and vision is the confidence leaders from other sectors of the economy expressed through their investment of funds. Indianapolis secured an appropriate financial return on its investment that indicated subsidies were, in actuality, shrewd investments.

Third, Indianapolis overhauled its image among its own residents and in the eyes of national leaders and institutions. In 1974 it would have been hard to imagine that Indianapolis would be a favored location for national or international events. Indianapolis would even host a Super Bowl, a dream that few thought possible in the 1970s or 1980s. As a result, today a very different reality exists with regard to the city's image. Downtown Indianapolis attracts people and events at a level unimaginable relative to the city's image in the 1970s. That success has helped create new employment and economic development opportunities related to tourism and the hospitality sector.

What can also not be overlooked, however, is that a local investment of $2.5 billion has meant that the civic leadership of Indianapolis must constantly lead efforts to advance real estate investment. Indianapolis is in essence the broker for the deals needed to complement the public funds committed to rebuilding the downtown area. No guarantee of any private sector investment accompanied the commitments made by Indianapolis. San Diego, Los Angeles, and Columbus—as will be described—had guaranteed levels of real estate investments made by private sector interests tied to the building of sport facilities. Indianapolis, more similar to Cleveland, had to secure development deals after it made commitments to build big-ticket items. If the commitment of public money for sports, cultural, and entertainment amenities was to reap dividends, Indianapolis had to become a broker, attracting events and other investors. The city then also had to be sure that an organizational structure was in place to assist in making events successful and to continue to attract other games and meetings. The city also had to have an agency focused on downtown—from addressing the needs of potential investors to advocating for needed improvements that maintain the downtown area's attractiveness.

Three organizations were created to perform the needed broker roles that steer the development of downtown Indianapolis. Indianapolis Downtown, Inc. exists to build partnerships between the private sector and the city to advance the growth, well-being, and user-friendliness of the core area. The Indiana Sports Corporation was created to be the catalyst to attract sporting events to the city and then to oversee the services the event organizers need to achieve their results. The Sports Corporation coordinates the activities and services needed from the public sector with and for event organizers. The corporation has also recruited, when needed, thousands of volunteers to help with an event. Lastly, the Department of Metropolitan Development as well as deputy mayors (depending on the mayor) work with corporations and others to focus development in the downtown area. These three organizations excel at making deals and cultivating the necessary public, private, and nonprofit partners to facilitate development.

Noting that three strong organizations—two of them nonprofit corporations—exist in a city to coordinate economic development would be seen by many as evidence of the exact sort of leadership expected or needed for rust-belt cities. In many other cities it is necessary to have executive leadership coordinate the economic development efforts, especially when different parts of the public sector fail to cooperate to achieve a common goal.[30] While coordinated leadership is not a problem for Indianapolis, the city must constantly create new partnerships to leverage returns from its big-ticket items. For example, immediately after closing the deal to build the new stadium for the Colts and expand the convention center, Indianapolis had to ensure a new hotel was built. The 34-story JW Marriott Hotel, with 1,005 rooms and 3 smaller hotels on the same site, involves $377 million from a private sector investment and $48 million from Indianapolis.[31] It is likely that several more deals will have to be brokered to be sure the public investment in the stadium is successful. Indianapolis will have to assist in attracting events and expand efforts to ensure that downtown Indianapolis remains inviting and user-friendly.

From the perspective of revitalizing and rebuilding a downtown area, leveraging funds from the private sector, maintaining a downtown area's centrality, and creating an entirely new image, Indianapolis' sports strategy made the city a major league winner. This gain, though, must be tempered by the reality that the sports and downtown redevelopment did not lead an economic transformation of the region or translate into higher family incomes. There was no loss of wealth, just less gained. Further, the hope for overall economic and population growth did not occur. The area still fails to attract a large number of in-migrants. Indianapolis was able to use sports and an emphasis on culture to rebuild its downtown area, dramatically changing its image and creating a management structure to coordinate the revitalization of the core area. The city attracted billions of dollars in new investment, and an enviable leveraging ratio. Indianapolis produced a set of benefits that has turned large sports subsidies into strategic investments and positive cash flows.

# Endnotes

1. No forms of city-county consolidation are identical. The UniGov legislation allowed smaller communities to decide to remain independent, and four decided not to join. The consolidated city-county government, however, was given authority for all economic development programs and efforts for the entire county and even for the excluded cities. The township structure of local government was maintained, and the consolidated government also included nine independent townships. For decades there were 11 different police departments and 9 fire departments. Those were not consolidated until the 21st century.
2. Leland, S., and M.S. Rosentraub, Consolidated and fragmented governments and regional cooperation: Surprising lessons from Charlotte, Cleveland, Indianapolis, and Kansas City, in *Who will govern metropolitan regions in the 21st century?* ed. D. Phares (Armonk, NY: M.E. Sharpe, 143–163, 2009).
3. Hudnut, W., *The Hudnut years in Indianapolis, 1976–1991* (Indianapolis: Indiana University Press, 1995).
4. Molotch, H., The political economy of growth machines, *Journal of Urban Affairs* 15(1): 29–53, 1993.
5. Rosentraub, M.S., and P. Helmke, Location theory, a growth coalition, and a regime in a medium-sized city, *Urban Affairs Review* 31(4): 482–507, 1996.
6. See, for example, McGovern, S.J., Ideology, consciousness, and inner city redevelopment: The case of Stephen Goldsmith's Indianapolis, *Journal of Urban Affairs* 25(1): 1–26, 2003. Also, Vogelsang-Coombs, V., Mayoral leadership and facilitative

governance, *American Review of Public Administration* 37(2): 198–225, 2007, and Wilson, D., Metaphors, growth coalition discourses, and black poverty neighborhoods in a U.S. city, *Antipode* 28(1): 72—96, 1996.

7. The building of a domed structure provides for some conventions covered space where large equipment can be displayed. The existence of a large stadium adjacent to a convention center also makes it possible to offer large-scale entertainment space if a convention wanted to offer to attendees a special experience or show.

8. Squires, G., ed., *Unequal partnerships: Political economy of urban redevelopment in postwar America* (New Brunswick, NJ: Rutgers University Press, 1989), 3.

9. Porter, P.R., and D. Sweet, *Rebuilding America's cities: Roads to recovery* (New Brunswick, NJ: Rutgers University, Center for Urban Policy Research, 1984), 214.

10. Eisinger, P., The politics of bread and circuses, *Urban Affairs Review* 35(3): 316–333, 2000.

11. Rosentraub, M.S., The local context of a sports strategy for economic development, *Economic Development Quarterly* 20(3): 278–291, 2006.

12. Logan, J.R., and H.L. Molotch, *Urban fortunes: The political economy of place* (Berkeley: University of California Press, 1987).

13. Harrison, B., and B. Bluestone, *The great U-turn: Corporate restructuring and the polarizing of America* (New York: Basic Books, 1988).

14. Eisinger, P., The politics of bread and circuses, *Urban Affairs Review* 35(3): 316–333, 2000.

15. The amount of money spent to revitalize downtown Indianapolis was compiled from reports released by Indianapolis Downtown, Inc. and tax records maintained by Marion County and other data from the consolidated city-county's Department of Metropolitan Development. From 1974 through 2008 a total of $9.593 billion (2013 dollars) was expended by the private, public, and nonprofit sectors. The total private sector investment made in 2009 was $183.1 million. In 2010, $190 million was invested by the private sector, and in 2012, the public and private sector investment in downtown Indianapolis exceeded $1 billion. All of these figures of building activity in 2009 through 2012 are in constant dollars (2013) and were drawn from reports published by Indianapolis Downtown, Inc.

16. These years were chosen and information for Lucas Oil Stadium is included (even though it did not open until 2008), since detailed information for each of the projects in those years and for Lucas Oil Stadium was available.

17. http://www.stats.indiana.edu/maptools/c2010/tracts.asp.

18. Birch, E., *Who lives downtown?* (Washington, DC: Brookings Institution, Metropolitan Policy Program, 2005).

19. Hudnut, W., *The Hudnut years in Indianapolis, 1976–1991* (Indianapolis: Indiana University Press, 1995).

20. Rosentraub, M.S., *Major league losers: The real cost of sports and who's paying for it* (New York: Basic Books, 1997).

21. Children's Museum of Indianapolis, *The economic impact and value of the Children's Museum to the Central Indiana economy* (Indianapolis: Children's Museum, 2005).

22. Rosentraub, M.S., D. Swindell, and S. Tsvetkova, Justifying public investments in sports: Measuring the intangibles, *Journal of Tourism* 9(2): 133–159, 2009.

23. The selection of 2-hour drive times represents a realistic assessment of the distance people are usually expected to travel for entertainment events. There are certainly weekend and holiday trips that would produce longer commutes to events (or games). When looking at a market for entertainment events, 2-hour drive times (or round-trip of 4 hours) are reasonable approximations of the time that could be anticipated from spectators.

24. The facilities do not compete for the home games of teams. The Colts will not play a game in Bankers Life Fieldhouse, and the Pacers will not play games at Lucas Oil Stadium. Where the two facilities do compete, however, are for entertainment and other sports events that could be held at either venue. Domed stadiums can be configured to replicate the seating patterns of arenas for 18,000 to 20,000 spectators, even given their larger size.

25. Forbes, NFL team valuations, 2012, http://www.forbes.com/teams/indianapolis-colts/ (accessed August 5, 2013).

26. In December 2011 the Indiana Pacers announced that the field house would be renamed the Bankers Life Fieldhouse. CNO Financial Group, formerly known as Conseco, has a 20-year contract for the naming rights to the facility. In 2011 the company's leadership decided to name the facility for its largest subsidiary, Bankers Life and Casualty Company.

27. Pacer Sports and Entertainment is comprised of the Indiana Pacers and the Indiana Fever, and is responsible for all entertainment and the operation of the field house. It is frequently in the public sector's interest to have a private sector organization operate a facility, especially if the contract between the company and the public sector includes incentives for profitable operation. Those incentives help ensure that the economic impact of the facility is greater for the city's and region's economy. Public sector organizations frequently do not have the staff to plan for entertainment events. Rather than hiring needed staff, it is probably more efficient for a government to contract with a private sector organization to manage an arena.

28. City to subsidize Pacers arena costs, http://sports.espn.go.com/nba/news/story?id=5373149 (accessed August 6, 2013).

27. Rosentraub, M.S., D. Swindell, and S. Tsvetkova, Justifying public investments in sports: Measuring the intangibles, *Journal of Tourism* 9(2): 133–159, 2009.

28. Larkin, B., How Cleveland fumbled away Eaton corporation, *Cleveland Plain Dealer*, October 5, 2008, D1, 3.

29. Swiatek, J., A work in progress: Even before designs are finalized, massive JW Marriott project is forging ahead, *Indianapolis Star*, October 5, 2008, D1, 4.

## Chapter 4

# Shared Risk, Shared Returns: San Diego's Unique Partnership for a Ballpark and a New Downtown Neighborhood

## 4.1 Introduction

The 1980s and 1990s was an era of unprecedented public investments for sports facilities. Arlington (Texas), Baltimore, Chicago, Cincinnati, Cleveland, Dallas, Detroit, Green Bay, Jacksonville, Milwaukee, Phoenix, Seattle, St. Louis, St. Petersburg, Tampa, and Toronto raised taxes to ensure the presence of teams. These tax increases repaid the bonds sold to pay for the public sector's share of the cost of building arenas, ballparks, and stadiums. With the teams given control of most, if not all, of the new revenue generated from luxury seating, naming and sponsorship rights, and the expanded retail venues included in these new facilities, it might be imagined that each franchise had the revenue needed to repay any debt it incurred. Instead, teams argued that without an investment from the public sector, their financial success would be unlikely. As *Forbes* would report each year, however, the additional revenue led to substantially increased values of most franchises. As a result, several owners were able to realize a substantial return on the money they had invested in the team when they decided to sell their franchise. In Cleveland, for example, the owners of the Indians and Cavaliers sold their teams in the years after the opening of new facilities. Richard Jacobs (Indians) and the Gund Brothers (Cavaliers) each enjoyed substantial gains from the sale of franchises that played their home games in facilities that offered numerous new revenue streams.[1]

Ironically, in no instance where a public sector partner provided a substantial investment in a facility was there a commitment or assurance given that similar returns in the form of new private investments in the downtown area would take place to produce additional tax dollars (or a return for the public sector's investment). Each city could follow in Indianapolis' footsteps and put forward a sports and entertainment strategy that included new venues for arts and culture and then actively broker additional real estate development deals that might generate additional tax revenues to offset its investment. But those returns were the responsibility of the government. While each city assured residents it would try to enhance development and secure new taxes, in essence, taxpayers were left to hope something positive in terms of real estate development and new tax revenues would occur. Voters in San Diego would not support a typical ballpark deal—a public investment without an assured rate of return. San Diego had a strained relationship with the San Diego Chargers. The Chargers secured a change in their lease prior to the Padres seeking a new ballpark that included a guarantee that the public sector would buy any tickets that were not sold for any Charger regular season game. That guarantee would, after its acceptance, create a substantial political backlash that made any public participation in the financing of another sports facility contingent on substantial investments by a team owner.

The San Diego Padres needed a new ballpark to ensure its fiscal viability. Unlike the Chargers, who enjoy an equal share of the benefits of the NFL's very large national media contracts, the Padres, like all other MLB franchises, have to rely on locally generated revenues to be financially secure. While San Diego has an extraordinary climate and an unparalleled coastline, the metropolitan area is relatively small. The market area available to the Padres has an estimated population of 3.2 million (2012). To the north of this market area lies Orange County, the home of the Los Angeles Angels of Anaheim, a team that also draws fans from San Bernardino County. To San Diego's south lies Mexico, and the wealth of its residents has not allowed that market to be a robust source of income for the Padres. The Padres must rely on the revenues they generate from businesses and residents of San Diego County.

For many years the team was owned by Ray and Joan Kroc. Their fortune from the McDonald's hamburger franchise business provided a degree of flexibility to address the team's financial requirements independent of the revenues generated from baseball operations. A few years after Mr. Kroc died, Mrs. Kroc decided to sell the team. A group of local businesses leaders who purchased the team could not stabilize the franchise's finances. In 1994, John Moores purchased the Padres and immediately began to focus on the team's precarious financial state. It was apparent to him and most other observers of the business of baseball that the Padres could not be financially viable without a new ballpark.

Despite its setting and the near-perfect climate, few large corporations have their headquarters in the region, and while residential property prices soared in the latter half of the 1990s and into the first part of the 21st century, the region had a relatively small base of high-income residents. The Padres also played their home games in a facility where the NFL's Chargers had secured control of important revenue streams before the MLB team was created. As a result, the Padres earned far less revenues than many other MLB teams. When the Padres were created, there was only one facility in the region where baseball games could be played. The Padres had to accept the terms dictated by the Chargers. The loss of some game day revenues to the Chargers and the small scale of the market made the team's finances perpetually unstable. It was difficult to imagine how the team could be both competitive and profitable unless a new ballpark was built.

Regardless of the validity of these market issues, a typical tax-supported subsidy for a new ballpark was not feasible. Years of contentious relations between San Diego and the Chargers had created a large and vocal opposition to tax increases for professional sports. In the absence of an innovative approach and the creation of a public–private partnership with risks and benefits equally shared, there would be no new ballpark. The plan developed between the Padres' owner and San Diego guaranteed an amount of new real estate development to generate new tax revenues equal to the city's investment in the ballpark. If insufficient real estate was built and the agreed to tax revenues were not generated, the team's owner, John Moores, would be responsible for any financial shortfalls.

No other owner had ever made a commitment like this in order to have a new sports facility built. This would be a unique public–private partnership for the revitalization of a downtown area and the building of a ballpark.

An assessment of the Ballpark District's successes and failures provides civic leaders and sport managers/team owners with an opportunity to consider whether a strategy with risk and new revenue streams for the public sector and the team creates a new way to revitalize a downtown area. This case study also illustrates the political value of such an arrangement. Prior to the guarantees, there was little hope that the city's voters would support the government's investment in a new ballpark. After the guarantees were presented to the public, almost 60 percent of the votes cast in the referendum supported the proposed public–private partnership. That support allowed the creation of the Ballpark District anchored by a new ballpark. This deal between a team owner and a city changed the ways in which franchises and the public sector can and should look at sports facilities for downtown real estate development. In a sense, the Ballpark District has fundamentally changed the sports business and illustrated to voters, public officials, and team owners how franchises and the public sector both can win when a new facility is built.

## 4.2 The Padres and the Need for a New Ballpark

The Padres began play in 1969, and the challenges of the local market almost led to their quick demise. In 1974, when the team's owners were threatening to move the team to Washington, D.C., Ray Kroc (founder of the franchise system that spawned the McDonald's chain) purchased the team to assure its continued presence in the city. His wife assumed sole ownership of the team after his death in 1984 and underscored their family's commitment to keep the team in San Diego. The Krocs (and Mrs. Kroc after her husband's death) wanted San Diego to have a MLB team. In 1990, however, Mrs. Kroc decided to sell the team to 15 local business leaders; local ownership met her goal of assuring the team's continued presence in San Diego.[2] Operational losses led this group to sell controlling interest to John Moores in December 1994. Mr. Moores, a Houston native, made his fortune in software, but was unable to buy his hometown Astros. With Mr. Moores at the helm, the Padres won four division titles and the National League pennant in 1998.

The Padres played their homes games in the San Diego Stadium, renamed for legendary sports writer Jack Murphy and later known as Qualcomm Stadium. The facility opened in 1967 as the home of the NFL's Chargers. When the Padres' franchise was created, the team became tenants in a facility controlled by the Chargers. The Chargers' lease gave them control of all revenues. John Moores understood that a baseball team in a relatively small market that did not (1) control all game day revenues and (2) have access to and control of all the revenue generating amenities in newer facilities would never be profitable and competitive in the San Diego market.

Baseball teams are located in 26 different metropolitan areas. The San Diego market, by population size, is the 16th largest (see Table 4.1, fourth column). Interpreting team markets is a bit complicated. Some teams play in markets that are basically a single metropolitan area; others play in market areas that are consolidated regions of several metropolitan areas. The most extreme case is the New York consolidated statistical area (CSA), which is home to more than 23 million people. In contrast, the San Diego Padres play their home games in a single metropolitan area of less than 3.2 million people. Several other teams also play in consolidated areas (Cubs and White Sox, Giants and Athletics, Dodgers and Angels), and in some smaller consolidated areas, there is but one team (Texas Rangers). This gives teams access to markets of varying size and with very different levels of discretionary income expended by residents and businesses located in their market areas. By population size (excluding Toronto), the San Diego market for the Padres ranks 16th. If the Toronto market were included, the Padres would be playing in the 17th

**Table 4.1   The Measures of the Value of Different Markets to MLB Teams**

| Metropolitan or Market Area | Metropolitan Area GDP 2011 | Extended Market Area GDP 2011 | 2012 Market Area Population | 2011 Market Area Personal Income | 2012 Metropolitan Area Personal Income |
|---|---|---|---|---|---|
| New York | 1,277,228 | 1,463,731 | 23,362,099 | 1,260,650,280 | 1,079,532,373 |
| Los Angeles | 747,306 | 897,207 | 18,238,998 | 742,168,596 | 575,044,998 |
| Chicago | 547,609 | 554,511 | 9,899,902 | 444,294,529 | 436,998,041 |
| Washington, D.C. | 433,097 | 594,845 | 9,331,587 | 489,107,234 | 338,498,235 |
| Philadelphia | 353,323 | 396,261 | 7,129,428 | 313,062,640 | 291,970,010 |
| Houston | 419,696 | 419,696 | 6,371,677 | 292,752,464 | 289,790,417 |
| Dallas–Fort Worth | 391,350 | 394,902 | 7,095,411 | 297,953,490 | 285,259,943 |
| San Francisco | 347,107 | 594,977 | 8,370,967 | 441,414,744 | 269,588,048 |
| Boston | 325,585 | 454,648 | 7,893,376 | 399,590,626 | 265,794,170 |
| Miami | 263,376 | 278,616 | 6,375,434 | 23,494,321 | 244,223,754 |
| Atlanta | 283,344 | 296,660 | 6,092,295 | 223,696,219 | 212,830,075 |
| Seattle | 239,710 | 264,209 | 4,399,332 | 209,159,363 | 178,306,642 |
| Detroit | 199,378 | 233,130 | 5,311,449 | 204,188,169 | 171,472,741 |
| Minneapolis | 207,819 | 215,575 | 3,759,978 | 173,551,781 | 161,468,259 |
| Phoenix | 194,793 | | 4,329,534 | | 157,026,115 |
| San Diego | 172,583 | | 3,177,063 | | 146,955,781 |
| Baltimore | 148,256 | | 2,753,149 | | 139,527,940 |
| Denver | 161,956 | 188,923 | 3,214,218 | 150,615,287 | 127,324,066 |
| St. Louis | 132,029 | | 2,900,605 | 122,592,111 | 120,763,454 |
| Tampa–St. Petersburg | 116,232 | | 2,842,878 | | 110,900,696 |
| Pittsburgh | 117,845 | | 2,661,369 | 109,176,370 | 106,145,736 |
| Kansas City | 108,144 | 116,391 | 2,376,631 | 90,504,705 | 88,391,888 |

*(Continued)*

**Table 4.1    The Measures of the Value of Different Markets to MLB Teams (Continued)**

| Metropolitan or Market Area | Metropolitan Area GDP 2011 | Extended Market Area GDP 2011 | 2012 Market Area Population | 2011 Market Area Personal Income | 2012 Metropolitan Area Personal Income |
|---|---|---|---|---|---|
| Cleveland | 106,810 | 148,056 | 3,497,711 | 118,864,734 | 87,622,449 |
| Cincinnati | 102,469 | 102,469 | 2,188,001 | 88,827,673 | 87,484,877 |
| Milwaukee | 87,539 | 94,347 | 2,037,542 | 77,198,860 | 69,691,155 |

*Note:* GDP = gross domestic product; GDP and personal income in thousands of dollars.

largest market (by population). What is also vital to each team's financial strength is the scale of their region's economy. Note that residents in the Padres' market had incomes below those of residents of more than half of the markets served by MLB teams. When one turns to a measure of wealth related to an area's gross domestic product (GDP), San Diego is again among the least most valuable markets. These data illustrate the challenge for the team's financial success. Without exclusive control of all revenue streams from their home games, the Padres were destined to either lose money or become noncompetitive (see Table 4.1, columns five and six).

When the Padres began to discuss a new ballpark with the city, the team compared its revenue earning potential to that of the Cleveland Indians, who had recently moved into a new, baseball-only facility. In 1997, the Indians—playing in what would become a market area smaller than metropolitan San Diego—were able to generate $134.2 million. The Padres earned $20 million *less* from the sale of tickets. The Padres also received only 29 percent of the revenue from the rental of luxury suites at Qualcomm Stadium, as the balance accrued to the primary tenant, the San Diego Chargers (Rosentraub 1998).

To more fully explain the revenue limitations that confronted the Padres, the team circulated Table 4.2a to elected officials and the community to illustrate the revenues earned by the Arizona Diamondbacks, Atlanta Braves, Baltimore Orioles, Cleveland Indians, Colorado Rockies, Texas Rangers, and New York Yankees for 1998. Every team except the Yankees had a new facility. The Yankees were included to illustrate the challenges faced by small market teams relative to the franchises in larger and wealthier regions. Each of these teams had total gross revenues that were at least $30 million to $40 million *larger* than the amount of money earned by the San Diego Padres. To amplify the challenge confronting the Padres' owner, team values for all franchises before PETCO Park opened, immediately after it's opening, and in 2013 are illustrated in Table 4.2b. Note that in 2002, prior to the opening of the new ballpark, the team's value was estimated

**Table 4.2a    The 1998 Estimated Earnings of Selected MLB Teams (in thousands of dollars; some estimates projected from 1997 figures)**

| Team | Revenue from | | | | MLB Shared Funds | All Other Sales, Advertising | Total Estimated Income |
|---|---|---|---|---|---|---|---|
| | Tickets Sold | Local Media | Luxury Suites | Club Seats | | | |
| Arizona Diamond-backs | 53,071 | 6,000 | 7,245 | 4,872 | 15,510 | 27,316 | $114,014 |
| Atlanta Braves | 57,740 | 7,000 | 10,075 | 10,427 | 15,510 | 27,316 | $128,068 |
| Baltimore Orioles | 72,846 | 14,000 | 5,940 | 11,134 | 15,510 | 27,316 | $146,746 |
| Cleveland Indians | 60,158 | 17,865 | 11,144 | 35,005 | 15,510 | 30,000 | $169,682 |
| Colorado Rockies | 60,152 | 7,600 | 4,531 | 9,979 | 15,510 | 27,316 | $125,088 |
| New York Yankees | 60,611 | 50,000 | 2,900 | 16,335 | 15,510 | 27,316 | $172,672 |
| Texas Rangers | 48,273 | 12,000 | 12,000 | 10,099 | 15,510 | 27,316 | $125,198 |

*Source:* Miller, W. S. and A. Friedman, 1998, eds. *Inside the ownership of professional sports*, Chicago: Team Marketing Report.

by *Forbes* magazine to be $207.3 million, making the team the 21st most valuable MLB franchise. In 2005, after the opening of the new ballpark, the team's value rose to $329 million, making the Padres the 13th most valuable franchise. In 2013, as the facility has aged and the population size and wealth of the market served by the Padres had not grown as fast as that of the other areas, the team's value of $600 million meant it was the 18th most valuable franchise. The need for the new ballpark is clearly underscored relative to the issues that San Diego confronted when John Moores made his proposal for a new ballpark and a new neighborhood.

In 1996, San Diego's mayor, Susan Goldberg, created a committee to explore the financial challenges the Padres faced. In 1997 the Task Force on Padres Planning—comprised of community and citizen leaders, many of whom were connected to leading local institutions and businesses—concluded (1) the team was losing money and (2) without a new ballpark, the team's fiscal position could not be improved. While there was little public surprise with the Task Force's support of the team's position, the lease given to the Chargers in effect had constrained the Padres' profitability. Despite the complexity of the arrangements

**Table 4.2b   Value of MLB Teams (in millions of dollars) (Padres' rank in parentheses)**

| Team | 2002 | 2005 | 2013 |
|---|---|---|---|
| New York Yankees | 751.3 | 950 | 2,300 |
| Los Angeles Dodgers | 435.9 | 294 | 1,615 |
| Boston Red Sox | 428.1 | 563 | 1,312 |
| Chicago Cubs | 286.3 | 398 | 1,000 |
| Philadelphia Phillies | 232.0 | 392 | 893 |
| New York Mets | 483.5 | 505 | 811 |
| San Francisco Giants | 353.7 | 381 | 786 |
| Texas Rangers | 357.0 | 326 | 764 |
| Los Angeles Angels of Anaheim | 195.7 | 187 | 718 |
| St. Louis Cardinals | 270.2 | 370 | 716 |
| Chicago White Sox | 221.9 | 262 | 692 |
| Seattle Mariners | 373.8 | 415 | 644 |
| Detroit Tigers | 263.3 | 239 | 643 |
| Washington Nationals | Did not exist | 310 | 631 |
| Atlanta Braves | 423.0 | 382 | 629 |
| Houston Astros | 337.1 | 206 | 626 |
| Baltimore Orioles | 319.6 | 341 | 618 |
| **San Diego Padres** | **207.3 (21)** | **329 (13)** | **600 (18)** |
| Arizona Diamondbacks | 271.7 | 286 | 584 |
| Minnesota Twins | 127.6 | 178 | 578 |
| Toronto Blue Jays | 182.4 | 214 | 568 |
| Milwaukee Brewers | 239.5 | 208 | 562 |
| Cleveland Indians | 359.8 | 319 | 559 |
| Cincinnati Reds | 202.7 | 255 | 546 |
| Colorado Rockies | 345.5 | 290 | 537 |

*(Continued)*

**Table 4.2b   Value of MLB Teams (in millions of dollars) (Padres' rank in parentheses) (Continued)**

| Team | 2002 | 2005 | 2013 |
|---|---|---|---|
| Florida/Miami Marlins | 137.4 | 424 | 520 |
| Pittsburgh Pirates | 240.9 | 218 | 479 |
| Oakland Athletics | 156.4 | 185 | 468 |
| Kansas City Royals | 153.0 | 357 | 457 |
| Tampa Bay Rays | 142.2 | 176 | 451 |

*Source: Forbes*, various years.

with the Chargers, it was made clear that the Padres needed a new facility, but a favorable response from voters would require a unique and unprecedented partnership. The task force agreed that it was unlikely that a short-term fix for the Padres could be secured at the existing stadium. In addition, it was hard to imagine how longer-term improvements to Qualcomm Stadium to improve sight lines for baseball would make the stadium a valuable resource for the team. In addition, any changes to the facility or adjustments to the lease would require the Chargers' approval. There were few incentives for them to agree to changes in their lease or the design of the venue unless they too received new revenues. Some suggested building two new venues, but that option was not politically viable. For the Padres, however, it was never in their interest to remain in a stadium that was never properly designed for baseball games. The dual sport facilities that were built in several cities in the 1960s and 1970s (Qualcomm opened in 1967) were circular in an effort to accommodate a rectangular football field and a diamond-shaped baseball field. Those designs, however, never fully satisfied fans of either sport, as sight lines were compromised, given the very different shape of the playing fields. Baseball teams also needed facilities that had far smaller seating capacities, given the crowds attracted to their 81 games. Football teams, playing eight regular season games, are able to attract far more fans. Smaller venues give fans improved sight lines and, as a result, the fans are more willing to pay higher ticket prices than they would in larger venues with seats located farther from the field.

# 4.3 The Politics of San Diego's Sports World

The economic arguments regarding the team's viability in San Diego and a potential loss of the franchise to another city would likely not be sufficient to convince skeptical voters to support a public investment in a new ballpark. Only something extraordinary or unique could do that. Just how poisoned was the political environment for sports-related issues? The Chargers' leadership had demanded a series of improvements to Qualcomm Stadium, and the generous lease also included a "trigger clause." The clause became a "lightning rod" for public opposition. The trigger meant that if the Chargers' annual revenues did not reach a designated level for consecutive years, the team could relocate. San Diego's residents had always feared the team would prefer to play in Los Angeles, although that option would involve resolution of a number of issues between the NFL and the Oakland Raiders. In any event, the trigger became a focal point for voters' resentment of partnerships between San Diego and its teams. The Padres could not ignore this environment, and the resentments that existed, even though their fiscal situation was substantially different from the one that confronted the Chargers. A bit of background is required to understand why the Padres eventually proposed what was at the time the most unique public–private partnership for a new sports facility.[3]

In 1995, the City of San Diego and the Chargers reached an agreement to remodel Jack Murphy Stadium and the team's lease was extended through 2020. The public perception was that San Diego's investment in the renovation had secured the team's presence for 25 years. The Chargers' leadership made public statements declaring their relief in having matters resolved while looking forward to another generation in San Diego. In 1996 and 1997, the Chargers released a letter to the public underscoring their commitment to the city but noting that if the team was ever under "severe financial hardship," it would have the right to renegotiate the terms of their lease. The Chargers also underscored that the renovations being made, while of extreme value to the team, were undertaken to assure that San Diego could host the 2004 Super Bowl. The tone of the letter started the public's distrust of stadium deals, but more disclosures would make matters worse.

The 1995 lease actually included two components that inflamed public resentment. First, the city guaranteed that the Chargers would be able to sell 60,000 nonluxury seats to every home game for at least 10 years, regardless of the team's performance. If 60,000 seats were not sold, then the city was responsible for buying any unsold tickets, regardless of their price. The so-called ticket guarantee was not only unique in the relationship between cities and teams, but the city's obligation was unconditional. In other words, the Chargers could perform poorly or set unrealistic ticket prices for seats with poor sight lines, and neither of these actions reduced or eliminated the city's liability to buy unsold tickets (Rother 2002). The guarantee was seen as a blank check for long-term access to tax dollars regardless of the team's performance and pricing policies.

The second element that ruffled political feathers was the triggering clause tied to the issue of severe economic hardship. Severe financial hardship meant that if the team's player costs exceeded 75 percent of a designated set of revenues, the team had the right to renegotiate the lease and could move elsewhere. With the team suggesting 2 years into the lease that the trigger point was already being reached, the public lost faith in any deal with a professional sports team. Voters and numerous community groups did not trust the city to protect taxpayers' interests. Proposing a new ballpark for the Padres in this environment required a deal or partnership that was quite different and even unique. Otherwise, a new ballpark was the proverbial nonstarter.

This was the political or social environment in which the Padres found themselves as they sought a new ballpark. Ironically, while the public referendum on the Padres proposal passed in 1998, a series of legal challenges, political situations, and a crisis would delay construction. The ballpark opened in 2004. During that time the Chargers' debate would continue and dominate local news. For example, in 2001 information surfaced that the Chargers had preliminary conversations with the Anschutz Entertainment Group (AEG) regarding their relocation to a new football-only facility in downtown Los Angeles. The implication for the public was clear. Even after approving the use of tax money to improve the stadium and a lease that included a ticket guarantee and a relocation option if revenue levels were not secured, the team was still trying to move to Los Angeles. In April 2002 the Chargers' owner unilaterally announced the lease had to be renegotiated as the triggering point had been reached. The team, however, would be unable to provide the financial data to sustain their position that the triggering point had been reached. Later in that same year, the team decided to relocate its preseason training facility to Los Angeles County, further exacerbating the public's confidence and patience with teams and their owners. Debates about the Chargers' future in San Diego continue. The team and the city in 2013 were discussing three different ideas or proposals for a new stadium. Whether or not any NFL team will play in Los Angeles is also unresolved, leaving fears that the Chargers still cling to their hope of becoming the Los Angeles Chargers.

While the drama with the Chargers unfolded, a federal corruption investigation linked Padres' owner John Moores to the substantial financial gains a San Diego council member had made from the public offering of stock for a company owned by Mr. Moores. There were also charges that Mr. Moores helped the council member receive medical treatments after she was diagnosed with cancer. The gifts involved help provided by the Moores family to facilitate treatments available at a medical center in another city. Those details regarding the support provided were slow to emerge, creating problems for the project as investigations were initiated.

Several different people filed a total of 17 lawsuits in an effort to convince one court or judge to overturn the council's decision to commit public funds to the building of the ballpark. Some of the plaintiffs seemed to have overlooked the guarantee made by John Moores that the city's investment would be supported by more than $450 million in new real estate development. The property taxes paid by owners of the new buildings, homes, and condominiums would generate enough taxes to match the public sector's investment in the ballpark.

Once all of those cases were resolved—none were successful in challenging the legality of the procedures followed—and the stock and the ethics issues were resolved (no crimes were found to have been committed), construction was allowed to continue. There was, however, one brief additional hiccup. In April 2003, the city found that the team had changed the agreed upon design so that fewer seats would be built. The city ordered that the ballpark be built as specified; the Padres immediately complied. PETCO Park—the naming rights to the facility were sold before the facility opened—hosted its first game in March 2004 and was ready for the Padres' 2004 season.

## 4.4 Task Force II and the Generation of Substantial Public Benefits

If a new ballpark for the Padres were built with any tax dollars, it would have to create important benefits for San Diego. The city's leadership established three requirements. First, the ballpark would have to be located where San Diego wanted. Second, there would have to be assurances provided that sufficient levels of new construction would take place to generate new tax revenues to offset the public's investment. Third, the team owner would also have to guarantee that a new headquarters hotel near the San Diego Convention Center would be built.

In the earliest negotiations three sites were discussed. The Padres preferred a Mission Valley location near Qualcomm Stadium. Any site in suburban Mission Valley area offered excellent access to the region's major east-west and two north-south freeways. The popularity of the Mission Valley area would have made it relatively easy to assure new development to generate property taxes; however, that development would have occurred even if a ballpark were not built. As a result, it would be difficult to claim the property taxes from new residences or commercial offices in the Mission Valley area represented new income for San Diego.

The other two sites were downtown. One preferred location was on the waterfront near the convention center. The city, however, favored the aging East Village district (the current site of PETCO Park), north and east of the convention center on the landward side of East Harbor Drive. The Gaslamp district north and west of the ballpark had become a successful entertainment district with numerous restaurants and pubs. The nearby Horton Plaza retail center was also successful, but no redevelopment had occurred in the East Village. San Diego was willing to invest in a ballpark located in the East Village, but wanted two other public benefits.

## 4.5 Public Benefits and the Stigma of Subsidies

San Diego wanted a headquarters hotel for the convention center in the East Village and a revitalization plan that would generate sufficient new tax revenues equal to its investment in the ballpark. John Moores wanted to limit his investment in a new ballpark to approximately $150 million. A debt of that magnitude would permit the team to pay competitive salaries to players and ensure that he did not lose money. It was initially anticipated that the ballpark would cost $411 million (Chapin 2002; City of San Diego 1998). The City of San Diego agreed to spend $186.5 million for the ballpark; the Padres committed $81 million to the ballpark's construction and $34 million for land acquisition and the building of needed infrastructure. The team also agreed to be responsible for any cost overruns. The City of San Diego's redevelopment agency pledged $88.5 million for land acquisition, and the Unified Port of San Diego agreed to invest $21 million. Of the anticipated $411 million investment, the public sector planned to spend $296 million. The public share was equal to 72 percent of the anticipated total cost.

In the end the ballpark cost $483.1 million; the team assumed responsibility for 38.8 percent of the project. San Diego paid 42.6 percent of the project's cost, and the redevelopment agency supported 17.2 percent of the project's costs. The Unified Port of San Diego (port authority) supported 4.3 percent, or $21 million. The public sector assumed responsibility for almost two-thirds of the project's cost if the port's contribution is included. If that is excluded, then San Diego's cost was the share supported by the city itself and its redevelopment agency, which amounted to $289.1 million, or 59.8 percent of the project's costs. The new property tax revenues guaranteed by John Moores would generate enough money to match the public sector's investment.

Voters were asked to approve the deal with the Padres; 59.6 percent of the electorate authorized San Diego to enter into a memorandum of understanding (MOU) with the Padres and the city's Centre City Development Corporation (CCDC) to:

1. Create a ballpark redevelopment district
2. Construct a baseball park
3. Redevelop the East Village area

The redevelopment area was designated as the Ballpark District. As noted earlier, the guarantee for sufficient real estate development to produce new tax revenues equal to the city's investment in the ballpark made the deal unique. Voters were reminded of this guarantee that was secured by a bond posted by John Moores. In addition, John Moores had made a guaranteed commitment to a redevelopment strategy for the East Village that would ensure development of more than 850 hotel rooms (to support the attraction of more events at the nearby San Diego Convention Center), new residences, and new retail and commercial properties. The most important public benefit, and the one that was the centerpiece of the campaign to secure voter approval for the financing plan and creation of the Ballpark District, was that sufficient levels of new real estate development had to occur before and immediately after the opening of the ballpark. Further, if the opening of the hotel were delayed past the opening of the ballpark, then the Padres would be responsible for paying a share of the lost hotel taxes (the room usage taxes that visitors would have paid). San Diego planned to use the new hotel taxes to pay its share of the maintenance costs associated with the operation of the ballpark.

On July 14, 1998, all parties agreed to a memorandum of understanding (MOU). San Diego and the Padres also agreed to complete a set of tasks by April 1, 1999, to secure the land and ensure that construction could begin later in the spring or early summer of 1999. San Diego also required John Moores to have in place by April 1, 1999, the financing for the headquarters hotel, which would have at least 850 rooms. As will be discussed, market conditions changed and it was agreed that instead of a single 850-room hotel, multiple properties could be built as long as at least 850 hotel rooms were added to the city's inventory in close proximity to the convention center.

The deal certainly looks like a familiar set of subsidies for an arena, ballpark, or stadium cleverly disguised by the participation of two public entities that are essentially led by the same people, the city council and mayor. This obfuscation between two entities can make some residents leery of the possibility for a lack of clarity and less transparency when two different entities led by the same elected officials are involved. The involvement of two entities can make it possible for elected officials to claim elements of the partnership were required by the involvement of another entity, and therefore make it more difficult for voters and residents to follow a clear division of responsibilities, funding, and financial commitment.

Regardless of the number of public entities involved and the complexity of their relationship to each other, the team, the ballpark, and the Ballpark District, the unique aspects of this deal were, as noted, the unprecedented commitments made to build the desired number of hotel rooms near the convention center and the guarantee of new development to generate new property taxes. In addition, the ballpark was to be built where the city preferred, and an entire new downtown neighborhood would be built. The existence of the new neighborhood was not a hope or a goal—it was to be built and guaranteed by the team's owner. Commitments of this nature had never been made before.

Before San Diego would make its substantial investment—through the city or through the redevelopment agency—the financing for the hotel and the promised level of new development had to be in place. On March 30, 1999, San Diego's city manager reported to the city council that the assurances were in place and John Moores' commitments were guaranteed. The council accepted the city manager's report and committed to acquiring the land and construction of any needed infrastructure improvements. On March 31, 1999, the Ballpark District was officially created (City of San Diego 1999). San Diego had guaranteed ticket sales for the Chargers, but the Padres' owner was required to provide assurances that the tax revenues needed to avoid a subsidy were going to be generated. This was the substantial difference from the deals the public sector had made with the San Diego Chargers. Those differences are what engendered a level of support from voters.

Relative to the public benefits secured, some could suggest that 850 hotel rooms to support the convention center's attractiveness was not as important as other needs. While San Diego's climate and amenities, as well as the coastal location of its convention center, made the city a meeting planner's delight, city leaders believed more nearby hotel rooms were needed to attract more conventions and meetings. San Diego did not want any responsibility for building a hotel or ensuring that 850 new rooms would be added to the city's inventory. In many other communities the public sector has indeed guaranteed the financing for a hotel near a convention center. In addition, city leaders had been frustrated by the lack of any private sector initiative to build new hotels or additional rooms near the convention center. The Ballpark District created an opportunity for the hotel rooms to be built that could meet the needs of convention attendees and attract out-of-town visitors to the ballpark. But to get the rooms built, the city had to invest in a ballpark. For its investment San Diego received a commitment to have a baseball team in the city for at least 22 years, a new ballpark, the hotel rooms that were needed, and real estate development assurances that would lead to a redevelopment of the East Village area and private sector investments that exceeded the city's investment in the ballpark.

Prudent perspectives on growth and development require acknowledgment of the possibility that the tax dollars generated by new hotel rooms and other forms of new development might not be *new* revenues for San Diego. The development in the downtown area could have replaced projects that would have taken place in *other* parts of the city. The public sector perceived great value from ensuring that the development took place in the East Village area. The movement of economic activity to conform to public plans can be as important as the occurrence of the economic activity itself.

Since the city council had declared it a matter of public policy and importance to (1) redevelop the East Village, (2) have 850 hotel rooms added to the city's inventory in close proximity to the convention center, and (3) secure a guaranteed assurance that real estate development would occur, the issues to evaluate or assess are the extent to which each of these goals was realized. The city also specified that a proportion of the residential units developed would have to be below market rate to provide a level of economic integration in the Ballpark District. The city and sports fans would have to rely on the public statements made by John Moores that if the ballpark were built, he would spend the money necessary to keep the team competitive. There was no protection for the city or guarantee that the team would spend a certain proportion of its revenues for players. While it is also appropriate to recognize that some residents of the region thought the city's leadership should not have focused as much on the redevelopment of the downtown area, sports, the convention center, or changing that character of the East Village, the council was responsible for making those decisions or choices. In addition, when the proposal was put before the electorate for a required referendum vote, almost 60 percent of those who voted supported the concept and the council's decision. In evaluating the returns secured, the goals established by the council and ratified by the voters need to be the factors evaluated or assessed. This is not meant to suggest that a different council or that the council could have specified different benefits or outcomes.

There could have been a different commitment requested for other infrastructure or community development projects. Logical and effective arguments could have been made for a large number of projects that could have also added luster to neighborhoods in San Diego. What is relevant is what was specified as the requirements for the public sector's participation, and whether or not those expectations or legally binding commitments were secured.

In noting what the public sector wanted and what voters approved, the financial challenges that emerged for San Diego in the years after the ballpark opened must also be included in the analysis and assessment. The financial challenges were related to an underfunded pension plan and inadequate funding for fire protection.[4] The surplus property taxes generated by the Ballpark District (beyond the revenues needed to repay the bonds) were not transferred to the city's general revenue fund. Instead, those funds remained with the redevelopment authority. The failure of redevelopment authorities in several cities in California to transfer revenue to their city's general revenue funds (to pay the bills for pensions and service delivery) led to the abolition of the authorities after Jerry Brown was elected governor in 2010. His campaign, against the backdrop of financial problems for several cities in California, included a promise to eliminate development authorities so that all property tax increments would be redirected to the general funds of cities to help meet their obligations, as opposed to only those of downtown areas.

## 4.6 The Scorecard on the Ballpark District: What Was Built

A headquarters hotel for conventions with at least 850 hotel rooms was not built, but two hotels did open in the Ballpark District. The change to smaller hotels was accepted by San Diego's City Council and was made to accommodate both the market shifts and concerns with security after the 9/11 terrorist attacks and changes that took place in the convention and hotel business. By 2008, a total of 747 new hotel rooms were built, and in 2009 the Hotel Indigo with 210 rooms opened. When that hotel was finished, John Moores Investments (JMI) would have exceeded the minimum number of guaranteed rooms. Today, the Hotel Salamar has 235 rooms, the Omni has 511, and the Residence Inn has 240. The Hard Rock Hotel has also opened in the area, bringing the total number of rooms built since the Ballpark District was created to more than 1,200. The total number of new hotel rooms near the convention center was realized.

The 2007 year-end report by the Centre City Development Corporation (CCDC) noted that more than 3,000 market rate residential units had been built in the Ballpark District and 594 price-restricted units had also been occupied. In addition, 546,670 square feet of commercial space had been built. The dollar value of this new construction was $1.13 billion, *360 percent more than what was specified in the MOU for phase I.* The Padres committed to a total of $487 million of new development in the Ballpark District across *two development phases* (Rosentraub 1998). The level of construction activity was not only surpassed during phase I, but the anticipated or promised development was actually more than double the amount included in the campaign literature urging voters to vote for the creation of the Ballpark District and the building of a new home for the Padres. Table 4.3 identifies construction completed by 2007. That was the year by which approximately $487 million in new construction had to be completed; at the end of 2007, $1.15 billion of new construction had been completed, or more than twice the amount guaranteed by John Moores.

A 2008 study by the Stanford Graduate School of Business reported that more than $4 billion in new investment had taken place in and around the Ballpark District.[5] Table 4.4 illustrates the planned construction in the Ballpark District through 2010. Those projects brought the total level of investment to more than $2.87 billion of new development, which was completely financed by the private sector, and did not include any of the expense associated with the ballpark or other public buildings in the area.

The total amount of money spent to build a new neighborhood was far more than anyone would have thought. More important than the amount of money spent is the design of what was built and the architectural accomplishments achieved. Several views of the Ballpark District are included to underscore several different facets of the design, demonstrating that the project was always focused on the creation of a new urban neighborhood. Figure 4.1 shows the ballpark and a view of the neighborhood fans enjoy from their seats. Notice the buildings that offer views of the field from windows and the grass seating area beyond the right center field area. The scale of the ballpark was designed to ensure that it fit within the new neighborhood but did not dominate the view or the landscape. The neighborhood itself, the Ballpark District, was to be the most dominant feature, and not the ballpark.

The commitment to build a new neighborhood and guarantee more than $450 million in new real estate development by the team's owner required that considerable attention be directed toward ensuring that the ballpark *complemented* the community. John Moores had to be certain that a neighborhood would be created where people wanted to live and work. Figure 4.2 provides an illustration of the ways in which a desirable place to live and work was created. Notice how the green space and condominium towers frame the ballpark on the left side of the photo. The globe rising on the right side of the photograph is the new public library, and its glass atrium is visible directly in front of the globe.

Two other views of the ballpark and development present a clear perspective on how the facility was designed to be the anchor of an urban development that created revenue streams for the team and the City of San Diego. Figure 4.3 is the family seating area in right center field. Notice that there is a sandbox for young children against the outfield fence. The bench-like seating in the foreground permits parents to enjoy the game and at the same time watch their children at play in the sandbox. Security

**Table 4.3  New Construction in the Ballpark District, through 2007 (in millions of dollars)**

| Project | Units/Rooms | Square Feet | Cost |
|---|---|---|---|
| 6th and K (offices, parking) | | 15,000 | $1.5 |
| Diamond Terrace (condominiums) | 113 | | 29.0 |
| Diamond View Tower (offices) | | 325,000 | 81.0 |
| Element (condominiums and offices) | 65 | 9,670 | 23.0 |
| Entrada | 172/40 | | 17.0 |
| Fahrenheit Lofts | 77 | | 27.0 |
| Hotel Solamar | 235 | 7,000 | 50.0 |
| ICON | 327 | 16,000 | 115.0 |
| Island Village (price controlled) | 280 | 5,000 | 16.0 |
| Lillian Place (price controlled) | 74 | | 14.5 |
| M2i | 230 | 12,000 | 82.0 |
| Market Street Village I | 225 | 43,000 | 38.0 |
| Metrome | 184 | | 51.0 |
| Nexus | 68 | 3,000 | 24.3 |
| Omni Hotel | 512 | | 110.0 |
| Padres Parkade (1,000 parking spaces) | | 3,000 | 23.0 |
| Palm Restaurant | | 7,000 | 1.0 |
| Park Boulevard East | 107 | | 30.0 |
| Park Boulevard West | 120 | 6,000 | 30.0 |
| Parkloft | 120 | | 83.2 |
| Park Terrace | 233 | 25,000 | 81.0 |
| Potiker Family Senior Residences | 200 | | 16.6 |
| Lofts at 677 7th Street | 153 | 5,000 | 23.7 |
| The Mark | 260 | 8,000 | 105.0 |
| The Metropolitan | 32 | | 62.0 |
| TR Produce | | 42,000 | 12.0 |

*Source:* Centre City Development Corporation, 2007, www.ccdc.com

*Note:* Where a / is used, the number to the right indicates units that were price controlled for affordability.

**Table 4.4    Projects in the Ballpark District with 2008 to 2010 Completion Dates (cost in millions of dollars)**

| Project | Units/Rooms | Square Feet | Estimated Cost |
|---|---|---|---|
| 14th and K | 222 | 9,000 | $79.5 |
| 15th and Island | 617 | 20,000 | 188.1 |
| 15th and Market | 274 | 25,000 | 100.9 |
| Alta | 179 | 11,000 | 64.9 |
| Axiom | 205/41 | | 72.0 |
| Ballpark Village | 1,600 | 517,000 | 1,400.0 |
| Cosmopolitan Square | 290 | 29,000 | 107.3 |
| Echelon | 183 | | 64.0 |
| Hotel Indigo | 210 | | 47.3 |
| Laundry Lofts | 208 | 2,000 | 73.0 |
| Library Tower | 174/16 | 12,000 | 69.0 |
| Market Street Village II | 244/24 | 14,000 | 88.2 |
| Parkside | 77/76 | 10,000 | 17.0 |
| Seventh and Market | 418/84/220[a] | 14,000 | 300.0 |
| Strata (hotel) | 236 | 12,000 | 84.0 |
| The Legend | 183 | 30,000 | 80.0 |
| The Lofts at 655 6th Avenue | 183 | 12,000 | 18.0 |
| Triangle | 57 | 4,000 | 17.0 |

*Source:* Centre City Development Corporation, 2007, www.civicsd.com

*Note:* Where a / is used, the number to the right indicates units that are price controlled for affordability.

[a] This project will have 418 market rate units, 84 price-controlled units, and 220 hotel rooms.

is maintained during the game and during batting practice to protect children from home runs or balls batted into the family section. On nongame days—this picture was taken on a day the Padres were on the road—the family seating area remains, allowing visitors and residents to enjoy a view of the facility as it was meant to be an integral part of the Ballpark District and not an isolated amenity.

Figure 4.1 PETCO Park and a new urban neighborhood. (Courtesy of Mark S. Rosentraub.)

Figure 4.2 Fitting a ballpark into a neighborhood.

**Figure 4.3    The family seating area and sandbox in PETCO Park and San Diego's Ballpark District.**

The other unusual amenity built into PETCO Park and the Ballpark District was a miniature baseball field for the neighborhood's residents and children. During Padres' games the space is open for young children and their family members to play in the space and to provide ways for even the youngest fans to connect to the team. (On the days that games are played in PETCO Park, access to this field is reserved for families that have purchased tickets.) This amenity is open to the public and neighborhood on nongame days, and its access is only controlled or limited to fans attending a Padres' game for a few hours before and during a game. Note in Figure 4.4 that the field is positioned near residential and commercial properties. In the foreground, which is not visible in the picture (but its shadow is caste across the diamond) is the left field stands and the center field area of PETCO Park.

The anchor for the Ballpark District, PETCO Park and its main entrance, framed by the surrounding green space, are shown in Figure 4.5. The pedestrian bridge built in 2011 underscored the Ballpark District's linkage or connection to the convention center. This connection allows visitors staying in more than 1,000 hotel rooms in the Ballpark District to have another access point to the convention center (see Figure 4.6).

Those opposed to the Ballpark District and the building of the Padres' new home included those who feared San Diego would again be subsidizing sports owners and those who thought the East Village should continue as a location for artists, start-up business, and some residents. Before any conclusions are reached

**Figure 4.4    The miniature baseball field in the Ballpark District, just outside of PETCO Park.**

**Figure 4.5    The main entrance to PETCO Park.**

**Figure 4.6    The pedestrian bridge linking the Ballpark District to the San Diego Convention Center.**

with regard to the fiscal merits of the project, the issue of the development strategy adopted by San Diego needs to be addressed.

San Diego lacked a large residential base in its downtown area; therefore, city officials were intent on anchoring a new residential flavor to the Ballpark District. Still others, impressed with Jane Jacobs' philosophy, suggest that the best course of action is to let regeneration occur through the reuse of properties by start-up businesses. To encourage regeneration, these advocates prefer transitional areas with live-work space. By the 1990s, the East Village was an area with some artists' studios, shops, and coffeehouses. There were also some fledgling business start-ups in the area. Some of the aging warehouses had been converted into live-work lofts, giving the area a small residential profile. The ballpark and the Ballpark District dramatically altered the development process. The East Village was an area where these perspectives on regeneration collided. San Diego's political leadership wanted a large-scale development—a sort of new downtown area—replete with new hotels for the convention center and an accelerated timetable for commercial and residential development. Some community leaders, however, had a different vision for the East Village. Mr. Wayne Buss, an architect focused on environmentally appropriate development, for example, was a champion for a perspective that would transform the East Village into a Greenwich Village (the area in Manhattan celebrated for its eclectic, artistic, and educational character) for San Diego (Williams 2004). The city's leadership from both the public and private sectors had another vision. As noted, San Diego's elected and appointed political leadership wanted a new downtown neighborhood anchored by hotels and the ballpark. To boost residential life in the downtown area, a large number of market rate homes with an appropriate concentration of houses for families with modest incomes were components of their vision. An eclectic area was desired, but the mix was quite different from what

Mr. Buss would have preferred. The city's elected leadership and city manager were concerned with ensuring that the downtown area would become a neighborhood with thousands of residents, new hotels, and new commercial space that might also provide employment opportunities. Development in their view had languished, and the there was little confidence that patterns would change without a catalyst. A plan that involved hundreds of millions of dollars of investment and that dramatically changed the area's development trajectory in a short period of time was needed. While any assessment of the Ballpark District has to look at the public's investment and taxes generated, it is also important to consider, in a qualitative sense, what was built. "Tens of thousands of condos, town homes, and apartments have been built as part of hundreds of housing projects. Retail and entertainment projects have injected vitality into downtown. This effort has transformed downtown from its gritty past into the hottest neighborhood around" (San Diego Union-Tribune 2004). It is now a realistic goal that as many as 50,000 people may live in the downtown area before 2020, where a new large-scale supermarket has opened. It is also important to note that the Ballpark District has helped to preserve some older facilities. For example, the TR Produce building, built in 1934, has been refitted with two stories of office space and new condominiums (Newman 2006: 10):

> Completed in 1934, the TR Produce building is one of about a dozen surviving structures from around 1870 to the early 1930s in the East Village. The old produce building and the new commercial condominium complex within its walls are a novel combination of historic preservation and new construction. Under an agreement struck with a local preservationist group, the old and new buildings barely touch each other. The new structure was built within the walls of the produce building. Standing on a stilt-like structure of steel columns, the new metal-and-glass commercial condominium complex rises above the old brick walls to peer into the ballpark.

There were approximately 12 older industrial buildings that remained in the area. Bruce Coons, executive director of the nonprofit Save Our Heritage Organization, "led the negotiations that set standards for the reuse of 11 historic buildings in the ballpark area with both the developer and city officials" (Newman 2006: 10). This led to the incorporation of the Western Metal Supply Company building as part of the left field wall in the ballpark. Chris Wahl, vice president and partner of San Diego-based Southwest Strategies LLC, and spokesman for the Downtown Residential Marketing Alliance, probably summarized things most accurately when he noted, "What the ballpark has done is opened up an entirely different part of downtown that didn't previously exist from a residential standpoint. East Village has completely taken off" (Broderick 2006: 40). In 2006, the *New York Times* reviewed the project noting that the goal of an extraordinary level of development had indeed taken place (Newman 2006). At the same time these accomplishments are recognized, it is important to note the destruction of the Bohemian character of the East Village and the implementation of a development strategy that dramatically changed its character and image. That character, however has been financially successful while being different from what existed.

## 4.7 Economic Integration and the Vitality of the Ballpark District

There were justifiable concerns that the Ballpark District would become economically segregated and an exclusive enclave for higher-income individuals and families. There was also concern that a master-planned neighborhood that was essentially built across less than 20 years would not be sustainable. The Ballpark District was largely built during the explosive growth of property values in Southern California and in many places in the United States. When the property value bubble burst in 2007, an opportunity was created to understand if a master-planned community that was artificially supported by a housing market bubble was economically sustainable. Cantor and Rosentraub (2012) examined both the extent to which the Ballpark District was economically integrated and how it fared in the aftermath of the collapse of property values.[6] They concluded that fears of economic segregation or an inability to sustain the economic viability of the master-planned community were misplaced (Cantor and Rosentraub 2012: 226):

> In total $2.87 billion of new real estate development took place through 2010 excluding the funds invested in the ballpark. If there was a concern that the neighborhood would gentrify and offer few or very limited residential opportunities for households with moderate incomes, that fear was misplaced. The neighborhood remains economically integrated and the increase in the number of higher income households has the area far more balanced than it was before investment of more than $2 billion by John Moores' real estate firm and those of other investors attracted to the area. The age demographics in the area are also well integrated as the Ballpark District has attracted older and younger residents…. There has also been an increase in the proportion of individuals who are employed in sectors where it is expected that people have higher levels of education…. The severe recession was a particular concern for any neighborhood where there were large numbers of new residences built in a relatively brief period of time. In areas that are less well established there is the possibility that housing prices would escalate sharply during the boom phase, and then collapse as soon as a "bust" settled into the region. Data through 2010 suggest prices in the Ballpark District

have remained relatively stable especially when compared with volatility throughout San Diego County and across the southwest.

The stability of price levels is especially important when it is realized that the Ballpark District is comprised only of condominiums and townhouses. The product that dominates in the region is detached single-family homes. This created the specter of reduced demand for a specialty product that was designed for a niche market. That fear relative to a master-planned neighborhood created in a relatively short period of time was also misplaced.

# 4.8 The Scorecard: Taxes Generated

San Diego was depending on increases in hotel taxes (transient occupancy taxes (TOT)) to meet its responsibilities to maintain the ballpark and pay for the bonds issued to build the ballpark. The new property taxes were to be equal to the public sector's investment in the ballpark. Table 4.5 illustrates the increases in the TOT since PETCO Park opened. The annual increments indicate that every year far more funds than those needed to maintain the ballpark have been generated. The available data do not provide the opportunity to indicate what effect the ballpark had on TOT revenue generation. The redevelopment agency did survey occupancy rates through 2007 in the Ballpark District and estimated that $6.9 million in new TOT was generated each year by the new hotel properties. That figure increased after new hotels opened. Regardless of the results of the survey, the issue of concern for San Diego was that sufficient funds would be generated to meet the possible need for approximately $2 million to $4 million in maintenance costs to sustain PETCO Park. Only in the 3 years since the ballpark opened was the increment from 2003 (the year before the ballpark opened) less than $8 million. In contrast, in 2009, 2011, and 2012 the increment was more than $30 million above the funds collected in 2003 (see Table 4.5). The additional hotel rooms in the Ballpark District are not solely generating this sizable increment in TOT revenues reported in some years. The essential point, however, is that the demands on TOT dollars that existed in 2003 have not been disadvantaged by the commitment to pay for maintenance of the ballpark, as sufficient new revenues have been generated to meet that responsibility. It should also be noted that in 2006 the Padres decided to make several enhancements to PETCO Park. The team paid 100 percent of the cost for those modifications, since certain modernization elements remain the responsibility of the team. That further reduces the demand for TOT funds for maintenance projects.

The financial model developed by San Diego called for the building of approximately $500 million of new real estate (excluding the funds expended to built the ballpark, which is exempt from city property taxes) to match the city's investment in the ballpark. With more than $2.87 billion of new real estate developed, more

**Table 4.5    Transient Occupancy Taxes (TOT) and the City of San Diego, 2002–2012**

| Year | TOT Collections | Increments from 2003 |
|------|-----------------|----------------------|
| 2002 | $95,175,000     |                      |
| 2003 | 105,263,000     |                      |
| 2004 | 113,209,000     | $7,946,000           |
| 2005 | 120,792,000     | 15,529,000           |
| 2006 | 136,803,000     | 31,540,000           |
| 2007 | 146,379,000     | 41,116,000           |
| 2008 | 159,348,000     | 54,085,000           |
| 2009 | 140,657,000     | 35,394,000           |
| 2010 | 123,332,000     | 18,069,000           |
| 2011 | 140,752,000     | 35,489,000           |
| 2012 | 148,184,000     | 42,921,000           |

*Source:* City of San Diego, Comprehensive Annual Financial Reports, City of San Diego, 2006–2012.

than four times the amount needed. No further analysis is needed to answer the question regarding the sufficiency of new property taxes to match the city's investment. One analysis that I did perform suggested the new taxes could amount to as much as $32 million each year for San Diego. Regardless, more revenue was produced across the term of the bonds to exceed the investment in the ballpark.

The issue of the production of more property tax revenue engenders a discussion of the relationship between central cities and the development authorities created to revitalize downtown areas. As is often the case when cities, counties, or states create special districts or authorities, there is a policy question of what is the appropriate use of any generated revenues. Some could argue the funds should be retained to sustain other investments that are less profitable, and that funds from more successful projects should be used for further enhancements. Such issues have been debated when some projects financed by port authorities generate revenues that are in excess of costs (Moss and O'Neill, 2014). Many downtown redevelopment districts never generate sufficient funds to support the expense of projects and are actually dependent on the infusion of funds from cities or counties.

The Ballpark District was far more successful than was envisioned, and that success took place at a time when San Diego was challenged to meet its pension obligations and enhance municipal service delivery, especially with regard to fire protection services. The property taxes generated by the Ballpark District accrued to the development authority and not to the City of San Diego. The authority could use those funds only in the downtown area for other projects. In 2011, during Governor Jerry Brown's first year in office, there was considerable discussion regarding the dissolution of development authorities so that excess revenues would be available for education and other services and to address San Diego's other financial issues. His administration noted that voters had expressed their desire to ensure that all locally generated funds would be available to fund local government services and obligations in a 2010 referendum. In 2011, the California Supreme Court upheld the legislature's and governor's authority to abolish community development authorities.[7]

There are two different policy perspectives on the use of the excess funds produced by special authorities created by state and local governments. As these organizations are created to produce and sustain particular initiatives or developments, one strain of thought is that revenues from successful projects should be used to offset any losses and support the long-term maintenance issues associated with successful initiatives. Placing this in the context of San Diego's Ballpark District, while real estate development was the responsibility of John Moores' JMI, the development authority could have used the extra revenue for other amenities or the maintenance of the area long after the private sector had made all of its investments. One of the considerations that underscored the creation of authorities has been to separate the initiatives and management of downtown areas or other assets from electoral politics. That has proved to be a naïve expectation. Development authorities are also subject to their own politics. Special interest groups seek to ensure that investments made by development authorities meet their needs or expectations. It must be recognized that those businesses focused on real estate development have a vested interest in protecting development authorities, and their revenue can be used to reduce the risk associated with new initiatives.

In San Diego's case there were concerns that leading business interests allied themselves with the development authority to ensure that all revenues would continue to advance development in the downtown area even at the expense of the needs of other communities in San Diego or the city's overall fiscal health.[8] At one level, however, the authorities were created to do just that. The authorities were actually created to focus on a single objective (downtown development) and were not created to focus on downtown development and the city's overall financial viability.

There are other perspectives in the debate of over the best use of excess funds produced by development authorities. One championed by Governor Brown in California in 2011 was that the revenues generated by development and community authorities had to be part of the overall set of fiscal decisions made by state and local governments. His leadership led to the demise of authorities. As a result, city councils and state legislatures (and the governor can also make recommendations for the legislature to consider) will have direct authority to decide where all the revenues are to be spent. Returning to the San Diego case, the situation is made more complex by the fact the board controlling the downtown development authority was the city council. While it is not clear if the city council meeting as the development authority board had the legal authority to transfer funds to San Diego's general revenue fund, it was clear that the issue of expending funds for other needs was not a major concern for the downtown development authority or the city council functioning as its board.

San Diego and California are not the only city and state to confront the issue of the ways in which special authorities and their revenues should be managed. Massachusetts and New York City have had similar experiences with port authorities. What is important for those pursuing careers with teams or cities and the building of sports facilities and real estate is to understand the politics of development authorities and the relationship of revenues generated to the welfare of the entire city. There are advantages for a team's image and its future to ensure that the product of its presence in a downtown area generates benefits for an entire city and not just the downtown area. The Ballpark District was a prudent investment. The financial returns, however, were assigned to the development authority and not the city. This was changed in 2011.

## 4.9 The Ballpark District and San Diego: Mutual Risk in a New Model for Public–Private Partnerships

While many cities had made very extensive commitments to build sports facilities, there were never assurances or commitments from a team's owner to ensure private sector investment. Indianapolis' sports strategy was tied to a large-scale revitalization effort, but there the city essentially was responsible for facilitating additional private sector investments. Neither the Colts' nor the Pacers' ownership made any assurances for any real estate investments or for the success of the downtown development initiative. The Pacers' owners did participate in the building and management of Circle Centre Mall, but that effort was not specifically associated with the city's investment in Market Square Arena or the Fieldhouse, and it also benefitted from financial support from the city. In addition, when Simon Development—the owners of the Pacers—built its new headquarters building in downtown Indianapolis, the firm negotiated for and received an abatement from property taxes. In scores of other cities, even with large public sector investments in facilities, most team owners have been reluctant to make any commitments or assurances that real estate development would take place.

San Diego, the Padres, and JMI created a new framework for a public–private partnership. Each took risks, but the potential for mutual success also existed. San Diego could realize substantial property tax revenue growth. JMI also assumed substantial risk, and it too could lose money. While the bargaining position between cities and teams is uneven, the establishment of development goals and linking them to the provision of public subsidies, as was done in San Diego, can ensure that the public sector's development goals are a priority, and in this instance, they were achieved. For the first time, a city's participation in the financing and maintaining of a sports facility was directly linked to assurances provided by a team's owner that new real estate development would take place where the public sector deemed it necessary and appropriate. This accomplishment cannot be minimized.

It is also important to note that JMI continues to assume a lead role in developing the Ballpark District. In that regard, while San Diego must continue to play a development broker role similar to the work Indianapolis must do to ensure its sports investments are paid off, San Diego has a specific private sector partner to lead efforts to expand and enhance the district. The tax revenues earned for the development in the Ballpark District may have not been new growth for San Diego, but it must be conceded that had the ballpark not been built in the East Village area, some of the development might have taken place elsewhere in the city. It is also possible that the development could have occurred beyond the city's borders. San Diego's goal to concentrate development in the East Village area was undeniably achieved, even though it meant changing the character of the neighborhood.

Finally, it must be recognized that the development of the Ballpark District was a decisive policy choice by San Diego to forego strategies related to Jane Jacobs' ideas and to transform the neighborhood in a relatively short period of time to a largely upscale downtown area. San Diego's leadership chose to infuse public and private money to substantially alter development. The leadership wanted a new residential and commercial area to create a very different image for the downtown area. Leadership also wanted new hotel rooms near the convention center. San Diego's leadership not only created a new model for other cities to follow when dealing with professional sports teams, but it also secured its development goals. While it is clear some community organizations would have preferred a different strategy, with almost $2.9 billion in private sector investment, the Ballpark District would be a welcome addition to the revitalization effort of any city. Most mayors and city council members would conclude that San Diego and its Ballpark District are major league winners.

# Endnotes

1. Richard Jacobs paid $45.5 million for the Cleveland Indians in 1986; he sold the team for $320 million in 1999. His investment in 1986 amounted to $69.2 million (in 1999 dollars), meaning a return of 462 percent on his investment. That figure, however, is misleading, as it is impossible to know exactly how much additional money he invested in the team across the tenure of his ownership and if those investments had returns as a result of higher levels of attendance and the sale of food, beverages, and merchandise at the ballpark. Even if the return on his investment was half of the gross calculation, the

point is sustained that substantial fiscal gains were secured by the owner as a result of the new revenue streams included in a facility that was built with a substantial investment by the public sector.

2. Mrs. Kroc's decision to sell the team was associated with ongoing stresses with MLB and her fellow owners, as described in a 1997 interview with the author. She also described her firm desire that the team had to remain in San Diego and stressed that to the new ownership group.

3. Some teams have paid all of the capital costs for a new facility in exchange for public support for needed infrastructure. The Washington Redskins (1997), Miami Dolphins (1987), and Carolina Panthers (1996) privately financed their new stadiums, but the economics of football create possibilities that did not exist for the Padres. In 2000 the Giants built a privately financed ballpark in downtown San Francisco, but that market offered options that were not viable in San Diego. The Padres had to find a different approach.

4. San Diego's problems with the funding of its pension fund and the need for more revenue for the delivery of appropriate and needed urban services have now emerged as issues for numerous cities. Chicago is the most recent city to have found its pension funds approaching insolvency (August 2013). These problems, as alluded to in Chapter 1, are a function of politics, the Great Recession, and the changing structure of the economy. What made the situation somewhat unique was the presence of revenue streams generated by successful downtown redevelopment efforts, including the Ballpark District, and the lack of initiatives to consider the best use of those revenues to ensure the city's fiscal future. This issue will be discussed in the last section of this chapter.

5. Hoty, D., San Diego Padres: PETCO Park as a catalyst for urban redevelopment, 2008, Stanford Graduate School of Business, Stanford University, http://www.portlandmercury.com/images/blogimages/2009/05/13/1242256908-petco_park_-_stanford_case_study_2008-02-19.pdf (accessed August 8, 2013).

6. Cantor, M.B., and M.S. Rosentraub, A ballpark and neighborhood change: Economic integration, a recession, and the altered demography of San Diego's Ballpark District after eight years, *City, Culture, and Society*, 3: 291–226, 2012.

7. Lin, J., and P. Elias, Jerry Brown, state lawmakers asserted right to eliminate community development authorities, 2011, http://www.huffingtonpost.com/2011/11/10/jerry-brown-redevelopment-agencies_n_1087360.html (accessed August 11, 2013); Roy, D., Dissolving community redevelopment, 2011, http://www.mckennalong.com/publications-519.html (accessed August 11, 2013); Garrison, J., Jerry Brown's bid to kill redevelopment agencies sets stage for fierce battle, *Los Angeles Times*, 2011, http://articles.latimes.com/2011/jan/15/local/la-me-local-budget-20110115 (accessed August 11, 2013).

8. Erie, S., V. Kogan, and S. MacKenzie, *Paradise plundered: Fiscal crisis and governance failures in San Diego* (Stanford, CA: Stanford University Press, 2011).

## Chapter 5

# A White Elephant, an Arena, and Revitalization: Using Location and the Glitz of L.A. LIVE to Rebuild a Downtown Area

## 5.1 Introduction

In the early 1990s, Los Angeles' image and stability were weakened by riots after police officers were acquitted in the beating of Rodney King. Gang violence not only made numerous neighborhoods dangerous places to live, but the killings and destruction of property destroyed families. The city's image as a place to live and work was severely damaged. Amidst a fear of cascading crime and increasing numbers of homeless people, the actions of Los Angeles police officers involved in the beating of Rodney King made it seem like violence defined life in Los Angeles. Parts of Los Angeles' descent into a state of lawlessness and chaos was captured in the popular 1991 movie *Grand Canyon*, in which the leading character and protagonist in the film laments that life should not be this hard after he rescues a white motorist taunted by a gun-wielding gang member.

In 1993 Richard Riordan, a Republican, was elected mayor after three decades of leadership by Democratic mayors. He promised voters that as a successful businessman he was "tough enough" to handle Los Angeles' violence and its other problems. Mr. Riordan personally financed his election campaign (he did not accept donations) and defeated city council member Michael Woo, in a city where a majority of the voters were nonwhite. Historians will debate Mr. Riordan's legacy, which included the hiring of 3,000 additional police officers and other changes designed to reduce crime, reduce levels of violence, and produce a new image for the city. Few would have imagined that when he asked a staff member to think about ways to improve the fate of downtown Los Angeles' $500 million convention center, an innovative public–private partnership for an arena and entertainment would both create a new brand and help revitalize downtown Los Angeles. In the years after the opening of L.A. LIVE, several other cities tried to create their versions of entertainment districts in their downtown areas, copying the design elements of L.A. LIVE.

The Los Angeles Convention Center opened in 1971 in the southern part of the downtown area with more than 200,000 square feet of exhibition space. When the facility failed to attract a robust number of conventions, public leaders focused on a dramatic expansion rather than on a set of complementing real estate developments to enhance the attractiveness of the adjoining area or neighborhood. Leaders were convinced that a convention center with 500,000 square feet available for meetings and exhibitions would succeed in ways that the smaller venue did not. While it is possible that a smaller facility discouraged some meeting planners from selecting Los Angeles, crime levels, the lack of adjacent hotels, the deterioration of the downtown area, and the lack of other amenities close to the center were likely contributing factors convincing convention planners to choose alternate Southern California destinations. Despite the logic that convention attendees are also attracted to centers close to a package of amenities, the convention center was expanded while downtown Los Angeles was losing residents and businesses to other parts of the city and region.

When Richard Riordan was elected mayor, the convention center had become a bit of a "white elephant," as public money was being used to cover both the capital costs supported by payments for the bonds sold for the center and its expansion and the operating costs not being funded by the events held at the venue. Mayor Riordan sought to reduce the hemorrhaging of tax money, and he also wanted ideas and a plan to improve the area around the facility. The convention center was located at the juncture of two of North America's busiest freeways. But when Dr. Charles Isgar started to think about what it would take to enhance the convention center and the adjoining area, even he did not envision what would take place. Two decades after being charged with the task of solving the convention center's problems, downtown Los Angeles was revitalized with a new arena and an entirely innovative entertainment complex. What made the project possible were the advertising and real estate development opportunities because of the presence of the freeways and land near the convention center that was available for redevelopment.

Almost two decades after the Staples Center opened and with the Nokia Theatre and L.A. LIVE completed, the impact from these efforts can now be assessed. Using its power of eminent domain and its willingness to transfer land to a private developer, the City of Los Angeles was able to achieve a set of goals charted by a mayor who wanted change and revitalization "fast tracked." Los Angeles is a major league winner, and the lessons learned can help other cities change subsidies for sports, entertainment, and cultural centers into investments for revitalization.

## 5.2 Thinking Outside the Box: Bringing the Lakers and Kings Downtown

When the new convention center expansion was dedicated, Dr. Charles Isgar, a member of Mayor Riordan's staff, attended the event. Looking at the deteriorating area surrounding the expanded center, he wondered why anyone would hold their annual meeting in an area with so little to offer visitors. San Diego's convention center, a mere 123 miles south, was set against the Pacific Ocean with easy access to a growing downtown area with restaurants. (The Gaslamp Quarter is across from San Diego's convention center and since 1986 had been redeveloped as an area for retail, restaurants, and entertainment.) Orange County's convention center was near Disneyland (28 miles from the Los Angeles Convention Center) and a host of other attractions in suburban Anaheim. Los Angeles had a convention center in a deteriorating downtown area that was crime-ridden, riddled by gang violence, and prone to race riots. A 500,000-square-foot facility could not succeed in that environment even if attractive alternatives were not nearby. If the downtown was to be revitalized, the image of the area had to be remade. Expanding a convention center's footprint would not change the image of downtown Los Angeles.

Dr. Isgar began to wonder what a new arena might mean for changing the area, and if an iconic facility could create an entirely new image for downtown Los Angeles. Why a new arena? The Los Angeles Lakers (NBA) and Kings (NHL) played their home games in a 30-year-old facility located in a suburban city. The Forum, while boasting an iconic image, was economically obsolete compared to the facilities being built for other teams. The Forum did not have any luxury suites or club seats, and those teams that played in facilities with those amenities were about to secure these new revenue streams. If they did, their ability to compete for the best players would make it more difficult for the Lakers and Kings to attract the talent needed to win championships. Several teams from the NBA and NHL were building or would soon plan for facilities with luxury suites, club seats, and numerous other revenue streams. The Lakers and Kings needed a new arena; Dr. Isgar recruited a respected developer, Mr. Steve Soboroff, to help convince the teams that downtown Los Angeles was the exact place for a state-of-the-art sports palace.[1]

If convincing the teams to relocate to downtown Los Angeles was not a sufficient challenge, there was one other political element that had to be addressed. The new facility would have to be built without any investment of funds from the City of Los Angeles. A majority of the members of the Los Angeles City Council were Democrats and would likely be eager to attack any plan from a Republican mayor offering subsidies for another big-ticket investment. A subsidy request by a mayor who himself was a wealthy real estate developer would be negatively portrayed as helping Los Angeles' regime gain/receive expanded access to public money. On the other hand, if the arena could be built with clear financial returns and no subsidies, Mayor Riordan would be a champion for a market-based approach to revitalize downtown Los Angeles. The challenge was to identify the peculiar and profitable assets that the downtown area could offer to the teams' owners that would make them willing to pay 100 percent of the costs for a new arena.

## 5.2.1 The Lakers, the Kings, and the Fabulous Forum

In 1947, the Lakers began play in Minneapolis as part of the National Basketball League (NBL). The team that was led by one of the first "big man" superstars, George Mikan, moved from the NBL to the Basketball Association of America in 1948, joining franchises from New York, Boston, Chicago, and Philadelphia. In 1949, the NBL and the Basketball Association of America merged and the NBA was created. The Minneapolis Lakers continued to be one of the league's dominant teams, attracting large crowds wherever they played. While the NBA had become a stable entity by 1960, the Lakers' owner sought a more profitable location. Watching the success of Walter O'Malley, who had moved the Dodgers to Los Angeles for the 1958 baseball season, the Lakers subsequently relocated to Los Angeles in 1960. The team decided to retain its nickname, the Lakers. The Lakers actually referred to the large vessels that traveled the Great Lakes. Some also linked the name to the ten thousand lakes of Minnesota. The Los Angeles area had neither ten thousand lakes nor the large ships that roamed the Great Lakes. Regardless, the Lakers have become one of the NBA's iconic franchises, and their trademark is recognized around the world.

The Los Angeles Lakers initially played their home games in the Los Angeles Memorial Sports Arena. Opened in 1959, the arena was adjacent to the Los Angeles Memorial Coliseum, and both facilities were in Exposition Park. Exposition Park is located directly across a large boulevard from the University of Southern California (USC). USC has played its home football games at the Coliseum for decades (and in 2008 signed a 25-year lease extension). The university also used the Los Angeles Memorial Arena for basketball games before opening its own facility, the Galen Center, closer to campus in 2006.

In 1965 the political and social geography of the Exposition Park area and downtown Los Angeles was severely impacted by the riots in the Watts neighborhood. While the Watts area is more than 5 miles from the sports facilities in Exposition Park and USC, the devastation from the riots and the impression of lawlessness had an impact on perceptions of the city and on its image. There were racial confrontations, riots, and violence in several other urban centers across the country. Several teams, including the Lakers, decided it was best to play their home games in arenas located in suburban cities distant from urban centers that were increasingly seen as unsafe and riddled by violence. Many teams also wanted facilities surrounded by acres of parking, given the increasing popularity and affordability of automobiles for an expanding middle class. The Lakers found a location for a new arena in suburban Inglewood. This location placed the Lakers closer to their largest concentration of their fans, even though it was a bit distant from the most robust employment centers. Inglewood, however, was much closer to the wealthier west side of the metropolitan area. Inglewood also provided convenient freeway access to basketball and hockey fans living throughout the region. As a developer-friendly city, Inglewood was willing to provide whatever resources were necessary to help build a new arena. Many believed that coordinating projects with Inglewood was much easier than working with either Los Angeles or the commissioners who oversaw the facilities in Exposition Park.[2]

In 1965 the Lakers' franchise was sold to Jack Kent Cooke, a Canadian-born entrepreneur who also wished to bring an NHL team to Los Angeles. Building a new suburban arena would make more sense and have a greater likelihood of being profitable if there were two tenants. In 1967 Mr. Cooke paid the NHL's $2 million fee to acquire the franchise rights for the region; consequently, the Los Angeles Kings was created. Mr. Cooke now had two teams for the new arena, meaning there would be at least 86 events (43 games for each team, plus additional games if either qualified for the play-offs) held in his arena. If he were successful in attracting entertainers, the circus, and other events, the Forum would be very profitable.

## 5.2.2 The Fabulous Forum and Its Limitations

The Forum was designed to be a showplace. Drawing inspiration from Rome's ancient forum, the arena's round shape permitted it to be surrounded by open parking lots that created the familiar look of a saucer-like building sitting amidst an asphalt ocean for cars. Convenient freeway access put the facility within easy reach of the overwhelming majority of the fans and the wealthiest parts of the region. While the Forum had no suites or club seats, its courtside seating became known as "Jack's seats" in honor of Jack Nicholson. These 2,400 folding chairs surrounding the court quickly became among the most expensive and desired seats for professional sports anywhere in the world. These seats not only were close to the great players that allowed the Lakers to make perennial play-off appearances, but also provided access to Jack Nicholson and other entertainers living and working in the region who became fixtures at Lakers' games.

Ironically, despite the notoriety of Jack's seats, the absence of luxury suites and club seats in the Forum created an opportunity for Dr. Isgar and Mr. Soboroff to see whether the Lakers and Kings would consider relocating to a new arena. When the Forum was built, the importance of luxury seating to a team's revenue streams and fiscal viability was still emerging. Although Jack's seats provided substantial revenue for the Lakers, combining luxury suites and clubs seats with Jack's seats would create a new level of prosperity for the team. When the Bulls opened their new arena in Chicago with luxury suites and club seats, it became clear the Lakers (and Kings) needed to have these same amenities if the teams were to be financially competitive. Arenas, however, need ample land in order to accommodate luxury seating and expansive corridors for the new additional retail selling points. It was not feasible to build the new arena adjacent to the Forum, as there was insufficient land available at the site for construction of a new venue while also providing fans with parking spaces for their cars. A search ensued to find a site large enough for a new arena that was near freeways, and where there was sufficient land for parking. Suddenly, downtown Los Angeles was "in the game," as it had land for an arena, space for parking, and it also offered access to the region's freeway system.

In the 1990s, luxury seating at sport facilities was a product that did not exist in the Los Angeles market. The Coliseum, where USC and UCLA, as well as the Rams and Raiders, played their home games for several seasons (but not at the same time; the Raiders moved to Los Angeles for a few years after the Rams had moved), had no club seats or suites.[3] The Rose Bowl also did not have luxury seating. A new arena, regardless of its location, would have the potential to offer businesses and sports fans a new product.

## 5.2.3 Arena Economics and the Appeal of Downtown Los Angeles

The people who would make the new arena a reality were the new owners of the Kings and Lakers. The ownership odyssey that brought the right set of entertainment and real estate entrepreneurs into place began in 1979 when Jack Kent Cooke sold the Lakers and Kings to Dr. Jerry Buss for $67.4 million ($231 million in 2013 dollars). At the time, this transaction was the largest ever for the purchase of sports teams in the United States. Since Dr. Buss' main interest, however, was basketball, in 1987 he sold the Kings to Bruce McNall. Mr. McNall would eventually sell controlling interest in the Kings to Philip Anschutz and Edward Roski. Then, in 1998, Dr. Buss would sell part of the Lakers to Mr. Anschutz for $268 million. Unlike Dr. Buss, who was focused on basketball, Mr. Anschutz was the head of an entertainment mega-corporation (Anschutz Entertainment Group (AEG)) and Mr. Roski was chairman of the board and chief executive officer of one of the largest privately held real estate companies, Majestic Realty. Their expertise and interests would attract them to the possibility of an arena becoming part of a larger entertainment district and real estate development project in which the teams would be the centerpieces or anchor attractions. AEG's main concern involved the assembly of land required for an arena and a large mixed-use entertainment complex.

Before officials from the City of Los Angeles contacted the owners of the Lakers and Kings, it turned out the teams' owners were already focused on building a new arena replete with luxury seating and an adjacent large-scale real estate development. There were three available options for the Lakers and the Kings, but two were impractical. First, the Forum could be extensively remodeled, or a new arena could be built adjacent to it in the parking lots that surrounded the existing facility. Remodeling the facility, however, presented a number of logistical problems. There were no viable options for the teams to play their home games during the renovation stages. If the renovations occurred during the off-season, the project would take several years. There would also be substantial opportunity costs, as closing the Forum for several months for 2 or 3 years would result in reduced revenues as concerts and other shows would have to be postponed. This would mean far less income for the owners of the Forum.

Second, building a new facility adjacent to the Forum would allow the teams to continue to play in the existing venue and avoid canceling concerts and shows. This option, however, had other problems or challenges. While the new facility was being built, there would be far less parking for fans attending games and shows. In the 1990s there was no realistic public or mass transportation option that could have been relied upon to provide fans an opportunity to attend games and shows.

The third or only realistic option was to assemble sufficient land elsewhere to permit the building of a new arena (and a large-scale entertainment center with additional opportunities for both commercial and residential development). As negotiations began and the team owners mentioned other locations for the project (in an effort to convince Los Angeles to offer more incentives), it became clear that a new arena was seen as a necessity and that there were few, if any, areas where sufficient land located adjacent to major freeways was available to permit the building of both a state-of-the-art arena and a large-scale entertainment and commercial complex. Indeed, the only area that offered exactly what was needed was in the downtown area less than 2 miles south of city hall.

## THE DISNEYFICATION OF SPORTS

A story that may or may not be an urban myth is that when Walt Disney looked at all of the development surrounding his Disneyland and the revenues others were realizing by locating near his park, he said, "If I do another park I would own all of the hotels and other activities that people enjoy when they visit Disneyland." Disney World was the result of that observation, containing several different amusement parks, numerous hotels and restaurants, and a host of other entertainment options and retail outlets to serve visitors.

Disney World established the concept of "tourism planning for the entire visitor's experience." Disneyfication refers to the inclusion of all consumption and related entertainment options being built within a lead entity or prime entertainment center and owned or controlled by the facility or team's owner. In the context of an arena, ballpark, or stadium, this would mean expanding the footprint of the facility to include space for all retail operations or associated entertainment options that fans or spectators would want on an event day. It would also mean that a franchise or facility owner could maximize its revenues if it controlled land adjacent to an arena, ballpark, or stadium where fans could be offered pregame and postgame entertainment or meeting places serving food and beverages to enhance the game day experience.

Disneyfication as a management strategy means that fans or spectators coming to a facility for an event are assured of a choice of complementing amenities. As a result, if a visitor is coming to a sporting event or a show, that person and his or her friends and family will have easy access to restaurants, hotels, and other public spaces that enhance their enjoyment and spending at the event. For Disney World this did not just mean offering visitors hotels for overnight stays, but also creating a mix of hotels providing higher-end luxury to those who want that product and more modest and moderately priced facilities for other families. Disney also wanted to offer families the opportunity to stay for several days or a week at his resort. To accomplish that goal of effectively providing enough amenities to offer a vacation, it also meant that other parks, events, and attractions needed to be created. Walt Disney World also offered a full range of restaurant choices and expanded retail outlets with expensive and moderately priced items. In later years, a Disney cruise line was added that included on-board day and evening camps to provide parents with a vacation after several days of chasing children around Disney World.

In relation to sports, Disneyfication means first and foremost a focus on the total experience and providing fans the luxury they want when attending a game and to offer a full set of clubs and other comforts and amenities. This leads to a wide range of price points, with more expensive seating providing the expected amenities. It also means providing improved sight lines for all fans to ensure that the team can meet the price points fans are willing to pay. Since fans usually enjoy food and beverages before and after events, it means building facilities with wide concourses that permit people to be served high-quality food and beverages in a relatively short amount of time. It means providing meeting spaces for people to network before and during the game. Every new facility also has expanded retail outlets for team merchandise. Lastly, it means also designing facilities to maximize the opportunities for advertising and for naming options. If an arena attracts a million or more visits in a given year, those attendees offer to advertisers the chance to deliver a sustained message about their products to an exclusive group of consumers who would be spending several hours in a set location watching an event.

The goal of the Disneyfication process is to offer to fans a complete, first-class experience that is perfect, clean, and comfortable. Dark and dank restrooms are artifacts of a bygone age, as are low-quality food and drink. In addition, the arenas and other sport facilities are designed to maximize the opportunity to use games and events as convenient and comfortable meeting places and places to enjoy sporting events and entertainment while engaging in extensive social networking. Facilities built in the 1960s were not designed with these assets or additional revenue sources.

Los Angeles' new arena was designed with 160 luxury suites that could be leased to clients for all Lakers and Kings games, and when the Clippers decided to play their home games at the new arena, the suites could also be leased for those games. The Staples Center also has 32 party suites that can be leased for an individual game or event. The facility has 2,500 premier or club seats (which offer food and beverage service at the seats and various other amenities). Staples Center seats 18,997 for basketball, 18,118 for hockey, and 20,000 for concerts. The facility itself contains 900,000 square feet with broad concourses and meeting places for people to network and watch the events at the same time. By comparison, the Fabulous Forum had seating for 17,505 fans for basketball, 16,005 for hockey, and 18,000 for concerts. It had no luxury suites; it did not have the broad concourses to support expanded sales and create meeting places. Without a new arena the team owners were leaving quite a bit of money on the table that fans were eager to spend.

The teams' owners, however, wanted to take Disneyfication to a new level. If they could also build an entertainment and mixed-use project adjacent to the arena, they could offer visitors multiple pre- and postgame activities as well as activities for fans who did not have a ticket to the game. All they needed was enough land close to the region's freeway system.

## 5.3 Downtown Los Angeles: Liabilities and Assets

In addition to a new arena, Los Angeles needed much more to change the image of the downtown area. While Mayor Riordan was initially focused on improving the performance of the convention center, he and his staff knew that the goal required changing downtown Los Angeles. Why did the downtown area have such a poor image and reputation while at the same time Hollywood and Westwood, both parts of the city, were still destinations valued by tourists and residents? Several factors contributed to the downtown's poor image. First, downtown is geographically distant from the city's preferred neighborhoods and tourist center. The downtown area is 7.3 miles from Hollywood and 13.7 miles from Westwood. For many residents and tourists, downtown was just not an important part of their experience or life in Los Angeles. Second, 53 people died during the riots that lasted 6 days after the verdict in the Rodney King case.[4] The riots accounted for more than $1 billion in property losses, and the damage to the city's image was incalculable. The beating of a white truck driver (Reginald Denny) hauled from his truck by African-Americans was broadcasted and then replayed countless times. Mr. Denny was not rescued by the police, but by black residents of the area who also saw the beating on television. All of North America saw rioters out of control, people being murdered, the wanton destruction of property, and a police department unable or unwilling to protect people and respond to a massive riot. Indeed, minutes after Mr. Denny was rescued, television cameras photographed the beating of Mr. Fidel Lopez by another mob. With both whites and Hispanics being singled out and violently attacked, Los Angeles appeared to millions to be a city locked into a series of endless racial violence and lawlessness.

Third, the entire Rodney King incident—from his arrest and beating to the acquittal of the police officers charged in the attack to the rioting where the police withdrew instead of rescuing innocent people—created an image that violence in Los Angeles was unchecked. While the events did not take place in the downtown area, it was impossible to separate images of civil unrest and wanton attacks from another part of the city. The announcement that the police were withdrawn while a white truck driver and Hispanic worker were singled out for attack further underscored to many that Los Angeles was a dangerous place for residents, visitors, and workers. Something spectacular was needed to create a new image. Fourth, the downtown area itself had other limitations. In 1993, office occupancy rates had declined by 30 percent[5] and hotel occupancy rates were also falling.[6] Downtown Los Angeles was hardly a place where a successful convention could be held. Only a truly extraordinary project could help to reverse these trends and images.

Ironically, while the downtown area had an image of being unsafe, crime rates actually declined in the area between 1993 and 1994. Property and violent crimes had been reduced by more than one-third since 1992, and the number of reported thefts declined 44 percent. Downtown Los Angeles, despite images of unlawfulness, was actually becoming a safer place to visit. Business owners reported that the perception of a lack of safety and gang violence was the reality they had to address regardless of the actual crime numbers released by the Los Angeles Police Department.[7]

Despite these problems or issues, downtown Los Angeles also offered some unique value or assets. Some of these were linked to the limitations of the Inglewood location. First, building a new facility in the parking lots adjacent to the Forum would have created 2 years' worth of severe parking problems. There were no other convenient locations available to replace the lost parking spots. In contrast, building a facility in downtown Los Angeles would mean operations could continue at the Forum. Second, while it might have been possible to build a new arena in Inglewood across from the existing facility, this location could not offer any other development opportunities, so an entertainment complex would not have been possible. The land surrounding the site to the west and east was primarily residential, and it was unrealistic to think it could have been acquired or taken in an eminent domain action. To the north was a cemetery, and unless the racetrack would be razed, there were really no possibilities for any additional development (see Figure 5.1). On the other hand, downtown Los Angeles had sufficient land for an arena and a large entertainment complex.

Third, Los Angeles was committed to assisting in the assembly of needed acreage. Land with convenient access to the region's freeway system was in short supply (this limitation still exists today and constrains the locations for a new stadium that could host a team from the NFL). Los Angeles County has more residents than any other county in the United States, but the large number of single-family homes produces a population density rate below that of San Francisco, Denver, and even neighboring Orange County. There are few, if any, large tracts of unencumbered land with convenient freeway access. The downtown Los Angeles site was adjacent to north-south and east-west freeways, and the city was willing to use its eminent

**Figure 5.1** The Forum (arrow), Hollywood Park Raceway, and the possible location for a new arena. (From Google Maps.)

**Figure 5.2    Land and location: The convention center, Staples Center, adjacent properties, and freeway access. (From Google Maps.)**

domain powers to ensure that land needed for an arena and an entertainment complex would be assembled and sold to the teams' owners.

The development opportunities available at the downtown Los Angeles site are vividly illustrated in Figure 5.2. Depicted is the convention center; the original building is the structure bounded by Pico Boulevard and Figueroa Street. The expansion that created the full-scale $500 million structure that prompted Mayor Riordan's call for a plan to enhance its fiscal performance includes the addition east of the Staples Center. The new development opportunity that became L.A. LIVE was the surface parking lots across from Chick Hearn Court. The land Los Angeles was willing to assemble through eminent domain, if needed, would provide ample space for a state-of-the-art arena and the dream that became L.A. LIVE. Notice also that the land offers excellent freeway access (see Figure 5.2). The Pasadena-Harbor Freeway (I-110) provides north-south access to the region. At the bottom left of Figure 5.3 is the intersection of I-110 with the Santa Monica Freeway (I-10), which provides the site with excellent east-west access.

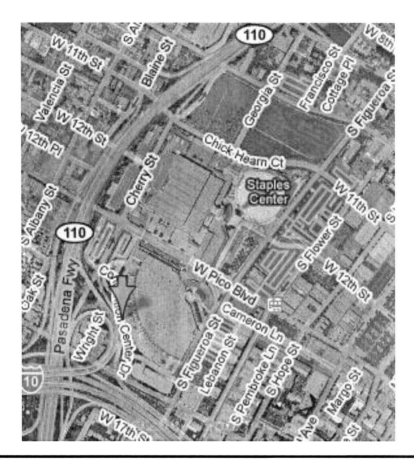

**Figure 5.3** Location, location, location: The intersection of the Harbor-Pasadena and Santa Monica Freeways and Staples Center. (From Google Maps.)

## 5.4 Sealing and Selling the Deal

Los Angeles had three goals it wanted to achieve during the negotiations with the teams' owners.[8] First, it wanted extraordinary facilities built as close as possible to the convention center in order to change the identity and image of the downtown area. Second, the city wanted all of the deteriorating buildings near the convention center replaced. Third, the new arena had to be built without any public subsidies. The assets of land, location near the freeway system, and a willingness to assemble the parcels needed for what became L.A. LIVE were obviously important to offer in exchange for the private sector's commitment to meet the city's goals. Given the risks associated with building a downtown arena in the 1990s, those assets might have not have been enough to get a new arena built without any tax dollars. Los Angeles, however, had one additional asset, and that one made building a facility without a subsidy possible. Los Angeles had a "deal maker."

The proposed site for the arena is adjacent to one of the busiest freeway interchanges in the world. The Santa Monica and Harbor Freeways have an average daily vehicle count of 325,000 (California Department of Transportation). This made the location extremely valuable in terms of the advertising *if* Los Angeles was willing to allow the team owners to strategically place advertising pylons so that messages would be visible to drivers on both freeways. Those pylons towering over the freeways would create a unique and extremely valuable revenue stream. In addition to a naming rights deal for the arena, the team owners would have an incentive no other city or location could offer. If the team owners were permitted to erect their advertising towers and Los Angeles assisted in assembling the land, each of the city's goals could be achieved.

Through creating the L.A. Arena Company, team owners agreed to build the arena and a large-scale entertainment complex directly across the street. The arena would be placed on land adjacent to the convention center, and the new headquarters hotel would be part of the entertainment complex. The L.A. Arena Company also had to sign a 25-year lease commitment guaranteeing that the Kings and Lakers would play at least 90 percent of their home games at the new venue. If for any reason the L.A. Arena Company went into bankruptcy, Los Angeles would own the arena and the land on which it stood. It was also agreed that Los Angeles would not incur any responsibility for debts created by the L.A. Arena Company if it defaulted. The teams' owners would be financially responsible for the obligations of the L.A. Arena Company.

To solidify the deal with AEG and Majestic Realty, Los Angeles was guaranteeing to agree to work with the convention center to permit the building of advertising towers (video displays) on land owned by the convention center. The desired video boards visible from both of the adjacent freeways would provide a substantial revenue stream for the L.A. Arena Corporation and its owners. Those entities would retain all revenues from the advertising sold, but would also be responsible for the total cost of building the new arena. In addition, the L.A. Arena Corporation would be required to pay a fee for use of the land upon which the arena would be built; a fee would also have to be paid for the land used for the advertising towers. The fee was approximately equal to the property taxes that would be paid if the land were owned by a private sector entity. In addition, to protect the public's interest in the sort of messages or advertising that would be displayed on publicly owned land within the City of Los Angeles, limitations were imposed on the sort of businesses and products that could be advertised. Los Angeles required that the arena not be named after any alcohol, beer, tobacco, or firearms company:[9]

> and no exterior signage will be placed on any Convention Center property which will contain alcohol (including beer), tobacco, or firearms advertisements. The Venture [L.A. Arena Company, LLC] would be allowed to place beer advertisements on a pylon on Venture property,

but would not be allowed to place tobacco, firearms, or other alcohol advertisements on the pylon. The Venture proposes a marquee and/or temporary display at the entrance to the Arena which would announce events being held at the Arena. If the name of the event sponsor is an alcohol, tobacco, or firearms company, the name may appear on the marquee or temporary display.

The L.A. Arena Company wanted two locations for its advertising towers/video displays that would be built on land owned by the convention center adjacent to the I-10 and I-110 Freeways. The locations selected had to be mutually acceptable to Los Angeles and the Venture, but the pylons at both sites had to be "viewed from the 10 Freeway and the 110 Freeway."[10] The Venture was given 7 years to develop a convention center hotel and a complex of restaurant and entertainment facilities. The Venture, before initiating construction of the entertainment complex and convention center hotel, had to submit a master plan for the proposed project. Los Angeles also had the authority to approve or request modifications to the plan, and its approval was required before construction on the project could begin.[11] One of the two advertising pylons at the heart of the public–private partnership for the arena and the entertainment complex is shown in Figure 5.4.

**Figure 5.4**  The advertising pylon that made an arena and entertainment complex possible. (Courtesy of Mark S. Rosentraub.)

## 5.5 Los Angeles' Investment and Returns

To assemble the land and build the needed infrastructure for the arena, the public sector had to invest $71.1 million. The cost of the arena has been estimated at between $375 and $400 million. With this much spent for the facility (in 1999 dollars), Los Angeles received a "Taj Mahal" of arenas. This was an important objective for Mayor Riordan's administration that was actively engaged with several partners in numerous projects to rebuild the entire downtown area. Los Angeles' goal was for the construction of a first-class arena and a venue that would help redefine the image of the downtown area. When the final cost was realized and announced, Los Angeles knew it had an extraordinary asset for its downtown redevelopment effort.

The breakdown of the investments made by each partner is detailed in Figure 5.5a and b. The private sector paid for 81 percent of the total cost if the final construction cost was $375 million. If the final cost of the Staples Center was approximately $400 million, the private sector was responsible for 82 percent of

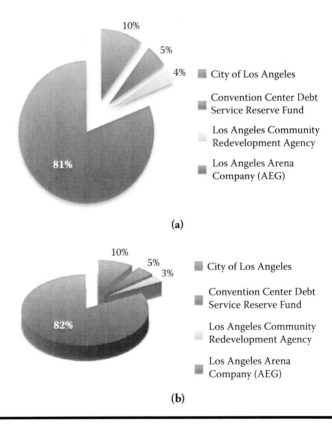

(a)

(b)

Figure 5.5    The investments made to build the Staples Center by each partner by percentage. (a) If the facility cost $375 million. (b) If the facility cost $400 million.

## PROTECTING THE PUBLIC'S INTEREST

The public sector's share of the costs for the Staples Center under either scenario would be considered somewhat larger than was typical or expected at the time for an arena built in a market as large as Los Angeles. Were Los Angeles and its public sector partners losers in the sense that a subsidy was provided? The answer lies in the terms of the lease and the revenue streams that were dedicated to the public sector.

The funds expended by Los Angeles and the convention center were to be repaid by revenues generated by the arena. The L.A. Arena Corporation and AEG guaranteed that if the pledged revenues did not materialize, the company would be responsible for providing the needed revenues to Los Angeles and the convention center. Thus, if it is assumed, just for the sake of argument, that the $12.6 million from the Community Redevelopment Agency was never repaid, the public investment declines to a maximum of 4 percent. That would have made the Staples Center deal among the most favorable negotiation at the time by any city.[13] The resulting private real estate development in the downtown area also produced sufficient new tax revenues to ensure that the city and the redevelopment agency both earned real economic benefits offsetting the total investment each had made in the arena. In summary, the new development downtown produced more than enough new revenues to provide Los Angeles and the development authority with sufficient income to give each a positive return on their investments.

the project's cost.[12] Los Angeles borrowed $38.5 million, equal to approximately 10 percent of the project's cost. The Los Angeles Convention Center committed $20 million (approximately 5 percent of the project's cost) drawn from the interest it earns on its reserve fund to pay its bonds. The Los Angeles Community Redevelopment Agency invested $12.6 million, and therefore was responsible for between 3 and 4 percent of the project's costs (see Figure 5.5a and b).

To ensure repayment of its investment of $71.1 million, the public sector received a portion of the parking fees collected and the proceeds from a ticket tax. Given projected attendance levels, the anticipated revenue was expected to produce more than enough new income to meet these obligations. When the contract was presented to the city council, there was concern that taxpayers might not be completely protected from any potential losses. While partisan politics might have played a role in the emerging opposition, the matter was quickly resolved when AEG agreed to be responsible for any financial shortfalls in Los Angeles' ability to retire the debt on the bonds or replace the lost interest from the convention center's bond repayment fund. As the $12.6 million investment by the Community Redevelopment Authority occurred later, the public sector received no guarantees on its repayment. That investment would have to be sustained or repaid by new taxes.

## 5.5.1 Were the Taxpayers Protected?

Los Angeles sold bonds to finance its investment. Those bonds obligated the city to annual payments of $3,872,694. The public sector had other costs. There was lost interest by using money from the convention center's repayment fund, amounting to $900,000 each year. The Arena Company was also responsible for paying $451,830 for the use of city-owned property (Los Angeles 1998: Annex B, Annex C).[14] This meant that Los Angeles needed to receive $5,232,099 each year in extra revenue to offset its investment. The revenues received from each source are identified in Table 5.1, and "Annual Balance" refers to the cash remaining after the $5,232,099 is repaid. The credits refer to Los Angeles' Jobs Incentive Credit Program. Firms that create jobs in Los Angeles receive tax credits, and the Arena Company was entitled to this benefit too. The value or credit given for each job created was specified in the gap funding agreement.[15] At the end of the 2008 fiscal year, the entire debt was repaid with a surplus of $6.2 million (see Table 5.1). That surplus grows each year as Los Angeles continues to receive income from the dedicated revenues. The ticket tax remains in effect, and the city continues to receive a share of all parking revenues.

In 2003, Los Angeles and AEG agreed that for a single one-time payment of $14,700,000 and a payment of $1,800,000 to cover related city administrative costs, the developers and teams would be released from any obligations to offset future revenue shortfalls. Given that a shortfall was encountered just once and

**Table 5.1 Payments to Los Angeles to Sustain Its Investment in the Staples Center**

|  | Admission Tax | Pre-payment | Parking | Interest | Credits | Total | Annual Balance |
|---|---|---|---|---|---|---|---|
| 2001 | $3,248,429 |  | $96,433 | $585,931 | $3,989,577 | $7,920,370 | $2,695,846 |
| 2002 | 4,474,167 |  | 172,658 | 4,674 | 1,330,872 | 5,982,371 | 757,847 |
| 2003 | 4,013,673 | 405,088 | 168,955 | 744,667 | 780,272 | 6,112,655 | 888,131 |
| 2004 | 4,005,049 | 828,277 | 348,859 | 110,250 | 479,418 | 5,771,853 | 547,329 |
| 2005 | 3,197,584 | 1,075,751 | 186,027 | 70,938 | 0 | 4,530,300 | −694,224 |
| 2006 | 5,250,282 | 1,031,652 | 482,968 | 20,044 | 0 | 6,784,946 | 1,560,422 |
| 2007 | 3,984,224 | 987,909 | 1,289,167 | 124,430 | 0 | 6,385,730 | 1,161,206 |
| 2008 | 4,000,000 | 949,000 | 800,000 | 100,000 | 0 | 5,849,000 | 624,476 |
| Estimated cumulative balance on June 30, 2008 |  |  |  |  |  |  | $6,184,034 |

*Source:* City of Los Angeles year-end financial reports and 2008 budget.

that the revenue streams were performing to expectations, the offer from the teams yielded a very favorable outcome for Los Angeles.

The column labeled "Credits" also involves expenses that AEG paid with the city's permission that were related to the arena and the development of the area. In 1998 the city and AEG agreed that a set of expenses for development that were under consideration by the city council to constitute Los Angeles' responsibility—if paid for by AEG—could be considered as part of the financial contribution of the company to the project. The Los Angeles City Council would review each expenditure to see if AEG's claim that the expense should be considered part of the city's responsibilities was valid.

Only in 2005 did an actual shortfall occur, but with the accrued surpluses from previous years, Los Angeles had more than enough revenue in its arena account to make its required bond payment. While there was no subsidy from the city to have the arena built—and Los Angeles continues to receive revenues from the dedicated streams and through the rental payments made by the Arena Corporation—there is still the matter of the $12.6 million from the Community Reinvestment Agency. That expenditure represents less than 2 percent of the money spent by AEG for Staples Center, the Nokia Theatre, and L.A. LIVE. Before moving on to the issue of the level of development in downtown Los Angeles, it is important to determine if the growth in property taxes or other revenue streams repays that commitment as well.

In a report prepared in 2003 for Los Angeles' controller, Professor Robert A. Baade found that new developments near the arena generated $3,399,034 annually in new property taxes. If it is assumed that the new buildings were only built because of the presence of the arena, these tax dollars represent new revenue. As the area was languishing for years prior to the building of the arena, it is reasonable to expect that these taxes represent new income.[16]

Using a 7-percent discount rate on the full increment of $3,399,034, and assuming there is no additional development, the investment of $12.6 million was completely repaid by mid-2006. If it is assumed that just half of the development was a result of the presence of the new arena ($1,667,952)—or that other development would have taken place generating 50 percent of the property taxes, even if the arena was not built in the downtown area or elsewhere in Los Angeles—the loan from the Community Reinvestment Agency was repaid by mid-2012. Under either assumption it can be concluded that the revenues to repay the Community Reinvestment Agency's investment were realized in a relatively short period of time (see Table 5.2). As a result, the entire public sector investment in the arena was repaid and the public sector continues to receive new income each year.

There are other taxes that are paid by AEG and the teams that were not included in this tabulation that yield returns for Los Angeles. For example, AEG pays $4 million each year in possessory interest charges based on its use of public land that is exempt from property taxes.[17] There is also a gross receipts tax paid by AEG for the arena's operations—approximately $300,000 each year. The Lakers and the

**Table 5.2    Repaying the $12.6 Million Investment by Los Angeles'
Community Reinvestment Agency (7-Percent Discount Rate Applied)**

| Year | Tax Growth 100 Percent | Repayment at 100 Percent | Tax Growth at 50 Percent | Repayment at 50 Percent |
|------|------------------------|--------------------------|--------------------------|-------------------------|
| 2002 | $3,399,034 | $3,399,034 | $1,667,952 | $1,667,952 |
| 2003 | 3,161,102 | 6,560,136 | 1,551,195 | 3,219,147 |
| 2004 | 2,939,825 | 9,499,961 | 1,442,612 | 4,661,759 |
| 2005 | 2,734,037 | 12,233,998 | 1,341,629 | 6,003,388 |
| 2006 | 2,542,654 | 14,776,652 | 1,247,715 | 7,251,103 |
| 2007 | | | 1,160,375 | 8,411,478 |
| 2008 | | | 1,079,149 | 9,490,627 |
| 2009 | | | 1,003,608 | 10,494,235 |
| 2010 | | | 933,356 | 11,427,591 |
| 2011 | | | 868,021 | 12,295,612 |
| 2012 | | | 807,259 | 13,102,871 |

*Source:* Baade, R.A., *Los Angeles City Controller's Report on Economic Impact: Staples Center* (Los Angeles: City of Los Angeles, Office of the Controller, 2003); Office of the Assessor, City of Los Angeles. Office of Controller, 200 N. Main Street, Room 300, Los Angeles, CA 90012. Laura N. Chick, controller.    Controller.lacity.org/stellent/groups/electedofficials/@CTR_contributor/documents/contributor_web_content/LACITYP_008662.pdf

Kings also pay taxes. These were *not* included in Tables 5.1 or 5.2, as an argument could be made that all of those taxes would have been paid as long as the new arena was built somewhere in Los Angeles County.

## 5.5.2 Rebuilding Downtown: Housing

The arena's development coincided with the building of a substantial number of new residences in downtown Los Angeles. From the date of the announcement of the agreement to build the arena through the fourth quarter of 2011, a total of 28,861 residential units were built in downtown Los Angeles. This means that there were almost four times as many residential units in the downtown area as there were prior to the opening of the Staples Center. More importantly, in 1999, 72.6 percent of the units were affordable, meaning the area was economically segregated. By 2011, market rate housing accounted for 50.3 percent of the residential units. Some might fear that an emphasis on market rate housing would mean an absence

**Table 5.3    Downtown Housing: Units Built through 2011**

| Time Period | Housing Type | | Total |
| --- | --- | --- | --- |
| | *Affordable* | *Market Rate* | *Total* |
| Prior to 1999 | 8,445 | 2,532 | 11,626 |
| 1999 to 2011 | 11,038 | 17,823 | 28,861 |
| Total | 19,483 | 20,355 | 40,487 |

*Source:* www.downtownla.com/pdfs/about/2011-DCBID-Annual-Report. pdf

of new units for families with limited budgets. The number of new affordable rate units built in the area more than doubled the supply of these homes from what existed prior to 1999. The downtown area is thus more economically integrated, and there has been a dramatic increase in the supply of affordable or below-market-rate housing that exists in the area (see Table 5.3). If there was a fear that building the arena and L.A. LIVE would lead to an elimination of housing opportunities for moderate-income households, the data suggest that such an outcome did not occur.

# 5.6  Rebuilding Downtown Los Angeles: L.A. LIVE

Within 7 years of the signing of all agreements, development on L.A. LIVE was to be initiated, including the hotel for the convention center. AEG began to purchase the land across from the arena soon after its construction began. The redevelopment agency acquired a few parcels through its power of eminent domain, and then sold the land to AEG for the price it paid, ensuring that taxpayers did not subsidize the land acquisition costs for the promised hotel or the new entertainment complex. The use of eminent domain to transfer property from one private owner to another—which the U.S. Supreme Court would uphold—remains a policy issue that raises important equity issues. After the Supreme Court's decision, several states passed laws making the use of eminent domain to transfer property from one private sector owner to another more difficult. Relative to the issue of developing downtown Los Angeles, or remaking it, the redevelopment authority purchased land and then transferred it at cost to AEG. The use of the public sector's power can be considered a subsidy or an incentive to ensure a type of development chosen by the city council does take place. To the extent that eminent domain reduces the costs to the developer, one could argue that a subsidy exists. There was, however, no fiscal subsidy by taxpayers in terms of the costs of land and its assembly for the proposed development. AEG even paid a price slightly higher than what was paid to secure the land through eminent domain to repay the public sector for the costs of the eminent domain process.

While construction was still underway in 2009, the Nokia Theatre at L.A. LIVE opened in October 2007 with seating for 7,100. The theatre is set at one end of the Nokia Plaza, which was designed to be Los Angeles' Times Square. The plaza has become a popular meeting place and open-air seating and hospitality services. When events and games are played or presented at the Staples Center, video is available to patrons enjoying the plaza. ESPN's West Coast broadcast center is located at L.A. LIVE. The complex is also home to a 14-screen multiplex movie theatre, the Grammy Museum, and the Staples Center hosts the annual Grammy Awards. A private theatre with 880 seats was also built for private screenings of movies. In 2013 there were also 18 restaurants or pubs at L.A. LIVE. L.A. LIVE is a destination and offers a wide-ranging set of amenities to residents of the downtown area, visitors, convention attendees, and spectators at games and events at the Staples Center.

When AEG was unable to attract a partner to share the cost of building a hotel, negotiations were reopened with Los Angeles. AEG wanted the city to make an investment to offset the additional capital it would need since no other partner was interested in building a hotel in downtown Los Angeles. This represented a material change in the original contract.

AEG proposed that Los Angeles invest all of the hotel tax revenue it would be receiving from guests for a period of 25 years. AEG wanted that money transferred to the company to allow it to pay part of the cost of building the hotel. It was estimated that this would represent an investment of $246 million by Los Angeles. AEG also asked the city for a $16 million interest-free loan to be repaid across 4 years, and that $4 million in development fees be waived.[18] Lastly, AEG asked the Community Redevelopment Agency to invest $10 million to pay for needed infrastructure costs. In 2006, the redevelopment agency also approved a transfer of $5 million in extra revenue from another downtown tax increment financing district to be used for infrastructure at L.A. LIVE. The Los Angeles City Council agreed to each of these requests.

To calculate the total public sector investment in the L.A. LIVE project (including the convention center hotel), a present value calculation was performed using a 5 percent discount rate.[19] The present value of the public sector's investment in L.A. LIVE was $167.6 million. The present value of the transfer of $246 million of hotel taxes across 25 years is $145.6 million. The present value of the foregone interest for the 4-year loan was estimated at $2.98 million. (The loan has since been repaid.) The waiving of development fees ($4 million) and the investment by the Community Redevelopment Agency ($15 million) were included at full value and not discounted.

What is Los Angeles getting in return for this investment?

The convention center hotel is 49 stories tall, adding to Los Angeles' skyline. Eighteen floors house a Marriott Hotel with 878 rooms. A Ritz-Carlton Hotel uses 5 floors and contains 123 rooms. A total of 26 floors are "Ritz Residences" with 224 condominium units. While there were hopes for a larger hotel, at 1,001 rooms the Los Angeles Convention Center will have an extraordinary convention headquarters hotel within a very short walk of its main entrance. While there is indeed disappointment that the promised hotel linked to the arena required a substantial investment by the city, it is equally true that the anticipated entertainment complex is far more elaborate than originally thought and beyond the scope of the original agreement. In exchange for the material adjustment to the original agreement, AEG was proposing to build a far more extensive complex and its investment in the project was at least $2.5 billion.

Many communities might conclude that a public investment of $167.6 million that leverages $2.5 billion in private funds is worth the change to the original agreement. That original agreement, however, did not include any additional public money for the entertainment complex or hotel. If that scenario were fulfilled, the gains for the public sector in terms of new tax revenues would have occurred without any public investment. With the new investments, the leveraging ratio is still an impressive commitment of 15 private sector dollars for every public sector dollar invested. Regardless of the rationalization used, Los Angeles invested $167.6 million to have the hotel built as part of a $2.5 billion entertainment, commercial offices, and residential project. Did Los Angeles need another entertainment center that warranted a $167.6 million subsidy?

Some critics suggested that the Nokia Theatre would just compete with the Staples Center, the Shrine Auditorium, the Gibson Auditorium at Universal City's City Walk, and the Forum in Inglewood.[20] The Nokia Theatre, however, was designed to capture events from New York and other cities and award presentations that were not held at those facilities (Riley-Katz 2007). Some of the events held at the Nokia Theatre have included the Grammy Awards and the American Idol competition (later moved to the Staples Center). These are important successes, but it also true that many entertainment venues in Los Angeles were built without subsidies.

In the absence of the building of L.A. LIVE it is possible that other forms of development might have taken place. Would it have been reasonable to expect $2.5 billion of activity within a few years? That seems highly unlikely, but just as in the case of the Ballpark District in San Diego, the public–private partnership established with AEG meant that the development would occur in a very short period of time. Los Angeles' elected leadership unanimously supported the idea of ensuring that the development took place in the shortest period of time. The Staples Center, the cornerstone of the development, is depicted in Figure 5.6; L.A. LIVE is depicted in Figure 5.7.

## 5.7  Rebuilding Downtown—Other Iconic Projects

The rebuilding of downtown Los Angeles included several other projects, two of which had no connection with Staples Center and L.A. LIVE. Together, however, the completion of Disney Hall (see Figure 5.8)—the new home of the Los Angeles Philharmonic Orchestra and the new cathedral, Our Lady of the Angels (see Figure 5.9)—identified downtown Los Angeles as a home to iconic projects. The arena and L.A. LIVE at the southern end of downtown and a cultural amenity,

**Figure 5.6   The Staples Center. (Courtesy of Mark S. Rosentraub.)**

**Figure 5.7   L.A. LIVE, the Nokia Plaza, and hotel complex. (With thanks to Mr. Chris Wells.)**

## COMMUNITY DEVELOPMENT AND L.A. LIVE

The focus of several cities, elected officials, and growth regimes on sports facilities for redevelopment of downtown areas has been criticized for an emphasis on tourism and consumption that produces few, if any, benefits for lower- and moderate-income residents. This has prompted calls for programs that advance community development. Economic development has as its focus the increment in wealth generated by projects without respect to the distribution of those benefits. Community development emphasizes a balance in the distribution of benefits and ensuring that groups and neighborhoods traditionally ignored or made worse off by revitalization efforts have their interests protected. With their focus on tourism, recreation, and consumption, the Staples Center and L.A. LIVE could easily fall in to the trap of displacing people and businesses that were part of a lower-income neighborhood while attracting and entertaining the wealthy.

Community benefits agreements have emerged as a tool by which neighborhoods or cities negotiate with developers to ensure that there is a set of direct benefits for lower-income individuals and neighborhoods. Professor Saito had observed that redevelopment programs in Los Angeles had an almost time-honored tradition of adversely impacting low-income and minority neighborhoods.[21] In response, the Los Angeles City Council passed legislation requiring the payment of living wages (1997) and created its first community benefits agreement in 1998.

To avoid any conflict, AEG agreed to a community benefits agreement that included several commitments. First, AEG agreed to fund an assessment of the need for parks, open space, and recreational facilities in an area south and west of L.A. LIVE, and to provide at least $1 million to develop the recommended assets. Second, AEG also agreed to create and manage a residents' parking program to ensure sufficient on-the-street automobile parking for residents not displaced by the redevelopment effort or living in newly constructed condominiums and apartments. AEG's investment in the program was set at not less than $25,000 for the initial 5 years of the program's operation.

Third, AEG also agreed that at least 70 percent of the jobs associated with L.A. LIVE's development, construction, and operation would offer living wages as defined by the Los Angeles City Council. The level established by the Council in 2001, as living wage, was $16,058 if health insurance benefits were also provided, and $18,658 in the absence of that benefit. Fourth, training programs were established to ensure that people living within 3 miles of the Staples Center and L.A. LIVE would have an opportunity to gain the skills required for employment. Fifth, AEG also agreed to ensure that between 500 and 800 new affordable rental units were built in the immediate area. These units had to remain affordable for 30 years, with minimum and maximum income levels established by the city council. These units had to be within a 3-mile radius of the Staples Center and L.A. LIVE development. Sixth, AEG pledged to work with local community groups to develop more affordable rate housing units in the area. Seventh, AEG also agreed to provide $650,000 to one or to a combination of identified community organizations to assist in the building of affordable apartments. Lastly, AEG also agreed to be responsible for the relocation of families displaced by the building of the arena or of the L.A. LIVE complex.

Disney Hall, on the north established the endpoints or bookends for the revitalization strategy. Los Angeles joined Indianapolis and Cleveland in using both sports and cultural amenities to anchor its redevelopment efforts.

Disney Hall—a project Lillian Disney helped launch with a $50 million gift to create a memorial for her father, Walt—would take more than 16 years to complete. The 1994 Northridge earthquake damaged the structure, raising costs, while several other crises led to additional cost overruns. In addition, the original cost estimate failed to include the expense for a new parking garage. After every problem

**Figure 5.8    Disney Hall. (Courtesy of Mark S. Rosentraub.)**

**Figure 5.9    Our Lady of the Angels Cathedral. (Courtesy of Mark S. Rosentraub.)**

was addressed, the $274 million edifice opened in 2003. Our Lady of the Angels cost $189.7 million and opened in 2002.

## 5.8  Conclusions

What became Staples Center and L.A. LIVE—and the thousands of housing units after the arena was built—was a result of an effort to resuscitate a "dying convention center." As described by Los Angeles' chief legislative analyst, the housing and the other developments were the "gravy" or "the very welcome and unexpected unintended consequences" of a project designed to save the convention center.[22] Even the fact that the arena and L.A. LIVE became bookends of the redeveloping area of downtown (paired with Disney Hall) was basically good fortune. There were broad strokes of a plan for revitalizing downtown Los Angeles that spanned the administrations of two mayors, yet there was no real strategic plan. Some community leaders reported that a vision and exciting ideas were lacking for the revitalization process of the downtown area. The money being lost by the convention center was just another example of the mismanagement of the entire downtown area. Many civic leaders concluded the convention center was placed in the worst part of downtown hoping something good would happen. Rarely, if ever, does hoping cause something good to happen.

The problems did not end with the lack of a strategic plan or vision. The city had failed for more than 20 years to find any investor interested in building a headquarters hotel for the convention center hotel. Have things improved for the convention center in the post-arena era? With a larger number of events, the convention center generates enough revenue to cover its operating costs.

Leaving the convention center issue aside, building the arena was a fiscal success. By assembling land and permitting the construction of two advertising towers, Los Angeles was able to have an arena built at no public cost. In addition, the city's receipt of specific revenues from the operation of the arena ensures that it will receive a positive cash flow for decades. The public sector did have to make a large investment to have the entertainment complex and hotel built, but that ensured that L.A. LIVE would be an extraordinary entertainment and commercial center replete with residences. Leveraging $15 in investments from AEG for each dollar it committed, made Los Angeles a major league winner when it comes to L.A. LIVE too.

The arena deal was also a success. In January 2013, *Forbes* valued the Los Angeles Lakers at $1 billion. The Lakers are the second most valuable NBA franchise, trailing the Knicks by $100 million.[23] *Pollstar* annually ranks the world's most successful arenas. The Staples Center is seventh in the world and ranked first in the United States by tickets sold for entertainment events despite the presence of four professional sports teams.[24]

Was the arena responsible for the revitalization of downtown Los Angeles?

Local officials and community leaders believe that had the arena not been built, and if L.A. LIVE was never created, not only would the convention center have never seen a new hotel, but the housing and office boom that propelled the redevelopment would also have never taken place. Carol E. Schatz, president and CEO of the Central City Association of Los Angeles, labels Staples Center as the catalyst for the downtown's resurgence. In her view, there was no real revitalization prior to the announcement that the arena would be built in the downtown area. Under her leadership and the support of the Center City Association, the adaptive reuse ordinance was also passed, which helped expedite the conversion of commercial properties into apartments and condominiums. The policy offers developers (1) expedited review and exemptions from commercial corner development regulations and (2) exemptions from updates in planning codes relative to floor area ratios, height, residential density, and parking. The ordinance also excludes mezzanines from floor area ratio calculations. This made conversions of commercial properties to residential condominiums and apartments easier to finance. The ordinance was passed in December 2001.

Los Angeles received a state-of-the-art arena built where it wanted and needed, and did so without offering a subsidy. Staples Center continues to produce annual revenues for Los Angeles. In terms of the convention center hotel and the L.A. LIVE complex, Los Angeles did make an investment. Its financial returns there, however, are substantial. Some would take issue with Los Angeles extending the Jobs Credit Program to the Arena Corporation and allowing those funds to be counted toward repayment of the obligation to the city. Again, the magnitude of the investment dwarfs the scale of the concession, and the program existed for all businesses, not just for the Arena Corporation. The jobs credit was another subsidy that raised Los Angeles' overall investment in the project.

Los Angeles, like San Diego, channeled development to a part of downtown that had languished for years. Many thought that without new investments steered by the public sector to the area, little improvement would occur. Critics of the L.A. LIVE project correctly noted that Los Angeles had many valuable and popular tourist and entertainment destinations. Did it really need another set of complexes, especially one that required a subsidy?

The answer to that question lies in Los Angeles' leadership's desire to change the location of some economic activity produced by entertainment and tourism from Hollywood to downtown Los Angeles. The investment of $500 million in the convention center had not produced any meaningful returns. Leadership feared that without a substantial relocation of economic activity, the convention center would continue to lose money and the area would also continue to deteriorate. Indeed, to thwart that deterioration, a far larger public investment might have been required. Instead, trading location, land assembly, and a small subsidy (compared to the private investment made), the area was rebuilt and transformed within a decade.

The transformation lead to an entirely different land use pattern, but a new neighborhood was created. Los Angeles ensured that a large number of below-market-rate apartments were built, and even required, through the community benefits agreement, that AEG provide a modest investment to permit community organizations to build additional housing to serve moderate- and low-income families. AEG's involvement with community organizations also created an opportunity for these groups to benefit from the substantial expertise that the corporation has in real estate development. While the neighborhood has been changed and some families were relocated, the benefits substantially exceeded the costs. Given the number of new below-market-rate apartments created, the benefits extend beyond those usually enjoyed by the upper and middle classes. The decision to use public resources to relocate a substantial amount of tourist and entertainment activity could also be criticized. That policy decision, however, was carefully weighed, and on numerous occasions was unanimously reaffirmed by the city council and different mayors.

It is also important to note that property values and the population in the downtown area have substantially increased. In 1999, 18,700 people lived in the downtown area. In 2011, 46,414 people lived in the downtown area. Los Angeles' downtown area is a residential community. While Mayor Riordan was initially focused only on making the convention center more successful, it is probably fair to conclude that he would have been very pleasantly surprised to know that in a span of 11 years, the residential population would more than double and the area would become an economically integrated community. As important as is the establishment of a viable, economically integrated downtown neighborhood, the growth in property values underscores the financial return to the public sector from the fiscal investments. In 1999, the assessed value of real estate in the nearby downtown area

**Table 5.4    Growth in the Assessed Value of Real Estate in Downtown Los Angeles, 1999–2010**

| Year | Assessed Value | |
| | Absolute | In 1999 Dollars |
|------|----------|----------------|
| 1999 | $4,838,421,305 | $4,838,421,305 |
| 2000 | 5,025,431,988 | 4,891,460,164 |
| 2001 | 5,260,525,694 | 4,936,061,516 |
| 2002 | 5,544,496,087 | 5,143,764,580 |
| 2003 | 5,688,391,189 | 5,143,658,076 |
| 2004 | 6,045,596,904 | 5,363,345,418 |
| 2005 | 7,002,900,943 | 6,033,437,991 |
| 2006 | 7,853,144,506 | 6,506,664,863 |
| 2007 | 8,695,487,916 | 7,058,081,696 |
| 2008 | 9,301,781,581 | 7,240,300,899 |
| 2009 | 9,326,410,136 | 7,257,305,169 |
| 2010 | 8,851,402,207 | 6,711,456,537 |

*Source:* Downtown Center Business Improvement District. "Downtown Los Angeles: Demographic Study, 2011."

was $4.8 billion. In 2010, in the aftermath of the recession, property was valued at $8.9 billion (unadjusted dollars). In 2009, property values had risen to $9.3 billion (unadjusted dollars), but declined in 2010 as a result of the severe recession and its effects on real estate values. Most importantly, in inflation-adjusted dollars, the value of real estate in the downtown area *increased* from $4.9 billion to $6.7 billion, or by 37.2 percent, from 1999 to 2010 (see Table 5.4).

Given its size, do any of Los Angeles' decisions, options, or actions offer lessons for other cities? There are indeed some important lessons. Los Angeles used a willingness to assemble land with excellent access to the region's transportation system with the unique value of outdoor advertising along transportation networks to secure a large-scale private sector investment. Other communities might have similar locations that could be used to leverage private investments, and all have the ability to assemble land. The ability to assemble land at a very desirable location that could leverage signage and advertising may well be the important lesson for all cities that Los Angeles offers. Los Angeles' leadership used those assets to attract private capital to what was regarded as a highly undesirable downtown area.

# Endnotes

1. Interview conducted with Dr. Isgar on March 10, 2008.
2. Several individuals interviewed for this book observed that they had found the Coliseum to be a difficult board with important differences that impacted different negotiations. While it may well be that the Coliseum Commission is just shrewd in its negotiations, Farmer observed that some of the commission's proposals and its public disclosure may have created an unwarranted and unfounded reputation for a lack of flexibility: Farmer, S., Commission, Coliseum Commission still trying to find solution, *Los Angeles Times*, December 14, 2007, http://articles.latimes.com/2007/dec/14/sports/sp-newswire14 (accessed March 10, 2008).
3. The Los Angeles Rams played their home games at the Coliseum from 1946 until 1979, and then moved to Anaheim, where they played at Anaheim Stadium from 1980 through 1994. The Rams relocated to St. Louis in 1995. With no professional football team in Los Angeles, the Oakland Raiders relocated and played home games in Los Angeles at the Coliseum from 1982 to 1994. For the 1995 season the Raiders returned to Oakland. UCLA played its home games at the Coliseum from 1928 through 1981, and then made the Rose Bowl its home field after the Raiders moved to Los Angeles. UCLA never enjoyed playing on a field adjacent to its archrival's (USC) campus, and the presence of the Raiders made UCLA the third tenant. Those factors each contributed to the decision to relocate.
4. On March 3, 1991, Rodney King was apprehended by Los Angeles police officers and during his arrest he was assaulted. Someone who lived in the area where the arrest took place was able to videotape the assault. Several officers participated in the assault, and others appeared to let it occur without trying to intercede. Four of the officers were subsequently brought to trial, and after they were acquitted of all charges, civil protest ensued. Some people in the protests initiated their own level of violence, and several days of riots ensued. During the riots the police withdrew from the area and failed to restore order.
5. Hamashige, H., Downtown L.A. office rents tumble more than 30%: but high-rise towers ride out quake with little damage—Los Angeles, California—Special report: Quarterly real estate, *Los Angeles Business Journal*, January 31, 1994, http://findarticles.com/p/articles/mi_m5072/is_n4_v16/ai_15125486 (accessed March 8, 2008).
6. Deady, T., L.A. County hotel room occupancy shows a significant increase in 1993, *Los Angeles Business Journal*, March 7, 1994, as cited in *High-Beam Encyclopedia*, http://www.encyclopedia.com/doc/1G1-15277102.html (accessed April 1, 2008).
7. Turner, D., Police crackdown causes crime rate to plummet in downtown LA, *Los Angeles Business Journal*, April 3, 1995, online edition contained at BNET, http://findarticles.com/p/articles/mi_m5072/is_n14_v17/ai_17015000 (accessed March 10, 2008).
8. The negotiations were actually between the City of Los Angeles and the representatives of the Anschutz Entertainment Group (AEG) (owned by Phil Anschutz) and Ed Roski (owner of Majestic Realty and the Los Angeles Kings). AEG owned a portion of the Los Angeles Lakers, but Jerry Buss retained majority ownership of the Lakers. Mr. Buss was not interested in the real estate components of the overall deal and signed a long-term lease to have the Lakers play in the new arena. Majestic Realty and AEG created a new company, the L.A. Arena Corporation. In short order, Mr. Roski would sell the

Los Angeles Kings to AEG. In essence, the overall deal involved at least four companies: the Los Angeles Lakers, the Los Angeles Kings, the L.A. Arena Corporation, and AEG, which owns L.A. LIVE.

9. Los Angeles, *Proposed arena at the Los Angeles Convention Center—Memorandum to the Ad Hoc Committee on the Sports Arena from Keith Comrie, City Administrative Officer and Ronald Deaton, Chief Legislative Analyst* (Los Angeles: Office of the City Council, 1997), 4.

10. L.A. Arena Company, LLC, *Proposal for L.A. Arena Company LLC to Los Angeles City Council, Mayor Richard Riordan, Los Angeles Convention and Exhibition Center, and the Los Angeles Community Redevelopment Agency* (Los Angeles: Office of City Council, 1996), 10.

11. Los Angeles, *Los Angeles Convention Center Arena: Proposal summary. Internal memorandum, City Council* (Los Angeles: Office of the City Council, 1997).

12. It might seem a bit peculiar that a decade or more after the building of the Staples Center there is still debate over the project's final cost. Readers are reminded that the agreement was that the arena cost at least $350 million. The owners of the L.A. Arena Corporation were not required to provide any documentation of costs incurred once the agreed threshold was met. As a result, the final cost is entirely a private matter, but it is known that additional expenses were incurred beyond the planned $350 million construction figure.

13. Baade, R.A., *Los Angeles City Controller's report on economic impact: Staples Center* (Los Angeles: City of Los Angeles, Office of the Controller, 2003).

14. Los Angeles, *Gap funding agreement between city of Los Angeles and L.A. Arena Company, LLC (Los Angeles Arena Project)*, March 26 (Los Angeles: Office of the City Council, 1998), Annexes B and C.

15. Ibid., Annex D.

16. It is possible that the development that took place near the arena would have been built in other parts of Los Angeles if no new facility were built near the convention center. If that took place, then the property taxes would not be new income but would represent a transfer of funds from one part of the city to another. It cannot be determined if the new buildings near the arena displaced activity from another part of Los Angeles. What can be stated with a high degree of confidence is that in the absence of the arena, it is extremely unlikely new development would have taken place near the convention center given that little, if any, construction had taken place for several years. The assumptions made in calculating the repayment of the $12.6 million in Table 5.2, however, effectively address the possibility that development would have taken place in other parts of the city, or even at the convention center site. Under the most strident restrictions, the $12.6 million is repaid by 2012, and Los Angeles continues to receive higher property tax revenues in every year beginning in 2013.

17. The $4 million figure is an approximate annual payment each year since the Staples Center opened and was confirmed by a telephone interview on June 17, 2008, with AEG's chief fiscal officer. In some years the amount paid was slightly less than $4 million, and in recent years it has slightly exceeded $4 million.

18. Zahniser, D., L.A. LIVE promoters tout Times Square West, *Daily Breeze*, September 18, 2005, http://www.joelkotkin.com/Commentary/DB%20LA%20Live%20promoters%20tout%20Times%20Square%20West.htm.

19. The use of a 5 percent discount rate, which some might argue is too low, actually increases the value of the public sector's investment in L.A. LIVE. Had a 7 or 10 percent discount rate been utilized, the present value or the public sector's investment would have been less. The 5 percent rate provides a conservative but higher estimate of the public sector's investment.

20. At the time that people included the possibility that the Forum could be a competitive venue it had not yet been transformed or refurbished. For a few years it was used as a church. Recently, however, it was purchased by Madison Square Garden Corporation, and its intent is to use the Forum as an entertainment venue. Whether or not it can compete for premier acts with Staples Center and the Nokia Theatre is not clear given the successful brand established by both venues and the popularity of L.A. LIVE.

21. Saito, L.T., *Economic revitalization and the community benefits program: A case study of the L.A. LIVE project, a Los Angeles sports and entertainment district* (Los Angeles: Department of Sociology, University of Southern California, 2007).

22. Interview with Gerry Miller, Chief Legislative Analyst, City Council of Los Angeles, conducted March 14, 2008.

23. Forbes, NBA team valuations, 2008, http://www.forbes.com/lists/2008/32/nba08_NBA-Team-Valuations_MetroArea.html (accessed December 4, 2008).

24. http://www.pollstarpro.com/files/charts2012/2012YearEndWorldwideTicketSalesTop100ArenaVenues.pdf (accessed September 11, 2013).

*Chapter 6*

# Columbus, a Successful New Neighborhood, but a Struggling Arena and NHL Franchise

A decade ago, a 75-acre area along the Scioto River less than a mile west of this capital city's downtown was an industrial no man's land, consisting of barren rail yards, old warehouses and a shuttered 19th century penitentiary. But that was before Nationwide Realty Investors, an affiliate of Nationwide Mutual Insurance, turned the area into the Arena District.[1]

## 6.1 Introduction

Columbus' Arena District is located 2 miles south of the main campus of the Ohio State University and less than 1 mile from Ohio's state capitol, which is at the center of the city's central business district. A few short years after the closing of a shopping mall built across from the state capitol in an effort to help revitalize the downtown area, a new downtown neighborhood thrives and has achieved what the retail center could not. Ironically, however, while the Arena District has become a successful mixed-use neighborhood, the arena built as the anchor for the new neighborhood has not been a financial success. Those individuals seeking an NHL franchise (the team would become Columbus Blue Jackets) initiated the process that led to the master development plan for the Arena District. The team, however, has struggled to attract a large fan base. *Forbes* recently ranked the team as the least valuable of the 30 NHL franchises.

What makes a study of Columbus, Ohio, important is that an arena that was designed to anchor an entire downtown neighborhood helped attract more than $1 billion in investments by the private sector. Slightly less than 1,000 people now live in the 75-acre neighborhood, and more than 14,000 people work in an area that was relatively moribund before the arena was built and a master plan was developed. Understanding the unique factors that contributed to the Arena District's success while the team and arena face severe challenges provides valuable lessons for urban planners, public administrators, and sports managers. Columbus' focus on redeveloping its downtown area is also interesting from another perspective. The city's population had continued to grow, and its downtown area was never in a state of decline that was similar to what was experienced in Los Angeles (or any of the other cities studied). From 2000 to 2010, more than 65,000 new residents moved to Columbus, giving the city a growth rate of more than 10 percent. In 2012, the city had an estimated population of 809,798; its growth continues even though it is at a slow rate (see Table 6.1). While Columbus has not suffered a loss of residents, its leadership still wanted a revitalized downtown area and a new neighborhood. The Nationwide Arena helped the city achieve that goal even while the Columbus Blue Jackets continue to struggle to be a valuable and competitive team and the arena's new management structure tries to chart a plan for its financial stability.

**Table 6.1   Population Changes by Decade, Columbus, Ohio**

| Year | Population | Percent Change |
|------|-----------|----------------|
| 1950 | 375,901 | — |
| 1960 | 471,316 | 25.4 |
| 1970 | 539,677 | 14.5 |
| 1980 | 564,871 | 4.7 |
| 1990 | 632,910 | 12.0 |
| 2000 | 711,470 | 12.4 |
| 2010 | 787,033 | 10.6 |
| 2012 | 809,798 | 2.9 |

*Source:* U.S. Bureau of the Census, various years, "Estimates of Resident Population and Population Change: July 1, 1950 to July 1, 2012."

# 6.2 Why Was Columbus' Elite on a Quest for a Major Sports Franchise?

In May 1997, voters in Franklin County—home to Ohio's capital city, Columbus—rejected a referendum to increase the local sales tax. The increment was proposed to voters so that a new arena would be built and ensure that the NHL would grant a local investor an expansion franchise. The referendum also called for the creation of the Downtown Family and Sports Entertainment District. The new arena, projected to cost $203.5 million, was touted as the lynchpin for a public–private partnership that would lead to an expansion franchise from the NHL. A local businessman was willing to pay the franchise fee to the NHL; the future team owner, however, wanted the public sector to be responsible for the full cost of the new arena. Had the sales tax increment been approved, Columbus would have had a team from one of the four older major leagues for the first time in its history. Columbus was home to the Crew soccer team (MLS), but some civic leaders had longed for a team from one of the other major sports leagues. The voters' decision seemed to bring to an end to that dream. For some, however, it was a bit of a mystery as to why Columbus needed another professional sports team. For decades the city had been one of the country's centers of college football. Would a team from one of the leagues really change the city's image? What drove leadership in Columbus to want another team?

Located in the middle of Ohio, 107 miles northeast of Cincinnati and 142 miles southwest of Cleveland, Ohio's two larger metropolitan regions were the long-standing home to the state's major league teams. The lineage of today's Cincinnati Reds, regarded as the first professional baseball team, begins in 1869. The Cincinnati club was not the first baseball team; it was, however, the first that paid its players to play baseball. Machinations ensued, but in 1878 the club changed its name from the Red Stockings to the Reds. The team joined the National Association that same year. The team was soon expelled from the league for selling beer. The Reds then became part of the American Association, and then later joined the National League for the 1890 season, along with numerous other baseball clubs. The Cincinnati Reds were one of the charter teams of the modern-day National League.

The Cleveland region has a similar history in the formation of the American League. The American League was founded as a competitor to the National League after the older circuit decided not to award an expansion franchise to a group of investors from Cleveland. The Cleveland Indians became a charter member of the American League in 1901 and played their first season in what is still called today the junior circuit. While Cleveland and Cincinnati both have had historical roles in the formation of the major leagues, Columbus has had to settle for minor league baseball and then a MLS franchise. Today the city is home to the AAA affiliate of the Cleveland Indians. This is another ignoble reminder that Columbus is a minor league city compared to Cleveland, despite the capital city's faster population growth rate and the presence of the state's flagship university (the Ohio State University) and its very successful sports teams.

Cleveland and Cincinnati are also home to the state's two NFL franchises; Columbus was bypassed when the American Football League expanded during its competitive battles with the NFL. The Cleveland Browns began play in 1946 in the All-America Football Conference, and then joined the NFL in 1950. When the team's owner decided to move the Browns to Baltimore for the 1996 season (renamed the Baltimore Ravens), the NFL created an expansion franchise for the city. The new Cleveland Browns began play in 1999. The Cincinnati Bengals were an expansion team in the American Football League, beginning play in 1968. The franchise was then part of the merger between the AFL and the NFL. The AFL chose not to place an expansion franchise in Columbus; competing for football fans in the midst of one of college football's premier teams was not viewed as a desirable strategy when another option existed in the state.

Columbus was also largely ignored by professional basketball. The NBA had a team in Cincinnati, the Royals; that franchise originally played its home games in Rochester, New York. The team then relocated to Kansas City in 1972 and was renamed the Kings. In 1985, the Kings moved to Sacramento, and in 2013, the team was sold to a partnership that will try to keep the team in California's capital city. Another ownership group had offered to buy the team, wanting to relocate the Kings to Seattle in order to replace the Supersonics, which now plays in Oklahoma City (the Thunder). The Cincinnati Royals' financial struggles convinced the NBA not to place another team in the area. In 1970, the NBA granted an expansion franchise to Cleveland (the Cavaliers) before the Royals moved west. The Cavaliers remain Ohio's only NBA franchise.

The history of Ohio's professional sports teams is provided to illustrate the frustration felt by some of Columbus' residents and civic leaders regarding their failure to attract a team. The four older sports leagues had repeatedly ignored the city and region as an option for expansion or the relocation of a team despite its population growth and increasing wealth. (The NHL had a team in Cleveland but supported its relocation to San Jose.) Different people had tried to buy teams, but their efforts to bring franchises to Columbus were rejected. The proximity of teams in other markets was certainly a factor in the decisions made by the leagues to look beyond Columbus to other areas. In addition, while the Columbus market was growing, it was still relatively small (see Table 6.2). With fewer than 2 million residents, the market was still relatively small compared to others in the United States with financially successful teams. As noted, what made the region's relatively small population base particularly problematic was the extraordinary success of the Ohio State University's sports program. Can a region with fewer than 2 million residents support the athletic programs of the Ohio State University and a professional sports franchise? This background is necessary to understand the fixation on securing a franchise from the NHL.

**Table 6.2    Population Changes in Ohio's Largest Metropolitan Regions, 1990 to 2010**

| Metropolitan Region | Years | | | Percent Change |
|---|---|---|---|---|
| | *2010* | *2000* | *1990* | |
| Columbus | 1,901,974 | 1,612,844 | 1,405,168 | 35.4 |
| Cleveland | 2,077,240 | 2,148,143 | 2,102,207 | –1.2 |
| Cincinnati | 2,172,191 | 2,050,175 | 1,880,332 | 15.5 |

*Source:* U.S. Bureau of the Census, "Estimates of Resident Population and Population Change: July 1, 1990 to July 1, 2010."

Despite rapid growth, the Columbus region is still smaller than its intrastate urban rivals. In 2010, the Columbus area's population of 1,901,975 made it Ohio's third largest region, behind the Cincinnati area with 2,172,191 residents, and metropolitan Cleveland's population of 2,077,240. Columbus has been Ohio's fastest-growing region from 1990 to 2010. The Columbus area grew by 35.4 percent during that 20-year period, while the Cleveland region lost 1.2 percent of its residential base. The Cincinnati region grew by 15.5 percent.

The relatively small population bases of each of these Midwest regions (compared to others with professional teams) meant that Columbus needed to focus on hockey if it was to have a team from one of the older major leagues. With MLB teams in Cincinnati and Cleveland, both franchises need to attract fans from the Greater Columbus region in order to meet their attendance and financial goals. Both teams also broadcast games throughout Central Ohio. Neither could afford to share the Greater Columbus media market with a third MLB team. Similarly, the NBA's Pacers located in Indianapolis, 170 miles to the west, count on fans from eastern Indiana and western Ohio to fill their arena. They too would oppose the presence of an NBA expansion franchise for Columbus or a relocation request by an existing team that would compete with them for fans living between the two metropolitan areas. If the NFL were to expand, it would likely focus its interest on the Los Angeles metropolitan region or foreign locations. In addition, NFL teams in Pittsburgh, Cleveland, Cincinnati, and Indianapolis also surround Columbus, and they would likely oppose an expansion in their midst.

The existing distribution of sports teams left hockey as the only possible option for Columbus, even though a competing franchise, the Pittsburgh Penguins, plays 167 miles to the northeast. (The Consol Energy Center in Pittsburgh opened in 2010 and would complicate issues for the financial success of the Nationwide Arena built for the Columbus Blue Jackets.) It was hoped, however, that the proximity of the Penguins might create a competitive relationship that would produce a new level of interest for fans in hockey. While many would argue that the separation between these two markets was too little to financially sustain another NHL franchise, there would clearly be less opposition than what would exist from teams in the NBA, NFL, or MLB to an expansion team in their leagues for Columbus. As there was no NHL team elsewhere in Ohio, nor in nearby Indiana or Kentucky, the path to having a team from one of the older four major sports leagues led civic leaders to a relationship with the NHL.

Ironically, of course, Columbus never really needed another professional sports team to be considered major league.

First, and almost as a side note in terms of Columbus' image as a major league city, the Columbus Crew of Major League Soccer (MLS) has played in the city since 1996. Second—and first in the hearts of all Ohioans—Columbus is home to the Ohio State University's legendary football team and the long-standing and successful men's basketball team. The university also has more NCAA Division I sports programs than any other university. The region does not suffer from a lack of excitement, sporting events, or even national championships. The success of the university's football team has led to the perennial selling out of all its 102,329 seats for every game, regardless of the quality of the opponent. There are few experiences in professional sports that can match the excitement generated by the Buckeyes and their football fans. The spectacle of games in the fabled "Horseshoe"—the nickname for the cavernous on-campus stadium—is an exceptional experience for all fans. Despite the extraordinary levels of athletic success for the collegiate teams based in Columbus, numerous civic leaders still wanted another professional sports team. Some believed that with a professional team from one of the older four major sports leagues, the city would enter the elite echelon of communities that were home to a high-profile professional sports franchise. Others, however, challenged the need for a team or the perspective that an NHL team would elevate the region's profile. This difference of opinion aside, a new arena—to serve as a home for an NHL team—was also looked to as an anchor to revitalize a new neighborhood that would revive a stagnating downtown.

During the campaign to increase sales tax in order to fund a new arena, proponents argued that the referendum was the last chance to bring a major league team to the city. Within 30 days of the rejection of the proposition known as Issue 1, a new proposal emerged with the Nationwide Insurance Company agreeing to pay for the arena. In addition, Nationwide Insurance would lead the effort to establish the Arena District.

What was accomplished in Columbus? What were the characteristics of this unique public–private partnership that led to the rebuilding of a lethargic part of downtown Columbus? How did Columbus, Ohio, become a model for cities that were considering sports or entertainment facilities as anchors for revitalization?

# 6.3 Fighting for a Team from the MLB, NFL, NBA, or NHL

The Arena District's roots are to be found in the quest for Columbus' Moby Dick—a franchise from one of the older four professional sports leagues—and a failure of another initiative to revitalize the downtown area. If a Moby Dick was to be captured, it would mean that the city's leadership would need to find a way to make the presence of an NHL team a possibility even after the voters rejected an add-on to the city's sales tax. The major initiative to revitalize the downtown area that failed was a retail mall located across from the state capitol and near one of the State of Ohio's largest office complexes for its administrative offices. Less than a decade after it opened, the mall closed and was razed. If downtown Columbus was to have a new residential and mixed-use neighborhood, something other than a retail center was needed.

In its efforts to secure an NHL franchise, a growth coalition was formed to secure political support for a new arena. The coalition included local developers, the local newspaper's owner, the owner of the local minor league hockey team, leadership from the Chamber of Commerce, Lamar Hunt (owner of the Columbus Crew), and leadership from several corporations, including Ameritech and Nationwide Insurance. A public–private partnership was created with the Franklin County Convention Facilities Authority (FCCFA). The linkage to the FCCFA was required to ensure that if the needed land for the arena could not be secured through market transactions, the threat of eminent domain could be used to convince reluctant owners to sell the needed parcels. The FCCFA's involvement also assured tax-exempt status for the new facility and access to reduced financing costs through the issuance of bonds likely to be classified as tax-exempt.

Voters rejected a sales tax increment for the arena's construction. The proposal presented to voters was also vague with regard to exactly how a new neighborhood would be developed and who would make the financial investments to create it. The political campaign for Proposition 1 brought forth the same sort of opposition that existed in San Diego and Los Angeles with regard to higher taxes to support subsidies for professional sports. No clearly understood private sector investment strategy existed for a new neighborhood when Proposition 1 was presented to the voters. Simply put, there were vague discussions about development, but a plan for a new neighborhood was not part of the package that was on the ballot. As mentioned, the Padres dealt in advance with the likely political opposition to a public subsidy with a guaranteed level of private sector investments in a hotel and other properties to ensure that the public sector's investment would be exceeded by private investment by the team's owner in a new neighborhood. That guarantee was made before asking voters to approve the use of public money in the partnership to build a ballpark. In Los Angeles, the Anschutz Entertainment Group (AEG) agreed to pay for a new arena while also building a hotel and an extraordinary entertainment facility before asking the city council for its support. Even though Los Angeles' investment grew by more than $167 million to ensure the building of the hotel, by the time the city had to make that commitment, AEG had already committed more than $2.8 billion to the projects (arena and L.A. LIVE).

In Columbus and Franklin County the growth coalition decided to follow the more usual tactic of first asking for a tax increase without guaranteeing any specific level of private sector investment for real estate development. The group also did not have a specific plan for the Arena District to share with voters before the election. The acknowledged or guaranteed private sector investment in the partnership at the time of the vote was limited to the payment of the franchise fee to the NHL to secure an expansion team. If the team were successful, that investor would enjoy any of the realized profits and the public sector would not share in those benefits. There was no guaranteed financial return for the public sector for the investment of tax dollars in the partnership. There were no guaranteed revenue streams for the public sector and no commitment to build a new downtown neighborhood. The private sector in Columbus did not appear to be prepared to make investments that were similar to those made in San Diego and Los Angeles.

The public sector in Columbus was actually asked to assume all of the risk associated with building the arena. If the team and the arena were not successful, the franchise could relocate, but Columbus and Franklin County taxpayers would be financially responsible for the arena. In this regard, the initial proposal was similar to those that had led to the creation of subsidies provided by cities to teams. The record of those partnerships was that they produced dubious financial returns for the public sector.

Throughout the Proposition 1 campaign, proponents argued that this was Columbus' last chance to become home to an NHL team. This threat, rather than the promise of private sector investment in a new downtown neighborhood, was thought to be sufficient to secure voters' support. Proponents also indicated there was no plan B or backup strategy if the voters rejected the tax increment. If the proposal failed, there would be no other effort to secure an NHL franchise, and Columbus would not have a state-of-the-art arena. (The Ohio State University, however, was building a new arena with seating for more than 18,000 fans. With the structure set to open, Columbus actually would have had a state-of-the-art arena.) Since the NHL was interested in expansion, all of the usual psychological factors were in play. Even with these implied threats, the referendum still lost.[3]

## 6.4 A Privately Built Arena, Real Estate Development, and a Unique Public–Private Partnership

After the defeat of the tax referendum—indeed within approximately 30 days—another plan was put forward. This plan would not require voter approval; the

Columbus City Council could accept what was proposed. In this plan, however, the public sector would not be asked to make a substantial investment in the arena. While there was still some risk for taxpayers, the private sector would be assuming the vast majority of the financial risk associated with the project. And, to reduce their risk, an entire new downtown neighborhood would be built. While the public sector would be directly involved in the financing of the arena, Nationwide Insurance Company (together with one minority partner, the local newspaper) would build the new arena. Nationwide would also guarantee that sufficient new real estate development would occur to generate new tax revenues to repay the bonds sold by the public sector to pay for its investment. The Nationwide Insurance Company's international headquarters buildings are located adjacent to the area that would become the Arena District. If insufficient real estate was built to generate the needed new property tax revenues, Nationwide Insurance agreed to assume responsibility for a substantial portion of any revenue shortfalls if new property tax revenues were insufficient to make the annual bond payments. In effect, the new plan B substantially reduced the possibility that there would be a substantial tax subsidy for the new arena. The new plan, whether it existed prior to the election or not, addressed most, if not all, of the concerns of the project's opponents who led the "vote no" effort.

The physical plan for redevelopment and the creation of the Arena District resulted in far more private investment than anyone envisioned. Indeed, an entire new neighborhood, and not just an arena, was built as a result of the private sector's investment of more than $1 billion in different projects. It cannot be underscored enough that this was a complete reversal of the original plan presented to voters that featured a $200+ million subsidy through a tax increase. In addition, what was presented to the voters was a request for an investment without a vision or plan for a new neighborhood. Ironically, both of these deficiencies were addressed in the new plan B presented to the Columbus City Council, the State of Ohio, and all residents of Franklin County.

The key participants in the growth coalition that argued for the tax increase created the new proposal. Its rapid development and presentation led some to suggest that this idea existed even while the sales tax increment was requested. The possibility of a large public investment would have reduced the risks for Nationwide Insurance and the individual who would own the team.[4] Had the tax increase passed, other commitments made by the public sector would not have been necessary. Whether or not a plan B had existed, what is important is that a new proposal was put forward. This proposal, while requiring important public sector commitments, involved a substantial level of private investment, and in the end would create a new model for the development of sports facilities while also redeveloping a downtown area.

## 6.4.1 The Arena District Plan

The key element in the plan for the Arena District was Nationwide Insurance Company's commitment to build the arena without any tax money. The company agreed to pay 90 percent of the cost of building a new arena; the corporation that owns Columbus' daily newspaper paid the balance of the cost. The public sector's contribution was limited to responsibilities for land assembly (use of eminent domain if required), approval of the development strategy to ensure that sufficient property taxes would be generated to repay the bonds sold to finance the infrastructure improvements, and issuing the bonds to finance the needed infrastructure improvements. Nationwide Insurance is the seventh largest employer in the Columbus metropolitan area, with more than 8,500 employees, and at the national level is a "top 100" in terms of the number of employees across the country (36,000). Annually, the corporation ranks among the largest insurance companies in the United States determined by policies sold. In 2007, the corporation reported $21 billion in revenues and $160 billion in assets. In 2012, *Fortune* magazine estimated its total revenues at $30.7 billion, and that the company had assets valued at $141.3 billion. The decline in asset valuation was a function of the recession.[5]

Columbus also agreed to a property tax exemption for the arena even though a private company would own the facility. The project, however, included more than just the arena. Nationwide Insurance wanted all of the parcels necessary for the arena's success to be exempt from local property taxes. The property tax exemption was also applied to the garage built adjacent to the arena and the restaurants and all other improvements near the arena; various valuations of the exemptions placed the value of the property removed from the tax rolls at "$44 million to $156 million."[6] The lost or foregone annual revenue to the units of local government was not between $44 million and $156 million. The foregone revenue was the assessed value multiplied by the property tax rates set by local governments (including Columbus, the Columbus public schools, and Franklin County), the community college district, the health and human services district, and any other districts created by the county in accordance with state law.

The local schools were eventually held harmless from the loss of any taxes as a result of property tax exemption. Nationwide Insurance agreed to make an annual in-kind payment to the public schools to partially offset their lost revenue. The revenue that Nationwide Insurance Company would pay to the public schools (K–12) was generated by a $1 tax on every ticket sold to an event held at the arena. (As noted, the taxable value of the arena and the surrounding property was contested, with Nationwide Insurance placing its value at $44 million and the school district arguing it was worth $156 million.) After 6 years, a compromise was reached and it was agreed that the school district would receive revenue from a $1 ticket tax surcharge. In addition, the City of Columbus would also transfer 50 percent of the annual municipal income tax revenue received from players and employees of the NHL teams (the Blue Jackets and all visiting team members too, as well as all other employees working in the buildings or on the land that was declared to be exempt from property taxes) to the school district. In essence, no value was ever agreed upon for the arena and other properties exempt from local property taxes. The school district settled its claim for the $1 ticket tax revenue and half of the City of Columbus' income revenues generated by everyone working at the facilities built on the exempt properties.

While this proposal or mechanism held the school district harmless relative to revenue flows, no income stream from the arena's operations was pledged to the City of Columbus. In addition, the city's transfer of a share of some of the municipal income tax revenue collected from those employed at the exempt properties reduced revenue that the city would have received. Columbus' investment in the project includes all of the foregone income and property tax revenues.

## 6.4.2 Financing the Arena District

The Columbus Blue Jackets agreed to pay an annual rent of $3 million for the initial 10 years of the lease. After that, the rental rate would increase to $3.3 million per year for the next decade. Nationwide Insurance looked to that income stream, parking revenues, and the advertising value of having its name on the arena as the return on its investment. The parking revenues were to come not only from attendance at arena events, but also from the scores of visitors attracted to extensive new development in the Arena District. Nationwide Insurance was committed to real estate development in an effort to ensure that there would be a steady stream of visitors, workers, and residents to build the value of its investment and secure a return on its financial commitments. As Nationwide's headquarters was located at the edge of the Arena District, the area's transformation from being characterized by decline and an absence of vitality to a vibrant residential and commercial district would also be of value to the firm.

As part of the public–private partnership for the development of the arena, Columbus agreed to give Nationwide Insurance a 10-year lease for an existing site the city owned. Nationwide was also granted an option to purchase the land in the seventh year at its fair market value. The city council agreed to declare the arena site itself a "blighted area," making it possible for the FCCFA to acquire it through its eminent domain powers (as a public entity). FCCFA would own the land and lease it to Nationwide for 99 years. The annual lease payments would be $150,000 for the initial 10 years. From year 11 to 25, the rental rate for the land was set at $165,000 per year. The rental rate in years 26 through 50 will be $165,000 plus an adjustment each year equal to the region's price changes (as measured by the consumer price index). The FCCFA paid $11.7 million for the land. Nationwide Insurance's plan was to use the funds it received from its lease with the Blue Jackets to make its payments.

Columbus was responsible for the environmental remediation of the sites and estimated that when all infrastructure costs were included, its total expense would be $32.6 million. Columbus' investment in infrastructure and the environmental remediation of the land was actually $36.6 million (or 12.3 percent higher than expected; an increment of that scale is not uncommon for a project as large as the Arena District).[7] A bond was sold and the increment in property taxes from the redevelopment of the Arena District was the anticipated source of the revenues generated to make the annual payments.[8] Similar to the strategies followed in San Diego and Los Angeles, a tax increment financing (TIF) district was created based on the anticipated development in the area. In this manner Columbus would likely have no or very little expense for the building of the arena, and increments to its general revenue fund would result if development levels produced more than enough revenues to repay the bonds. If development levels did not generate the funds needed to make the annual payment, Nationwide Insurance Company agreed to provide most of the funds needed to make the annual payment. In other words, the property taxes collected from the new development first had to be used to make the payments on the bonds sold in order to raise the $36.6 million. If the new development resulted in more tax revenues than what was needed to make the bond payments, Columbus would enjoy an increment to its general revenue fund.

The total public investment was $48.3 million (Columbus' costs plus the investment by the FCCFA) reduced by the annual lease payments to the FCCFA and any new property tax income (revenue that exceeds what was needed to repay the bonds sold). The private sector investment was $150 million for the arena (cost of constructing Nationwide Arena) plus the $75 million franchise fee paid to the NHL. Nationwide Insurance spent $140 million, and the *Columbus Dispatch*, the region's newspaper, invested $10 million. The shares of the public–private partnership are depicted in Figure 6.1 with regard to the arena construction. The total public sector investment amounted to less than one-quarter, 23 percent, and the private sector investment was equal to the rest. With the public sector investment guaranteed by

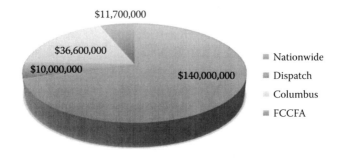

**Figure 6.1   The financial commitments to the public–private partnership to build Nationwide Arena and provide the land for the Arena District by source.**

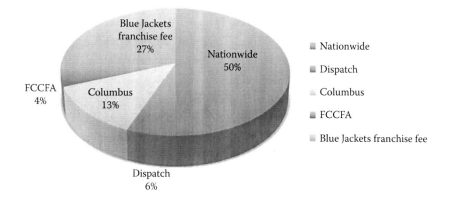

**Figure 6.2   The percentage of public and private investments in the partnership by source: Franchise fee included.**

Nationwide Insurance, the plan could be considered 100 percent funded by the private sector.[9]

When the franchise fee paid by the team's owner is included in the calculation of the total costs for the partnership—without the team there might have been no interest in an arena and thus no reason for a public–private partnership—the public share declines to 17 percent (see Figure 6.2). Regardless of which scenario is chosen as the most accurate depiction of the partnership, the public sector's investment, just like those of the private sector partners, was tied to revenue streams designed to cover the cost and perhaps even generate a return. Columbus was not pledging increases in property tax revenues to repay the bonds it sold to raise the money needed, but also was optimistically expecting a financial return to enhance its general revenue fund. The FCCFA would receive lease payments, and while there was no expectation that the payments would repay the investment, the authority would now have access to more space and anticipated more conventions and other events to increase its overall revenue levels and contributions to the region's economy. Nationwide Insurance pegged its return to the lease with the team, the income from other events staged at the arena, and the parking revenues throughout the district. For the *Columbus Dispatch*, the added advertising revenue from having a NHL team in the city was the source of its optimism. As noted by many, the great advantage to a newspaper from a team's presence is the advertising revenue generated as a result of increased readership.[10]

There were some cost estimates that place the total price of the arena at $175 million. Some of those estimates may well have included the infrastructure payments made by the public sector. Other reports reduce Nationwide's commitment by subtracting the payments made by advertisers and others that made investments for luxury seating (suites) or from sponsorships. Those payments, however, simply transfer the construction cost of the arena from Nationwide to others while reducing the profits to the team or arena operator from future operations of the facility.

The land for the facility was secured through condemnation and the use of the FCCFA's eminent domain powers. As in Los Angeles, when the land was acquired, Nationwide Insurance paid the full costs for acquisition. AEG made the same arrangements with Los Angeles, but also agreed to increase its payments by 10 percent to cover all administrative costs incurred by Los Angeles' staff. Regardless of the payment made, a relevant issue is that the public sector—Columbus, in this instance—was transferring land from one private sector actor to another to realize the city's development goal. Some critics suggest that allowing any government to steer land use decisions by choosing one land use or developer over another to meet a city's objectives can lead to an abuse of power and interference with an individual's rights. There is also the issue of disrupting economic development patterns that are more evolutionary (as opposed to the product of a master-planned area), and the recognition that what was developed—an arena and a high-income neighborhood—was a project that would mostly serve wealthier segments of society.

Proponents for the Arena District, just as those who supported the projects in Los Angeles and San Diego, would note that development levels had stagnated in the area. As a result, a concerted public–private partnership was needed to change and reinvigorate the area. In Columbus, for example, the number of people living in the downtown area had declined from 44,000 in 1960 to an estimated 3,500 in the late 1990s.[11] Waiting more than 40 years for development to take place was evidence for some civic leaders that without substantial public intervention to redirect economic activity, growth would not occur. In the global competition for economic development confronting cities, Greater Columbus might be growing and expanding, but the downtown area was moribund. This was a real lost opportunity given the proximity of the Ohio State University and the extraordinary level of talent and the number of younger people in the city each year. Columbus' leadership wanted to capture this talent (and convince that talent to build their careers and lives in the city) and, to that end, wanted a lively downtown. Waiting for development in the downtown area to occur without a master plan and a substantial stimulus seemed akin to letting another great opportunity pass by the city.

## 6.5 Columbus' Arena District: What Was Built and What Was Accomplished

In September 2000, Nationwide Arena opened with the Blue Jackets playing their first home game a month later. The arena was designed to be an anchor for development in the district. An important design feature relative to accomplishing the development goals was the building of the team's practice facility—the (Columbus) *Dispatch*[12] Ice Haus—as an adjacent component. The practice facility was designed so that many of the team's practices were open to the public. More importantly, when the team was not using the Ice Haus, community events including youth and amateur hockey or other activities could take place. The facility became an anchor for a wide-ranging number of events attracting thousands more people to the district. The practice facility added to the "neighborhood feel" of the arena by creating a public space where children and other residents of Columbus could use the facility as well as enjoy watching the team practice. This community element to a professional sports facility had never been attempted on this scale before. Some new ballparks are designed with public viewing areas so that practices can be watched as people stroll by the outside of those facilities. No other facility, however, has a component that is also available for amateur use. The *Dispatch* Ice Haus creates an impression that Nationwide Arena is also a neighborhood center for youth and amateur hockey—or where residents can watch their professional team—at the same time that it also serves as a home for professional sports and high-end entertainment events. San Diego's Ballpark District includes a miniature baseball field that is part of a public park, and it too has a public viewing area where area residents can watch the team practice and play games, but there is no full-scale field for amateur and youth baseball. In this regard, what was built or included in the Arena District was quite unique, and very successful in advancing its image as a new and very different downtown neighborhood. Nationwide Arena was designed to host the usual array of entertainment events and hockey games, but it was also planned to be a home to scores of neighborhood and community events. MSI (now MKSK), a Columbus-based planning, urban design, and landscape architecture firm, worked with the city to develop the master plan for the area. Figure 6.3 is the 2004 vision plan for the entire Arena District presented to the community.

The arena appears in the center of the figure to the immediate right of the parking/vacant lots. The proposed minor league baseball facility, to the left of the parking/vacant lots, opened in 2009. The district is relatively small at 75 acres, but it would be inappropriate to consider this 75-acre plot the entire area impacted by the arena project. Legally, of course, and from a planning perspective, the 75-acre Arena District was designated or created by Columbus. The district was the area in which the TIF district was designated to pay for the public's investment. Immediately north of the Arena District is the "Short North" community that has enjoyed a renaissance of development activity that includes numerous restaurants and several hundred new residences. This area has enjoyed new development in the years immediately after the arena plan was presented to the city council.

Short North extends to the beginning of the area adjacent to the campus of the Ohio State University. The university initiated a development of its own at the intersection with Short North called Gateway. Gateway, operated by a commercial firm, is anchored by the university's main bookstore. The store is one of the largest college bookstores in the United States, and the development adjacent to it includes

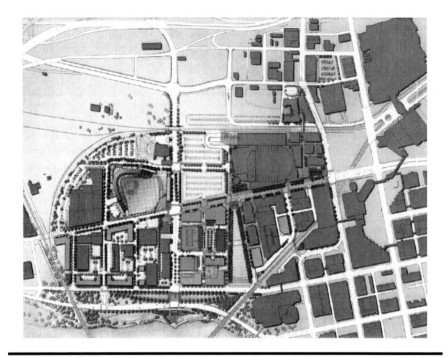

**Figure 6.3    The master vision for Columbus Arena District. (From MSI Columbus, Ohio.)**

residences and numerous restaurants and pubs. There is now a set of three neighborhoods joining the university to the downtown area—Gateway, Short North, and the Arena District. This has created a sort of Greenwich Village atmosphere for Columbus complementing other well-established and successful inner city neighborhoods. The Arena District is relatively small; its impact and linkages to other development efforts are substantial, and it may well be the "glue" that has helped to finalize the building of a residential and mixed-use urban corridor from the Ohio State University to downtown Columbus.

## 6.5.1 Real Estate Development

From 1999 through January 2008 there was a total of $374.6 million of private sector development in the Arena District. This figure excludes parking garages and the pedestrian walkways built as part of the infrastructure required or needed to facilitate development. The $374.6 million was for projects initiated as early as 1999 and as recently as 2006. When the construction budget figures are presented in 2006 dollars, the total private sector investment was $399.5 million (see Table 6.3).

A study prepared by the John Glenn School of Public Affairs of the Ohio State University in 2008 concluded that the total investment in the Arena District was

**Table 6.3    Development in the Arena District through January 2008**

| Arena District Projects | Project Initiated | Construction Budget | In 2006 Dollars |
|---|---|---|---|
| West Street office building | 2006 | $10,500,000 | $10,500,000 |
| Condominiums at North Bank | 2006 | 50,000,000 | 50,000,000 |
| Marconi Boulevard office building | 2005 | 16,500,000 | 17,157,577 |
| Burnham Square Condo | 2004 | 25,000,000 | 26,768,359 |
| Eye center | 2003 | 17,000,000 | 18,553,110 |
| Jones Day office building | 2003 | 25,000,000 | 27,283,985 |
| Arena Crossing Apartments | 2002 | 35,000,000 | 39,189,723 |
| Schottenstein, Zox, Dunn office building | 2001 | 15,000,000 | 16,987,436 |
| Lanman Building | 2000 | 800,000 | 905,997 |
| PromoWest Pavilion | 2000 | 5,500,000 | 6,228,726 |
| Arena Grand Theatre Complex | 2000 | 125,000,000 | 141,561,965 |
| URS office building | 2000 | 13,300,000 | 905,997 |
| 191 West Nationwide Boulevard | 1999 | 15,000,000 | 18,104,078 |
| 401 North Front Office Boulevard | 1999 | 9,000,000 | 10,862,447 |
| McFerson Commons Apartments | 1999 | 5,000,000 | 6,034,693 |
| Ohio Moline Plow office building | 1999 | 7,000,000 | 8,448,570 |
| Total | | $374,600,000 | $399,492,660 |

*Source:* City of Columbus, Downtown and Economic Development Department, annual reports, 1999–2006.

expected to surpass $1 billion. That estimate was based on the new buildings already completed ($635 million expended by the private sector) and $406 million in planned investments for which permits had already been secured. There were 5,449 full- and part-time workers in the area (2007). Most importantly, by 2008, the assessed valuation of property in the area increased by 267 percent since 1999.[13] In 2008, 800 people lived in the area and 172 businesses had opened stores or offices in the area.

The expectations for further development discussed in the 2008 report have been met. Table 6.4 identifies all of the buildings in the Arena District (as of September 2013), the projects under construction (as of September 2013), and those currently

**Table 6.4  Development in the Arena District through September 2013**

| Arena District Project | Size | Description |
|---|---|---|
| **Commercial** | | |
| 125 W. Nationwide Boulevard | 75,000 | 4 floors, 1st floor retail space |
| 155 W. Nationwide Boulevard | 105,000 | 5 floors, 1st floor retail |
| 191 W. Nationwide Boulevard | 134,000 | 6 floors, 1st floor retail |
| 277 W. Nationwide Boulevard | 95,000 | 5 floors, 1st floor retail |
| 230 West Street | 130,837 | 1 floor, office space and retail space |
| 250 West Street | 127,000 | 7 floors, office space and 1st floor retail |
| 325 John H. McConnell Boulevard | 165,000 | 6 floors, office and retail |
| 375 N. Front Street | 67,000 | 4 floors, 1st floor retail space |
| 401 N. Front Street | 129,000 | 4 floors, 1st floor retail space |
| Moline Plow building | 70,000 | 4 floors, 1st floor retail space |
| **Entertainment and Hospitality** | | |
| Arena District Athletic Club | 11,000 | |
| Crowne Plaza Hotel | | 377 guestrooms |
| Huntington Park Ballpark | | 10,000 seats |
| The Hyatt Regency | | 20 floors, 631 rooms |
| Lifestyles Communities Pavilion | 3,000 seats | Indoor-outdoor concert venue |
| The Lofts Hotel | | 44-room boutique hotel |
| Nationwide Arena | | 18,500 occupancy |
| **Residential** | | |
| Arena Crossing Apartments | 419,325 | 252 total units |
| Burnham Square Condominiums | 338,643 | 98 condominium flats |

*(Continued)*

**Table 6.4    Development in the Arena District through September 2013 (Continued)**

| Arena District Project | Size | Description |
|---|---|---|
| The Condominiums at North Bank Park | 375,340 | 109 total units |
| Flats II | 610–1,050 per unit | 120 units |
| Flats on Vine | 500–1,200 per/unit | 232 total units |
| Buggy Works | 750–2,500 per unit | 68 condominium lofts |
| 415 N. Front Street | | Retail, 252 luxury apartments |
| **Projects under Construction** | | |
| Goodale Apartments | | 180 units |
| Neighborhood Launch—Long Street | | 260 units |
| 463 N. High St. apartments | | 12 units |
| 51–53 E. Gay Street | | |
| HighPoint at Columbus Commons | | 302 units |
| Columbus State—Union Hall | 17,600 | Renovation underway |
| Old Police HQ renovation | | |
| Columbia Gas building | 286,000 | |
| LeVeque Tower renovation | | Renovation underway |
| 34–38 W. Gay St. | | Storefront replacements |
| **Projects Proposed** | | |
| Adler Building | | |
| Hawthorne Grove Apartments | | 40 units |
| LC South High Apartments | | 100 units |

*(Continued)*

**Table 6.4 Development in the Arena District through September 2013 (Continued)**

| Arena District Project | Size | Description |
|---|---|---|
| Neighborhood Launch—6th and Gay St. | | 28 units |
| Neighborhood Launch— future phases | | 199 units |
| Atlas Building renovation | | 99 units |
| Discovery District Commons | | 100 units |
| Museum of Art—addition | 50,000 | |
| Scioto Dam removal/park development | | 33 acres |
| North Bank Park public art | | |
| 101 S. High St. | | |
| 101 S. High St. | | |
| 112 E. Main St. | | |
| Capital Square streetscape | | |
| Creative campus streetscape improvements | | |
| Pearl and Lynn Alley improvements | | |

proposed and seeking permit approval from Columbus. Within two decades of the opening of Nationwide Arena it is probable that total private sector investment in the area will exceed $1 billion.

The importance of this level of investment—relative to the success in changing development patterns of the Arena District—is best underscored by the failure of the retail mall built in the downtown area across from the state capitol, which is a short distance from the activity taking place around the sport facility.[14] Given the continuing growth of Columbus' more distant suburban areas, it is likely that development would have been concentrated in those areas if the arena had not been built. For example, the fastest-growing county in Ohio is Delaware County, which lies north of Columbus. Delaware County's growth from 2000 to 2012 illustrates a familiar trend (see Table 6.5). Columbus and Franklin County are growing, but suburban Delaware County is growing much faster. Delaware County, even with its faster growth rate, is still far smaller than Columbus. What underscores the

**Table 6.5  Population Changes in Central Ohio**

| Community | Population | | | | Percent Change, 2000–2012 |
|---|---|---|---|---|---|
| | *2000* | *2006* | *2010* | *2012* | |
| Columbus | 711,470 | 757,117 | 788,033 | 809,798 | 13.8 |
| Franklin County | 1,068,978 | 1,111,018 | 1,163,414 | 1,195,537 | 11.8 |
| Delaware County | 109,989 | 162,689 | 174,214 | 181,061 | 64.6 |

importance for the development of the Arena District, however, is the income differential between the residents of Columbus and those of Delaware County. In 2012, the U.S. Bureau of the Census reported that the median household income in Columbus was $43,348; in Delaware County it was $90,022. Columbus, just like many other central cities, is home to a large portion of its region's lower-income households. Economic segregation is taking place, and Columbus has to ensure that some neighborhoods attract and retain wealthier residents. Columbus also has to attract and retain sufficient economic activity to produce the tax revenues needed to pay for the services its residents need.

## 6.5.2  Property Tax Revenue Generation

The pace of new real estate development in the Arena District did not generate the tax revenues needed to make the payments required on the bond sold in the project's earliest years. Through 2007 Nationwide Insurance provided Columbus with $7.9 million to offset the difference between the new property taxes generated by the development in the Arena District and the payments for the bond sold for the city's investment in the needed infrastructure. Nationwide Insurance Company agreed to be responsible for 65 percent of any financial shortfall if the new projects built in the Arena District did not generate sufficient new property taxes to repay the debt assumed by Columbus for the Arena District's creation and development.[15] This commitment guaranteed that Columbus' investment would not require the use of existing tax revenues. A subsidy was not needed after the effects of the 2008 recession ended. Had the TIF district produced no revenues at all, Columbus would have been responsible for 35 percent of the bond payments, and if the projects produced less than 35 percent of the revenue, Columbus would have had to pay a small portion of the bond's cost. Columbus has never had to make a payment for the bond using any revenue from any tax source.

It is still possible to suggest that the property tax increment to Columbus derived from the development that is taking place in the Arena District is a subsidy. Had that development taken place elsewhere in Columbus, it is likely the city would have been able to retain a substantial portion of the tax revenues generated by that development if it were located elsewhere in the city. If that had happened, the property tax revenues received by Columbus could have been used to deliver services or for other projects. If the development took place in Delaware County, however, Columbus would have lost the revenue. To the extent that the development would have taken place elsewhere in Columbus, there is indeed an opportunity cost loss for Columbus taxpayers. If any or all of the development had taken place beyond the city's borders, then there is no subsidy, as the money is a direct result of the arena's presence and the transfer of economic activity to downtown Columbus. Further, given Nationwide's commitment to pay for almost two-thirds of the revenue shortfalls in repaying the city's debt, few would argue that the benefits generated for Columbus were not worth some opportunity costs or foregone property taxes.

### 6.5.3 Employment Growth

In 2002 there were a total of 7,584 full- and part-time jobs in the Arena District; by 2011, 14,407 jobs existed. In addition to the overall job growth, it is important to note that the number of jobs in the finance and insurance sector grew from less than 2,000 to almost 7,000 (see Table 6.6). The number of professional or scientific positions grew by more than 1,000. The Arena District is also contributing to the retention of jobs in the downtown area. In the absence of the Arena District, it is possible that all of these jobs could have been located elsewhere in Columbus, or even in the downtown area. The presence of the Arena District, however, ensured that these positions were located in downtown Columbus. From a fiscal perspective, the retention of jobs is also important, as Columbus collects an earnings tax. An earnings tax is an income tax based on where money is earned (or where a job is located, not where a worker lives). Columbus administers a 2.5 percent earnings tax. As a result of the presence of high-paying jobs, important revenues for the city are generated. Although a credit is earned if the individual lives in a city with an income tax, 2.5 percent of the gross income earned by each worker is paid to Columbus less any credit to the city where live to a maximum of 0.5 percent.

## 6.6 Views of Columbus' Arena District

The Arena District is quite similar to San Diego's Ballpark District. It was designed to be not only an entertainment center, but also a neighborhood. Green space was maximized, as were areas for people to live, work, and stroll in a park-like atmosphere. Staples Center and L.A. LIVE are primary destinations adjacent to mass transportation linkages and freeways, two downtown neighborhoods, and a commercial center. San Diego's Ballpark District and Columbus' Arena District, in contrast, were designed as neighborhoods with an anchor attraction. Nationwide Arena had to be a "good neighbor" and fit within the confines of a neighborhood much like San Diego's vision for PETCO Park.

**Table 6.6   Job Growth in the Arena District: Number of Jobs in Selected Years**

| Sector of the Economy | Year | | | | | |
| --- | --- | --- | --- | --- | --- | --- |
| | *2011* | *2009* | *2007* | *2005* | *2003* | *2002* |
| Utilities | 529 | 677 | 619 | 585 | 551 | 501 |
| Construction | 110 | 27 | 138 | 81 | 42 | 27 |
| Wholesale trade | 105 | 70 | 74 | 66 | 74 | 73 |
| Retail trade | 159 | 175 | 156 | 132 | 188 | 225 |
| Information | 120 | 121 | 94 | 80 | 75 | 21 |
| Finance and insurance | 6,968 | 6,413 | 6,621 | 5,519 | 2,099 | 1,951 |
| Real estate and rental and leasing | 341 | 252 | 260 | 241 | 100 | 59 |
| Professional, scientific, and technical services | 1,868 | 1,393 | 1,566 | 992 | 879 | 868 |
| Management of companies and enterprises | 35 | 26 | 168 | 115 | 117 | 54 |
| Administration and remediation | 517 | 663 | 468 | 180 | 239 | 215 |
| Health care and social assistance | 384 | 393 | 432 | 246 | 236 | 306 |
| Arts, entertainment, and recreation | 588 | 228 | 299 | 206 | 256 | 239 |
| Accommodation and food services | 684 | 769 | 613 | 500 | 594 | 440 |
| Other services | 231 | 42 | 46 | 39 | 42 | 75 |
| Public administration | 1,731 | 1,933 | 2,193 | 1,871 | 2,306 | 2,369 |

Nationwide Arena is the anchor tenant in the Arena District. To be sure, the arena fit into the neighborhood. The building's external height was limited to 80 feet, and its exterior utilized brick, glass, and steel components that matched other buildings in the area. The extensive use of glass allows pedestrians to look into the facility at all times and provides spectators with a view of Columbus' skyline. The arena can seat 18,500 fans for hockey games and up to 20,000 for basketball games, concerts, and other events. The arena has 58 suites and 3,200 club seats (see Figure 6.4).

**Figure 6.4    Nationwide Arena. (Courtesy of Mark S. Rosentraub.)**

Views of the Arena District and its movie theatres, green space, residential space, and commercial space are provided in Figure 6.5. Nationwide Arena enjoys a seamless fit into its own neighborhood, with the adjacent Short North area providing ease of access for pedestrians and a walking area for visitors. The first residential units did not open until 2004, and by 2008 four complexes of apartments and condominiums were completed. By 2008 there were also 13 restaurants and pubs operating in the Arena District, and an 11-screen Arena Grand movie theatre opened in 2006.

## 6.7 Problems with Nationwide Arena and Challenges for the Columbus Blue Jackets

During the Blue Jackets' initial years in Columbus, the team was very popular. From 2000 through 2004 the team enjoyed an average game attendance of at least 17,339. For the 2007–2008 season, however, average game attendance declined to less than 15,000. Two seasons later, average game attendance would be below 14,000. Average game attendance has remained below 15,000 since the 2010–2011 season. The team has not been successful and has qualified for the play-offs only twice in its history. The contraction of Ohio's manufacturing economy and the lingering recession beginning in 2008 has led to fans having less discretionary income to spend on tickets for hockey games. At the same time, however, Ohio

(a)

(b)

**Figure 6.5** The Arena District. (Courtesy of Mark S. Rosentraub.) (Continued)

(c)

**Figure 6.5 (Continued)    The Arena District. (Courtesy of Mark S. Rosentraub.)**

State football has continued to enjoy sellout crowds. The supply of spectator sports in a relatively small and crowded market cannot be discounted as a contributing factor to the team's overall financial performance. Some of the long-standing concerns with the ability of a major sports team to be financially successful in a market as small as metropolitan Columbus given the popularity of the athletic programs of the Ohio State University may have been valid.

The financial problems in the Arena District were not limited to the Blue Jackets. Nationwide Arena has also struggled. As discussed in Chapter 3 which looked at outcomes in Indianapolis, there may well be too many facilities in the Ohio-Indiana-Kentucky-Missouri-Michigan-Pennsylvania market regions, and too few residents to ensure the financial success of each. The situation in Columbus is even more complicated by the Ohio State University's decision to build the Value City Arena at the Jerome Schottenstein Center. Located across from its campus and 2.2 miles from the Nationwide Arena, the 18,809-seat facility opened in 1998. It is home to the Ohio State University's basketball and hockey teams and events that could as easily be held at the Nationwide Arena. In October 2013, for example, the Schottenstein Center hosted an NBA exhibition game, a concert, and the Disney Junior Live on Tour presentation of the *Pirate & Princess Adventure*. During the same period, the Nationwide Arena hosted only one event that was not a Columbus Blue Jackets' game. The Columbus market is too small to have two successful arenas that are about the same size and just 2.2 miles from each other.

The financial struggles for the Nationwide Arena are hardly surprising given the size of the Columbus metropolitan market and its proximity to other arenas in Cleveland, Cincinnati, Pittsburgh, and Indianapolis. People living between each of these cities have convenient access to new modern venues and each can offer concerts and shows. Too few people in even a geographically dispersed area will lead to financial failure.

The financial issues confronting Nationwide Arena in 2010 convinced the insurance company and the *Columbus Dispatch* to sell the arena to the FCCFA for $43.3 million. Nationwide Insurance loaned the FCCFA $43.3 million to pay for the facility, which will be paid back by 2039 through casino revenues received from Columbus and Franklin County. The Ohio Department of Development also agreed to loan $10 million to the FCCFA for the arena's purchase and renovations. Nationwide Insurance will also pay the FCCFA $28 million to retain the naming rights on the facility through 2022. To support the financially struggling Columbus Blue Jackets, Nationwide Insurance also acquired a 30-percent ownership share in the team for $58 million. Nationwide's participation in ownership of the club allowed the team to commit to play in the arena until 2039. If the team relocates before 2039, the franchise would have to pay $36 million to the FCCFA. Such a figure would be rather inconsequential if the team were able to relocate to a more valuable Canadian market or Seattle. Finally, in an effort to thwart competition with the Schottenstein Center, the Ohio State University agreed to accept short-term responsibility for managing the facility. The University, Nationwide Insurance Company, Columbus Blue Jackets, and FCCFA formed the Columbus Arena Management Company, which now oversees the finances and management of the Nationwide Arena.

# 6.8 Conclusions

Columbus provides insight into the contribution that arenas can make relative to the master-planned community even when a team is not as successful as anticipated. The success of the Arena District is even more impressive when noting that the arena had to share events with a second and similarly sized facility located 2.2 miles away in a region with less than 2 million residents. The Arena District has succeeded, and Columbus was able to minimize its investment. The private sector has invested more than $1 billion in the Arena District. The only properties to be exempt from local property taxes include the arena, the adjacent garage, and some small adjacent facilities. The vast majority of the development in the Arena District is producing important property tax revenue for Columbus. In addition, the more than 14,000 employees in the 75-acre district pay a local income tax equal to 2.5 percent of their earnings that is partially reduced only if the city where the employee lives also administers an income tax.

Columbus achieved something that has eluded many similar-sized center cities and metropolitan areas. Columbus was able to avoid a tax increase and have a private firm build the arena that it needed to secure an expansion franchise. The public sector's investment was limited to supplying the needed infrastructure and land. The public sector's investment will be repaid by the new property taxes generated from the new buildings in the Arena District and Nationwide Insurance. Columbus is also giving to the Columbus public schools 50 percent of the income tax it receives from players, entertainers, and other employees of the Blue Jackets and the visiting NHL teams.

Even if it is argued that the property tax increment used to repay the $48.3 million bonds sold to finance the needed infrastructure and land assembly represents foregone income, the overall outcomes still make Columbus a major league winner. It is also unlikely that all of the development that has taken place in the Arena District would have occurred elsewhere in Columbus. Growth patterns in the region suggest that some of the new residences, restaurants, and entertainment venues may well have occurred in the growing county north of Columbus.

Columbus also received far more than an arena for its investment. The lesson from Columbus and the secret to the city's success in this partnership lies in the incentives for Nationwide Insurance to create the Arena District. To secure the highest possible return on its investment in the arena and its commitment to other real estate development, Nationwide has a vested interest in the Arena District's success. This led to the need or incentive to (1) create a vision for a new neighborhood; (2) present a unified plan integrating residences, entertainment, and commercial properties into this new neighborhood; (3) attract and encourage other entrepreneurs to invest in the area; and (4) coordinate activities with the adjacent Short North neighborhood. These outcomes produced a successful redevelopment effort in Columbus' downtown area that had previously eluded the city's leadership. Earlier downtown redevelopment efforts involved the building of a retail mall and hotels across from the state capital. The hope was that the return of retail to the downtown area would attract residences and slow the rapid outmigration to the northern parts of the city, county, and region. Columbus' City Center could not compete with Eaton—the new lifestyle center built on the northeast side of the region—nor with Polarius, a large retail mall and shopping district located near the Franklin and Delaware County borders.[16] The Arena District succeeded where the retail mall failed because it offered a unique urban neighborhood incorporating residences into an area with unique entertainment venues, businesses employing thousands of people, a wide array of restaurants and pubs, pedestrian-friendly paths and areas, and easy access to other vibrant urban neighborhoods. In short, the Arena District was everything that could not exist in a suburban area that was built to accommodate cars, large retail centers, and single-family homes with large lots. The Arena District offered an entirely different lifestyle and residential product, and its success creates a model for other cities to emulate.

As important as the creation of a new urban neighborhood for the redevelopment of Columbus' downtown area was the city's achievement relative to negotiating with a team owner and a growth coalition for professional sports. Columbus' Arena District highlights how cities can avoid excessive subsidies through a focus on using a sports facility to anchor the development of a unique neighborhood. That neighborhood then offers a lifestyle that is unavailable or impractical to build in suburban areas. That uniqueness attracts residents, employers, and most importantly, other investors, who then extend and enhance the assets and amenities in the immediate and adjacent areas.

For sports teams, the lesson of the Arena District is that integrated development of a facility with an urban neighborhood can create extraordinary opportunities for returns on an investment on adjacent real estate anchored by an arena or ballpark and team. Simply put, making teams and their facilities good neighbors and part of a unique urban neighborhood is good business. The Arena District's design meant a commitment to the brick facades that characterized the area, as well as the inclusion of green space, made the Arena District a neighborhood in which people lived, worked, and enjoyed professional sports and entertainment. San Diego's Ballpark District and its success also underscore what can be accomplished when teams or other organizations link together in a larger metropolitan area of almost 3 million people. Columbus' Arena District shows it is also possible in a smaller metropolitan area of less than 2 million residents located in the center of a slower-growing region with far colder winters. Indeed, perhaps the Arena District identifies the redevelopment path that can help smaller and slower-growth regions build the images and reputations needed to attract and retain the human capital that has for the past decades decided to settle in other parts of the country.

Given the returns, the public sector's investment of less than $50 million and the sharing of income tax money with the school district was a prudent investment. The public sector also had to acquire land and make it available for the development plan presented by Nationwide's planners. It is true that land was taken from one set of individuals and transferred to others to ensure that the neighborhood could be built. Few who walk the streets and pedestrian alleys of the Arena District, or sit in its green spaces, would disagree with the observation that the long-term public interest was indeed served by the building of the Arena District.

Columbus and Franklin County were also able to bring another sports venue to the Arena District without large subsidies. Columbus has been the long-term home to an AAA minor league baseball team and a new ballpark opened in the Arena District in 2009. The new ballpark and related infrastructure improvements cost $81 million. More than $40 million was secured from a naming rights agreement and prepaid corporate sponsorships, a grant from the State of Ohio, the sale of the old ballpark, and interest income earned on the project's finances. A $42.4 million revenue bond was sold to complete the financing, and it will be repaid through the use of the remaining naming rights payment, sponsorships, and a ticket tax. If the ticket tax and further corporate sponsorships are sufficient to retire the bond, the public investment will amount to $7 million from the state, plus $3.3 million from the sale of the land on which the old minor league ballpark stood. This public investment would complement the Arena District and help ensure additional real estate development in the downtown neighborhood.

Despite these achievements, there is one other issue for Nationwide Arena and Columbus. While Columbus and Nationwide were focused on building a new arena for an NHL team, the Ohio State University built a new arena for its basketball and hockey teams and other events. Early losses required the Ohio State University to restructure repayment of the construction bonds. "It [the Schottenstein Center] netted $1.9 million over expenditures in fiscal 2004, its record year, and $1.2 million in 2006. But that amount has plunged in the past two years as higher fees for performers ate into profits: $367,000 in fiscal year 2007 and $175,000 in fiscal year $175,000."[17] When the Schottenstein Center was conceived and built there was a commitment that it would not compete for regional events, but rather concentrate on serving the university's requirements or needs for a venue to host indoor events. That commitment made it possible for Columbus to still pursue its dream of an arena to anchor a revitalization program for the downtown area. Economic pressures may have led to the decision to host events that could also be held at Nationwide Arena. Two competing arenas in a small market cannot succeed, and resolving the operational issues of both facilities remains a challenge for leaders of the university and the city.

# Endnotes

1. Schneider, K., A waterfront revival in the Midwest: Home and businesses enliven an old industrial district in Columbus, Ohio, *New York Times*, December 3, 2008, B4.
2. Forbes, The business of hockey, November 2013, http://www.forbes.com/nhl-teams/Columbus-blue-jackets/ (accessed April 10, 2014).
3. A detailed history of the electoral battle, campaigns, and the defeat of the sales tax referendum for the new arena is provided by Curry, T.J., K. Schwirian, and R.A. Woldoff, *High stakes: Big time sports and downtown redevelopment* (Columbus: Ohio State University Press, 2004).
4. Curry, T.J., K. Schwirian, and R.A. Woldoff, *High stakes: Big time sports and downtown redevelopment* (Columbus: Ohio State University Press, 2004).
5. http://money.cnn.com/magazines/fortune/fortune500/2012/snapshots/10192.html (accessed October 8, 2013).
6. Burns, M., Nationwide, schools settle arena valuation dispute, *Columbus Business First*, December 5, 2007, http://columbus.bizjournals.com/columbus/stories/2007/12/03/daily22.html (accessed April 3, 2008).
7. Bach, A., Arena District, *Urban Land*, January–March 2007, Case C037003.
8. The bond was guaranteed by the City of Columbus. This means that even though the expectation was that the new property tax revenue would be used to repay the bonds, the city itself was legally responsible for the bonds. To minimize the extent of the city's

loss if the real estate development needed did not take place, an agreement was made that Nationwide Insurance would cover approximately two-thirds of any loss realized by Columbus.

9. The possibility that some of the development would have taken place elsewhere in Columbus is considered at a later point in the chapter. If the Arena District displaced development would have been fully taxed, then Columbus' investment proportion increases as a result of the opportunity costs associated with projects that would have occurred elsewhere in the city.

10. Trumpbour, R., *The new cathedrals: Politics and the media in the history of stadium construction* (Syracuse, NY: Syracuse University Press, 2007); Rosentraub, M.S., *Major league losers: The real cost of sports and who's paying for it* (New York: Basic Books, 1997).

11. Sheban, J., Rise in urban housing cheered, *Columbus Dispatch*, June 3, 2004, 1E.

12. Naming rights for the practice facility was part of the participation agreement that included the $10 million investment by the newspaper.

13. Wirick, D., et al., *Assessment of the gross economic impact of the Arena District on Greater Columbus*, 2008, John Glenn School of Public Affairs, Ohio State University, http:// glennschool.osu.edu/faculty/greenbaum_pdf/Phase2_report.pdf (accessed September 19, 2013).

14. Pramik, M., City Center might close once Macy's leaves, *Columbus Dispatch*, September 27, 2007, http://www.dispatch.com/live/content/local_news/stories/2007/09/27/ city_center.html (accessed April 5, 2008); Rose, M.M., Forlorn downtown mall waits, *Columbus Dispatch*, August 1, 2008, 1.

15. City of Columbus, Capital improvements project development and reimbursement agreement for Nationwide Arena District, September 15, 1998, City of Columbus, Office of the Mayor.

16. Rose, M.M., and M. Pramik, Goodbye, City Center, *Columbus Dispatch*, February 4, 2009, 1. The City of Columbus in February 2009 decided to not only close the City Center Mall, but to demolish it. Demolition was scheduled for the summer of 2009, and the plan was to build a park area and prepare the land for residential and commercial development. It is hoped that the Columbus Commons will become similar to the Arena District, and perhaps even link to it.

17. Bush, B., Rivals to this day: As Ohio State's Schottenstein Center turns 10, its bumpy history with Nationwide Arena hasn't been forgotten, *Columbus Dispatch*, 2008, http:// www.inscleveland.com/apps/pbcs.dll/section?category=fram...es_2008_11_17_arena_ anniv.ART_ART_11-17-08_A1_KOBTM3E.html_sid=101 (accessed November 17, 2008).

*Chapter 7*

# Rebounding in the Mountain West: Denver and the Strategy for Matching Suburban Growth Rates and Sustaining Job Levels in a Downtown Area

## 7.1 Introduction

While part of the growing West of the United States, Denver shares some of the same challenges that confront central cities in the Midwest and East. In 1950, 67.9 percent of the region's population lived in the City of Denver. By 2010, the city's 600,158 residents accounted for less than a quarter of the region's population. Just like central cities in other parts of the United States, Denver has become a smaller proportion of its region. It has a smaller demographic footprint, and its leaders are rightly concerned that its smaller scale could lead it to have insufficient tax revenues to sustain levels of urban services.

What makes a study of Denver so important, however, is not that it is a western city facing some of the same challenges that have confronted former industrial centers in other parts of the country. What is important to understand is the strategy the city implemented that has allowed it to establish a population *growth* trajectory that now matches the rate of expansion taking place in the region's suburban areas. Simply put, the population of Denver is increasing at a rate that matches the region's growth rate. That level of growth exceeds what is taking place in most other central cities compared to population growth in their respective regions. The suburban areas of the Indianapolis region, while still having fewer residents than does the consolidated city-county, are enjoying far more robust levels of growth. The same observation could be made with regard to Columbus and its suburban counties. Yet Denver's population growth rate is similar to what is taking place in its suburban counties. How did Denver achieve this level of success?

Despite its smaller number of residents, Denver's focus on redeveloping its downtown area anchored by higher-density residences, several sports complexes, numerous theatres, and a convention center has allowed it to maintain its centrality and prominence, as the region has grown to be home to almost 2.9 million people. The Metro Denver Economic Development Corporation expects the region to have as many as 3 million residents by 2015. If that goal were achieved, Denver's anticipated 651,000 residents would account for approximately 22 percent of the region's population.[1] The population in Denver increased by 28.3 percent from 1990 to 2010. In the suburban areas, the growth rate was 28.5 percent. While the population bases are dramatically different—far more people live in the suburban areas—few if any central cities have enjoyed a growth rate that matches that found in suburban parts of a region. How that was accomplished is the subject of this chapter.

From 1950 to 1980 the suburban areas in the Denver metropolitan area enjoyed a 377-percent increase in the number of people who lived outside of the central city. At the same time, the number of residents in Denver increased by only 18.9 percent. In addition, in the 1970s, as will be discussed, state laws were changed that in effect eliminated the possibility of the City of Denver (which is also a county) to expand its territorial boundaries. Denver was thus precluded from annexing any additional land to ensure new neighborhoods could be created or that real estate developers could have the option of building new commercial or retail properties in the central city that would be able to enhance the tax base. Despite extraordinary growth in the suburbs and the restrictions placed on Denver's ability to change its boundaries, from 1990 to 2010 the population's growth rate (in percentage terms) in both the suburbs and Denver was virtually identical. Critics could argue, of course, that after decades of substantial growth the suburban areas were reaching a saturation point that made it impossible to continue to match the growth rates that were achieved before 1980. Some of the suburban areas were either partially or mostly built out, meaning vacant land was less plentiful (or more expensive). As a result, new residential development was less attractive. Those observations, while valid, obscure Denver's accomplishments. It is those achievements that fashion or shape an important urban planning case study of the ways in which a central city can enjoy growth rates that are more aligned with those in suburban areas even when territorial expansion is *not* possible. Sports facilities assumed a major role in helping to make downtown Denver a destination for visitors and the region's residents while also anchoring neighborhood revitalization efforts that made downtown Denver a desirable place to live and work.

Denver changed its trajectory through the building of a new downtown area that remains a magnet for the region. By 2010, more than 60,000 people lived in several distinct downtown neighborhoods defined by high-rise residences (high-rise by Denver's standards), a new arena (for the Denver Nuggets and the Colorado Avalanche), a ballpark (for MLB's Colorado Rockies), and a new stadium (for the NFL's Denver Broncos). Denver's revitalization strategy was not limited to sports and entertainment. Just like Indianapolis, Denver also expanded its convention center and added or renovated several theatres for the performing arts that further enhanced the number of attractions, events, and activities in the downtown area. All of these venues and the restaurants that opened near each facility created the market or demand needed to successfully support numerous neighborhood-level retail establishments that are possible when more than 60,000 people live in an area and millions of visits are made by the region's residents to a well-planned downtown area. Downtown Denver, however, eschewed regional-scale shopping centers, even conceding the development of new lifestyle centers that mimicked downtowns to the surrounding suburban areas (see Figure 7.1). Downtown Denver and the city's leadership focused on building neighborhood retail that included unique stores that catered to residents who preferred an urban lifestyle. Denver also encouraged the opening of restaurants and other amenities to serve residents and those working in the downtown area as well as people attending events (see Figure 7.2). Denver also supported the expansion of a regional public transportation system that made the sports, arts, and culture amenities located in the downtown area accessible to all suburbanites and residents of each of the downtown neighborhoods. Denver's rebuilding of its downtown area and investments in a set of amenities have allowed its downtown area to remain vibrant. Downtown Denver has become the location for high-rise apartments and condominiums and a prime location for well-trained and young talent that is steering the state's economy. Denver made a set of strategic investments that have reaped substantial returns. Its investments in sports facilities were not subsidies but shrewd investments that secured the city's centrality in the region's growth.

# 7.2 Denver's Early Growth and 20th-Century Challenges

The expansion and completion of the transcontinental railroad that connected the eastern, midwestern, western, and far western portions of the United States drove

Figure 7.1   Lifestyle mall in a suburban setting in Denver metropolitan area. (Courtesy of Mark S. Rosentraub.)

Figure 7.2   Typical street in downtown Denver. (Courtesy of Mark S. Rosentraub.)

Denver's early growth. In 1862 the U.S. Congress gave residents in Denver the right to build a railroad across the Rocky Mountains. This commitment to the emerging city in the Colorado territory was part of the Pacific Railway Act. The authorization would prove pivotal, as the Union Pacific Railroad had designated Cheyenne, Wyoming (108 miles north of Denver), as its major depot or stop for the transcontinental line. Denver preempted Cheyenne's development when it built a connection between (built by the Denver Pacific Railway Company) the existing Kansas Pacific lines already in Denver and the Union Pacific's track in Wyoming. That investment made the Denver Pacific Railway a vital part of the transcontinental connection and established Denver as the center of the mountain region of the American West. Cheyenne's development slowed, just as did other cities that did not become major junctions on the transcontinental rail line. Cheyenne was initially seen as the city that would be the center for the new rail line in the mountain region of the United States. Denver's preemptive investment redirected future economic development to its region and changed its economic destiny and that of Cheyenne.

The investment in a railroad line was the first of several large-scale public sector investments to engender economic development in the Denver region's effort to establish its prominence. Denver's physical isolation from other major cities might have contributed to a willingness to advance economic development through collective investments supported through the raising of taxes. Aggressive strategic investments for economic development became part of Denver's culture and were designed to help create and advance the interests of the private sector and enhance the region's economy.

Geographic isolation likely contributed to the interest from residents in collective initiatives for economic development, even if that meant higher taxes. Those living in the region could not depend on interregional connections to drive local economic development. In contrast to Denver, for example, Indianapolis is located within a web of other cities (Chicago, Cincinnati, Columbus, Louisville, and St. Louis; none is more than 250 miles from Indianapolis), and that made it a crossroads of the eastern part of the Midwest. As a result, Indianapolis offered businesses a desirable location with the potential to provide investors with access to lower real estate costs (compared with a location in Chicago or St. Louis) that could produce or store products that could be efficiently delivered to very large market areas within a business day. Indianapolis also enjoys a location that permits it to be within 24 hours (driving time) or a 90-minute flight of a large proportion of all markets in North America.

Denver's geographic isolation means that it is not a part of any web or cluster of large urban centers. Denver is also not conveniently located near a substantial segment of North America's markets. The Kansas City and St. Louis areas, for example, are 604 and 850 miles east of the Denver region. Sacramento and San Francisco are 1,171 and 1,258 miles west of the region. A smaller metropolitan area, Salt Lake City, is 525 miles west of Denver. This relative isolation might have convinced a majority of the region's residents to be more open to the pooling of public resources to ensure that economic activity could or would be deflected to the region. Urban areas in more densely populated parts of the country could depend on spillover effects from growth taking place in other metropolitan areas that would generate investment opportunities in nearby metropolitan areas with lower land costs. Denver's residents implicitly or explicitly recognized that they lived in a region largely isolated by physical distance from the economies of other metropolitan areas. That would mean large collective investments would likely be necessary to advance the Denver region's development.

After World War II, population growth patterns in the Denver region were similar to those found in other metropolitan areas. From 1950 to 1980, for every new resident of Denver, the suburban areas added almost 10 residents (see Table 7.1). In addition, in the 1970s, Denver's ability to annex land was severely restrained. Denver was created as a consolidated city and county separated from Arapahoe County in 1902. Prior to that year, Denver was the county seat of Arapahoe County.

## 7.3 Denver and the Fate of Central Cities

To limit the consolidated city and county of Denver from extending its boundaries, the Colorado legislature created a board to review any proposed annexations. The created board included one county commissioner from each of three suburban counties surrounding Denver—Adams, Arapahoe, and Jefferson—and three representatives from the city and county of Denver. This law enacted in the 1970s effectively precluded the annexation of any land by Denver in any county outside of Adams, Arapahoe, and Jefferson unless all six members of the commission agreed. Annexation of land in Adams, Arapahoe, or Jefferson Counties required the approval of a majority of the board. This state law meant that Denver's boundaries would never change; the representatives from any of the suburban counties had no incentive to support any request from Denver to annex land. Similar to most cities to its east (excluding Oklahoma City), the consolidated city-county of Denver was now landlocked. The suburban counties were free to implement any zoning ordinances that would contribute to economic segregation (minimum lot sizes or minimum square footage sizes required for residential development). Policies similar to those had been successful in accelerating the relocation of higher-income households to suburban areas in most of the other parts of the country. If such policies were implemented by suburban communities, the City of Denver not only would be unable to expand, but also would soon have a larger proportion of the region's lower-income households living within its borders. That could mean that Denver would find itself in a fiscal situation similar to those confronting central cities in the Midwest and eastern parts of the country.

Denver's physical size was fixed at 155 square miles. The metropolitan area covers more than 8,200 square miles (excluding Denver). Suburban areas had vast tracts of land to develop that could offer residents lower tax rates and isolation from

**Table 7.1   Population Changes in the Metropolitan Denver Region, 1950–2010**

| Area | 1950 | 1960 | 1970 | 1980 | Change 1950 to 1980 | Percent Change | 1990 | 2000 | 2010 | Change 1990 to 2010 | Percent Change |
|---|---|---|---|---|---|---|---|---|---|---|---|
| Suburbs | 196,342 | 366,058 | 591,706 | 936,471 | 740,129 | 377.0 | 1,512,530 | 1,554,646 | 1,943,324 | 430,794 | 28.5 |
| Denver | 415,786 | 493,887 | 514,678 | 492,365 | 76,579 | 18.4 | 467,610 | 554,636 | 600,158 | 132,548 | 28.3 |
| MSA | 612,128 | 859,945 | 1,106,384 | 1,428,836 | 816,708 | 133.4 | 1,980,140 | 2,109,282 | 2,543,482 | 563,342 | 28.4 |

*Note:* MSA = metropolitan statistical area.

lower-income communities. If Denver were to grow, the city needed to focus on revitalizing its downtown area *and* high-rise development to maximize its population and tax base. High-rise developments would be needed to encourage population levels that could not be achieved with lower-density policy approaches given Denver's smaller geographic footprint. Downtown Denver had to become a set of desirable neighborhoods and a center for the region's entertainment and cultural amenities while also embracing a higher level of residential density. To attract people to a very different lifestyle—and one with higher urban densities that would sustain population growth—Denver had to offer a set of amenities that were not available elsewhere in the region.

How could such objectives be achieved? Denver had to take advantage of its central geographic location relative to the growing suburban areas in its region. The amenities that had to anchor downtown Denver had to be unique in that they could not also be offered or available in suburban locations. Sports, of course, by their structure mean that if MLB, NBA, NHL, and NFL teams were located in Denver, there would not be a second franchise elsewhere in the region (given the size of the region's market). If Denver could attract and retain the teams in its downtown area, it could leverage those assets and include them in its economic development strategy. Similarly, the region is only able to have one major convention center. The Denver regional market can sustain just one major set of venues for live performances, concerts, and other performing arts. As the geographic center of the region and conveniently located relative to all suburban counties, Denver could become the region's destination for all of these cultural and entertainment amenities. That location and the advantage it affords could be enhanced by mass transportation options too. A new mayor for Denver, Federico Pena, elected in 1983, would pursue that option—public transportation—even as work began to concentrate cultural and entertainment amenities in the downtown area.

# 7.4 The Plan for a New Downtown Denver

The same changes and pressures that were impacting central cities throughout the United States in the 1980s buffeted Denver. Keating and Krumholz noted that when Mayor Pena was elected[2] racial minorities comprised more than 30 percent of the city's population. These residents of Denver had income and educational attainment levels that were far less robust than those of the white residents of the region.[3] The Denver Partnership, a coalition of pro-growth advocates that included business, civic, and elected leaders, developed a new master plan for the downtown area in the 1980s. While there were numerous public meetings, there was criticism that the elite coalition essentially steered the process. The vital element in the plan was a transportation hub for the region's bus system that created a spine across 16th Street. Several new neighborhoods were also planned. The Denver Partnership provided leadership and direction for the planning process. If broader public participation was not included, it should be noted that numerous elements of the plan would, in the future, require approval from voters, and at those times there was substantial debate and opportunities for public input. The plan required the raising of taxes, and each investment or commitment of taxes required the approval of voters. In that sense, then, numerous vital components of the overall plan were subject to substantial levels of public participation and the approval of a majority of voters.

Two maps illustrate the end product of the vision put forward in the 1980s that were then altered or adjusted to respond to changing market conditions. Google Earth provides a perspective of the scale of the city's redevelopment as it stretches from the new home of the Denver Broncos on the west edge of the downtown area (Sports Authority Field at Mile High) to Coors Field at the northeast corner of the area. The distance from the stadium to the ballpark is 2 miles. Midway between Coors Field (located at 20th Street and Blake Street) is the Pepsi Center that is home to the Denver Nuggets (NBA) and the Denver Avalanche (NHL). In the Google Earth map the Pepsi Center is north of Auraria Parkway and south and west of Speer Boulevard. The downtown area includes an educational complex that is home to the University of Colorado at Denver and a very large community college. At the very south edge of the downtown area and the lower part of the map is the Denver Health Medical Center. The central business district is north of Colfax Avenue and east of Speer Boulevard (see Figure 7.3).

The second map is a detailed depiction of downtown Denver created by Nick Trotter (see Figure 7.4). The advantage of this map is the identification of all of the major assets or amenities built in the downtown area and downtown region's various neighborhoods. This presentation identifies all that has been concentrated into the downtown area and the relationship of each amenity to the 16th Street mall. That mall has become the spine that was envisioned in the 1980s with two bus stations at either end and Union Station at its northwestern endpoint. Note that the Art District, the convention center, and the Denver Performing Arts Complex also help define the downtown area. In effect, downtown Denver has concentrated all of the region's unique sports, entertainment, and cultural amenities in the greater downtown area. These amenities cannot be replicated elsewhere within the region (as the market is too small to financially sustain more than one of each of these assets). The extensive revitalization process created the opportunity to stabilize downtown Denver. Before looking at outcomes, however, it is important to consider the process and factors that led to the collective investments made and the public's support for tax increases to support major elements of the redevelopment plan and strategy.

**Figure 7.3    Downtown Denver. (From Google Earth.)**

## 7.5  Public Investments in Sports

### 7.5.1 MLB, the Colorado Rockies, and Coors Field

The Denver region's investments in facilities to attract and retain professional sports teams are particularly interesting from at least two perspectives. First, the Denver metropolitan region is among the smallest with a team from *each* of the older four major sports leagues. The region is also home to a major league soccer team, the Colorado Rapid. The University of Colorado's Division I sports programs are also available to the residents of the region. In 2010 the region's population was the 21st largest in the United States. The Nielsen Corporation ranked the region as the country's 17th largest media market in 2013, having 1,574,610 households with televisions. The region had 1.36 percent of the country's households with televisions.[4] The next largest market areas with a team from each of the older four sports

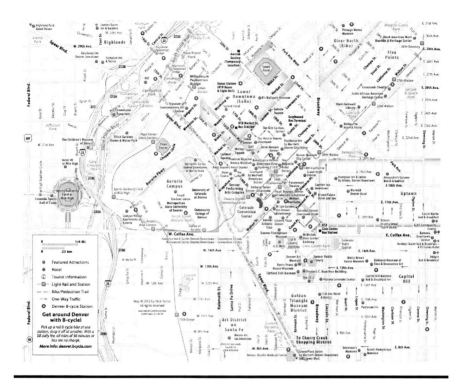

**Figure 7.4  Another view of downtown Denver. (Courtesy of Nick Trotter.)**

leagues are Miami and Phoenix. In the Phoenix region the Coyotes sought bankruptcy protection and the team's ownership reverted to the NHL. After 3 years and the promise of a substantial additional investment in the arena by taxpayers (residents of Glendale), new owners purchased the team. These owners have a right to relocate the team to another region if after 5 years of operations in Glendale the team is still losing money. In the Greater Miami region, Dade County made a substantial investment to permit a new ballpark to be built for the renamed Miami Marlins. After attendance levels did not meet expectations, the team's owner substantially reduced the Marlins' payroll by trading away a number of the franchise's best players. The Denver market is smaller than either the Phoenix or Greater Miami markets, but the franchises located in downtown Denver have been more financially stable. Their success is related to the support provided by the public sector and the commitment of individuals and businesses to buy tickets and luxury seating from the four teams.

Second, the two largest investments in sports facilities—the ballpark that brought Major League Baseball to the region and the new stadium for the Denver Broncos—involved a regional or multicounty tax. While both facilities are vital to the continued development of Denver and its downtown area, taxpayers across the metropolitan region supported the investment. Regional support for Denver's downtown development is noteworthy, as those investments have contributed to some of the outcomes that have improved Denver's financial status and the relocation and recentralization of economic activity that will be reviewed later in this chapter.

Denver's early investment was in Mile High Stadium. Built in 1948, the stadium was home to a minor league (AAA) baseball team. The Denver Broncos—a charter member of the American Football League—played in the facility from the team's creation (1960) until a new stadium opened in 2001. The public sector also assumed responsibility for $25 million in renovations to Mile High Stadium in 1977 ($96.4 million in 2013 dollars). The building of the stadium and its renovations were both financed by the public sector, but the suburban areas were not initially involved in the financing of the sport venue. This changed when the region decided it was in its best interest to host an MLB team.

The region's collective investment (uniting Denver with its surrounding suburban cities and counties) in a partnership to build a ballpark and stadium began with the decision to compete with other regions for an expansion franchise from MLB. Voters in the metropolitan area were asked to add 1/10 of 1 percent to each county's local sales tax to pay for 78 percent of the $215 million cost of a new ballpark ($348 million in 2013 dollars) if MLB granted the region a franchise. The public sector's investment in 2013 dollars was approximately $272 million. Voters were asked to approve the investment before MLB's team owners would select regions for expansion, and as a result, the imposition of the tax was conditional on the award of a franchise. If a franchise were not awarded, the ballpark would not be built. The generous investment by the public sector illustrated the commitment of the Denver metropolitan area to ensure the financial success of a new team.

The region was still growing and home to a successful NFL team. The Denver Nuggets, an American Basketball Association team that joined the NBA when the leagues merged, had been playing in the area since 1978. From 1980 through 1992 the Nuggets averaged fewer than 13,500 fans per game.[5] That relatively modest support for a second major sports team provided some evidence that the region might not have the financial capacity to sustain three teams. At the time the effort began to attract an MLB team, there was no NHL franchise in the region. The return of the NHL to the area took place after the region received an expansion MLB franchise.

The substantial public investment in the ballpark and the generous lease terms were designed to illustrate the region's collective commitment to baseball. The public sector's investment in the ballpark and the generous lease terms that eliminated rent payments from the team in exchange for their acceptance of responsibility for maintenance expenses convinced MLB that a team could be financially successful in the region. The public's support for the investment in a new ballpark convinced MLB to award an expansion franchise to the region.

NHL franchises in the region have had an uneven financial history. There was a Colorado Rockies (NHL) franchise that played six seasons in the area before moving to New Jersey (Devils) in 1982. The Devils serve the very large New Jersey and northeastern Pennsylvania areas. Northern New Jersey, by itself, had more than 3.5 million residents (2010). Central New Jersey has more than 3 million residents. The market available to the Devils is substantially larger than the 2.9 million residents of Greater Denver. Relocation made a great deal of financial sense and underscored the Denver region's challenge in ensuring the financial success of each of the four franchises that now call Denver home.

The relocation of the hockey team provided another piece of evidence suggesting that the region might not be able to guarantee the financial success of an MLB team. The large investment by the public sector reduced the financial pressure on the MLB franchise, especially when the public sector was willing to provide a lease that limited the team's financial obligations for the ballpark and maximized its control of revenues produced by the facility. In 1995 the NHL returned to the region when the Quebec Nordiques relocated to downtown Denver. The Nordiques were a franchise in the World Hockey Association and then joined the NHL when the leagues merged in 1979. The possibility of playing in a larger market and at a new arena was sufficiently attractive to entertain the idea of leaving a very small market (less than 600,000 residents) for one that had slightly more 2.5 million residents. Of course, the Avalanche would have to compete with far more entertainment options available to residents of the area. And as the franchise's ownership would learn, in many seasons attendance in Denver would not be much different from what was enjoyed in Quebec City.[6]

The less robust financial performance of the basketball and hockey franchises might have been a cautionary note for some with regard to the likelihood of success of another professional sports team. Certainly that record would be a topic that MLB executives and other team owners would discuss in their efforts to secure lucrative commitments from the public sector. Indeed, it was in MLB's interest to use every available tactic or negotiating tool to secure generous financial terms from the public sector and local governments in the region. There is debate, however, regarding the insight that can be drawn from attendance levels or support for teams from other sports. Some argue that each sport has a core base of fans that do not elect to follow another if their favorite sport is not available. This debate—are fans focused on individual sports or willing to transfer their interest to others if their favorite game is not available?—is referred to as the cross-elasticity of demand argument. There is some empirical evidence to suggest that when a particular sport is not available to local residents, attendance levels rise for teams in other sports. There is also a core base of fans devoted to each sport that will not shift their demand to another if their favorite game is not played by a home team. With some fans focused on a particular sport, it could mean that if one team in another sport is not successful, a team in another could succeed.[7] The aggregate spending for tickets to all games, however, is part (or a function) of the discretionary income available to households to spend for entertainment. If a consumer's preferred sport is not available, it is reasonable to expect that some shifting among other entertainment choices will occur. Sports could be part of that shift, although it is also possible that a consumer would choose another diversion or even travel to another market to view a game in his or her most preferred sport. The failure of one or more teams from different sports in a market could also mean that there is simply insufficient discretionary income in a market to permit another form of entertainment to thrive. If that form of entertainment—in this case MLB—was more desirable than other types of diversions, then it is possible that a team would be quite successful. Too few studies are available to indicate what will happen in a market as small as the Denver region when and if an MLB franchise were granted. Today, however, the Colorado Rockies is among the least valuable franchises in MLB, suggesting the area may well not have as much discretionary spending available to sustain each team at a level that makes each very profitable.[8] Even with the substantial public investment in the ballpark and the very favorable lease terms provided to the team, the Colorado Rockies are not successful (from a financial perspective). This would suggest that the presence of four teams in the market has provided residents with a rich array of amenities, and those choices have placed MLB in a market where there is a substantial level of competition for consumers' discretionary income. In addition, since the NHL has returned to the market, the Colorado Avalanche enjoyed robust attendance in the seasons when the team competes for the Stanley Cup. When the team has had less success, attendance levels average less than 16,000 fans per game.[9] This provides additional evidence that some regions might well need to have far more residents to ensure the financial success of each team. The Denver region could well be a challenge for each team until the anticipated population growth occurs. Given anticipated growth, there are certainly reasons to be optimistic. If that anticipated or projected population growth does not occur, it is possible one team might not achieve the level of profit anticipated given the number of entertainment choices available to residents.

It is also interesting to note that a majority of voters living in the City of Denver who cast ballots to decide whether or not to provide funds for a ballpark voted *against* the 1/10 of a percent increase in the sales tax. The referendum's support came from voters in three suburban counties. This outcome is somewhat surprising in that the ballpark was an amenity that was to be built in downtown Denver and was planned as an anchor for a revitalized neighborhood. In essence, suburban residents were more supportive of a public investment that would produce benefits for Denver than were those voters who lived in the city. Some might argue that Denver's residents were more concerned with traffic and other environmental factors that would, in their view, make the city less desirable. Yet the site for the facility was at an edge of the downtown area and was to be an anchor for development that would add residents to an area extending from the center of the downtown area to the ballpark. Given that more people live outside of Denver, suburbanites would be paying a larger proportion of the investment in the ballpark that would produce more development opportunities for Denver. Some might argue that regardless of the geographic location of taxpayers and the development options and benefits that Denver might enjoy, a sales tax increment, no matter how small, is an increased reliance on a regressive tax. With a larger proportion of the region's lower-income households living in Denver, it is possible that some reticence by voters from the city manifested itself in a reluctance to support even a small increment in a tax that would be a burden on people with lower incomes.

As noted, the Colorado Rockies were offered a generous lease. The team was able to use the facility without paying any rent. The team, however, would be responsible for day-to-day operating expenses of the ballpark and the repair and maintenance of the facility. The payment for day-to-day operations was capped at $150,000. The fee could be less if sales tax revenues were sufficient to retire the bonds and support operational expenses. The public sector receives 25 cents from any ticket sold when attendance exceeds 2,250,000 (25 cents per person from the 2,250,001 attendees at games up to the 2,500,000th visitor). The public sector receives 50 cents for attendees between 2.5 million and 3 million per year, and then $1 for each visitor in excess of 3 million attendees. In essence, the annual rent could not exceed $150,000, with the team's obligations limited to maintenance, operations, and repairs. That effectively meant the team would enjoy minimal expenses for the initial years of use of the ballpark. In addition to retaining all revenue generated by the ballpark, the club would also receive 80 percent of all parking revenues collected at garages built as part of the ballpark district. These generous terms convinced MLB to offer an expansion franchise, and the Colorado Rockies began play in 1993 in Mile High Stadium and moved into Coors Field for the 1995 season.

## 7.5.2  Sports Authority Field at Mile High

The Denver Broncos also wanted (or needed) a new stadium. As noted, Mile High Stadium opened in 1948, and while it had been renovated and properly maintained, it lacked many of the revenue generating amenities commonly part of the more modern facilities used by NFL teams. With the 1/10 of 1 percent sales tax performing better than expected, sufficient funds had been generated to retire the bonds sold to pay for the ballpark's construction several years earlier than anticipated. The Broncos' owner wanted to capitalize on the success of the 1/10 of 1 percent increment in the sales tax and approached the region's elected leadership to support an extension of the tax to help pay for a new football stadium. Continuing the tax beyond the mandate supported by voters for the ballpark would require a new ballot referendum. In the aftermath of the Broncos' winning of a Super Bowl championship, the tax extension was supported by 57 percent of voters. Voters supported the extension of a 1/10 of a percent increase in the sales tax to ensure a new stadium for the Broncos would be built in downtown Denver.

The building of the new stadium was presented to the voters as a public–private partnership. The new facility was projected to cost $364.2 million ($518.7 million in 2103 dollars), with the team's owner agreeing to pay 25 percent of the total cost and accepting responsibility for any extra expenses above the projected cost. The final cost of the facility has been estimated to be $400.8 million (or $570.8 million in 2013 dollars). If the facility cost $400.8 million, the team owner and the NFL paid for 28 percent of the cost of the stadium. In addition, the new lease extended the team's commitment to the region for 30 years. There was fear among some voters and others that if a new stadium was not built, the team might have relocated to another market. Extending the sales tax ensured that the Broncos would be in Denver for several decades.

### 7.5.3 The Pepsi Arena

The home of the Denver Nuggets, the Denver Avalanche, and the Colorado Mammoth (National Lacrosse League) opened in 1999. Responsibility for building the facility was accepted by the private sector. Denver's investment in the facility consisted of an annual property tax exemption that was initially valued at $2.1 million (per year). The private sector partners also received a $2.25 million sales tax rebate on the purchase of construction materials. As the arena is privately owned, the public sector is not responsible for any maintenance expenses. The public sector's investment also included $36.5 million from the Denver Urban Redevelopment Authority (financed through bonds repaid from a tax increment financing district). The City of Denver also made an investment of $4.5 million for required or needed infrastructure improvements to sustain the arena. The present value of the annual property tax abatement for 30 years is $84.9 million (in 1999 dollars). The public sector investment (in 1999 dollars) to ensure the arena would be built and that the Nuggets would remain in Denver was $125.9 million. The private sector's investment was at least $180 million; it is likely the cost of the facility was slightly larger. The total cost of the arena project was at least $309.6 million, and the private sector's share was at least 58.8 percent. In addition, with the private sector responsible for the facility's maintenance and for any renovations, the total investment by the arena's owners will exceed the $180 million for construction (see Figure 7.5).

The investments in sports venues were not the only ones made in big-ticket items. For example, in November 1999, 55 percent of those voting in an election in Denver approved an investment of $261.5 million to expand the Colorado Convention Center. The bond was supported by a tax on hotel rooms (the rate paid by those staying in hotels each night) and a tax on short-term car rentals. A similar proportion of voters approved a property tax increase of $2.5 million in November 2007 to pay for infrastructure enhancements to the downtown area. That particular election also included funding for the Denver Zoo, the art museum, and public transportation. Each of the particular initiatives had to be supported by a majority of voters. The largest support was for public transportation (73 percent of the voters). Funding for the zoo and art museum received the support of at least 61 percent of the voters.[10]

As in other regions—a point that will be considered at length in Chapter 8, which focuses on the revitalization of downtown Cleveland—Denver's mayors and other elected officials did not limit their focus on economic development to sports

**Figure 7.5    The Pepsi Center. (Courtesy of Mark S. Rosentraub.)**

venues, the convention center, or entertainment districts. There were numerous job development initiatives, an emphasis on historic preservation, a renewed effort to revitalize one of the city's historic centers, Larimer Square, and a commitment to remove dilapidated buildings that could not be renovated. Denver also dramatically expanded public transit to provide easy access to service sector jobs emerging in the four major neighborhood development districts and the educational center established by the presence of the University of Colorado at Denver and the region's leading community college.

# 7.6  What Was Accomplished in Denver

While some of the pictures already included in this chapter provide some insight into what downtown Denver has become (see Figure 7.2), other views are required before economic and demographic outcome shifts can be considered. Figure 7.6 is a view of the covered plaza that connects several of the theatres for live performances in addition to an adjacent parking structure and restaurants. Figure 7.7 is a view of the 16th Street Mall together with a regional transit bus system that links to the light rail transit system. The historic clock tower has been restored to provide the mall with a distinctive meeting place. Spaces in the tower are available for social events. The tower was once home to a department store and would have been demolished had it not been for the work of preservationists. It now stands as a

**Figure 7.6  Part of Downtown Denver's theatre district.**

symbol of the rebuilt downtown area. The integration of Coors Field—the home of the Colorado Rockies—with downtown neighborhoods is depicted in Figure 7.8. Coors Field is at the very end of the street. The important or critical element in this photograph is not the ballpark, but the way in which the approach to it is defined by new buildings built on the existing downtown grid. The buildings in the photograph are a mix of commercial and residential properties melding with the ballpark to create a distinctive urban neighborhood. The last illustration, Figure 7.9, is across from the Pepsi Center (arena). This photograph illustrates the city's commitment to integrating older buildings in its revitalization efforts and the connectivity achieved by using jogging and bicycle trails to link various parts of the downtown area to each other. The walking, jogging, and bicycle route is built along the Denver River and is adjacent to new residential properties. The bridge that connects the neighborhood streets to an arterial roadway provides access for cars and pedestrians while protecting the neighborhood from the larger stream of traffic. The walking and bicycle path is below grade and isolates walkers and those using bicycles from vehicular traffic.

For most of the 21st century, the proportion of the region's jobs that are located in downtown Denver has remained relatively stable. In 2002, there were 109,023 full-time jobs in the downtown area. The recession had little effect on employment levels. In 2010 there were 121,913 full-time workers in the area; that declined slightly to 115,401 in 2011. The proportion of the region's jobs in the downtown area has remained relatively constant, ranging from slightly less than 9 percent in

**Figure 7.7    16th Street Mall and Clock Tower. (Courtesy of Mark S. Rosentraub.)**

2003 to 10 percent in 2010. There was then a stabilization of employment levels across the decade, and the relative concentration of the region's jobs in the downtown area did not decline. There was no loss of centrality relative to the location of primary jobs even if there was little evidence of extensive recentralization or the recreation of a dominant downtown (see Table 7.2).

There was, as would be expected, variation in regional concentration by job type, and in that sense, evidence of some degree of recentralization is apparent. Where there was a level of concentration relative to the overall level of jobs, it was in some important and high-profile areas of the economy. For example, in the finance and insurance sector of the Denver regional economy, between 13.5 and 17.8 percent of the full-time positions in this segment have been located in the downtown

Figure 7.8  Downtown street and approach to Coors Field, home of the Colorado Rockies. (Courtesy of Mark S. Rosentraub.)

Figure 7.9  Integrating the past with the future, downtown Denver. (Courtesy of Mark S. Rosentraub.)

area. These proportions should be compared with the 9.4 percent of the region's full-time jobs in the downtown area to appreciate the degree of success or concentration of positions and the character of employment in downtown Denver. While the downtown area has not enjoyed a measurable difference in jobs in the information sector, there were important concentrations of jobs classified as professional, scientific, or technical and in the management of companies. The concentration of theatres and other entertainment venues led to an expected concentration of positions in that area of the regional economy. The opening of restaurants, hotels, and pubs linked to the entertainment and sports venues also led to a slight concentration of jobs in the hospitality sectors (see Table 7.2).

Returning to residential patterns, downtown Denver is home to more than 60,000 residents, and the popularity of the various neighborhoods in the downtown area has helped Denver enjoy a population growth rate that matches that of the suburban areas. Denver's residential population base, similar to the employment base, represents a small portion of the region. But the similarity of the growth rate and the stability of the employment levels do illustrate that downtown Denver is vibrant and has protected the centrality of the city that once defined the region. What now underscores or underlines Denver's contribution to the region is the downtown area.

## 7.7 Conclusions

Denver, in a manner similar to Indianapolis, has been focused on redeveloping its downtown area in an effort to recentralize or stabilize regional economic activity that takes place inside the city. Similar to Indianapolis, Denver has been focused on this policy initiative across four decades and throughout the administrations of several different mayors. While some might also suggest that Denver as a county was also similar to Indianapolis that consolidated with Marion County, the spatial dimension of UniGov actually allowed the central city to expand its territorial footprint. In the 1970s territorial expansion was politically minimized as a policy option for Denver. The inability to expand its boundaries may well have been a factor that encouraged a focus on a redeveloped downtown Denver. For Indianapolis, the impetus for revitalization of its downtown was the absence of a national identity or image combined with a realization that consolidation of the city with most of the surrounding communities in Marion County did not slow the deterioration of the downtown area. Regardless of the factors that focused attention on revitalization of its downtown areas, Denver included elements of Indianapolis' approach, but included one important difference.

Denver's initiative was anchored to a transit system that linked the suburban areas and neighborhoods throughout the city and region to its 16th Street mall. The sports facilities were also vital elements, and each of the region's major professional sports teams plays its home games in venues in the downtown area. Just as

**Table 7.2 The Location of All Full-Time Jobs and Jobs in Selected Areas Downtown and in Metropolitan Denver, 2002–2011**

| Area/Jobs | 2002 | 2003 | 2004 | 2005 | 2006 | 2007 | 2008 | 2009 | 2010 | 2011 |
|---|---|---|---|---|---|---|---|---|---|---|
| **Primary or Full-Time Jobs** | | | | | | | | | | |
| Downtown | 109,023 | 101,984 | 105,379 | 106,464 | 109,951 | 116,001 | 108,820 | 116,885 | 121,913 | 115,401 |
| Region | 1,171,357 | 1,143,330 | 1,145,915 | 1,177,243 | 1,192,644 | 1,222,115 | 1,226,813 | 1,179,621 | 1,212,672 | 1,232,317 |
| % Downtown | 9.3 | 8.9 | 9.2 | 9.0 | 9.2 | 9.5 | 8.8 | 9.9 | 10.0 | 9.4 |
| **Finance and Insurances** | | | | | | | | | | |
| Downtown | 11,383 | 11,505 | 11,420 | 11,797 | 11,693 | 10,350 | 10,954 | 12,590 | 11,926 | 9,089 |
| Region | 71,950 | 73,662 | 72,122 | 73,021 | 73,191 | 68,492 | 71,778 | 70,601 | 69,514 | 67,333 |
| % Downtown | 15.8 | 15.6 | 15.8 | 16.2 | 16.0 | 15.1 | 15.3 | 17.8 | 17.2 | 13.5 |
| **Information** | | | | | | | | | | |
| Downtown | 8,960 | 8,477 | 9,709 | 8,799 | 8,258 | 9,160 | 7,329 | 7,283 | 6,642 | 5,490 |
| Region | 66,480 | 58,565 | 56,600 | 51,303 | 48,452 | 52,653 | 52,246 | 51,487 | 47,188 | 52,679 |
| % Downtown | 13.5 | 14.5 | 17.2 | 17.2 | 17.0 | 17.4 | 14.0 | 14.1 | 14.1 | 10.4 |
| **Professional, Scientific, and Technical Services** | | | | | | | | | | |
| Downtown | 18,744 | 17,390 | 16,924 | 16,349 | 17,460 | 18,445 | 19,541 | 19,252 | 17,590 | 19,151 |

| | | | | | | | | | | |
|---|---|---|---|---|---|---|---|---|---|---|
| Region | 90,527 | 86,762 | 87,555 | 91,163 | 96,829 | 103,009 | 109,456 | 105,616 | 107,406 | 108,454 |
| % Downtown | 20.7 | 20.0 | 19.3 | 17.9 | 18.0 | 17.9 | 17.9 | 18.2 | 16.4 | 17.7 |
| **Management of Companies and Enterprises** | | | | | | | | | | |
| Downtown | 1,902 | 1,903 | 2,004 | 3,067 | 3,281 | 3,585 | 3,802 | 3,496 | 3,995 | 4,433 |
| Region | 17,250 | 21,222 | 20,851 | 22,465 | 24,109 | 25,253 | 25,991 | 26,446 | 27,421 | 27,567 |
| % Downtown | 11.0 | 9.0 | 9.6 | 13.7 | 13.6 | 14.2 | 14.6 | 13.2 | 14.6 | 16.1 |
| **Arts, Entertainment, and Recreation** | | | | | | | | | | |
| Downtown | 2,709 | 2,629 | 2,808 | 2,848 | 3,229 | 3,491 | 3,841 | 3,478 | 3,450 | 3,255 |
| Region | 19,514 | 19,066 | 20,625 | 21,727 | 21,937 | 21,970 | 22,589 | 21,514 | 22,292 | 21,920 |
| % Downtown | 13.9 | 13.8 | 13.6 | 13.1 | 14.7 | 15.9 | 17.0 | 16.2 | 15.5 | 14.8 |
| **Accommodation and Food Services** | | | | | | | | | | |
| Downtown | 12,048 | 13,660 | 12,525 | 12,527 | 13,335 | 12,682 | 14,277 | 13,378 | 13,847 | 13,880 |
| Region | 96,838 | 96,036 | 99,549 | 99,869 | 102,373 | 108,264 | 110,509 | 105,935 | 107,057 | 109,560 |
| % Downtown | 12.4 | 14.2 | 12.6 | 12.5 | 13.0 | 11.7 | 12.9 | 12.6 | 12.9 | 12.7 |

*Source:* Bureau of the Census, U.S. Department of Commerce, *On the Map*, 2002–2011.

Indianapolis is the smallest market with two teams (and of course the major events at the Indianapolis Motor Speedway), Denver is among the smallest markets with four teams (one from each of the most successful leagues). The Indianapolis market is also a vital part of the base for the Division I athletic programs of Indiana and Purdue Universities. As a result, what is most interesting, however, is that in both regions there was a need for regional financing efforts to ensure the building of at least one of the sports facilities. In Denver, a regional tax was used for the ballpark and stadium. A regional tax was used to pay for the new home for the Indianapolis Colts. The State of Indiana, however, also contributed to the building of the arena for the Indiana Pacers through the deflection of some state tax revenue to the project (through the creation of a sports tax district that captured state and local taxes). Both central cities received financial help from other governments to advance the redevelopment of the downtown area. Whether or not intergovernmental transfers for activities other than sports would have been possible is well beyond the scope of this book. It has to be noted, however, that in an era when intergovernmental transfers to central cities have become more difficult, both Denver and Indianapolis benefited (as did Cleveland, as will be discussed in Chapter 8) in finding support from other local governments and the state if the investment of other taxpayers was linked to sports.

Both downtown areas are home to numerous theatres and performance centers for live entertainment, very successful convention centers, state capitols and office complexes, large-scale commuter campuses of their respective state universities that are increasing their residential characters, a major community college (a bit outside the downtown area in Indianapolis), and numerous museums that serve their respective regions (and extensive sections of their states). Denver, however, has been far more successful in attracting residents to live in the downtown area.

First, Denver sustained a level of its centrality by building mass transit links to the suburbs. The public transit system made the amenities of downtown accessible. This was accomplished at the same time that convenient linkages throughout the interstate system were also made available to commuters and visitors. The revitalization of Denver's downtown area was aided by a trimodal approach to transportation. Within the downtown area there are protected trails and paths for bicycles and pedestrians. Public transit options exist for suburban residents. For those who prefer to use their cars, the highway system is also convenient.

Second, as depicted in several of the pictures, Denver's redevelopment mixed new construction with restoration and the repurposing of buildings throughout the area. There was in a sense an application of some of Jane Jacobs' ideas with regard to urban design, while also incorporating large-scale developments and master-planned areas. Downtown has become an area populated by higher-income households, and that has meant a level of income segregation in some parts of the downtown area. The restaurants and pubs surrounding the sports venues and the cultural centers clearly serve an up-scale market and clientele. The city, however, remains home to a large portion of the region's lower-income households. Denver's median household income (2007–2011) was $47,499, while in the state the median household income was $57,685. In nearby Arapahoe County the median household income was $59,937. Downtown Denver needs to attract and retain higher-income households to ensure the city's long-term fiscal stability, and the downtown area is contributing to that goal.

## Endnotes

1. Metro Denver EDC, http://www.metrodenver.org/demographics-communities/demographics/population.html (accessed December 8, 2013).
2. Keating, W.D., and N. Krumholz, Downtown plans of the 1980s: The case for more equity in the 1990s, *Journal of the American Planning Association*, 57(2): 136–152, 1991.
3. Judd, D.R., From cowtown to sunbelt city: Boosterism and economic growth in Denver, in *Restructuring the city: The political economy of urban redevelopment*, ed. S.F. Fainstein et al., 167–201 (New York: Longman, 1983).
4. http://www.tvb.org/media/file/TVB_Market_Profiles_Nielsen_TVHH_DMA_Ranks_2013-2014.pdf (accessed October 13, 2013).
5. The history of per game attendance at Denver Nuggets games is available at http://www.databasebasketball.com/teams/teamatt.htm?tm=den&lg=n (accessed October 13, 2013).
6. The attendance at Quebec Nordiques' games averaged more than 14,000 in most of their seasons: http://www.hockeydb.com/nhl-attendance/att_graph.php?tmi=7584 (accessed October 13, 2013).
7. Rascher, D.A., T.B. Matthew, M.S. Nagle, and C.D. McEvoy, Where did National Hockey League fans go during the 2004–2005 lockout? An analysis of economic competition between leagues, *International Journal of Sport Management and Marketing*, 5(1–2): 183–195, 2009; Winfree, J., and M.S. Rosentraub, *Sports finance and management: Real estate, entertainment, and the remaking of the business* (Boca Raton, FL: CRC Press/Taylor & Francis, 2012).
8. Franchise values are estimated by *Forbes* and are available at http://www.forbes.com/mlb-valuations/list/ (accessed October 12, 2013).
9. http://www.hockeydb.com/nhl-attendance/att_graph.php?tmi=5307 (accessed October 12, 2013).
10. http://www.ciruli.com/election11299.html (accessed November 1, 2013).

*Chapter 8*

# Can a City Win When Losing? Cleveland and the Building of Sports, Cultural, and Entertainment Facilities in the Midst of Population Declines and Job Losses

## 8.1 Introduction

Cleveland also embarked on a path that mirrored Indianapolis' effort to use entertainment, cultural, and sports facilities to (1) arrest downtown decline, (2) create a new image, and (3) slow or reverse the city's and the region's economic contraction. Cleveland's dramatic loss of residents and businesses—and the region's precipitous decline—required different institutional relationships and financing mechanisms. Its geographic footprint is far smaller than that of San Diego, Los Angeles, or Columbus. The rapid movement of middle- and upper-class residents to independent suburbs and the loss of firms to the suburbs and other parts of the country weakened Cleveland's financial base. As a result, any solutions or policy initiatives had to involve other levels of government or foundations. Simply put, as Cleveland did not consolidate with its surrounding county, it had far fewer financial tools and options for independent action than other cities studied in this volume. Similar to Cleveland, Denver had to fashion financial plans that included surrounding cities and counties. Cleveland, however, has not been able to duplicate Denver's success in building downtown neighborhoods that became the home for tens of thousands of residents. Events in 2013 and 2014 may permit Cleveland to enjoy a new level of success. There are several lessons to learn from Cleveland's experiences, including the cost of delaying aggressive policy initiatives and the possibility that even the most ambitious plans cannot change the flow of economic activity out of a region without substantial shifts in market dynamics. Cleveland's lack of success could be a function of too general a plan or vision for its downtown redevelopment effort. It is also possible that the lower levels of success in Cleveland were a function of a failure to concede that in order to revitalize the city, the size and scale of the downtown area had to be dramatically shrunk. Part of that smaller geographic sense of downtown means that investments have to be concentrated in a small area, as seen in Indianapolis.

In Cleveland, the restored theatre district, Playhouse Square, is at the eastern end of the downtown area. Two of the new sports facilities are at the southern extent of the downtown area with the football stadium, and two new museums located on the downtown area's northern edge adjacent to Lake Erie (see Figure 8.1). It may be that Cleveland's leaders tried to spread new investments across too much geographic space. This reason for the lack of success and other lessons from Cleveland's reliance on sports, entertainment, and culture as the anchors for its redevelopment strategy are explored and considered in this chapter. Throughout the early years of the 21st century, numerous vacant buildings and storefronts were interspersed between new assets and amenities. The failure to concentrate the new facilities and completely restore one part of the downtown area as opposed to initiatives in several parts of a shrinking core was surprising given the city's rich planning history that emphasized carefully detailed plans and focused redevelopment.

At the beginning of the 20th century, Cleveland commissioned urban visionary Daniel Burnham to produce a master plan for part of its downtown area when a new city hall, county courthouse, public library, railway station, and convention center were to be built. That plan led to a unified design for a core area surrounding and adjacent to Public Square. A similarly focused master plan for the downtown's revival in the last decades of the 20th century was not developed. Instead, redevelopment activities were undertaken in many different parts of an extensive downtown area defined when Cleveland was one of America's most prosperous central cities.

Dispersed revitalization efforts usually mean vacant and, in some cases, deteriorating properties will be mixed among newer assets, creating an air of decay amidst redevelopment. Why? Too often when regional economies are decentralizing there is reduced demand for land in larger-scale downtown areas that were created when the central cities dominated their regional economies. In response to the lower

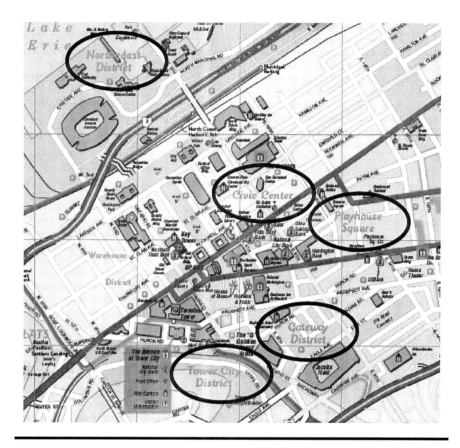

**Figure 8.1    Downtown Cleveland and the dispersion of facilities. The Cleveland Browns' stadium, the science museum, and the Rock and Roll Hall of Fame are in the Northeast District on the shores of Lake Erie. The ballpark and the arena are in the Gateway District (southern edge of the downtown area) at the map's bottom (center), and Playhouse Square lies on the right-hand side of the map (the eastern edge of downtown). (From Positively Cleveland.)**

demand it is necessary to concentrate renovated or new assets in designated areas in an effort to produce a more successful revitalization strategy. If development can be secured in a smaller downtown area, it is possible to encourage entrepreneurs to seek opportunities within an area that concentrates amenities to ensure a lively environment or atmosphere. The residential or commercial projects that surround the revitalized core area then permit the redevelopment effort to expand outward from a strong and successful center. In contrast, placing assets in diffused sections of a large downtown area that is based on what existed decades ago, as was done in Cleveland, will lead to the presence of abandoned or underdeveloped properties that reduce confidence that even a smaller downtown area can thrive.

From a design standpoint, it would seem that it may be too premature to use Cleveland's effort as a case study of how not to revitalize a downtown area in contrast to the successes elsewhere. The scale of the public subsidies for the three sports facilities and the Rock and Roll Hall of Fame and Museum further complicates classifying Cleveland's effort as a success. In the early part of the 21st century the leases with the Indians and Cavaliers would be renegotiated, and the subsidies for annual maintenance of the ballpark and arena from the public sector would be effectively eliminated. The public sector, however, would remain responsible for structural maintenance (roof of arena, foundation of both facilities, etc.). Before the leases were renegotiated, the Indians and Cavaliers were recipients of some of the most generous subsidies given to any MLB or NBA team. Finally, the public sector's investment of tax dollars was not tied to any specific commitments of private capital to rebuild part of the downtown area. Cleveland and Cuyahoga County invested tax dollars in sports facilities and then in the Rock and Roll Hall of Fame, hoping the private sector would recommit to the future of Cleveland. Why then should Cleveland be included in a book focused on cities that successfully used sports and culture for revitalization?

The private sector investments and revitalization efforts that took place decades *after* the building of the sports and cultural facilities in a city with long-term population losses make Cleveland's experiences critical for this volume. The public sector's investments were made to bolster confidence in Cleveland's future at a time when population losses, racial conflicts and riots, the severe contraction of the manufacturing sector, and the relocation of several large corporations created an image of an urban area in the midst of a rapid decline. It is not an overexaggeration to note that a crisis of confidence dominated conversations about Cleveland. The public sector made a strategic and dramatic decision to make very large investments in big-ticket items to create an image of confidence and present a vision for a future anchored to new first-class amenities. The goal of these investments was to convince residents, visitors, and private investors that Cleveland and Northeast Ohio's future was as bright in the 1980s and 1990s as it was that day in 1902 when Daniel Burnham was hired to present the city with a new plan for its downtown area. Their efforts may not have achieved the hopes expressed until 2014.

Many cities and regions that were former manufacturing centers around the world found themselves in situations similar to that of Cleveland. Population and job losses abound amidst calls for concentrated public efforts coordinated with private sector partners to reverse the trend across North America and in several European centers (Belfast, Bilbao, Manchester, etc.). What happened in Cleveland after these large investments to inspire confidence even if delayed is important to understand as many older manufacturing centers continue to reinvent themselves through a focus on sports, entertainment, and the arts. Was Cleveland's effort successful? This chapter looks at delayed success from a revitalization effort in a former manufacturing capital.

At the abyss of the loss of confidence and at the height of outmigration, George Voinovich (at that time the lieutenant governor of Ohio and a former Cleveland official) agreed to run for mayor *if* the private sector would reengage with the city. He wanted a commitment that the business sector would agree to form an organization to help him rebuild Cleveland. After being elected mayor, Voinovich empowered a regime that then dedicated substantial resources to community development projects while championing the use of sports and cultural amenities to rebuild downtown Cleveland and its image. Could Cleveland's public–private partnership change the city's fate? This chapter addresses this difficult question by looking at private investments in the downtown area, the city, and the county in the years before and after the big-ticket strategy and in ensuing decades after a billion dollars of public investments. This assessment will help community leaders in other areas experiencing severe economic contractions to better understand what is possible from a confidence building strategy focused on big-ticket items and neighborhoods when a region's economy and population levels decline. A study of Cleveland's longer-term success from the public sector's investments also adds to the understanding of the options available for formerly dominant manufacturing centers in their efforts to create new images and a 21st-century economy.

# 8.2 The Crisis of Confidence

## 8.2.1 Racial Conflict and White Flight

The crisis of confidence in Cleveland's future began with an extraordinary population shift. During the 1960s and 1970s, the number of people moving out of Cleveland was equal to 34.5 percent of its 1960 population. The desire for a suburban lifestyle and newer houses probably initially steered some people from Cleveland and into dozens of surrounding suburban cities. The slow but steady outflow of people became a torrent after two riots rooted in the city's long-standing racial conflicts figuratively divided the area into a spatially segregated region. The first riot occurred in the summer of 1966 in the Hough area, a predominantly African-American neighborhood on the city's northeast side, and lasted for 6 nights. The riot began with a confrontation between a white bar owner and two or three black patrons (Lackritz 1968). The confrontation spilled into the streets and led to wide-scale attacks against businesses owned by whites. Hundreds of fires were set, and the violent attacks led to four deaths. The riots and looting spread across more than 20 blocks and unleashed simmering frustrations between blacks and whites.

In 1968, a second and more violent riot engulfed Glenville, another east side neighborhood. In the initial confrontation three police officers and four African-Americans were killed. The exchange of gunfire and the subsequent fires, looting, and destruction of property continued from July 23 to July 27 and gave Cleveland an image of being unsafe and at war with itself. It was later revealed that some of the guns used in the riot had been purchased with funds donated by business leaders to help advance the city in the aftermath of Carl Stokes' election as mayor.

Mr. Stokes was the first African-American elected mayor of a major American city. The business community donated $4 million to a "Cleveland Now" development campaign and placed the resources at the disposal of the new mayor. It was hoped these funds would help Mayor Stokes initiate new programs to unify residents and advance community and economic development. It was later discovered that a city employee authorized the use of some of these funds to buy the guns used by the rioters (Hanson et al. 2006). Cleveland's image was now one of complete disarray and racial conflict. The resulting white flight left Cleveland's east side a predominantly black community. In the aftermath of the riots, the large Jewish community that had lived on Cleveland's east side for decades moved to the region's eastern suburbs. By 1990, almost all of Cleveland's Jewish religious and cultural centers had moved to different eastern suburbs.[1]

The eastern part of Cleveland was soon completely separated by race and economic class from its western half and from the adjacent eastern suburbs. In later years the divide would be predominantly economic as the growing black middle and upper class also moved to the eastern suburbs. Family median income in the eastern part of Cleveland would be less than half of that of families living in the adjacent suburbs. Cleveland's school system that was once the pride of the region was soon among the most unsuccessful in Ohio. Most people who could afford to live in other cities moved out of Cleveland. The resulting racial and economic segregation would scar the city and region for decades and led to a loss of more than half of Cleveland's 1950 population. Between 1960 and 1970 more than 125,000 people left, and then another 177,000 people moved out in the 1980s. The decline continued for the next decades. By 2010 the city had fewer than 400,000 residents, and by 2012 the U.S. Bureau of the Census estimated that 390,928 lived in Cleveland. Cuyahoga County's population also began to decline in the 1970s. By 2012 it was estimated that 1,265,111 people lived in the county. This meant that from the county's apex of 1,720,835 in 1970, almost 500,000 fewer people lived in the county in 2012 (see Table 8.1a). Since the late 1990s, the immediate metropolitan area has also been losing residents. By 2012 the MSA had lost more than 250,000 residents since the riots (see Table 8.1b). Is it possible to consider what has taken place in downtown Cleveland as evidence that the city is a major league winner? Far more insight and history are required before any conclusions can be offered. What is clear, however, is that the city, county, and metropolitan statistical area (MSA) have yet to enjoy a resurgence with regard to the number of people who live in Cleveland, Cuyahoga County, or the immediate MSA.

## 8.2.2  Economic Contraction and Fiscal Default

If racial tensions and the loss of residents were not enough to tarnish the region's image and weaken confidence in the city's future, the 1970s also ushered in a prolonged period of economic change that led to the loss of more than 100,000 manufacturing jobs. The loss of jobs in the region has not ended. From 2002 through

**Table 8.1a    Population Changes in Cleveland and Cuyahoga County**

| | Cleveland | | Cuyahoga County | |
|---|---|---|---|---|
| *Year* | *Population* | *Change* | *Population* | *Change* |
| 1920 | 796,841 | | 943,945 | |
| 1930 | 900,429 | 103,588 | 1,201,445 | 257,500 |
| 1940 | 878,336 | –22,093 | 1,217,250 | 15,805 |
| 1950 | 914,808 | 36,472 | 1,389,532 | 172,282 |
| 1960 | 876,050 | –38,758 | 1,647,895 | 258,363 |
| 1970 | 750,903 | –125,147 | 1,720,835 | 72,940 |
| 1980 | 573,822 | –177,081 | 1,498,400 | –222,435 |
| 1990 | 505,616 | –68,206 | 1,412,140 | –86,260 |
| 2000 | 478,403 | –27,213 | 1,393,978 | –18,162 |
| 2010 | 396,815 | –81,588 | 1,280,122 | –113,856 |
| 2012 | 390,928 | –5,887 | 1,265,111 | –15,011 |

*Source:* U.S. Bureau of the Census, various years.

**Table 8.1b    Population Change in the Cleveland MSA**

| *Year* | *Population* | *Change* |
|---|---|---|
| 1970 | 2,320.572 | |
| 1975 | 2,237,500 | –83,072 |
| 1980 | 2,173,734 | –63,766 |
| 1985 | 2,131,240 | –42,494 |
| 1990 | 2,102,207 | –29,033 |
| 1995 | 2,150,203 | 47,996 |
| 2000 | 2,148,143 | –2,060 |
| 2005 | 2,111,699 | –36,444 |
| 2010 | 2,077,240 | –34,459 |
| 2012 | 2,063,535 | –13,705 |

*Source:* U.S. Bureau of the Census, various years.

2011, the Northeast Ohio region lost approximately 81,000 full-time jobs. In the manufacturing sector there was a loss of more than 74,000 jobs, underscoring the changes taking place across the region's economy. Job growth was the largest in the health care and social services sector. The extent of the decline in the regional market is detailed in Table 8.2. In less than one-third of the job sectors was there any increase in the number of jobs. Employment growth was concentrated in the health care and social assistance category. That growth was related to the expansion of the Cleveland Clinic and the University Hospital systems. There was also some growth in the management sector. The consolidation in the banking sector associated with the mortgage crises led to the loss of more than 13,000 jobs.

Employment levels in Cuyahoga County also declined between 2002 and 2011. In 2011 there were 33,000 fewer jobs. The county lost slightly less than 24,000 jobs in the manufacturing sector. The greatest job growth was in the health care and social assistance sector, where more than 42,000 full-time positions were created. Despite growth in one part of Greater Cleveland's economy, the loss of more than 33,000 jobs in Cuyahoga County underscored the ongoing concern with economic growth. These numbers were particularly dispiriting after more than a decade of revitalization efforts in the downtown area (see Table 8.3). This lack of progress will be discussed later in this chapter.

At this point within the case study of Cleveland, it is important to return to events in the latter part of the 20th century that were defined by the riots and the loss of manufacturing jobs. The loss of those jobs and the relocation of numerous major businesses signaled in no uncertain terms that Greater Cleveland's economy was being restructured by external events. Local politics, issues, and the actions by particular elected and civic leaders, while also important, were dwarfed by the changing nature of manufacturing (increasing use of more efficient production processes) and increasing levels of domestic and foreign competition. All of these changes contributed to a growing lack of confidence in the city and region's future. As the economic restructuring began to shake the city and region, Cleveland endured another fiscal-political crisis. While these events would encourage even more people to leave the city, they would also set in motion the beginning of Cleveland's revitalization effort.

A young reformer, Dennis Kucinich (who later served for 16 years as member of the U.S. House of Representatives) was elected mayor for a 2-year term in 1978.[2] The young and idealist reformer assumed leadership of the city as its fiscal problems were increasing and deficits were becoming an annual occurrence. To balance the budget, the city frequently borrowed money, and during Mr. Kucinich's tenure the banks demanded the sale of the municipal power company to repay several loans (the principal amount was due and the banks wanted full payment). Mayor Kucinich refused to sell the asset and the banks refused to "roll over" the debt or extend the loan. With no other revenues available to repay the loan, Cleveland became the largest city to be in a position to default on its loan payments since the Great Depression. Cleveland never actually had to declare bankruptcy, as payment

**Table 8.2   Job Changes in Northeast Ohio, 2002–2011, Selected Job Categories (job losses in italics; job increases in bold)**

| Job Categories | 2011 | 2009 | 2007 | 2005 | 2003 | 2002 | Change 2011–2002 |
|---|---|---|---|---|---|---|---|
| Utilities | 8,405 | 10,384 | 8,762 | 9,686 | 10,441 | 10,263 | *–1,858* |
| Construction | 52,509 | 54,801 | 66,609 | 66,630 | 67,671 | 68,287 | *–15,778* |
| Manufacturing | 211,277 | 202,957 | 250,912 | 267,496 | 270,821 | 285,982 | *–74,705* |
| Wholesale trade | 78,356 | 80,403 | 87,229 | 85,606 | 83,988 | 87,489 | *–9,133* |
| Retail trade | 173,355 | 173,313 | 181,097 | 185,421 | 190,721 | 186,676 | *–13,321* |
| Transportation and warehousing | 46,384 | 47,594 | 53,010 | 50,155 | 48,167 | 47,380 | *–996* |
| Information | 27,395 | 31,403 | 31,426 | 34,648 | 38,557 | 40,178 | *–12,783* |
| Finance and insurance | 63,816 | 68,727 | 73,066 | 74,955 | 76,174 | 77,472 | *–13,656* |
| Real estate and rental and leasing | 20,375 | 20,744 | 22,034 | 22,617 | 22,618 | 23,394 | *–3,019* |
| Professional, scientific, and technical | 79,088 | 79,347 | 82,153 | 77,702 | 76,886 | 79,503 | *–415* |
| Management | 44,461 | 38,752 | 38,388 | 36,608 | 33,102 | 34,108 | **10,353** |
| Administration and support, waste management | 92,082 | 80,802 | 96,374 | 93,247 | 85,407 | 82,484 | **9,598** |
| Educational services | 128,733 | 131,464 | 125,308 | 123,737 | 140,180 | 136,196 | *–7,463* |
| Health care and social assistance | 271,224 | 222,911 | 251,724 | 233,450 | 228,821 | 210,299 | **60,925** |
| Arts, entertainment, and recreation | 18,433 | 19,176 | 19,774 | 20,478 | 20,902 | 21,457 | *–3,024* |
| Accommodation and food services | 119,008 | 115,357 | 122,811 | 122,150 | 118,494 | 117,830 | **1,178** |
| Other services | 45,622 | 45,929 | 48,788 | 48,198 | 49,714 | 52,233 | *–6,611* |
| Public administration | 54,294 | 50,745 | 49,942 | 51,158 | 52,168 | 53,286 | **1,008** |

**Table 8.3   Job Changes in Cuyahoga County, 2002–2011**

| Job Category | Job Loss/Gain 2002–2011 |
|---|---|
| Utilities | –316 |
| Construction | –6,154 |
| Manufacturing | –23,787 |
| Wholesale trade | –7,251 |
| Retail trade | –11,272 |
| Transportation and warehousing | –1,951 |
| Information | –7,303 |
| Finance and insurance | –12,984 |
| Real estate | –1,435 |
| Professional, scientific, and technical | –2,353 |
| Management of companies and enterprises | 5,284 |
| Administration and support, waste management | 859 |
| Educational services | –1,734 |
| Health care and social assistance | 42,353 |
| Arts, entertainment, and recreation | –1,321 |
| Accommodation and food services | –1,411 |
| Other services | –4,301 |
| Public administration | 2,185 |

on the loans was not demanded. As a result, the city never actually defaulted on its responsibilities. Cleveland's financial difficulties, while extremely critical, were far different in magnitude than those that confronted Detroit in 2013 when the governor of Michigan had to appoint an emergency financial manager. Detroit's financial difficulties led to the emergency financial manager's decision to seek bankruptcy protection for Detroit. While there were many residents and groups that opposed the decision to enter bankruptcy, the right of the governor and financial manager to seek bankruptcy protection was upheld by a federal judge. Through 2014 the city and its creditors, together with the bankruptcy court, began the process of negotiating a settlement of the more than $18 billion of debt that Detroit could not repay. Similar events never engulfed Cleveland.

The loss of residents and businesses was a result of a feeling that the city's best days laid in the past. The standoff between the banks and Cleveland's young mayor infuriated a number of residents who signed a petition demanding that a recall election be held to remove Mayor Kucinich from office. Mayor Kucinich narrowly survived the vote and was able to complete his term of office. Yet the damage to Cleveland's image was substantial, and the movement of people and businesses from Cleveland accelerated. Lastly, the businesses that remained had lost confidence in the mayor's leadership even after Mr. Kucinich survived the recall vote. Business leaders were also frustrated that the city was unable to deal with the national publicity concerning Cleveland's brush with bankruptcy, supplying additional evidence of a disintegrating city.

In this cauldron of population decline, confrontations between the business sector and Mayor Kucinich, and the economic restructuring taking place in the region, a handful of leaders from the city's largest remaining companies sought a candidate to replace Mayor Kucinich. George Voinovich, a resident of Cleveland, a moderate to conservative Republican, and the standing lieutenant governor, had lost an earlier election for mayor. He agreed to run again for mayor and vacate his statewide office *if* the business community would agree to help him reform the city's finances and administration. He also wanted an assurance from several members of the business community that they would join an effort to advance the city and the region's economy. George Voinovich wanted to restore or reestablish a growth coalition or regime and have that group become the leading partner in an effort to rebuild downtown Cleveland. He had two other tasks or demands. He wanted this regime or growth coalition to also help him restore the city's financial stability through the formation of a management team that would study the city's operations and recommend efficiencies and cost savings. More importantly, he wanted this group to help generate a new image for Cleveland through the rebuilding of the downtown area. In effect, a precondition for George Voinovich before committing to a campaign to be mayor was a guarantee from the business community to form a public–private partnership to rebuild the downtown area and create a new image for Cleveland. In essence, the building of an arena, new ballpark, and a set of commercial, retail, and residential projects was the *quid pro quo* for bringing George Voinovich back from Columbus to Cleveland. He would forego his statewide office if a commitment from the remaining leaders of the business community existed to work with him to rebuild Cleveland. Those public–private partnerships would ultimately require very large commitments of public tax dollars to secure investments from the private sector. Investing in Cleveland after riots, the emergence of financial challenges, the loss of thousands of jobs, and the relocation of numerous corporations was fraught with too much risk for most, if not all, investors. There were far more attractive locations where private investments could be made and more profits earned. Investing in Cleveland would require a reduction of the risk through public sector investments, tax abatements, and loans guaranteed by tax collections.

# 8.3 Cleveland's Hail Mary Pass: Downtown Revitalization as Symbols of Confidence

## 8.3.1 Playhouse Square and a Citizen-Driven Public–Private Partnership

In some ways George Voinovich and Cleveland's leadership actually "backed into" a focus on entertainment, culture, and sports to rebuild confidence in the city. In the throes of the confrontation between Mayor Kucinich and the business community, a historic preservation effort led by community activists was launched to protect an extraordinary part of Cleveland's past. Through the 1950s, downtown Cleveland had a thriving theatre district anchored by five grand facilities built in the 1920s for live performances and movies. By 1969 all the theatres had closed. As more and more people left the city, entertainment facilities were built in the suburbs. The racial riots gave people additional justification for avoiding the "unsafe" city and downtown. In the 1970s plans were afoot to raze the theatres.

A group of citizen-activists concerned with preservation and restoration organized a nonprofit corporation, the Playhouse Square Foundation, to save the theatre district. With the assistance of the Cleveland and Gund Foundations, individual donors, and eventually Cuyahoga County itself—but in the absence of strong or committed leadership from the public sector—each theatre was saved and eventually restored. Today the Playhouse Square Foundation operates the largest theatre district outside of New York City, and more than 1 million tickets are sold annually for shows, plays, concerts, speeches, and other performances. To advance real estate development in the adjacent area, leadership from the Playhouse Theatre Foundation created the Cleveland Theatre District Development Corporation. This community development corporation (CDC) has restored some buildings and built new commercial space, parking facilities, a hotel, and a public plaza for performances, celebrations, and concerts. For a city searching for a success story and evidence that downtown life could be restored, Playhouse Square became a symbol of what was possible. The restoration of Playhouse Square also underscored the value of partnerships between community groups, leading foundations, the private sector, and individual benefactors. The crowds that attend shows and other events created a lively atmosphere in a part of the downtown area that had been largely abandoned. Entertainment thus became a vehicle for rebuilding confidence and optimism. Playhouse Square's success in attracting crowds and financial commitments for its restoration from foundations, businesses, and people across the region amidst dismal news for Cleveland created a blueprint for a revitalization strategy. Cleveland would follow Indianapolis and focus on entertainment, sports, and culture, and cultivate public–private partnerships to achieve its goals. Three of Playhouse Square's theatres along a restored Euclid Avenue are visible in Figure 8.2.

Figure 8.2    Playhouse Square—Theatres and restored buildings, products of a public–private partnership on the eastern edge of the downtown area. (Courtesy of Mark S. Rosentraub.)

## 8.3.2 The Public–Private Partnership Mayoralty of George Voinovich and the Reinvigoration of a Regime

George Voinovich needed no prompting or convincing that the city and region's future was linked to (1) downtown and (2) strong partnerships between the public and private sector. He recognized that a massive rebuilding effort was needed to restore confidence in the city and generate excitement about its future.[3] During Mr. Voinovich's tenure, a declining industrial area adjacent to downtown and located along the Cuyahoga River, known as the Flats, was redeveloped as an entertainment destination with restaurants and pubs. A perfect complement to the attractions at Playhouse Square, the Flats, unfortunately, was located more than a mile from the theatres. The Flats would go through a second decline in the aftermath of violence at a nightclub. After 2003 it became the site of new residential developments and a planned new neighborhood (which in turn was delayed by the credit and financial crisis of 2008 and 2009). With the recovery of the credit markets, there was a renewed commitment of funds, and the Flats reemerged as a site for new real estate development. By 2014, the Flats had finally emerged as the development site that the Voinovich administration had envisioned (www.flatseast.com) decades after redevelopment efforts were first initiated.

Focusing on the Flats was a logical extension of the success of Playhouse Square. If people would return to the city for unique entertainment venues, a restored Flats area that turned abandoned warehouses and industrial properties into restaurants, clubs, and pubs, along with some new condominiums and apartments, might breathe life and vitality into the downtown area. It would take several decades before the Flats would become the development that Cleveland needed.

Mayor Voinovich's focus, however, was on projects that could rapidly change impressions that the city's best days had already passed. The Flats had promise, but in addition to the redevelopment of the Flats, the Voinovich administration and its private business partners were focused on a new ballpark for the Cleveland Indians. In 1984, a proposal for a domed stadium financed by a property tax increase was defeated by a 2-to-1 margin. Undeterred, in 1986, the Greater Cleveland Domed Stadium Corporation acquired the land and buildings that housed the deteriorating Central Market providing a *de facto* location for a new ballpark. To purchase the land the Domed Stadium Corporation received a $6 million grant from the State of Ohio and borrowed $18 million from area banks. With no revenue streams to repay the debt, the Domed Stadium Corporation turned to Cleveland Tomorrow. Cleveland Tomorrow was created and funded by the city's business leaders as part of their commitment to help Mayor Voinovich in his efforts to restore the city's luster. Cleveland Tomorrow assumed responsibility for the debt, and this initiated the first of many neighborhood and downtown real estate development deals that would be financed by the city's leading businesses through Cleveland Tomorrow and other organizations that its board would create.

Cleveland's Central Market mirrored the downtown area as it too was in decline. By 1981 it had fewer than 40 tenants and was but a shell of its former prominence as a retail and wholesale produce, meat, and fish market for the region. Some buildings were completely dilapidated. The private acquisition of the land was an effort to reengage the process to build a new downtown ballpark and to remove the stumbling block of assembling the needed land. The 28-acre site was actually large enough to accommodate a ballpark and an arena, as advocates for changing downtown Cleveland into a sports and entertainment center also wanted to convince the region's NBA team to return from their suburban home in distant Richfield. In 1988, a new proposal was presented to voters to build a ballpark and arena. This time property taxes would not be raised, but taxes would instead be increased on the sale of alcohol and tobacco products. It too failed; voters again refused to support higher taxes for sports and entertainment facilities.

Disappointment with the public vote for a domed stadium and then a ballpark and arena did not stop interest in other redevelopment efforts. A public–private partnership was created to remodel a deteriorating and abandoned train station affixed to the city's landmark Terminal Tower. Reopened as a mall in 1990, new commercial space was added in 1991 that included a Ritz-Carlton Hotel. The BP America Building opened in 1985 in the downtown area (without any tax abatements), and the adjacent Key Tower opened in 1991, but work on this structure was initiated during George Voinovich's administration (Hanson et al. 2006).

### 8.3.3 Mayor Michael White and the Ballpark and Arena Proposal's Redux

In November 1989 Michael White was elected mayor. A surprise winner, the city's second African-American mayor was not a sports fan, but indicated he would be inclined to urge voters to support a tax increase for a ballpark and arena if he could be convinced the facilities would advance economic development in downtown Cleveland. Impressed with the possibility that the arena could return a large number of events from the suburbs to the city, Mayor White endorsed and then strenuously campaigned to increase taxes to build two sports facilities. Framed as an economic development and revitalization program, the proposal focused on (1) the investments that would be made by the Cleveland Indians (and the support anticipated from the Cleveland Cavaliers if they too returned to Cleveland to play in a new arena), (2) the financial support from the business community through Cleveland Tomorrow, and (3) the changes for the downtown area from the presence of sports and entertainment events all year. Voters were again asked to support a new tax on the sale of alcohol and tobacco products to build a 42,000-seat open-air ballpark for the Indians and an arena for the Cavaliers with seating for approximately 20,000 spectators. The arena would also host a number of other entertainment events. Cleveland lacked a venue for major entertainment events since the Cleveland Arena that was built in the 1930s had been razed. The facility was closed after the Cavaliers moved to Richfield, Ohio, a suburban city located midway between Cleveland (to the north) and Akron to the south.

With Mayor White's enthusiastic endorsement, the countywide referendum to build both facilities passed with support from 51.6 percent of the voters. A majority of the voters who lived in Cleveland, 56 percent, voted *against* the tax increase, illustrating the inability of both white and black mayors to secure support for the concept from the city's voters. Support for the new ballpark and an arena to encourage the Cavaliers to move back to downtown Cleveland came from suburban residents. It took 6 years to secure public approval for a new ballpark and arena (Stoffel 1990). While the plans for the new facility were advanced by a regime, the defeat of two previous proposals and the time it took to secure public support suggest local politics were not as firmly controlled as some critics of regimes and their influence have argued (Squires 1989). The support from suburban voters and the opposition by residents of Cleveland were also somewhat counterintuitive. Residents of the county and businesses would pay a substantial proportion (a vast majority) of the taxes that would constitute the public sector's investment in the facilities. In addition, Cleveland retains all of the earnings taxes that would be generated by people working at the facilities and the athletes and entertainers. Cleveland would also retain revenue generated by ticket taxes at the ballpark (the ticket taxes collected at the arena would be part of the city's investment in the arena) and the taxes collected from people parking their cars while attending events at the ballpark and arena.

The 1990 campaign for the tax increase for the two facilities was conducted amidst an implied threat from MLB that it would approve any request from the Indians to relocate if the new ballpark was not built. The Indians' ownership never said it would move the team if a new ballpark was not built. MLB's commissioner, Fay Vincent, in testimony before Cleveland's city council, declared that the team's situation satisfied the criteria the league used to approve relocation requests. The intent of his message was clear (Rosentraub 1997a). Without a new ballpark, the Indians would be supported in their efforts to join other corporations that had also left Cleveland.

Voters' concerns with the deal for the new facilities that produced their relatively modest levels of support were a result of four issues, none of which dealt with opposition to an investment by the public to restore confidence in the region and city's future. The concerns raised during the campaign were nothing if not prescient. First, firm agreements with both teams regarding the cost of the facilities and the teams' contributions and financial responsibilities did not exist. As a result, the public sector's actual financial responsibility or investment was unclear. Second, leases had not been negotiated with either team, meaning there was no agreement regarding responsibilities for ongoing and long-term maintenance expenses. Third, voters were not presented with a plan that explained how the sports facilities would be included in any revitalization effort. Fourth, neither team was asked to make any commitment for real estate development adjacent to the facilities to complement or advance the revitalization of downtown Cleveland.

## 8.3.4 Large Subsidies and the Dispersion of Assets

Asking voters to approve a new tax, a tax increase, or any form of an investment by governments before leases, firm construction estimates, and a memorandum of understanding regarding responsibilities for short- and long-term maintenance gave the team owners substantial negotiating advantages when it came time to create leases and construction agreements. With voters having approved a tax, elected officials had to deliver a deal with the teams or face public criticism for campaigning to raise taxes and then being unable to secure the agreements necessary to retain and attract the teams. The approach taken—get the money and then finalize the plans—actually minimized the political leverage the public sector had to secure larger investments from the team or any commitment from them for related real estate development. Convincing reluctant voters to support tax increases for sports facilities is usually easier when there is a firm commitment from the teams to pay designated amounts of money. Voters had already rejected two different proposals for new taxes to pay for sports facilities. Those actions created an environment in which leaders could have asked for commitments from the teams to reduce voters' opposition to higher taxes. With voter approval secured, the owners could seek to reduce their financial responsibilities and force elected and other community leaders to endure any criticism for having campaigned to raise taxes and then failing to get the teams to commit to Cleveland. The teams used their bargaining strength to secure extraordinary lease arrangements and minimize their financial responsibilities for capital and operating costs (Rosentraub 1997b).

The excessive subsidies did not end with sports facilities. Cleveland also added big-ticket museums to its quest to create a new image, and those were also heavily subsidized. In 1983, music company executives in New York City created the Rock and Roll Hall of Fame and selected its first members even before a home for the hoped for facility was identified. After also considering New York and Memphis as possible locations, Cleveland was selected. Cleveland's link to the history and evolution of rock and roll was limited to legendary disc jockey Alan Freed, who popularized the term *rock and roll* to describe the new, emerging music style. Mr. Freed also organized numerous rock and roll concerts that provided a showcase for emerging performers at several Midwest venues. Cleveland's selection, however, was not related to this connection to rock and roll's history, but to the public sector's willingness to provide $65 million in tax money to build the new hall of fame.

The Rock and Roll Hall of Fame's leadership had recruited renowned architect I.M. Pei to design the facility and had expended a great deal of time to convince him to accept the commission. Mr. Pei was not attracted to any of the more central locations for the hall's location in downtown Cleveland. He preferred a more dramatic and dynamic location for his forthcoming masterpiece and chose a site on the shores of Lake Erie. Technically, the location east of Municipal Stadium (and the new stadium for the Cleveland Browns that is now known as First Energy Stadium) is north of downtown, or at the most northern part of what should be properly referred to as the greater downtown area. The Rock and Roll Hall of Fame and Museum is also 1.7 miles from the Flats area, and most walking maps estimate that it takes about a half hour to walk between that area and the Rock and Roll Hall of Fame and Museum. The spectacular building is distant from the center of downtown and the Flats area, where a great deal of new development is taking place. As a result, the extraordinary building designed by one of the world's greatest architects actually contributed to the dispersed nature of the revitalization effort taking place in a central city and region that was suffering from a loss of residents and businesses.

After several delays, construction began in 1993 and the Rock and Roll Hall of Fame and Museum opened in 1995. A science museum located nearby opened in 1996, establishing this part of downtown Cleveland as a mini-museum area on what was initially described as America's "north coast." The science museum was also paid for by the public sector. The nearby new home for the Cleveland Browns, 4/10 of a mile away from the Rock and Roll Hall of Fame, opened in 1999. Before the Flats redevelopment was completed, and before the downtown area was revitalized, and long after the Playhouse Square initiative was launched, greater downtown Cleveland had its fourth area in downtown undergoing revitalization.

The new ballpark and arena opened in 1994, and with construction of the Rock and Roll Hall of Fame and Museum and the science center underway, there was some hope that the revitalization effort might be enhancing confidence in the city and region's future. That exuberance lasted only for a short period of time. In 1995, Cleveland and the region were traumatized when Art Modell, owner of the Cleveland Browns, announced he was moving the team (a Cleveland icon) to Baltimore. Mr. Modell was frustrated by the deals given the Indians and Cavaliers while his team continued to play in a stadium built in the 1930s and which was commonly referred to as the "mistake by the lake." In contrast, Maryland and Baltimore agreed to build a new stadium for the Browns and give the team control of most, if not all, revenues without asking Mr. Modell to accept any financial responsibility for building the new facility.

Losing the Browns was as traumatic for Cleveland as was the loss of the Dodgers for Brooklyn. Leadership in the stunned city and region mobilized support, and the NFL decided to create a new Cleveland Browns franchise *if* a new stadium was ready for the 1999 season. To meet this condition, Cleveland would need to use the foundations of the existing facility (Municipal Stadium), meaning the new stadium would also be on the northern edge of the greater downtown area. This location, distant from the other sports facilities, also used very valuable lakefront property, reducing the public's access and opportunities to use this asset for residential development or the creation of new areas for the public's enjoyment of the lakefront. Assembling land for a stadium located closer to the two other sports facilities would have taken too long to satisfy the NFL's schedule. It was also possible that environmental and construction challenges at other sites would have substantially increased the cost for the stadium at a more central location. Cleveland accepted the NFL's condition, and Cuyahoga County taxpayers assumed responsibility for more than 70 percent of the cost of building the new stadium in exchange for a new franchise that would retain the name and colors of the beloved Browns.

Cleveland's Hail Mary pass to revitalize its downtown, change its image, and instill confidence in the city and region's future included the:

1. Building of three new sports facilities (see Figure 8.3 depicting Quicken Loans Arena before a planned renovation expected in 2014–2015)
2. Restoration of the five theatres that constitute Playhouse Square
3. Opening of two retail venues/shopping centers
4. Building of the Rock and Roll Hall of Fame and Museum
5. Building of the science center and IMAX theatre
6. Building of several new commercial office towers, each supported with property tax abatements

The next section of the chapter focuses on what was achieved from this investment in an image of confidence in the future.

Figure 8.3 Quicken Loans Arena, the arena that was part of the Gateway Redevelopment Authority and one of three sports facilities built in downtown Cleveland. (Courtesy of Mark S. Rosentraub.)

## 8.4 The Results of Cleveland's Hail Mary Pass

The major goal for the big-ticket investments was to give investors confidence that downtown Cleveland, and the city itself, was poised for growth and a far more robust future. The initial step in this confidence building exercise was to use entertainment and sports to increase the number of people visiting the downtown area. The excitement from sports and entertainment, it was hoped, would convince the businesses that were still located in the downtown area to remain. If businesses stopped relocating, then the employment base in downtown Cleveland could be stabilized. The revitalization strategy anchored to entertainment and sports was an effort to jump-start private investment and convince the remaining corporations to give Cleveland a chance to revitalize the downtown area. If the exodus of firms could be curtailed, and if millions of visits to downtown venues could be achieved, then perhaps the city's decline could be reversed. If the sports and entertainment amenities created a sufficient level of activity in the downtown area, and if a few businesses could be convinced to remain, then perhaps some other businesses would consider the downtown area as a place for their offices and a new residential base could be built, turning downtown Cleveland into a residential neighborhood for young professionals and others interested in an urban/downtown lifestyle.

It is difficult to measure the connections between any single investment and elevated levels of confidence. It is also impossible to associate the presence of one more sports venue—or one less amenity—with new private investments. Instead, what has to be studied is the association or correlation between a package of amenities, the design and location of the individual assets, and the overall changes in job location and residential growth before and after the building of the big-ticket items. Insight can be gained, from a comparison of private sector investment levels, job locations, and residential choices prior to and after the building of the sports and entertainment venues, but causality cannot be statistically illustrated, as numerous other macro- and microeconomic factors also affect outcomes.[4]

## 8.4.1 Private Investment Levels in Cleveland: Nonresidential Projects

A view of private sector investments in Cleveland in the years surrounding the initiation of the revitalization effort was produced through an analysis of construction data collected by the FW Dodge Corporation. This firm tabulates construction costs for all nonresidential projects. Data for Cleveland and Cuyahoga County were available for the years 1994 through 2003. This information was analyzed at the zip code and neighborhood level so that figures for downtown Cleveland could be tabulated. To compare outcomes in the years after many of the big-ticket items were built with those figures from the 1980s, information was collected from Cuyahoga County government offices in association with staff from the Greater Cleveland Partnership. This information, however, could not be classified by neighborhood or zip code area, and exists only as totals for each city. Finally, as FW Dodge's data do not include residential construction, data from the Cuyahoga County tax files were used to tabulate private sector investment in residential properties.

Between 1994 and 2003, there was a total of $3.6 billion in construction activity in nonresidential projects throughout Cleveland and $632.3 million in construction activity in the downtown area. This period corresponds to the initiation and completion of several of the sports and cultural amenities. The year-by-year totals for the downtown area and Cleveland, as well as the value of the projects in constant dollars, are contained in Table 8.4. Construction figures for 1980 through 1989—the years immediately before the investment in several big-ticket amenities—are also tabulated.

Comparisons across time periods are always difficult in that national and regional economic conditions vary and contribute to any observed differences. Further, there are numerous tangible and intangible factors that influence investor confidence. In the absence of any binding agreements that firms would make

**Table 8.4 Construction Costs for All Nonresidential Projects in Cleveland and Downtown Cleveland (2004 Dollars)**

| Year | Yearly Construction Costs Downtown | Yearly Construction Costs Cleveland | Construction Costs—2004 Dollars Downtown | Construction Costs—2004 Dollars Cleveland |
|---|---|---|---|---|
| 1995 | 38,923,393 | 118,108,363 | 47,961,493 | 145,533,392 |
| 1996 | 82,521,064 | 149,483,906 | 98,982,520 | 179,303,234 |
| 1997 | 46,646,432 | 156,259,076 | 54,298,675 | 181,893,029 |
| 1998 | 90,953,454 | 2,359,125,487 | 104,236,260 | 2,703,651,239 |
| 1999 | 184,384,537 | 306,025,561 | 207,839,417 | 344,953,949 |
| 2000 | 64,695,993 | 120,163,442 | 72,925,733 | 135,448,992 |
| 2001 | 60,159,490 | 169,771,013 | 63,629,569 | 179,563,630 |
| 2002 | 55,949,990 | 120,443,538 | 58,508,968 | 125,952,249 |
| 2003 | 8,051,997 | 115,529,928 | 8,207,099 | 117,755,326 |
| Total | 632,286,350 | 3,616,060,311 | 716,589,734 | 4,114,055,040 |
| 1980–1989 | Not available | 1,006,959,500 | Not available | 1,842,735,885 |

*Source:* Data from 1995 through 2003 from the FW Dodge Corporation; data from 1980 through 1989 from Cuyahoga County public records and reports collected and maintained by Greater Cleveland Partnership.

specific investments if a particular public–private partnership was created, it is not possible to attribute any observed outcomes to the building of a particular asset.

With these caveats in mind, from 1980 to 1989 private construction projects in Cleveland had a value of slightly more than $1 billion. When these figures are converted to 2004 dollars, the value of the construction projects was $1.85 billion. For the period 1995 through 2003 (a 9-year period), the present value of the nonresidential construction projects was $4.1 billion, or more than twice the figure for the 1980s. In downtown Cleveland alone, an area marked by the loss of many businesses in the 1980s, $717 million (in 2004 dollars) was spent for new construction.

### 8.4.2 Private Investment in Residential Properties

From 1980 to 1989, Cuyahoga County records indicate that $54.8 million was invested in residential properties in Cleveland; the value of these expenditures in 2004 dollars was $100.3 million. From 1990 through 2002, almost four times as much was invested in residential real estate in Cleveland (see Table 8.5). Baade (1996), among others, has noted that some large civic projects such as sports facilities

**Table 8.5   Construction Costs for Residential Projects in Cleveland, Property Tax Abatements Received**

| Years | Annual Construction Cost | Construction Cost—2004 Dollars |
|---|---|---|
| 1980–1989 | $54,827,800 | $100,334,874 |
| 1990 | 10,880,991 | 15,817,579 |
| 1991 | 7,574,744 | 10,422,307 |
| 1992 | 6,968,739 | 9,345,478 |
| 1993 | 14,592,407 | 18,951,710 |
| 1994 | 26,992,227 | 34,192,616 |
| 1995 | 24,257,806 | 29,890,523 |
| 1996 | 32,109,205 | 38,514,409 |
| 1997 | 30,389,211 | 35,374,493 |
| 1998 | 35,767,450 | 40,990,914 |
| 1999 | 40,869,604 | 46,068,476 |
| 2000 | 33,711,063 | 37,999,324 |
| 2001 | 35,278,693 | 37,313,615 |
| 2002 | 39,325,609 | 41,124,239 |
| Total | $338,717,749 | $396,005,683 |

*Source:* Data from 1980 through 1989 from Cuyahoga County public records and reports collected and maintained by Greater Cleveland Partnership; data from 1990 through 2002 from the Maxine Goodman Levin College of Urban Affairs, Cleveland State University.

have no positive effects on regional economic development. These same facilities, however, can move economic activity within a region, and in many instances that is an important policy objective. The movement of economic activity to the center city can improve the tax base of that community and reduce sprawl by increasing the reuse of existing infrastructure. It is important to note after the building of a number of big-ticket items, during a period of substantial expansion of the U.S. economy and of a very low level of population growth in Northeast Ohio, there was a large increase in private sector investment in both nonresidential and residential properties in Cleveland and in the downtown area. These investments, and the tax revenues that result for Cleveland and its public schools, are the returns from the public–private partnerships that have been formed. In reviewing these data, causality (that the new private sector investments are a result of the public–private partnerships) is not implied. In an analysis of private sector job retention in the downtown areas of Cincinnati, Cleveland, Columbus, and Indianapolis, however, it was found that Cleveland did far better than the other areas and actually had job growth despite the prevailing decentralization trends in the Midwest and the United States (Austrian and Rosentraub 2002). Those jobs in Cleveland and the resulting tax increases for the city and public school system were one of the returns from the public's investments.

The residential development that took place in Cleveland was also aided by the city's creation of a program to grant property tax abatements to owners of new homes. Cleveland's program requires owners to pay the full taxes due as a result of increments to the value of land. The program established the value of all land at 20 percent of the purchase price, with the remaining portion of the home's sale price removed from the calculation of property tax liabilities for 15 years. The property tax abatement could be transferred to subsequent buyers. Many other cities in Cuyahoga County also provide tax abatements to new buyers. Cleveland's elected and appointed civic officials hoped that investment in the sports and other amenities, combined with a competitive abatement program, would bring new residents to the city, or attract existing residents to buy a new and more expensive home in the city. There was also hope that the abatement would convince homeowners to improve their homes. Prior to the existence of the abatement program, some had observed that the virtual absence of new homes with values in excess of $150,000 forced residents seeking new and larger homes to leave Cleveland.

A report card on the performance of the property tax abatement program is contained in Table 8.6. The number of properties returning 100 percent of their value to the property tax rolls beginning in 2007 will produce $53.8 million (2008 dollars) in new property taxes for Cleveland each year beginning in 2020. A survey of people who bought these homes found that 60 percent would have lived elsewhere if the abatements were not available (Mikelbank et al. 2010). This suggests that the amenities in Cleveland likely produced $21.5 million in new annual property taxes, with the balance of the gain attributed to the presence of the abatements and the other amenities in Cleveland.

There was also a general upswing in private sector investment activity (residential and nonresidential) in the years after the opening of the sports facilities. While the new investments took place during a time of a general expansion in the national economy, Cleveland was still in the throes of the severe economic restructuring that gripped the manufacturing sector and was still suffering from population losses. While it is impossible to answer whether or not this level of private sector investment would have taken place if the public sector had not made its investments in the sports facilities, interviews with community leaders indicated that several believed the public sector investments were critical, especially given the substantial job losses in the manufacturing sector.[5]

**Table 8.6  Property Tax Revenues to Cleveland, the Cleveland Public Schools, and Cuyahoga County from Homes That Received Abatements**

| Year Taxed | Number | Assessed Value | Cumulative Assessed Value | New Property Taxes | Cumulative New Property Taxes |
|---|---|---|---|---|---|
| 2007 | 65 | $2,695,595 | $2,695,595 | $170,410 | $170,410 |
| 2008 | 132 | 5,980,835 | 8,676,430 | 374,460 | 544,870 |
| 2009 | 96 | 4,038,895 | 12,715,325 | 252,875 | 797,745 |
| 2010 | 53 | 2,377,340 | 15,092,665 | 148,845 | 946,591 |
| 2011 | 35 | 1,125,075 | 16,217,740 | 70,441 | 1,017,032 |
| 2012 | 273 | 10,364,935 | 26,582,675 | 648,949 | 1,665,980 |
| 2013 | 237 | 10,218,565 | 36,801,240 | 639,784 | 2,305,765 |
| 2014 | 147 | 8,221,150 | 45,022,390 | 514,726 | 2,820,491 |
| 2015 | 288 | 17,089,450 | 62,111,840 | 1,138,714 | 3,959,205 |
| 2016 | 261 | 15,705,305 | 77,817,145 | 1,021,551 | 4,980,755 |
| 2017 | 270 | 22,937,250 | 100,754,395 | 1,602,706 | 6,583,462 |
| 2018 | 181 | 11,306,540 | 112,060,935 | 731,434 | 7,314,895 |
| 2019 | 481 | 34,615,105 | 146,676,040 | 2,270,324 | 9,585,220 |
| 2020 | 327 | 22,671,810 | 169,347,850 | 1,485,638 | 11,070,858 |
| Total | 2,846 | | | | 53,763,279 |
| Taxes paid, properties bought because of abatements | | | | | 32,257,967 |
| Taxes paid, properties probably bought without abatement | | | | | 21,505,312 |

*Source:* Mikelbank, Post, and Rosentraub, 2010.

## 8.4.3 Tax Revenue Changes

The existence of the earnings tax as the largest source of revenue for Cleveland is why the city's policies and practices are focused on securing and maintaining jobs. Regional growth that involves new jobs outside of the city does not directly enhance Cleveland's fiscal situation. The redevelopment of downtown—with its majority financial support from Cuyahoga County—if it contributes to job attraction and retention in Cleveland, has the potential to substantially protect and perhaps enhance revenue streams for the city. Corporations are also subject to a 2-percent tax on their earnings.

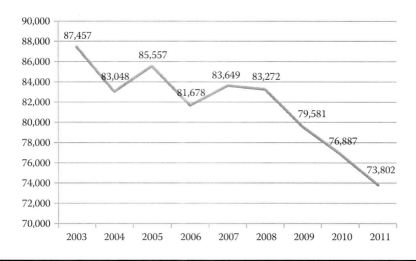

**Figure 8.4a   Downtown Cleveland full-time jobs by year, 2002 to 2011. (From U.S. Department of Commerce, *On the Map*.)**

Cleveland's largest source of "own source" revenues (funds that a city collects as a result of the taxes it administers) is a function of property and income taxes. Ohio permits its cities to collect an earnings tax which means people pay this income tax to the city in which they work (not where they live). As described in Figure 8.4a, in the downtown area, employment levels declined from 87,457 in 2011 to 73,802; that could imply that income tax receipts would decline. In contrast, however, in the University Circle area, 4 miles east of the downtown area, more than 15,000 jobs were added during this same period (see Figure 8.4b). Across the entire city, in 2003 there were a total of 273,412 jobs. In 2011 there were 256,480, meaning the city lost 16,932 as the recession came to an end and a slow recovery began (see Figure 8.5). During this same period, Ohio lost 4.1 percent of its full-time jobs. Cleveland lost 6.2 percent which while quite unfortunate was still an accomplishment given the collapse of two banks headquartered in downtown Cleveland and the loss of manufacturing jobs. University Circle's growth was able to offset some of the losses resulting from the contraction of employment in the downtown area. In that part of Cleveland the job losses were a partial result of the consolidation of two failed banks and the loss of employment in other sectors including management and finance. The gains recorded in the University Circle area were a result of the expansion of the Cleveland Clinic and the University Hospitals system. This meant the growth in the University Circle area surrounding Case Western Reserve University was in the health care sector with some new jobs in the education sector as well. In addition, many of these jobs were quite high paying generating important new income taxes for Cleveland.

What did these changes mean for Cleveland's tax collections? During the recession, as would be expected, earnings tax revenues declined. But by 2012, revenue

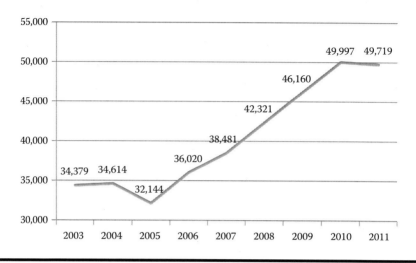

**Figure 8.4b** University Circle (Cleveland) full-time jobs by year, 2002 to 2011. (From U.S. Department of Commerce, *On the Map*.)

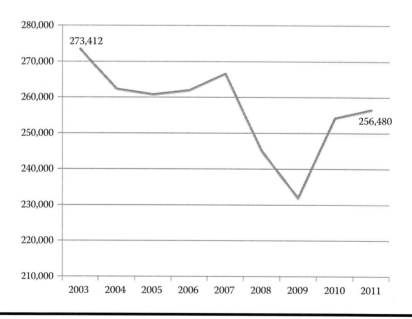

**Figure 8.5** Cleveland (entire city) full-time jobs by year, 2003 to 2011. (From U.S Department of Commerce, *On the Map*.)

levels rose to (unadjusted) levels that were enjoyed prior to the recession. More importantly, the income tax now accounts for 74.9 percent of the own source revenues collected by Cleveland. As large factories continued to close or "down size," property tax revenues continued to decline and in relative terms were slightly less than 17 percent of the value of the income taxes collected. These changes, illustrated in Table 8.10 are discussed in greater detail in the last section of this chapter. What is important to note, however, is that while Cleveland did lose jobs at a faster rate than what was observed for the state, it was able to stabilize its financial base by the retention of a sufficient number of higher income jobs.

As should be expected given the economic restructuring taking place and outmigration, the situation regarding property tax receipts was not as favorable. Large manufacturing plants traditionally generated high levels of property taxes, and as those facilities closed or were downsized, revenues declined. Greater Cleveland lost more than 43 percent of its more than 500,000 manufacturing jobs between 1980 and 2007 (Austrian 2008), and the closing of plants left the city with a declining property tax base. Lastly, in those sectors of the economy that are expanding, some of the facilities (hospitals) are exempt from local property taxes.

The Indians, Cavaliers, and Browns were permitted to retain all the revenue generated at the ballpark, arena, and stadium, but to ensure that some tax benefits accrued to Cleveland to help offset the investment made by its residents through the higher taxes, the teams agreed to support the creation of an amusement tax. An 8-percent tax is applied against all tickets sold for all events held at the ballpark, arena, and stadium. Economists have repeatedly underscored that ticket taxes represent foregone income for teams (Sandy et al. 2004). In the absence of an amusement tax, ticket prices do not decline. Teams simply price at the highest level the market will support. A tax does not increase the price. If the government passes a tax, it shares in the revenue. If the tax does not exist, then the team realizes additional revenue. Cleveland pledged ticket tax revenue from the arena to its construction.

In 1995 Cleveland collected $7.2 million from the amusement taxes, and this grew to $13.9 in 2007. In constant dollars the increment was approximately $4.3 million. The differences from year to year reflect changes in attendance levels that are linked to the teams' performance. In the years that the Indians and Cavaliers have been in their respective play-offs, revenues rose, and when the teams have less success, revenues decline. The Browns have not played a home play-off game since their return to the NFL (see Table 8.7).

## 8.4.4 Job Retention and Employment Changes

Another view of changes in Cleveland after the investments in the big-ticket items is provided in Table 8.8 and look at changes prior to the recession. The total payrolls of all businesses in Cleveland for the entire city and for the two largest employment centers, downtown and the University Circle area, are included in the table. University Circle is home to two of the region's largest employers, the

**Table 8.7 Amusement Tax Revenue Collections**

| | Amusement Tax Revenues | | |
|---|---|---|---|
| Year | Annual Revenues | In 2007 Dollars | Play-Offs |
| 1995 | $7,173,059 | $9,659,529 | Indians, Cavaliers |
| 1996 | 7,505,426 | 9,838,719 | Indians, Cavaliers |
| 1997 | 9,977,427 | 12,692,843 | Indians |
| 1998 | 8,932,106 | 11,187,242 | Indians, Cavaliers |
| 1999 | 9,750,710 | 12,011,830 | Indians |
| 2000 | 13,249,323 | 15,886,629 | |
| 2001 | 12,067,391 | 13,948,829 | Indians |
| 2002 | 12,581,373 | 14,378,712 | |
| 2003 | 11,291,310 | 12,577,662 | |
| 2004 | 10,071,768 | 11,007,159 | |
| 2005 | 11,082,443 | 11,762,383 | |
| 2006 | 11,879,154 | 12,124,764 | Cavaliers |
| 2007 | 13,930,166 | 13,930,166 | Indians, Cavaliers |

*Source:* Department of Finance, City of Cleveland, Comprehensive Annual Financial Reports, 1995, 1996, 1997, 1998, 1999, 2001, 2002, 2003, 2004, 2005, 2006, 2007.

**Table 8.8 Payroll Earnings in Cleveland, 1993 and 2007 (in millions of dollars; all figures in 2007 dollars)**

| | 1993 | | 2007 | | |
|---|---|---|---|---|---|
| | | | | | Percent |
| Cleveland Community | Amount | Percent | Amount | Of Total | Change |
| Downtown | $6,758 | 53.5 | $6,808 | 48.1 | 3.3 |
| University Circle | 1,211 | 9.6 | 1,988 | 14.1 | 51.9 |
| Elsewhere in Cleveland | 4,674 | 36.9 | 5,344 | 37.9 | 4.7 |
| Total | 12,643 | 100 | 14,140 | 100 | 11.8 |

Cleveland Clinic and University Hospital. Both health care centers are also at the center of Ohio's strategic plan focused on bioengineering, research into new therapies, procedures, and equipment, and new systems for the delivery of healthcare. It is also important to look at these data in light of the population losses suffered by Cleveland and the state's overall lower economic growth rates. Payroll levels in Cleveland rose, in real terms, by almost $1.5 billion from 1993 to 2007 (prior to the recession). The concentration of payroll dollars in the downtown area grew by a modest $50 million. Most importantly, however, there was no real decline even as population levels in the city and county declined. Given the growing importance of the health care sector for the region, it is not surprising that the real increase in wages in the University Circle area was equal to $777 million in the years immediately after the opening of the sports venues (see Table 8.8). As will be discussed later in this chapter, this job growth in the University Circle section of Cleveland continued through 2011, leading to higher earnings tax revenues for the city.

## 8.5  Extra Benefits from Building Amenities: Regional Cooperation

In Cleveland, as in many areas when economic contraction and restructuring occur, there are calls for greater regional cooperation among local governments (Leland and Rosentraub 2009). There have been repeated claims that the failure to have higher levels of regional cooperation has contributed to the economic declines for Cleveland. Too often the countywide levels of cooperation achieved through the building of the amenities in downtown Cleveland are ignored (Rosentraub and Al-Habil 2009). The big-ticket projects were undertaken to maintain some degree of centrality and vibrancy for Cleveland, but were financed at the county level, requiring cooperation for development from residents of 57 different cities.

Cuyahoga County was responsible for most of the public investment in the big-ticket items. This meant that the wealthier residents of suburban cities paid a large portion of the costs for the big-ticket items. Cleveland residents also saw their taxes increase. Since there are twice as many people living in the suburbs (compared to the number of residents of Cleveland), the burden for rebuilding downtown Cleveland was shifted to nonresidents. Cuyahoga County's main source of revenue is the property tax. Since the county's residents are far wealthier, the value of residential property in the county is also far greater, further shifting the burden of financing the rebuilding of downtown Cleveland to nonresidents. Countywide taxing instruments were used for the public's investment in all three sports facilities, the Rock and Roll Hall of Fame and Museum ($65 million), Playhouse Square ($18.7 million), and the Tower City retail center ($7 million). What makes these investments and the tax base sharing more notable is that all of the tax revenue generated by the facilities and the income tax paid by employees and the athletes accrues to Cleveland.[6] In addition, a substantial majority of the earnings taxes paid to Cleveland comes from commuters who work in the city but live in one of the suburbs (Mikelbank et al. 2010). The revitalization of downtown Cleveland is an unheralded example of regionalism and intergovernmental cooperation among a county's taxpayers.

## 8.6 Amending Cleveland's Major League Loser Status: New Leases

The efforts to improve Cleveland and Cuyahoga County were not limited to attracting private sector investments after the subsidies were provided. An effort was also led by the commissioners appointed by the city and county to oversee the maintenance and operation of the ballpark, the arena, the related parking garages, and the two public plazas. To oversee those tasks and the building of the facilities themselves, Cleveland and Cuyahoga County created the Gateway Economic Development Corporation of Greater Cleveland (Gateway). This nonprofit corporation was also responsible for ensuring that property tax payments were made. Even though the sports facilities were owned by a public agency (Gateway), they were exclusively used to generate profit for the two teams. From the revenues it received from the rents paid by the teams, it was agreed that Gateway would pay property taxes to support the Cleveland public schools and hold the school district harmless from the tax effects of removing the land from the property tax rolls.

Five volunteer commissioners lead Gateway: Cleveland's mayor appoints two of these individuals, and each of Cuyahoga County's three elected county commissioners (this form of county governance has been changed; the county's elected executive and a new county commission now select Cuyahoga County's representatives to Gateway's board). The five commissioners have the authority to hire the needed professional staff (general manager and accountant) and attorneys to represent the board in its negotiations with the teams. The rent paid by the teams was supposed to generate sufficient revenues for Gateway to meet its responsibilities to maintain the facilities, hire the needed staff, and also pay the facilities' property taxes. To appreciate why the rental payments were not sufficient and the political environment within which the leases could be substantially renegotiated, some of the history surrounding the negotiations of the leases is required.[7]

### 8.6.1 The Provision of Extraordinary Subsidies

Separate deals were negotiated with each team. The Indians agreed to immediately pay $20 million for the ballpark's construction and to make annual payments of $2.9 million until the construction bonds were retired. Those funds were to be used to reduce the public sector's financial responsibilities for constructing the ballpark.

The present value of this commitment was $31 million. It was originally anticipated that the ballpark could be built for approximately $130 million, but the total cost was $193 million, and the public sector was responsible for all of the additional costs. The Indians paid 26.4 percent of the capital cost of the new ballpark.

The Cavaliers agreed to use 27.5 percent of their annual revenue from the leasing of suites and 48 percent of the revenue from the sale of club seats to help pay for the arena's construction. The Cavaliers also provided an up-front payment of $4 million. Originally expected to cost $75 million, the arena's cost was $154 million. The public sector was also responsible for the cost overrun. Voters were told that the arena and ballpark would cost approximately $200 million. The cost for both facilities was 71 percent more than the voters were told to expect. These cost overruns would plague local politics and issues involving the facilities for years. With the tax on alcohol and tobacco sales unable to retire the debt associated with a combined capital cost of more than $340 million, Cuyahoga County had to rely on its revenues to cover the extra costs.

Both teams also agreed to pay rent based on attendance; those were to be the funds that Gateway used to meet all of its financial responsibilities. When both facilities opened, Gateway had enough revenue to meet its obligations. The Indians, averaged 3.4 million for four years. Within three seasons that had fallen to 1.7 million. Gateway now had insufficient revenue to meets its obligations.

The situation with the Cavaliers was quite different and even more contentious.

The Cavaliers embarked on a strategy of changing several things during construction of the arena, and then argued that those costs represented part of the team's investment in the facility's construction. The team's owners wanted those expenses subtracted from any required rent (reducing the revenue available to Gateway to meet its responsibilities). The team's calculations led them to conclude that the public sector owed them several million dollars. The team also took the position that it had the unilateral right to make the construction changes it deemed necessary, and then to deduct those expenses from any required rental payments without the concurrence of the city or county. The expenses it incurred were so high that it annually presented the public sector with a statement indicating the balance owed to the team. As a result, the Cavaliers never paid rent for the use of the arena and only made the required capital construction payments. It was thus hardly surprising that Gateway would soon not have enough money to meet its expenses. Initially the teams wanted the public sector to simply transfer funds from their budgets to meet Gateway's responsibilities. Gateway's board refused to ask either the county or city for more money, especially given the public sector's responsibility for 100 percent of the cost overruns associated with both facilities.

Negotiations were initiated to modify the leases in order to ensure that Gateway's financial responsibilities could be met and the facilities appropriately maintained. Gateway was not receiving sufficient funds from the team to meet its financial responsibilities raising the specter of fiscal insolvency for the public corporation. With Cleveland and Cuyahoga County losing people and businesses to the suburbs, the team owners recognized new lease terms improving Gateway's finances were necessary to avoid a confrontation or default.

Cleveland and Cuyahoga County faced an important challenge in their efforts to attract the Cavaliers back to downtown Cleveland. The Cavaliers were drawing sellout crowds, generating robust parking and other revenues for the Gunds. The Cavaliers' owners made it appear that they were quite content to remain at their suburban location at the geographic center of the region, especially given current demographic trends. What Cleveland's leadership may not have appreciated was that the Richfield Coliseum had become economically obsolete. As teams grew more reliant on luxury seating, the sale of food and beverages in a facility, and space to provide more complete experiences for fans, the Coliseum had too few of the amenities that would allow the team to match the revenues earned by other franchises. The Cavaliers needed a new arena and might have been more flexible in their negotiations if Cleveland and Cuyahoga County had threatened to cancel construction of the arena. But with Cleveland's leadership worried about the need to instill confidence in the city's future, the Cavaliers were able to secure a very favorable lease (Rosentraub 1997a; Delaney and Eckstein 2003).

## 8.6.2 New Owners, New Possibilities

While Richard Jacobs and the Gunds initially exploited the advantages of their negotiating positions, as the Gunds prepared to sell the team and the Indians' new owners studied Gateway's issues, it became possible to renegotiate the leases.

The Indians were sold to Larry Dolan (with financial support from the Dolan family trust). Charles Dolan, Larry's brother, founded HBO and also owns Cablevision in New York City, Madison Square Garden, and the Knicks and Rangers (and other entertainment venues). The Dolan family is from the Greater Cleveland area, and Larry Dolan and his sons and their families live in Northeast Ohio. The older Dolan brothers were interested in buying an Ohio-based sports franchise. After an unsuccessful effort to purchase the Cincinnati Reds, the Dolans turned their attention to the Indians when Mr. Jacobs made it clear he was interested in selling the team.

Richard Jacobs had positioned the team for sale through the building of a championship franchise. In the years after acquiring the team, Mr. Jacobs increased the team's payroll, but the fiscal losses mounted, playing in antiquated Municipal Stadium. In 1992, with a new facility on the horizon, Mr. Jacobs slashed the payroll, making strategic investments in new and younger players. Then, with the new revenue streams made available in 1994 from the ballpark, the team's payroll grew by 20 percent or more each year (except 1998). In some years the increase was more than 50 percent. The Indians responded by winning their division each year from 1995 through 1999. The team also made the play-offs in 2000 and won its division in 2001, the two seasons immediately after the Dolans assumed control (see Table 8.9).

How did this strategy position the team for sale? Revenues were at record levels during this period, as each game was sold out and the team's popularity was at an all-time high. The new ballpark offered many new revenue streams (luxury seating,

**Table 8.9**    **The Cleveland Indians' Payrolls and Winning Percentages: 1988–2008**

| Season | Opening Day Payroll | In 2008 Dollars | Percent Change | Winning Percentage |
|---|---|---|---|---|
| 2008 | $78,970,066 | $78,970,066 | 22.8 | |
| 2007 | $61,673,267 | $64,324,242 | 7.8 | **593** |
| 2006 | $56,031,500 | $59,648,258 | 29.8 | 481 |
| 2005 | $41,502,500 | $45,942,201 | 17.4 | 574 |
| 2004 | $34,319,300 | $39,118,813 | −30.7 | 494 |
| 2003 | $48,584,834 | $56,446,111 | −40.0 | 420 |
| 2002 | $78,909,449 | $94,058,637 | −15.8 | 457 |
| 2001 | $92,660,001 | $111,710,601 | 16.8 | **562** |
| 2000 | $76,508,334 | $95,680,742 | 0.8 | 566 |
| 1999 | $73,857,962 | $94,896,018 | 23.1 | **599** |
| 1998 | $59,033,499 | $77,116,161 | 7.4 | **549** |
| 1997 | $54,130,232 | $71,822,074 | 15.9 | **534** |
| 1996 | $45,317,914 | $61,959,920 | 25.4 | **615** |
| 1995 | $35,185,500 | $49,418,889 | 20.1 | **694** |
| 1994 | $28,490,167 | $41,137,307 | 76.8 | 584 |
| 1993 | $15,717,667 | $23,267,879 | 84.8 | 469 |
| 1992 | $8,236,166 | $12,589,824 | −56.1 | 469 |
| 1991 | $18,270,000 | $28,653,767 | 14.1 | 352 |
| 1990 | $15,152,000 | $25,106,650 | 49.3 | 475 |
| 1989 | $8,928,500 | $16,813,616 | 17.8 | 451 |
| 1988 | $7,819,500 | $14,267,039 | | 481 |

*Note:* Bold indicates seasons in which a division championship was won. The Indians also won the American League pennant, but lost the 1995 (Atlanta) and 1997 (Florida) World Series. Salary figures are from *USA Today's* database.

state-of-the art retail facilities, electronic displays), and Mr. Jacobs was able to demonstrate the team's revenue potential to any prospective owner. It was also a good time to sell the team. The players that gave the Indians their winning series were becoming more expensive and getting older (and were thus beginning to be less productive). A decline in performance was likely for some, and retaining others was going to be quite costly. Mr. Jacobs found the Dolans to be very interested buyers and sold the franchise for $323 million.

Richard Jacobs acquired the team for $35.5 million in 1986 and assumed $12 million of the team's debt for a total purchase price of $47.5 million. That investment in 1999 dollars was $74 million, and with a sale price of between $320 and $323 million, the gross profit was between $246 million and $249 million. An argument could be made that the team might have had operating losses in some years before and after the move to the new ballpark, thus reducing the gross profit figure. It is safe to assume that Mr. Jacobs made a substantial return on his investment and enjoyed extraordinary financial benefits as a result of the level of the public sector's investment in the ballpark. Simply put, that investment reduced his costs in securing new revenue streams that had increased the value and profitability of the team. General knowledge of the profitable return also made it politically dangerous to argue for additional subsidies.

In 1983, the Gund brothers bought the Cavaliers and the Richfield Coliseum (together with Ted Stepien's advertising business and a cable television station) for $20 million. This expense was not their only investment cost. Prior to selling the team, Ted Stepien had traded away or sold the team's first-round draft picks for successive years, and the NBA allowed the Gunds to buy those rights back from other teams. The value of the advertising business and the cable station are unknown, but for a conservative estimate of the profit made by the Gunds when they sold the team, the value of those assets were estimated to be zero. A generous estimate of the cost to reacquire the draft picks is $2 million.

In 2005 the Gunds sold the Cavaliers to Dan Gilbert for $375 million. In 2005 dollars their initial investment was $42.9, leaving a gross profit of $332.1 million. There were likely other expenses and losses incurred by the Gunds, but even if those had a 2005 value of $25 million or $50 million, the profit levels produced for them by the public sector's subsidies were clearly quite robust. This is not to suggest that other factors, including the demand to own teams, did not also contribute to the price Dan Gilbert was willing to pay. At the same time, however, the team's value would have been dramatically lower if the Gund brothers paid for the building of a new arena or a larger portion of the facility's cost and maintenance. On a very positive and important note, the Gunds did bring respectability back to the franchise in the 1980s, when the team regularly competed for the conference's championship. That was quite a reversal from the team's performance under previous owners. In the years prior to the sale of the team, it once again faltered, and the Gund brothers' most important achievement might as well have been winning the draft rights to LeBron James. The marquee value and talent of this one player not only carried the team to the NBA Finals, but elevated demand for tickets. Again, the substantial return earned by the Gunds made it politically difficult to ask the public sector for more money to maintain the facilities. Prior to selling the Cavaliers, the Gund brothers joined the Dolans in agreeing to new lease terms.

After purchasing the Indians and Cavaliers, both of the new owners made substantial improvements to the ballpark and arena, and did so without any financial contributions from the public sector. In the 2007–2008 season, Dan Gilbert spent slightly more than $31 million to enhance the arena.[8] The Dolan family spent $8.5 million for a new scoreboard and other electronic displays. The Cavaliers have also spent $20 million for a new practice facility to ensure that the team has the assets to attract and retain the best players in an effort to build and maintain a championship caliber franchise. Both of the new owners supported the idea of discussing Gateway's needs and resolving its financial crisis. Between 2008 and 2014 the Cavaliers paid $17.8 million to maintain the arena and Gateway. The Indians paid $22.5 million for the ballpark and Gateway.

## 8.6.3 The New Leases for the Ballpark and Arena

After lengthy negotiations and exchanges of proposals and ideas, the teams agreed to assume responsibility for all maintenance of the arena and ballpark for repairs or renovation projects that cost $500,000 or less. Individual projects could not be amalgamated to subvert the $500,000 cap. In other words, as with repairing the carpet in the luxury seat areas, each suite was an independent project, as was any enhancement to different parts of the club seating area or of the arena or ballpark. When the sound system at the ballpark had to be replaced, each speaker or unit was considered a separate element. The Indians paid all of the expenses associated with upgrading the sound system throughout the ballpark, replacing each of the 150 individual speakers (estimated at $2.6 million). Furthermore, if the teams wanted to make any new capital investments in the facilities, they had to assume full responsibility for those expenses. The teams also agreed to ensure that Gateway had sufficient funds to pay its property taxes and support Gateway's administrative budget. In turn, Gateway agreed that its annual budget would be subject to review by the teams, but that its responsibilities for maintaining the arena, ballpark, and common areas and plazas would remain inviolate. In addition to the capital investments made by the teams in the facilities, the new leases raised each team's annual costs by more than $2 million. In essence, the public sector was left with financial responsibility for the roof of the arena, the air conditioning and heating system in the arena, the arena's ice-making system, and the foundation and steel supports for both facilities. In 2014, voters living in Cuyahoga County were asked to renew the "sin" tax to support those responsibilities. On May 6, 2014, 56.4 percent of the voters suppported extension of the sin tax to pay for the public sector's responsibilities.

While these new arrangements substantially reduced the public sector's financial exposure and responsibilities, the teams wanted something of value in exchange for their acceptance of the new lease terms. Each team was given support to place more advertising on the outside of the facilities and the authority to lease advertising on additional spaces inside each facility. Placing additional signage on the venues required the approval of the City of Cleveland's architectural review board. Gateway's board of commissioners agreed to support the teams' efforts to add advertising on the venues which are owned by the public sector.

One issue involving the Cavaliers that Gateway's leadership wanted to resolve lingered. Prior to selling the team, the Gund brothers had their administrative staff continue to record all of the expenses the team incurred to improve the facility. As noted earlier, the brothers believed expenditures should have been considered construction expenses that were the public sector's responsibility. Rather than challenge the accounting, it was agreed that these expenses could be counted toward any excess rental income that needed to be offset (if attendance exceeded 1.6 million people at all events held in any calendar year at the arena) during each year of the lease. At the end of the lease period, however, any remaining debt would be erased and the public sector would have no responsibility to make any payments to the Cavaliers. Since the Cavaliers had also agreed to pay for all of the needed maintenance at the arena (excluding the roof and the machine that makes ice for hockey and other events), there was little need to press the issue of extra rental payments for higher attendance levels and to let any possible liabilities for the team be offset by the accrued list of expenses prepared by the previous owners.

## 8.7 A Regime and Downtown and Community Development

The building of the arena and ballpark—followed by a new stadium for an NFL franchise—represented important accomplishments for the growth coalition or regime cultivated by Mayor George Voinovich. The work of the regime was institutionalized in the creation of two organizations, Cleveland Tomorrow and its successor, the Greater Cleveland Partnership. The regime advocated for the investment of public money for several of the big-ticket items. Were these activities typical of those feared by many social scientists (Squires 1989)? Or, did the regime orchestrate a wide-ranging set of activities that included community development projects as well as countywide financing programs to stabilize Cleveland?

George Voinovich clearly linked corporate leaders and the regime to Cleveland's future. It began with his call for their participation as a condition of his candidacy. He only agreed to stand for election as mayor if the corporate community would agree to reengage and help improve the operations of the city. He also wanted the corporate leaders to be partners in the rebuilding of Cleveland. In 1980, Cleveland lacked a regime, as business leaders had effectively disengaged from civic affairs as a result of the conflicts with Dennis Kucinich. Hanson et al. (2006) concluded that the detachment was a product of the staggering problems Cleveland faced, including huge population losses, racial tensions, a deteriorating school system, the staggering loss of manufacturing jobs, and the famed fire on the Cuyahoga River. In the aftermath of the Kucinich administration there appeared to be a level of disinterest and disengagement of corporate leaders from Cleveland's affairs. Several corporations had relocated to the suburbs, and their leaders were all too eager to turn away from the complex problems Cleveland faced. In the midst of this chaotic situation—population declines, businesses leaving for the suburbs or other regions, and a destructive relationship between the private sector and the Kucinich administration—a small group of leaders from some of Cleveland's remaining large corporations convinced George Voinovich to run for mayor. Then, fulfilling their commitment to him, these same leaders convinced other business executives to reengage and help the new administration rebuild Cleveland.

A team of local business executives was recruited to review the city's operations and made more than 700 recommendations, of which several hundred were implemented by the new mayor's administration (Harvard Business School 1996a). Eight business executives honored the commitment to Mayor Voinovich to lead the reengagement of the business community sector. This group called themselves the Cleveland Tomorrow Project Committee. The committee would be institutionalized as Cleveland Tomorrow, whose membership was limited to the city's leading corporate executive officers. This group was initially created to "provide a forum where the CEOs of the major companies can come together to discuss what they see as the critical issues and try to develop a focused agenda for action" (Harvard Business School 1996a: 1). Projects that would change the city and region's economy were chosen, and for each there had to be a champion. The champion was a CEO who would agree to lead the effort. A venture capital fund was created, as was an organization to improve management-labor relations.[9]

To counter the severe contractions in the manufacturing sector, an advanced manufacturing program was also created. Each of the new organizations was designed to increase employment opportunities and advance the local and regional economy. Cleveland Tomorrow had three objectives: "make manufacturing competitive, foster the creation of new companies, and assist in rebuilding the city center" (Hanson et al. 2006: 7). These objectives did not conflict with any community goals. Cleveland Tomorrow then worked with local foundations to create Neighborhood Progress, Inc. (NPI). NPI worked with community development corporations to rehabilitate existing homes and build new ones in a city where the housing stock in several neighborhoods was rapidly deteriorating. Cleveland Tomorrow led the effort to raise $50 million to be used to help finance housing and retail development projects in the city's neighborhoods. Cleveland Tomorrow also worked to convince ShoreBank to open offices in Cleveland. ShoreBank is a commercial bank committed to community development and it originated in Chicago. It now has offices in Cleveland and Detroit. In Cleveland the bank has assumed a leadership role in rebuilding neighborhoods and funding new residential programs in several inner city neighborhoods. Cleveland Tomorrow's (and its successor organization's) success in securing new market tax credits has also led to the building of new retail centers in neighborhoods. In some neighborhoods there were few, if any, retail outlets left, as many stores closed after the riots and entrepreneurs preferred more suburban locations. Cleveland Tomorrow's decision to expand its focus to include redevelopment of inner city neighborhoods has led to the building of several shopping centers and new apartments and houses in the areas that were destroyed by the riots in the 1960s. More recently, Cleveland Tomorrow's successor organization, the Greater Cleveland Partnership, led the redevelopment of an arts district in another inner city neighborhood.

When Cleveland Tomorrow merged with two other organizations (one formed to address minority inclusion as part of the work of the region's chamber of commerce and the other on public education and workforce development), the Greater Cleveland Partnership became the regime or corporate partnership that George Voinovich envisioned as a necessary component of any revitalization strategy. But the group did not focus only on big-ticket items. Early in the formation of the Cleveland Partnership, and then continuing through 2014, a set of initiatives was created with the Cleveland public schools. The Greater Cleveland Partnership even became the leading advocate for tax increases to provide more funding for the Cleveland public schools, even though it would mean higher property taxes for many of its corporate leaders. The business community supported Mayor White's call for the schools to be placed under the mayor's authority in an effort to increase accountability and improve performance. Corporate leaders also created and funded several new programs. One of these programs encouraged businesses to adopt a school and have their employees serve as tutors and mentors in the schools to improve students' reading and math skills. Cleveland's corporate leadership also committed to the creation of an annual fund of $1 million to support new initiatives to enhance the management and administrative skills of teachers and principals in the Cleveland schools. These funds were given to the superintendent to use for any special initiatives that would enhance teaching skills or the administrative expertise of teachers, principals, or other school district employees. These discretionary funds in the cash-strapped district were sometimes the only resources available to augment professional development within the district.

As noted, the Greater Cleveland Partnership also supported and financed each of the campaigns to increase local taxes to support the Cleveland public schools. This is notable since the largest proportion of the local taxes for the schools is paid by the businesses located in downtown Cleveland. What this meant was that the Greater Cleveland Partnership was paying for a campaign to raise its own taxes. Businesses in Cleveland account for more than 60 percent of the school district's tax base. If voters agreed to support an increase in the tax rate, the largest increase would fall on the business sector. Rather than opposing any increment and claiming that higher taxes would make a Cleveland location an impediment to expansion or the attraction of new firms, the Greater Cleveland Partnership funded the campaign to secure passage of every tax increase sought by the district.

Cleveland Tomorrow and its successor organization focused on job creation, the attraction and retention of businesses, enhancing the competitiveness of the manufacturing sector, and the redevelopment of downtown. In addition to that extensive agenda, neighborhood development and then a commitment to public education were included. Cleveland Tomorrow was a regime, as is its successor organization, the Greater Cleveland Partnership. It is fair to recognize that the goals of the organization may well have served the self-interests of its members, but it also needs to be acknowledged that job retention, programs to enhance the manufacturing sector, and venture capital funds each had the potential to create needed jobs in a region losing a substantial number of employment opportunities. Regime leadership in Cleveland was not narrowly focused on enhancements that only created direct benefits for its members (Harvard Business School 1996b).

## 8.8 An Update—Cleveland, Downtown Cleveland, and Northeast Ohio in the Aftermath of Big-Ticket and Community Development Initiatives

That revitalization strategy, as already noted, did not change population growth trajectories for either Cleveland or Cuyahoga County. In both jurisdictions, population losses continued through 2010, along with the continuation of job losses throughout the region. There has been a resurgence in the number of people living in downtown Cleveland. It is estimated that 12,000 people now live in the downtown area, and when the Flats redevelopment is completed, a few thousand additional residents can be expected (http://www.theatlanticcities.com/jobs-and-economy/2013/08/if-you-build-it-they-will-come-how-cleveland-lured-young-professionals-downtown/6406/). In the aftermath of the building of sports facilities, entertainment centers, restaurants, pubs, theatres, and museums, downtown Cleveland has become a vibrant and desirable neighborhood. That is a notable accomplishment, even as the region's population and economy have continued to contract.

There are, however, other bright highlights in the aftermath of the downtown revitalization strategy or program. While there might be fewer jobs in Cleveland, a substantial number of higher-paying positions have been retained. Table 8.10 illustrates the major tax revenue streams that support the City of Cleveland. The income tax has been growing each year; and in 2012 the income tax accounted for almost three-quarters of the selected revenue sources. Included in Table 8.10 is the declining level of support received by Cleveland each year from the State of Ohio's local government fund. The State of Ohio had to reduce its support for local governments throughout the recession. Note, however, that during the recession Cleveland's annual income tax revenue collections declined, but then

**Table 8.10   City of Cleveland Major Revenue Sources, 2005–2012, and Percent of Revenue from Income Taxes (in thousands of dollars, unadjusted)**

| Revenue Source | 2005 | 2006 | 2007 | 2008 | 2009 | 2010 | 2011 | 2012 |
|---|---|---|---|---|---|---|---|---|
| Income tax | 288,191 | 302,084 | 317,268 | 329,316 | 296,507 | 298,209 | 311,492 | 330,863 |
| Percent income tax | 66.5 | 66.9 | 68.0 | 69.6 | 69.2 | 64.3 | 69.8 | 74.9 |
| Property tax | 64,390 | 66,762 | 69,313 | 65,398 | 63,573 | 88,087 | 63,839 | 56,086 |
| Other taxes | 25,051 | 26,492 | 28,567 | 25,918 | 25,053 | 28,450 | 27,312 | 28,680 |
| State revenue | 55,696 | 55,905 | 51,164 | 52,450 | 43,420 | 49,266 | 43,821 | 25,966 |
| Subtotal | 433,328 | 451,243 | 466,312 | 473,082 | 428,553 | 464,012 | 446,464 | 441,595 |

*Source:* City of Cleveland, Comprehensive Annual Financial Reports, 2005–2012.

quickly rebounded within 2 years and then exceeded the levels in 2008. It is impossible to link the downtown revitalization program to the growth of the earnings levels of workers in Cleveland that sustained the recovery of income tax revenues.[10] It is possible that the revitalized downtown area assumed no role in the decision of businesses to hire higher-income individuals. It is also possible that the attractiveness of downtown Cleveland and the amenities it offers assumed no role in the decision of these employees to work in Cleveland. Nevertheless, it is interesting to note that the growth in income tax revenues and its rapid recovery has helped provide a level of financial stability for Cleveland. Further, it is also important to note that while Cleveland's population and job levels were declining, the earnings tax receipts increased. This can only occur when salary or earnings increased, meaning that higher-income jobs were available in Cleveland. What were these jobs and where were they located?

There has been a continuing loss of jobs in downtown Cleveland. In 2003 there were 87,447 full-time positions located in the downtown area. At that point in time, Cleveland's leaders could point with pride to the contribution of the downtown revitalization strategy to sustaining employment levels despite the loss of residents in the region. Job levels declined but remained relatively stable through 2008, but the recession and crisis in the banking industry led to a sharp loss of full-time positions. Two banks with headquarters in downtown Cleveland failed in the aftermath of the collapse of real estate prices. By 2011 there were 73,796 full-time positions, but there was a loss of more than 13,000 positions (see Figure 8.4a). Job growth, however, as noted has been concentrated in University Circle. This area is home to the Cleveland Clinic and University Hospitals. Between 2003 and 2011 the total number of full-time jobs in this part of Cleveland increased by more than 15,000 (see Figure 8.4b). The increasing salary levels in the health care sector have led to enhanced earnings tax receipts for the city.

It is not possible to link the improved job growth in the University Circle area to the revitalization of the downtown area. In the last several years, new amenities have been added to the downtown area, including the building of a new medical mart (capitalizing on the presence of the Cleveland Clinic and University Hospitals), the renovation of the convention center, and the opening of a new casino. The owner of the Cleveland Cavaliers and the casino, Dan Gilbert, is poised to invest hundreds of millions of dollars as part of a project to enhance the arena that is part of the Gateway complex.

The region's newspaper, *The Plain Dealer*, reported that $5.4 billion of construction would likely occur before the end of the decade (http://media. cleveland.com/ business_impact/other/CLEVE-2011-DEVELOPMENT-MAP.PDF). The projects totaled in the July 2011 enumeration did not include the substantial renovation of the Quicken Loans Arena and the related projects being planned by Dan Gilbert's real estate development corporation. Statistically linking any of these commitments to the initial investment by the public sector to revitalize downtown Cleveland is not possible. It is reasonable, however, to observe that substantial levels of private sector investment are likely to take place, dwarfing what has been done in the past. Those investments, if made, would be a valuable financial return on the public sector's investments in big-ticket items.

# 8.9 Conclusions

Cleveland and Cuyahoga County provided extraordinarily large public subsidies for three sports facilities and two museums. The investments were made without any assurances from the private sector, and the most recent data suggest those larger private sector investments did not occur for more than two decades after the sports facilities and cultural centers opened. This makes it possible for critics to argue that the private sector investments that took place in later years were unrelated to the stabilization of the downtown area that was anchored by public sector investments in sports. Proponents of the public sector's aggressive stance on sustaining downtown Cleveland might make a different argument. They might suggest that if those investments had not been made, large-scale private sector investments would never have occurred. These same proponents could also argue that the public sector investment was necessary to stabilize the downtown real estate market until such time that it became more practical for private investments to be made. The population decline in the city and the region, combined with the movement of wealthier residents to suburban areas, clearly underscored the observation that market forces made private sector investments in downtown Cleveland very speculative and, as a result, highly unlikely to occur. That noted, however, each set of proponents is unlikely to be convinced of the arguments of the other side.

That being observed or conceded, there are still several important lessons to be learned from Cleveland's experiences and the case of using sports, entertainment, and cultural amenities to change development patterns in this former manufacturing center and rust-belt city. Before dealing with the issues of the role of regimes or growth coalitions dominated by business interests, Cleveland's redevelopment strategy was *shaped* or directed by external actors who controlled assets essential for the revitalization plan. Political pressure from the NFL and the trustees of the Rock and Roll Hall of Fame led to the new assets being built in locations distant from the other amenities anchoring the revitalization effort. While there may well have not been a coordinated strategic plan for revitalization of the downtown area that would fit a much smaller city than Cleveland was in the mid-20th century, the NFL and the Rock and Roll Hall of Fame and Museum wanted timetables and locations that met their needs. Cleveland's public and private leadership were convinced to meet both sets of demands and taxpayers were asked to underwrite the fiscal stability of both projects.

Could Cleveland's leadership have negotiated for a different set of outcomes to better fit with a development strategy that concentrated all amenities in a space that matched what a smaller central city needed? There is no clear answer to that question, partly because some leaders were not willing to concede that the entire downtown area could not be fully revitalized. Indianapolis' leadership planned a revitalization strategy that was concentrated into a 4-square-mile area. There was implicit and explicit recognition that downtown Indianapolis would never be as large as it was in the mid-20th century. Perhaps that was not a recognition that Cleveland's leaders were willing to concede.

Beyond acquiescing to the demands of external actors, why was the public–private partnership that guided Cleveland's revitalization effort willing to support large public sector investments? Simply put, decades of population losses in Cleveland and in Cuyahoga County, two devastating racial riots, and the severe economic restructuring that led to the loss of more than 100,000 jobs had shaken, if not destroyed, confidence in the city's future. Leaders believed dramatic actions were needed to create an air of optimism to attract investors and restore residents' confidence in the city's future. With a great deal of the money coming from businesses and their property taxes and residents of the suburbs, the sacrifice was shared across all income groups. While it is fair to note that some of the investment in a revitalized downtown Cleveland was sustained by lower-income residents of the city—and that means there was a regressive component of the investment—it is also important to recognize that the largest component of the public's funds were provided by local businesses through the higher property taxes they paid and the property and sin taxes paid by residents of Cuyahoga County's suburban cities.

It is also important to note that private sector investment—while not pledged or assured at the time the public sector's investments were provided—did dramatically increase in the years after the facilities opened. Newer investments in more recent years may well make the revitalization of downtown Cleveland one of the best examples of leveraging sports, entertainment, and culture for redevelopment. Causality cannot be determined and it is not possible to conclude that the private sector investments were a result of the public sector investments for the sports facilities and museums. In addition, there were other investments made by the public sector, including property tax abatements for new home construction. In addition, the late 1990s and the early years of the 21st century were "boom times" for America. Some might argue the private sector investment would have taken place even if the public sector investments in sports, culture, entertainment, and new homes were not provided.

While such a claim cannot be statistically rejected, it is important to point out that in the years of substantial increments in private sector investments in real estate in downtown Cleveland and in its neighborhoods, the city continued to lose residents. At the same time that job levels were stabilized in the downtown area and earnings tax revenues increased, Cleveland and Cuyahoga County continued to shrink. This suggests that the public sector investments in the downtown area's future did create some confidence that the city's future was going to improve and be different from its immediate past. Faced with extraordinary declines in its population and job base, Cleveland and Cuyahoga County made a decision to invest in specific amenities to change the look and feel of the area. The subsequent investment in real estate could well lead many to observe that the expenditures were appropriate and, in retrospect, prudent investments that generated appropriate returns in private sector investments.

It is also important to acknowledge that the public sector was able to undo part of the subsidies through new leases with the Indians and Cavaliers. While the city and county did give the teams expanded opportunities for exterior advertising, the teams not only assumed responsibility for most of the maintenance expenses associated with both facilities, but both have made their own investments to update the ballpark and arena. In total, the teams have invested more than $40 million to enhance the facilities, and the Cavaliers are poised to make another very substantial investment. Finally, the new lease arrangements now make the teams responsible for the facilities except for major structural items.

The outcomes for Cleveland—in the absence of assurances and commitments—do not mean that other cities should follow in its footsteps and enter into deals without substantial private sector assurances and investments. There are cities that may find themselves in a similar position where there is crisis of confidence in the future as a result of population and job losses. In that regard, there is good news from Cleveland's experiences. Building on its assets and making important commitments in sports, culture, and the arts did lead to new and far higher levels of private investment in real estate projects. This outcome suggests redevelopment efforts that are associated with sports do have a potential for elevating private sector investments (Rosentraub and Joo, 2009).

The positive outcomes for Cleveland—(1) new leases with the Indians and Cavaliers that eliminate ongoing subsidies to the teams, (2) substantial commitments from the Indians and Cavaliers to invest in the ballpark and arena, and (3) higher levels of private sector investments in the city's revitalization made after the extensive subsidies raised confidence in Cleveland's future—do not obscure the three distracting negative outcomes.

First, as noted, external actors increased pressure that may have changed the shape of the revitalization plan. Second, the original subsidies, even understanding the need to generate confidence in the future, meant that owners of the Cavaliers and Indians were able to enjoy extraordinary profits when they sold their teams. Those returns were a direct result of the public sector's assumption of a large portion of the cost to build the new venues. Far more aggressive negotiations by the public sector should have established a cap on these profits given the subsidies provided. Third, and more importantly, despite clear success in attracting private sector capital to help revitalize downtown and other parts of the city and county, the population outflow has not ended. Indeed, Cleveland and Cuyahoga County continue to lose residents, creating the possibility that the public sector cannot win or create the kind of change desired (higher family incomes and stable or expanding population bases) from success with its big-ticket investments. Critics may well bristle at the notion that the big-ticket strategy had any level of success. If success is measured by stronger levels of private sector investment, a stabilized level of jobs in the city, and the improvement of earnings tax revenues at a time when the city continued to lose residents (as compared to outcomes prior to the big-ticket strategy), then it is appropriate to recognize some level of success was achieved. Disappointment reigns in that even becoming a major league winner from its sports, entertainment, and downtown development strategy at some levels, Cleveland and Cuyahoga County's residents and leaders were still left scrambling for ideas to reverse population declines. It may well be possible that an amenity policy—even when successful—is not sufficient to reverse population trends, and that cities and regions cannot win when they are losing residents.

Finally, Cleveland's story also sheds important light on the role of regimes in redevelopment efforts. While these groups may be initially focused on big-ticket items, they are not adverse to more neighborhood-based initiatives. The evidence from Cleveland's experiences suggests that regimes clearly understand the need for and support initiatives to enhance the public education systems and the quality of life in inner city neighborhoods. Few, if any, of the new retail centers in Cleveland's inner city neighborhoods would exist without the funding provided by Cleveland Tomorrow and then the Greater Cleveland Partnership. The regime has also provided some level of fiscal flexibility for the superintendent of the Cleveland public schools while also financing all of the campaigns to raise public support for public education. More recently, numerous downtown businesses created a business improvement district (BID) to pay for improved public safety and new programs for the homeless. While critics might still argue the capitalized value of the subsidies for the sports and entertainment facilities exceeds these commitments, it is also true that the suburban areas and their wealthier residents and the business community pay a far larger proportion of the taxes used to build the amenities. At a minimum, then, some of the negative images conveyed about the motives and objectives of regimes need to be amended based on the work of Cleveland Tomorrow and the Greater Cleveland Partnership. Their work should encourage other cities to engage their business communities in downtown and neighborhood revitalization efforts.

# Endnotes

1. In September 2008 the Jewish Federation of Cleveland, citing the need to be located closer to the Jewish community, announced that a new primary headquarters would be built in Beachwood (one of the area's eastern suburbs). This action left only one small synagogue in the City of Cleveland (on its west side). In contrast, there are more 30 synagogues located in suburban areas, and every Jewish communal organization also has its headquarters or offices located in the suburbs.
2. Cleveland's mayors served 2-year terms at this point in history. There was a failed recall movement to remove Mayor Kucinich. The term of office was changed to 4 years during his successor's tenure.
3. Position restated in discussion and presentation by U.S. Senator George Voinovich in interviews in September 2008 in his Washington, D.C., office.
4. The limitations inherent in using even complex regression models to isolate the effects of amenity package investments on economic development are discussed in Rosentraub (2006) and Rosentraub and Joo (2009).
5. Business leaders that would each be described as members of Cleveland's regime underscored the importance of the public investments in making people think there was a future for the downtown area. While it could easily be argued many of them or their companies benefitted from the presence of the sports and entertainment facilities, they would respond that as national companies they are expanding elsewhere and needed reasons to convince their boards and shareholders that continued investments and presence in downtown Cleveland were in the companies' best interests. Exchanges like that, as well as the inevitable self-interest issues, make it difficult to predict causality, but underscore the pressure on Cleveland's civic leaders. The outcomes at least give those leaders some comfort that their investments were not a waste of the public sector's money.
6. In 2007 Cleveland and the suburban City of Independence agreed to an earnings tax sharing plan when the Cavaliers decided to build a practice facility separate from what was available at the arena. With that facility located in Independence, that city is entitled to the proportion of the earnings tax that results from the players and coaches "working" within their city limits. The tax sharing agreement protects Cleveland's long-term interest while allowing the team to build the needed facility and offices. An earnings tax is a tax on income and is paid to the city in which an employee works, not the city in which the employee lives.

7. During the time the leases were negotiated the author was one of the five commissioners serving on the board of the Gateway Economic Development Corporation of Greater Cleveland and a participant in the process. The author was first recruited as an advisor to the board as the renegotiations began and was then appointed to a vacant seat by one of Cuyahoga County's commissioners.

8. Confirmed through email exchanges with Mr. John Wolf, Vice President for Finance and Administration, Cleveland Cavaliers, September 2008.

9. Cleveland Development Advisors (CDA) was established in 1989 to manage the real estate investment funds raised by Cleveland Tomorrow. These funds were used for economic and community development projects in the downtown area and in other neighborhoods. The community projects funded through CDA include retail centers, arts and entertainment centers, and new construction, as well as the rehabilitation of existing residential properties. The Arbor Park Place Shopping Center, for example, is a 39,000-square-foot retail center in the midst of an east side neighborhood abandoned by store owners decades ago. The Gordon Arts project is an investment designed to stabilize and enhance a west side neighborhood.

10. Cleveland collects a 2-percent earnings tax from all individuals working in the City of Cleveland. An earnings tax differs from a traditional income tax in that it is paid based on where an individual works (as opposed to where he or she lives). At the same time that Cleveland's population and job levels were declining, the earnings tax receipts increased. This can only occur when salary or earnings increased, meaning that higher-income jobs were available in Cleveland.

*Chapter 9*

# Maintaining Downtowns in Smaller Cities: Can Little Brothers in the Shadow of Larger Cities Lead Revitalization Efforts with Sports, Entertainment, and the Arts?

## 9.1 Introduction: Economic Change in a Small City

The economic changes that transformed large metropolitan areas and their central cities have also impacted smaller regions. As leadership in some smaller cities focused on revitalization strategies, they usually encountered the additional challenge of more limited wealth that sometimes constrained options. Smaller cities are less likely to be home to large community or private foundations that could make investments in assets such as Cleveland's Playhouse Square. Smaller communities are also likely to be home to fewer large corporations. If one or more of these businesses moves to other regions, the economic effects are frequently devastating in terms of the loss of jobs and the resulting depreciation in land values. Of equal significance, however, is the loss of executive talent, and that often means the availability of fewer people to work with public leaders and involve the private sector in the design and implementation of a revitalization strategy. The loss of corporations in smaller towns can also result in a shortage of leadership for positions on the boards of arts and cultural organizations, weakening the ability of these institutions to participate in redevelopment efforts. The loss of executive talent for these organizations is often staggering when communities strive to maintain amenities to underscore their attractiveness and potential as a location for new and expanding businesses. If some of the arts and cultural organizations fail, then the ability to attract other businesses is further constrained, as new businesses could fear that the absence of amenities would reduce their ability to attract and retain the human capital needed to be competitive and profitable. The acquisition of local businesses by out-of-town corporations can also reduce the availability of local executive talent to help a smaller city with its revitalization strategies. If a community is seen as a place where younger executives stay for a short period of time before resuming their climb on the parent company's corporate ladder, they might be less likely to participate in community building activities.

Smaller cities and regions also suffer from the revitalization efforts undertaken by nearby central cities seeking to revitalize their own downtown areas. In addition, the growth of suburban and exurban cities at the edge of larger metropolitan areas means that there are areas of development seeking to offer some of the same town center or downtown experiences that smaller cities might also try to offer. For example, at the same time that Fort Wayne was focused on its downtown development activities, Indianapolis, located 125 miles to the southwest, was advancing its own initiatives. Other cities in the greater metropolitan Indianapolis area, Carmel and Noblesville, were also emphasizing new town centers. These suburban or exurban cities are located 115 and 105 miles from Fort Wayne. If that competition was not sufficient, Muncie and Anderson, Indiana, 79 and 85 miles south of Fort Wayne, were also trying to revitalize their core communities. Reading, Pennsylvania, once a prototypical smaller city offering opportunities for quality jobs and a small downtown city experience for its residents, is located 63 miles from Philadelphia, 81 miles from Baltimore, and 56 miles from Wilmington, Delaware. Each of those cities is engaged in extensive revitalization efforts. Reading has to also compete with suburban cities such as King of Prussia and West Chester, as well as other smaller cities, such as Hershey and Lancaster. Within this dynamic environment of urban change and competition from larger and similar sized cities, can a smaller city establish a niche for itself through a focus on sports, culture, and entertainment amenities in a revitalized downtown? This chapter looks at some of the efforts in two smaller cities and the outcomes within two very competitive environments where several cities are engaged in revitalization efforts to attract residents and businesses.

# 9.2 Changes in a Small City: Economic and Racial Separation

## 9.2.1 Reading in Brief

Reading is located too far from Philadelphia, Baltimore, and Wilmington to be a convenient suburban or exurban part of those metropolitan areas. In addition, there is no passenger rail connection between Reading and those cities' central business districts, making it very inconvenient for residents of Reading or surrounding Berks County to work in those metropolitan areas or central business districts. Founded prior to the Revolutionary War, Reading's iron industry provided arms to George Washington's army. The city's manufacturing base and role in the coal industry attracted immigrants, creating its first wave of wealth and growth in the early 19th century. In later years (the last half of the 19th and the early part of the 20th century) the production of clothing and eyewear propelled Reading into becoming the home for one of eastern Pennsylvania's most successful department store chains. Reading continued to grow, and by the onset of the Great Depression, the city's population exceeded 110,000. A period of general decline began in the post-1950s, and by 1990 the city had almost 30 percent fewer residents than it did in 1930. Then, in the 1990s and the first part of the 21st century, the city enjoyed a small population increment. Indeed, the population growth from 2000 to 2010 seemed to suggest that a rebound of sorts was taking place in this formerly declining city. The city's population in 2010 was larger than at any time in the past 40 years and would seem to suggest that the revitalization strategy had had a positive effect on the city's growth (see Table 9.1).

At first the city's population decline was part of the general suburbanization trends taking place in the post-World War II environment, as families with increasing wealth sought a more suburban lifestyle, newer large homes, and homes with large front and back yards. The expansion of some manufacturing and other businesses in the suburban areas of surrounding Berks County also brought increased prosperity to other parts of the region. Berks County has continued to grow, and by 2000 had more than 350,000 residents. The county's planning department had estimated that a population of 400,000 residents by 2020 was expected (see Figure 9.1). These estimates were actually too conservative. The U.S. Bureau of the Census estimated the county's population in 2012 was 413,491, and had actually exceeded 400,000 by 2010 (411,447 residents).

## 9.2.2 Reading and Berks County Today

The increasing population growth in Reading was not accompanied by an influx of wealthier residents. In 2011, the U.S. Bureau of the Census reported that Reading was the city in the United States with the largest proportion of its residents with annual incomes at or below the poverty level.[1] Job growth in Reading has, as would

**Table 9.1 Population Changes in Reading, Pennsylvania**

| Year | Population | Percent Change |
|------|-----------|----------------|
| 1880 | 43,278 | |
| 1890 | 58,661 | 35.5 |
| 1900 | 78,961 | 34.6 |
| 1910 | 96,071 | 21.7 |
| 1920 | 107,784 | 12.2 |
| 1930 | 111,171 | 3.1 |
| 1940 | 110,568 | –0.5 |
| 1950 | 109,320 | –1.1 |
| 1960 | 98,061 | –10.3 |
| 1970 | 87,643 | –10.6 |
| 1980 | 78,686 | –10.2 |
| 1990 | 78,380 | –0.4 |
| 2000 | 81,207 | 3.6 |
| 2010 | 88,082 | 8.5 |

*Source:* U.S. Bureau of the Census, "Estimates of Population and Population Change," various years; Berks County, Pennsylvania Planning Department.

be expected, continued to decline. In 2002 there were 34,969 full-time positions in the city; by 2011 there were 32,497, or 2,472 fewer jobs. In the metropolitan area job levels have remained relatively stagnant. There were 153,240 jobs in 2002 and 153,846 in 2011, for an increase of 606. The region actually saw far more growth; there were as many as 162,337 jobs in 2008. There was a contraction in the aftermath of the recession, with the loss of more than 1,400 jobs in the finance and real estate sector and 5,000 fewer jobs available with manufacturing companies. Job growth has taken place in the health care and social assistance sector, along with the professional, scientific, and technical services sector, where 1,180 jobs have been added since 2002.

The rising level of poverty in Reading means that the median income of people living in suburban Berks County was more than twice that of Reading's residents. The dropout rate from the Reading public schools is extremely high. The Pennsylvania Department of Education placed the dropout rate at 7.5 percent in 2007; it had improved to 5 percent in 2012. The dropout rate in 2007 was the

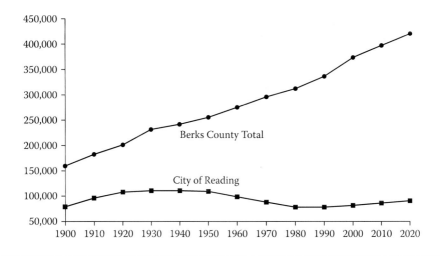

**Figure 9.1   Population trends in Reading and Berks County, 1900–2020. (From Berks County, Pennsylvania Planning Department.)**

highest in Pennsylvania.[2] The *Washington Post*, however, reported that 67 percent of the students enrolled in Reading High School did not graduate in 2007.[3] According to the Pennsylvania Department of Education, the graduation rate had improved to 61 percent by 2011. These performance measures contribute to a poor image for Reading's schools. More affluent residents have an incentive to send their children to private schools or to live in suburban Berks County, where they have access to more successful public schools.

Crime rates in Reading have continued to rise. Despite its small-town appearance and status, statistically, crime rates in Reading are far above national averages. For example, in 2003, FBI statistics indicate that the murder rate in Reading was 2.59 times the national rate (see Table 9.2). The rate at which forcible rape crimes were reported was almost double the levels for the United States, and the overall violent crime rate was also almost twice (1.96) the national level. These rates contributed to an image that Reading was an unsafe and dangerous place to live, work, shop, or visit for entertainment, and its downtown area and neighborhoods were places to be avoided. In 2012, City-Data's crime index for Reading was 479.9; the national average was 307.5, suggesting there has been no improvement in the level of safety in the city. In 2012, Reading's violent crime rates were 2.4 times the national average, and the rate of property crimes was 43 percent above the national average.

Reading's population growth has been driven by an influx of lower-income Hispanic households and accompanying migration of whites to suburban Berks County. This has created a highly segregated situation. In 2000, 30,302 residents of Reading described themselves as Hispanic. In 2010, 51,230 of Reading's 88,082 residents described themselves as being Hispanic. The number of white residents

## Table 9.2 Crime Rates in Reading, 2003

| Crime | Local Rate Compared to National Levels (2003) | Local Rate Compared to National Levels (2010, 2012) |
|---|---|---|
| Murder | 2.59 | 2.56 |
| Rape | 1.91 | 0.93 |
| Robbery | 2.46 | 3.96 |
| Aggravated assault | 1.50 | 1.71 |
| **All violent crime** | **1.96** | **2.40 (2012)** |
| Burglary | 1.66 | 2.50 |
| Larceny or theft | 1.03 | 0.97 |
| Car theft | 2.16 | 1.35 |
| Arson | 2.30 | 1.19 |
| **All property crime** | **1.30** | **1.43 (2012)** |

*Source:* For 2003, all data from the Federal Bureau of Investigation, rates adjusted per 100,000; U.S. national rates equal 1.0. Numbers greater than 1 indicate rates above the U.S. averages, and a number of 2.59 would mean a rate more than 2.5 times the national rate. For 2010, data from http://www.usa. com/reading-pa-crime-and-crime-rate.htm. The crime rates for 2012 are from the Federal Bureau of Investigation, http://www.fbi.gov/about-us/ cjis/ucr/crime-in-the-u.s/2012/crime-in-the-u.s.-2012/tables1table-datadecoverviewpdf/table1_crime_in_the_united_states_by_volume_ and_rate_per_100000_inhabitants_1993-2012.xls.

shrunk from 48,059 to 42,617. In contrast, 299,531 of the 323,360 residents of suburban Berks County described themselves as white (see Table 9.3). By 2000, Reading and Berks County had become two very different communities, defined and separated from each other by high degrees of racial and economic segregation.

Finally, Reading's housing stock has deteriorated, and there are blighted properties throughout most neighborhoods. A 2004 study for the city found 1,241 vacant buildings, of which 1,088 were single-family homes. The study observed that "Reading has critical problems: many vacancies in the downtown area; some residential blocks overwhelmed by vacant houses and lots; abandoned or mostly-vacant factories; graffiti; and evidence of drug sales and other criminal activity."[4] The report also strongly recommended a renewed commitment to code enforcement. Community and government leaders noted that in the 1980s and 1990s the city had reduced its code enforcement activities.[5] The city also lacked a housing counseling service, and the Fels Institute study noted that as early as 2004,

**Table 9.3  Demographic Change in Reading and Suburban Berks County, 2000–2010**

| | City of Reading | | Berks County[a] | |
|---|---|---|---|---|
| *Race* | *2010* | *2000* | *2010* | *2000* |
| Total population | 88,082 | 81,207 | 323,360 | 292,431 |
| Native American | 794 | 356 | 491 | 255 |
| Asian | 1,309 | 1,296 | 4,076 | 2,489 |
| Black | 11,624 | 9,947 | 8,519 | 3831 |
| Islander | 72 | 32 | 56 | 45 |
| Other race alone | 26,538 | 18,125 | 5,563 | 2,192 |
| Multiracial | 5,398 | 3,392 | 4,854 | 2,218 |
| White alone | 42,617 | 48,059 | 299,531 | 281,401 |
| Hispanic | 51,230 | 30,302 | 16,125 | 6,055 |

*Source:* U.S. Bureau of the Census, 2000 Census of Population and Housing; 2010 Census of Population and Housing.

[a] Berks County figures *exclude* residents of Reading.

approximately 12 houses per month were lost to foreclosures. These homes added to the larger number of vacant properties. It was recommended that Reading establish a housing counseling service to work with homeowners to prevent foreclosures.[6]

# 9.3 Into the Breach: A Volunteer Leadership Group and Its Focus on Entertainment

The effort to revitalize Reading is clearly tied to a group of older business leaders (hereafter, leadership group). Unlike some of the groups in other cities, however, there was no direct economic return that any of these individuals or their firms would receive if the city's stature were revived. Most of the members of Reading's leadership group were retired or had sold their main businesses years ago. Each had amassed their personal fortunes or achieved their financial stability decades ago. Several had homes and new businesses or offices (ventures started during their retirement years after selling their main businesses) in Berks County, near Reading's airport. These individuals were not the rentiers described by Logan and Molotch,[7] as they had long ago sold the businesses that generated their wealth or retired as executives from the region's largest firms.

The group's commitment to Reading was tied to their psychological attachments to the city and a lifetime of memories. Several members of the group had grown to maturity in Reading and, as immigrants to the United States or the children of immigrants, yearned to restore to the city the quality of life they remembered. Other members of this small group had relocated to the area decades ago when they joined some of the area's growing and successful manufacturing concerns. These individuals grew to love the city and decided to spend their active retirement years committed to efforts to revitalize Reading. Each member of the group could have chosen to live his or her retirement years in other parts of the country or could have simply spent his or her retirement years doting on children and grandchildren. Instead, each decided to spend a substantial portion of his or her active retirement years as stewards of a pronounced redevelopment effort for Reading. In addition, each had committed personal capital and, in some instances, substantial amounts of money to projects designed to revitalize downtown Reading.

Prominent among these projects was a hoped for hotel; ground was not broken for that facility until December 2013, but several other cultural assets were renovated or built prior to 2010. Group members have also made a commitment to underwrite the operational expenses of one or more of the arts and cultural organizations at the heart of the revitalization effort. Through 2008 that annual obligation was in excess of $1 million, and it was continued through the end of the decade. Group members also used their personal political power and influence (undoubtedly linked to campaign contributions and efforts on behalf of state and federal office seekers) to present the city's case for grants and assistance. Members of the leadership group were also willing to commit their private funds to efforts that had received state assistance, in essence providing the needed or required "matching funds" that the city could not provide. Even the most critical analysis of this group's activities could not conclude that any member could or would realize a financial return on the personal funds they had spent.[8]

With a customer-oriented business approach from their years of private sector success, this group of community leaders recognized that if Reading could not again become a center of activity through the attraction of people to the city, it would never again thrive. One of the business group's members had made his fortune from a set of department stores built across eastern Pennsylvania. Attracting customers to safe and exciting venues was ingrained in his personal and business philosophy. As he looked at Reading, the city had lost its excitement and was perceived as an unsafe place to visit.

For decades Penn Street, from 4th to 8th Streets, was the retail and social hub of Reading and Berks County. The legendary stories that people tell of the "good old days for Reading" describe trips to this part of downtown for shopping, dining, and entertainment.[9] Middle and upscale retail shopping now takes place in two suburban malls. The Berkshire Mall is located approximately 3 miles west of downtown Reading and is surrounded by acres of free parking. Vanity Fair's outlet mall is located less than 2 miles west of the downtown area and 1.2 miles east of the

Berkshire Mall. It too is surrounded by parking lots, removing the need to venture downtown for retail shopping. As Reading's demography changed, the stores that now fill Penn Street cater to lower-income families. Just as the Fels Institute study noted, the business group members knew that without a venue to bring some level of economic integration to Reading, the city's decline would continue. The initial hope was not to attract higher-income families to return as residents to stem the outmigration. To be sure, if that did occur, it would be an exceptional benefit. The goal was more limited. What was wanted was an attraction or venue that would bring people into the city for entertainment. The small group of retired business leaders understood that they needed to reinstill a sense of security and confidence in people that downtown Reading was a safe and fun place to visit. Reading needed a new image and attractions to give the middle and upper class throughout Berks County and the region faith in the city's future. Without something different, Reading would continue to be seen as crime-laden and filled with cut-rate stores and venues catering only to its growing lower-income population. In many ways the challenge for Reading in the early years of the 21st century was similar to that which Cleveland addressed through the successful renovation of the theatres that became Playhouse Square. Those theatres attract approximately 1 million visits each year to a downtown area once seen as crime-ridden. Reading did not need as many visitors; however, it needed something quite unique and special to change its image. Reading needed something that would make people venture into a downtown area that was viewed as dangerous.

Reading's leadership group decided to focus on sports, entertainment, and culture to remake the city's image and attract people to the downtown area. The projects selected would not include retail development. Downtown Reading was not going to be able to successfully compete with the nearby Berkshire and Vanity Fair (VF) Outlet Malls. Those two venues were well established, convenient, surrounded by acres of free parking, and very close to Penn Street. Penn Street is not going to succeed as a retail center with these two far larger and more successful malls located so close to the downtown area. If people were going to be attracted to the downtown area, the focus would have to be on sports and entertainment, and then, perhaps, the development of other unique or complementary activities. To be sure, there was substantial risk in focusing on sports, entertainment, and culture and the building of new venues.

Allentown, a short 26 miles northeast of Reading, opened a new arena in late 2000, and ground was broken for Hershey's Giant Center (another arena) complete with luxury suites and club seats in November 2000. The Giant Center is located 55 miles from downtown Reading, and residents of Berks County can easily drive to events at that facility in about 1 hour. Moving forward with a new arena for Reading would mean that there would then be three venues within a relatively short driving distance of each other competing to attract events and attendees. Could three facilities similar in scale and purpose survive serving a combined market of approximately 1.5 million people? Some people could have reasonably feared that one or more of these facilities would need large public subsidies to survive.[10]

Despite these risks and concerns, Reading and Berks County moved forward with plans for a new arena, and the Sovereign Center, costing $32 million, opened in September 2001. A grant from the State of Pennsylvania provided $14.5 million toward the project's cost. Sovereign Bank paid $2 million for the naming rights (and the right to erect an advertising pylon in front of the facility), and the bank provided a $12 million loan to the Berks County Convention Center Authority. The loan was secured by a 5-percent tax on hotel rooms charged at all facilities located within 15 miles of the Sovereign Center. A total of $3.5 million was secured through private donations from members of the leadership group focused on revitalization and the sale of sponsorships and advertising inside the facility. There is also an admissions tax that is charged on tickets sold for all events held at the center, with the revenues accruing to Reading. The center has 7,083 seats for hockey and more for concert events. The arena was initially home to a minor league hockey team and an arena league football team. A minor league basketball team suspended operations for the 2008–2009 season. Currently, the minor league hockey team still plays its home games at the arena. The other sports anchor is an indoor lacrosse league team.

The Santander Arena (formerly the Sovereign Center; Santander Bank of Spain acquired Sovereign Bank and placed its name on the arena) was not the only facility that opened in the downtown area to give Reading its concentrated focus on sports, arts, and entertainment. The Berks County Convention Center Authority also oversaw the acquisition and renovation of the historic Rajah Theatre. The theatre was built in the early 1900s to host vaudeville and other live entertainment events. The facility was completely renovated in the late 1990s. With concert and theatre seating for more than 1,500 patrons the performance hall is now the home of the Reading Symphony Orchestra and the "Broadway on 6th Street" theatre series. The renovation cost $10 million, with funds coming from state grants and the proceeds from a loan also guaranteed by the Convention Center Authority from its hotel room receipts.

Despite the stiff competition from the arenas in Allentown and Hershey and other venues for live performance, both of Reading's new entertainment venues have been a financial success. In every year but one, the facilities have generated more revenues than they need to meet their capital and operating expenses. "The Sovereign Center on Penn Street reported $193,000 in profits for the year ending June 30 (2008), and the Performing Arts Center on North Sixth Street reported a smaller-than-expected loss of $29,000. Authority Treasurer Carl Herbein said that's a combined operating profit of $164,000, according to unaudited figures and compares with an operating profit of $40,000 for the prior year."[11] The Berks County Convention Center Authority receives 80 percent of the revenues collected from a hotel tax and a ticket tax. Those revenues have made it possible to ensure that the arena is financially viable. The annual hotel and ticket tax receipts from

**Table 9.4   Hotel and Admission Tax Receipts through 2012**

| | Hotel Tax | | Admissions Tax | |
|---|---|---|---|---|
| Year | Receipts | Percent Change | Receipts | Percent Change |
| 2012 | $1,647,698 | 3.6 | $504,000 | 12.0 |
| 2011 | 1,590,516 | 8.1 | 450,000 | 0.0 |
| 2010 | 1,471,283 | 10.2 | 450,000 | 30.7 |
| 2009 | 1,335,233 | –18.2 | 650,000 | 18.2 |
| 2008 | 1,632,693 | –2.7 | 550,000 | –17.3 |
| 2007 | 1,677,537 | 8.3 | 665,000 | 6.4 |
| 2006 | 1,548,341 | 6.9 | 625,000 | 15.6 |
| 2005 | 1,448,340 | 10.9 | 540,587 | –12.8 |
| 2004 | 1,306,154 | –7.1 | 620,202 | 22.0 |
| 2003 | 1,406,733 | 6.5 | 508,472 | 14.8 |
| 2002 | 1,320,880 | | 442,892 | 43.4 |
| 2001 | | | 308,913 | |

*Source:* City of Reading, Berks County Convention Authority; admissions tax revenues estimates are from the city's budgets and are therefore estimates or projections of anticipated revenue.

2002 through 2012 are reported in Table 9.4. Notice that except for a sharp decline at the height of the recession, the hotel tax has been stable, providing a strong financial base for the arena's operations and for repaying the construction bond. There is increasing optimism that with the opening of a new hotel across the street from the arena in 2015 (as noted, construction was finally initiated in December 2013), revenues might be enhanced. Admissions tax collections have been far more inconsistent related to the number of events and the number of minor league teams that play their home games at the venue. At the current time, there are only two professional teams playing at the arena.

Both facilities are managed by SMG, and they have been successful in bringing leading entertainers to both venues. Elton John, Neil Diamond, Jerry Seinfeld, Dolly Parton, and Cher have each appeared in Reading. Few, if any, members of the leadership group that convened to change Reading's image or residents of the region who had long given up on the city would have believed that a roster of entertainers like that would appear in downtown Reading. That was as improbable an outcome when one looked at downtown Reading in the late 1990s as holding a

Super Bowl in Indianapolis was when leaders put forward a strategy for revitalization there in the late 1970s.

To make attendance at events easier, convenient, and safe, parking is available behind, in front of, and diagonally across from the arena. In this regard, leaders in Reading followed the same strategy used in revitalizing Cleveland's Playhouse Square. In Cleveland, people were similarly afraid of the high crime levels, and therefore to reduce their anxiety, parking facilities were built adjacent to the theatre complex. Reading's placement of convenient and abundant parking in very close proximity to the arena helped to respond to the fears some might have had in attending events in a downtown area thought to be crime-ridden. With attendance at the arena increasing, a surface lot across from the arena was made available for a new hotel, with parking options included in the hotel's design. By having sufficient parking for all attendees adjacent to the arena, the city and the leadership group of retired business leaders and entrepreneurs wanted to ensure that any safety concerns would be immediately addressed. The availability of close parking, however, reduces the ability, in the short run, to increase pedestrian traffic on the streets that could patronize local businesses. The higher priority, as with the building of Playhouse Square in Cleveland, was to ensure that attendees were comfortable and willing to come to events in downtown Reading. To further enhance safety and attractiveness, the facility, as well as all of the others built to make downtown Reading a destination, is ringed with high-power streetlights. These lights have sufficient candlepower to keep the area and its parking facilities well lit, generating additional feelings of safety (see Figure 9.2). With more than 100,000 visits each year to events hosted at the arena, that objective has been achieved. The advertising pylon available on Penn Street is also illustrated. Reading—at an obviously smaller level than Los Angeles—was able to capitalize on advertising to reduce the public subsidy required through the granting of permission to erect an advertising pylon (see Figure 9.2).

# 9.4 Reimaging Reading: From the Outlet Capital to a Mid-Atlantic Arts Center

Sports and entertainment helped to bring people back to downtown Reading, but the leadership group was interested in a new image for the city. Reading was a railroad and manufacturing center for decades, earning it a legendary spot on *Monopoly* gaming boards. When that part of its legacy passed, the city became known for its outlet malls. The unique aspect of its identity has been lost among the proliferation of similar retail centers across the nation. The leadership group wanted a more compelling image, and one that would draw people from the region to the downtown area on a regular basis. Reading's mall did nothing to aid the city's revitalization process.

**Figure 9.2  Reading's Sovereign Center, the powerful new street lights, and the center's advertising pylon. (Photo courtesy of John Ravert.)**

Inspired by Alexandria, Virginia's Torpedo Factory and Bethlehem, Pennsylvania's Banana Factory, the group's leader, Albert Boscov, envisioned a much larger arts center as an anchor for a mixed-use entertainment center for the southern part of downtown Reading. In 2002, a complex of factory buildings where safety goggles, glasses, and sunglasses were long manufactured was closed. Alexandria's Torpedo Factory Art Center is, as its name implies, the home of a center for the creative arts in a former torpedo factory. Since the factory to be used as the arts center in Reading was formerly used to make safety goggles, its name became goggleWorks, and it too was envisioned as a center for the creative arts. Mr. Boscov wanted a center that would be more than a studio; he wanted a center for the arts that attracted people throughout the day, every day. Such a facility in his mind would have opportunities for classes that would be part of the curriculum of the public schools. There could also be classes from the local colleges taught at goggleWorks, and adult education in the afternoon and evenings. To oversee the transformation of the former factory into exhibition space, studios for artists, a movie theatre, numerous classrooms, and rehearsal space for the performing arts, Mr. Boscov hired the director of the Banana Factory and gave her the financial support and authority to make the center a far larger and grander version of Bethlehem's center. Some financial support was secured from Pennsylvania, but the leadership group not only funded the remaining capital costs, but also continues to provide sufficient funding to sustain any shortfalls in goggleWorks' operating budget.

GoggleWorks has sufficient space to be home to more than 34 artists. Each artist leasing space is expected to use the facility to produce his or her work (with opportunities for the public to watch the "artist at work") and showcase his or her pieces. As part of his or her lease, each artist agrees to be present for at least 20 hours per week and on Second Sundays (of each month) when the entire facility is open all day to attract more visitors. GoggleWorks was envisioned to be far more than a showroom for art. It was to be a place where people could watch artists at work and talk to them about their style, techniques, and works of art, and where students of all ages can attend classes in both the creative and performing arts. GoggleWorks also has a small restaurant, coffee shop, and showroom where works of art by the resident artists can be purchased. The sale of their work encourages artists to take advantage of the exhibition space, creating a unique gift shop and retail center for Reading.

The executive director was also successful in convincing many of the region's performing arts schools (ballet and dance) to relocate, and now those students fill the halls of goggleWorks. The Reading public high schools use the facility for their art classes, ensuring that there is activity in the building every school day from 9 a.m. until 3 p.m. The performing arts schools, open to visitors and artists from 9 a.m. until 10 p.m., maintain a flow of students in the late afternoon, and classes for adults as well as motion pictures shown in the theatre each night. Attendance reports indicate that there are 80,000 visits per year to goggleWorks. In 2008 there were 25 different arts organizations and 34 artists in residence (see Figure 9.3). In January 2014 there were 33 artists in residence, illustrating the sustained viability and success of the facility.

The State of Pennsylvania provided a $3 million grant for the development of goggleWorks. The total cost of the complex was $12 million. The members of the leadership group raised $7 million in donations and also contributed $2 million. To meet the center's operating expenses, the plan was to raise

Figure 9.3   Reading's goggleWorks. (Courtesy of Mark S. Rosentraub.)

one-third of needed revenues from programs, one-third from the rent paid by resident artists, organizations, and schools, and then to raise any additional needed money from gifts.

Mr. Boscov's dream or vision was to have the art center anchor an "entertainment square," around which new condominiums and townhouses could be built. His hope was that an arts center and other entertainment amenities would encourage higher-income individuals and families to live, once again, in downtown Reading. Two other amenities were planned in coordinated fashion by the leadership group with the city to complete this Entertainment Square. Group members assumed responsibility for arranging the financing for a new movie multiplex complete with the region's first IMAX theatre. Another member of the group provided support for the building of a performing arts center for the Reading Area Community College that is within three short city blocks of goggleWorks. By 2008 the two new parts of the Entertainment Square were open. The Miller Center for the Arts is home to a 512-seat theatre and provides the community college with needed classrooms and space for performing arts seminars (see Figures 9.4 and 9.5). In the background of the Miller Center (Figure 9.4), the IMAX theatre can be seen, and Figure 9.5 illustrates the movie complex and the street lighting. A multistory parking garage across from the theatres and googleWorks serves visitors to each of the venues in Reading's new Entertainment Square.

**Figure 9.4   Reading Area Community College's Miller Center for the Arts. (Courtesy of Mark S. Rosentraub.)**

**Figure 9.5** Downtown Reading's new 11-screen movie theatre and IMAX center across from goggleWorks and part of Entertainment Square. (Courtesy of Mark S. Rosentraub.)

## 9.5 Reading's Leadership Group and Community Development

The ability to attract residents to a city with so many abandoned homes was another issue that concerned the group of community leaders. To reduce the number of dilapidated properties in the city, the group established Our City Reading to finance the reconstruction of some of the abandoned residential properties. Group members paid all of the expenses associated with rehabilitating these houses and then sold them at below market rates so that lower-income families could afford the mortgages. Basically, the goal was to ensure that lower-income families could be homeowners of a quality house for the same money that they paid for rent. Through October 2008 the group had paid for the renovation of and had sold 375 homes to lower-income families that formerly rented apartments in the city. Only two of the new owners have defaulted on their payments. The average loss or cost to the group is approximately $20,000 per home, and buyers are required to provide a down payment of just $500. Group members have contributed $7.5 million to the Our City Reading program (through October 2008). That figure is the result of the loss of $20,000 per unit sold to each of the 375 lower-income families. The Pennsylvania Housing Financing Agency provides public support for the program by paying for the closing costs associated with the issuance of the mortgage. In effect, the $20,000 expenditure by the group of civic leaders in each house becomes the down payment, leaving mortgage balances of approximately $29,500 on each home (accounting for the $500 down payment provided by each new owner).

# 9.6 Measures of Success

The assets that comprise the sports, entertainment, and arts amenities that anchored Reading's revitalization effort have been open for just a few years. The movie and IMAX theatre complex opened its doors for the 2008 holiday season. As a result, their cumulative effect on longer-term development trends will not be known for a few years. The credit crisis and recession of 2008 and 2009 will also postpone some of the anticipated benefits. As a result, it is too soon to note if the revitalization is a success and if the amenities can increase the economic integration in Reading and reverse the deterioration of many of the city's neighborhoods. There are, however, a few very encouraging signs of improvements.

First, there were steady increases in both the hotel and admission tax receipts through 2007, indicating rising demand for hotel rooms and for the events held in the arena and performing arts centers. After the recession and a decline in tax revenues, there was a robust recovery. The facilities were successful in bringing people to downtown Reading for events. Many of these people had probably avoided the downtown area for entertainment for years, meaning the goal of bringing people into the city for entertainment activities is being met.

Second, goggleWorks is attracting 80,000 visits each year, and on the special Second Sundays, when all artists are present, attendance averages 1,500 people. The small theatre permits films that would not normally be seen in Reading, and demand has reached the point where these types of films are shown every night. Capacity crowds are routine on the weekends in the 131-seat auditorium. With the relocation of performing arts schools to the downtown facility and the availability of evening classes, the amenity attracts people to the downtown area from 9 a.m. to 10 p.m. 4 days a week and on weekends.

There is no evidence yet available that the attraction of people to the new downtown amenities has translated into a substantial uptick in new residential development projects. Through 2008 there was considerable discussion of a $2 billion project along the Schuylkill Riverfront, a short distance from Entertainment Square. As the table and graph in Table 9.5 illustrate, there was a peak of activity in 2007, prior to the recession, and then a steady decline in new building permits for residential development through 2013. The steady decline in the value of residential building permits suggests that Reading may well never achieve the goals that its leadership is striving to achieve.

**Table 9.5   Total Value of Building Permits Issued for Reading, 2004–2008**

| Year | Value |
|------|-------|
| 2004 | $149,652,000 |
| 2005 | 129,742,000 |
| 2006 | 133,486,000 |
| 2007 | 118,308,000 |

*Source:* Economagic.com.

**Value of Building Permits (×$1,000); Reading, PA (MSA); Total**

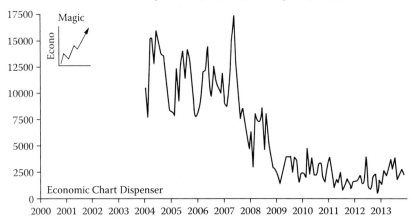

*Source:* Economagic.com. With permission.

## 9.7  Fort Wayne, Indiana

Unlike most aging center cities, Fort Wayne has been able to maintain its dominant economic role in its region. In 1990, 37.9 percent of the metropolitan area's residents lived in the city. In 2010, the city was home to 47.9 percent of the region's residents. Fort Wayne's growth, however, was substantially assisted by its annexation of an adjoining suburban township. Just as Indianapolis had done in the 20th century, Fort Wayne increased its centrality by adding suburban neighborhoods to the city. In 1990 the city had slightly more than 173,000 residents, and in 2010 it had 253,691 residents. In 2010 there were 35,765 residents in Aboite Township, meaning that within the old boundaries of Fort Wayne there were 217,926 residents. Fort Wayne did enjoy a level of growth within its preannexation boundaries. The total population declined slightly to 47.6 percent of the region's population in 2012, but such a small change based on population estimates could mean that there has been no real shift from the 2010 Census. Regardless, Fort Wayne has achieved

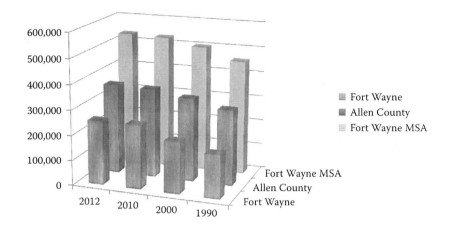

**Figure 9.6 Population trends in the Fort Wayne region. (From U.S. Department of Commerce, Bureau of the Census, various years; annexation takes place between the 2000 and 2010 Census dates. As noted in the text, however, there was also growth within Fort Wayne's older neighborhoods.)**

a degree of centrality that is a function of both annexations and growth within its preexisting borders. This is an outcome that has eluded many other cities, as the economy has changed and decentralization rates have increased. Figure 9.6 illustrates the centrality of Fort Wayne as a home for the region's residents.

While Fort Wayne has been successful in sustaining its centrality through annexation and the attraction of residents to neighborhoods within its preannexation borders, it too has been challenged to attract and retain higher-income residents. Latest estimates from the U.S. Bureau of the Census place the median household income of the city's residents at $44,599 (even after the annexation of a suburban township). The comparable figure for the entire county was $50,030. As that figure also includes residents of Fort Wayne, it is reasonable to expect that suburban households did have higher incomes. The concentration of higher-income households in Allen County is illustrated in Figure 9.7. The darker shaded areas or census tracts are those with higher median household incomes. Fort Wayne is where there is the *only* concentration of lower-income households. While the depiction does not permit a precise representation of the boundaries of Fort Wayne and the balance of Allen County, the concentration of lower-income areas for the county inside Fort Wayne underscores the challenges with regard to income segregation. That challenge has encouraged a focus on the revitalization of downtown Fort Wayne in an effort to retain jobs, residents, and higher-income households in the city.

Fort Wayne's challenge to redevelop or develop its downtown area was not hampered by the crime issues that plagued efforts in Reading. Crime rates have remained stable or actually declined. For example, in 2003, the violent crime rate

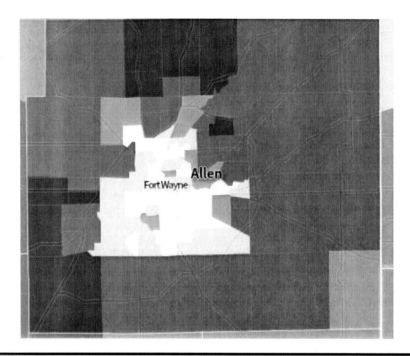

**Figure 9.7** Median household income, Fort Wayne and Allen County, 2012 estimates (darker shading indicates higher median income levels). (From U.S. Department of Commerce, Bureau of the Census, Census Explorer, http://www. census.gov/censusexplorer/censusexplorer.html.)

in Fort Wayne was 37 per 10,000. The comparable figure for the United States was 47.5, meaning that Fort Wayne's rate relative to the United States was 0.78 (or 78 percent of the national violent crime rate). Property crime rates, however, were higher than the national average in 2003. In that year the property crime rate in Fort Wayne was 433, or 121 percent of the national rate. The property crime rate declined to 345 per 10,000 people in 2010, but that rate was still 117 percent of the national rate. Violent crime remained well below the national average (71.8 percent of the national rate).

## 9.7.1 Redeveloping Downtown Fort Wayne

Revitalizing downtown Fort Wayne has been anchored by many amenities, including the Grand Wayne Convention Center that opened in 1985. The facility was renovated, and its reopening took place in 2005. The enclosed botanical garden opened in downtown Fort Wayne in 1983. Fort Wayne's elegant theatre (now named the Embassy Theatre) opened in the downtown area in 1928, adjoined to the 250-room Indiana Hotel. Following numerous ownership changes, the Indiana Hotel closed in 1971. In 1972 there were even plans to demolish the theatre, but as in Cleveland, a group of community leaders raised sufficient funds to avoid razing the historic structure. Several renovations followed, and the Fort Wayne Philharmonic began to hold its concerts at the venue. In 2005 a new marquee entrance was constructed. The Embassy Theatre remains a vibrant cultural and entertainment center for the entire region and an anchor for revitalizing downtown Fort Wayne. In addition to the concerts of the Fort Wayne Philharmonic Orchestra, the Embassy hosts touring shows and concerts by popular artists, an annual Broadway series, and numerous other live entertainment and civic events. These events ensure that there are a large number of visitors to downtown Fort Wayne in all years.

Professional sports, however, were not an initial component of the revitalization of the downtown area. In the 1940s, a group of civic leaders wanted to build a field house as a memorial to the veterans of the two world wars. Eventually voters agreed to fund the building of a new venue 3.1 miles north of the downtown area. Due to the emerging interest in private automobile transportation, the field house, which opened in 1952, offered abundant parking. The facility was also built, in part, to be the home for the Fort Wayne Zollner Pistons. The Zollner Pistons were an original franchise of the NBA; the agreement to form the league and the documents that led to the creation of the NBA were actually signed in Fort Wayne at a restaurant across from the Allen County War Memorial Coliseum. A few seasons after beginning play at the Coliseum, Fred Zollner moved the Pistons to the larger Detroit market and renamed the franchise the Detroit Pistons. A minor league hockey team, the Fort Wayne Komets, continues to play at the Coliseum.

An exhibition hall was added in 1989, creating a competitive venue with the Grand Wayne Center. The Coliseum has also hosted many entertainment events and was renovated again in 2001. Today the Coliseum can seat 13,000 spectators for sports and entertainment events. Any events held at the Coliseum reduce the attractions or activities that take place in downtown Fort Wayne. It is interesting to note that where entertainment events take place does not matter, as the Allen County War Memorial Coliseum is located in Fort Wayne too. As in the case of Cleveland, however, having two competing venues dilutes the development effects for downtown Fort Wayne. That is an ongoing issue for Fort Wayne.

## 9.7.2 Using Sports for Downtown Redevelopment: A New Ballpark and the Fort Wayne Tin Caps

The enhancements to the Grand Wayne Convention Center and other amenities were vital to the revitalization of downtown Fort Wayne. The largest project, however, was a $31 million ballpark for the Fort Wayne Tin Caps (Class A affiliate of the San Diego Padres). The state-of-the-art venue opened in 2009 and is part of a $110 million development known as Harrison Square. Adjacent to the ballpark (with views of the field) is a 42-unit apartment building; the first floor of that

**Figure 9.8 The ballpark and the parking deck (with party seating and retail space outside of the parking deck and beyond the right field fence, and the Marriott Hotel located beyond the right center field fence). (Courtesy of Mark S. Rosentraub.)**

building has commercial space that is occupied by a law firm. A new Marriott Courtyard Hotel is part of the complex, as well a 900-car parking structure (see Figure 9.8). Aboveground and covered walkways (skywalks) connect the Marriott Hotel and parking structure to another downtown hotel and the Grand Wayne Convention Center. The public sector invested at least $64.3 million in the overall project (ballpark and Harrison Square). The private sector investment was approximately $56.1 million. The owners of the Tin Caps paid $5 million for the construction of the ballpark; the balance of the costs was paid by the City of Fort Wayne. In addition, the ball club pays no rent unless attendance exceeds 275,000, and then only $1 for each fan in attendance at games the threshold figure is exceeded. Fort Wayne receives 10 percent of the gross revenues (excluding taxes collected) on the sale of food and beverages. Fort Wayne was also responsible for providing $230,000 each year toward the maintenance of the ballpark. The team retains all revenue from operations, including all advertising and sponsorship revenues earned.

Fort Wayne and the team, however, share the revenue generated by the naming rights sold for the ballpark. If the naming rights agreement exceeded $300,000 per year, all additional revenues are assigned to Fort Wayne. The team was responsible for building the apartment complex that is located outside of the facility (behind the left field fence; see Figure 9.9). Fort Wayne was responsible for furnishing the

**Figure 9.9** The residential complex built by the owners of the team and the party deck at the ballpark. (Courtesy of Mark S. Rosentraub.)

suites, including the inclusion of flat-screen televisions and the usual amenities expected (carpeting, couches, etc.). While the facility was owned by the city and therefore exempt from property taxes, the team was responsible for the property taxes on its personal property.

## 9.7.3 Outcomes in Fort Wayne

The relative population stability of Fort Wayne has already been noted, as well as the impact of annexation. But there has also been a movement of higher-income families to the suburban areas outside of Fort Wayne. As a result, it is fair to observe that the revitalization of downtown has not had a pronounced effect on economic integration relative to residential choices. To be sure, there are higher-income households living in the city; however, for the most part, wealthier families live elsewhere. For Fort Wayne the extent to which jobs are retained may be the measure of success that has to be considered when evaluating the return on its large investment in Harrison Square.

Looking first at the total number of jobs in the metropolitan area, 73 percent of all jobs were located in Fort Wayne in 2002. In addition, 90.6 percent of the region's jobs in the finance and insurance sector were also located in Fort Wayne. The proportion of the jobs in this sector of the economy located in Fort Wayne increased to 94.6 percent in 2011. The city has also retained a substantial proportion of the region's professional, scientific, and technical services jobs (82.6 percent in 2002 and 83.9 percent in 2011). There has been a slight decrease in the proportion of management jobs in the region located in Fort Wayne, but 83.8 percent of those positions are still located in the city. The jobs in the hospitality and in the entertainment sector have also remained relatively stable from 2002 to 2011. In short, the downtown effort has permitted the city to retain its leading role as the region's employment center.

## 9.8 Conclusions

While Fort Wayne has been able to protect and perhaps even enhance its employment base through its focus on downtown revitalization, its lack of success with regard to changing residential patterns reflects outcomes in Reading. For Reading, however, there has been little success with regard to changing employment or residential patterns. Indeed, it is safe to conclude in Reading's case that in the absence of a civic group of former corporate executives and company owners led by Albert Boscov, Michael Ehlerman, Carl Herbein, Marlin Miller, and others, few, if any, of the projects that were built to lead Reading's development would exist. Mr. Boscov's focus on the building of a new hotel took almost a decade of effort.

In Fort Wayne, however, while a large public investment was required to attract investors to the Harrison Square project, it is notable that new entrepreneurs were attracted to the area and purchased the minor league team. The investors in the new hotel are also from outside of the region. Reading, in contrast, has had to rely on individuals with long-standing linkages to the city and who are in effect using philanthropic commitments in an effort to preserve a city they hold dear in their memories. While major investments in Fort Wayne require substantial levels of public participation, job levels are being sustained and new investors are being attracted to the area.

Simply put, in Reading, older business leaders have pledged resources from their own personal wealth, and they have also used their political capital to secure financial support from Pennsylvania and the federal government for the needed projects. The local tax burden to sustain the projects is limited to a hotel tax that, while paid by visitors, inevitably has a slight negative impact on hotel operators and other businesses. That short-term loss, however, may well be offset by higher levels of consumption generated by attendance at the events at the arena. For example, if more out-of-town visitors stay at hotels and eat at nearby restaurants as a result of their attendance, then it is possible that any economic losses generated by the higher-priced room costs are compensated by a larger number of visitors. Assuming that the entire hotel tax is negatively capitalized, the local investment amounts to less than $1.7 million per year. The balance of the funding for the assets has come from the personal wealth of individuals or through grants from the state or federal agencies. This should be properly identified as net gains to the local economy, as those resources could easily have been invested in other communities or elsewhere in the international economy.

Members of this group have also committed personal funds for an important community development program. Neither the City of Reading nor the State of Pennsylvania had sufficient resources to rebuild abandoned or dilapidated houses, remodel them, and then sell them to lower-income households at a per unit cost (loss) of approximately $20,000. With 375 homes revitalized and sold through this program through 2008, at least $7.5 million has been set aside for community development focused on housing for lower- or moderate-income households.

There also is little doubt that the new amenities have achieved the two most important goals for Reading. First, large numbers of people (for a small city and region) are coming to downtown Reading for entertainment. Downtown areas that people avoided for decades because of crime rates and the fears generated by economic and racial segregation are now frequently visited by families and middle-aged and older residents of the region. Some minor league sports teams, however, were not able to continue operations in Reading. The number of people visiting goggleWorks each day and on each Second Sunday is another example of the success of the amenities in changing Reading's image and appeal.

Second, while it might be too early to proclaim that Reading has completely changed its image, or that it has a new image, things have improved from the time that the downtown area was completely avoided and regarded as unsafe for any sort of visits or tourism. The city might not yet be an arts capital, but its reputation has prompted attention from the *Washington Post*,[12] US Airways,[13] *American Craft*,[14] and *American Style*.[15] Such attention was not directed toward the city prior to the investment in the amenities. The appearance of leading entertainers also has an effect on the city's image in the minds of people throughout the region.

It is extremely unlikely that the retired business executives and owners that led this effort will ever earn any economic returns on their investments. The investments made by them fit Nowak's description of investments designed to be market building efforts; unfortunately, through 2013 it is necessary to observe that a market has yet to be developed that warrants substantial private sector commitments.[16] In essence, the group of retired executives and business owners is trying to revitalize Reading into a market for private investment. While Nowak points to the need for market building commitments to earn market-based rates of returns—or some appropriate financial return—it is highly unlikely that any level of financial success will be realized by members of the leadership group that planned the revitalization strategy. It is also possible that some future residential development might be profitable, but the time horizon on that is still difficult to project. The return to the members of this group of civic leaders will be largely intangible—making the city worthy of private investments in new homes and businesses. Tangible returns would come if the assets built achieve the hoped for levels of success and the members of the group then capitalized on the excitement created with additional residential or commercial investments. Because of the commitment and motives of the individuals in the civic group that focused on rebuilding the city, Reading is an example where minor league sports, entertainment, arts, and culture have led an effort to revitalize a declining city. While more time is needed to determine if the city becomes more financially integrated, its image is being changed and crowds are again part of the downtown life of a small city. In that regard, the city could become a major league winner, sporting a new image, new crowds, new confidence, and even for more growth. In the long-term, however, it is not yet possible to conclude that Reading will be stabilized.

For Fort Wayne, however, the prognosis is far more optimistic. With stable job levels, the public sector's investments might well convince people that Fort Wayne has used sports and entertainment to stabilize itself and reposition itself in the aftermath of a recession and a substantial restructuring of the economy. While it is too soon to declare Fort Wayne a major league winner, there is a basis to be quite optimistic about its future.

# Endnotes

1. Tavernise, S., Reading, Pa., knew it was poor. Now it knows just how poor, *New York Times*, September 26, 2011, http://www.nytimes.com/2011/09/27/us/reading-pa-tops-list-poverty-list-census-shows.html?pagewanted=all&_r=0 (accessed January 3, 2014).
2. Heister, M., *Public secondary school dropouts, 2006–2007* (Harrisburg, PA: Pennsylvania Department of Education, 2008).
3. Montgomery, D., The engine of change: Reading, Pa. has proven it's deft at switching tracks. As residents head to the polls, the question is: Where to next? *Washington Post*, April 22, 2008, C01.
4. Fels Institute of Government, *Vacancy inventory and reinvestment strategies for Reading, PA* (Philadelphia: University of Pennsylvania, 2008), 18, http://www.readingpa.gov/documents/fels_report.pdf (accessed November 1, 2008).
5. Confirmed in interviews conducted in October 2008 with city employees, private sector business leaders, and leaders of nongovernmental economic and housing development organizations by the author.
6. Fels Institute of Government, *Vacancy inventory and reinvestment strategies for Reading, PA* (Philadelphia: University of Pennsylvania, 2008), 38, http://www.readingpa.gov/documents/fels_report.pdf (accessed November 1, 2008).
7. Logan, J.R., and H.L. Molotch, *Urban fortunes: The political economy of place* (Berkeley: University of California Press, 1987).
8. The number of individuals involved in the leadership group is small and their identities and names widely known. Some members of the group have been portrayed in regional and national publications. To honor the commitment made regarding confidentiality, the names of the group's members interviewed are not included in this text relative to specific statements or actions taken by the group.
9. Interview with Cindy Herninitz, October 2008.

10. Some hotel operators in Reading filed a lawsuit against the imposition of a tax on room nights to pay for part of its cost. Experts testified that there was indeed substantial risk that multiple arenas in close proximity to each other could lead to operating losses for one or more of these facilities. The court ruled that there was nothing irregular in the procedures followed by Berks County and Reading, and the case was dismissed.

11. Spatz, D., Reading's two civic centers combine for $164,000 profit, *Reading Eagle*, August 21, 2008, https://www.readingeagle.com (accessed September 6, 2008).

12. Fidler, J., Reading: It's not just outlet malls anymore, *Washington Post*, July 19, 2006, C2.

13. US Airways, The man with a plan, *US Airways Magazine*, November 2006, 136.

14. American Craft, goggleWorks, Reading, PA, *American Craft*, October/November 6, 2006.

15. Tiger, C., See for yourself: A former eyeglass factory brings a Pennsylvania city's vision to life, *American Style*, August 2008, 70–75.

16. Nowak, J., The market-building potential of development finance in older industrial cities, in *Retooling for growth: Building a 21st century economy in America's older industrial areas*, ed. R.C. McGahey and J.S. Vey, 373–410 (Washington, DC: Brookings Institution, 2008).

*Chapter 10*

# Reversing Urban Decline: The Role for Sports, Culture, and Entertainment and What Is Required to Turn Subsidies into Strategic Investments

## 10.1 Introduction

A popular quip is that economists rarely agree; indeed, it almost seems that those who study economic issues informally agree to disagree with one another. There is, however, one issue where there is complete agreement. Teams and sport venues have little effect on regional economies. At best, professional sports are one of the amenities that contribute to a region's appeal. But other amenities are also valuable, and if professional sports are absent from a particular market, collegiate sports or other forms of entertainment could fill any void. The inconsequential nature of the effect sports have on a region's economy is not limited to professional sports. Little, if any, evidence suggests that mega-events such as the Olympics or the World Cup, or special one-time events such as the Super Bowl or World Series, change regional economies. So what is the value of the eight case studies, and why do I argue that sports, culture, and entertainment are important to cities? The answer lies not in the negligible increment sports generate for a region, but in the ways in which sports can facilitate the redistribution of regional economic activity. That redistribution can have a substantial effect on the financial stability of central cities.

At a symposium organized by Roger Noll and Andrew Zimbalist at the Brookings Institution in 1996, urban economist Professor Edwin Mills advised other scholars in attendance that it might be more important to study the ways in which sports (and venues) shift economic patterns in a region instead of occupying any more time trying to understand if teams and events affect regional economies. His advice was accurate. His observation or direction changed the focus of my research.

The importance of sports, culture, and entertainment is not to be found in the effect any or all have on a region's economy; the economic value of teams and venues lies in the ways in which each can reallocate or reposition where economic activity occurs within a region. The importance of Professor Mills' observation would not be so critical if all local governments in every metropolitan area shared tax revenues with each other. If local governments shared revenues, or if states, provinces, or national governments compensated local governments with grants to offset seg-regated housing patterns and the lower tax revenues produced by lower-income residents, then the spatial effects of sports would not matter. With economic segre-gation in housing patterns increasing, every public leader has to focus on attracting and retaining as much regional economic activity as possible. If they are not able to attract and retain regional economic activity, then a local government could lack the financial resources required to provide needed urban services to its residents. Detroit is but the most extreme example of what happens when regional economic activity occurs elsewhere in a region, leaving a central city without the tax revenues needed to support the services its residents require and deserve.

As noted throughout this volume, sports have a great potential to reallocate or redirect some of the spending that takes place in a region. What needs to be focused upon in this last chapter are the steps cities can take to ensure that they can benefit from the repositioning of regional economic activity that does occur when sports venues are built. The relocation of economic activity by sports cre-ates viable financial returns for a host city when the appropriate mix of real estate development projects take place and are connected to a venue. If substantial levels of real estate development based on private sector investments do not take place, any public investment in a venue is merely a subsidy, and the potential to redirect regional economic activity is lost.

Each of the cities studied tied sports, entertainment, and arts and culture to a revitalization strategy in order to enhance the financial stability of a central city that had declined or had a deteriorating downtown area. The size, location, and demographic differences between the communities did not substantially change the goals and hopes leadership had for their rebuilding efforts. Leaders in each city wanted to rebuild a deteriorating or stagnant part of its downtown area. They also recognized the need to attract and retain highly skilled workers to advance *local* economic development and the fiscal stability of the central city. In each area a revitalized downtown was also part of the effort to increase or extend a region's attractiveness. What needs to be summarized is the ways in which cities have succeeded in changing the flow of regional economic activity. What worked and what failed is the advice that other cities need.

For central cities or the downtown areas to be perceived as places to visit, work, or live, each of the case study cities looked to restore people's confidence in a central city's future through strategic investments in venues to host sport and entertainment events. A new or energized downtown area was also pursued to help the region offer educated labor a sense of diversity and to add the option of an urban lifestyle to the region's mix of living environments. The paths taken to finance revitalization varied, and in the use of different tools, important lessons have been learned to help other communities achieve their goals.

In pursuit of revitalized downtowns, some cities relied only on their own tax money to build amenities in an effort to convince entrepreneurs to make related private investments. In several cities, however, regional financing plans involved contributions from the residents of suburban cities, creating a level of regional investment to ensure that a level of economic activity was concentrated in an area's central city. While it is unclear if intergovernmental transfers would be possible for the provision of services to inner city residents, it is interesting to note that voters in the Cleveland and Denver regions supported proposals to pay for sports facilities built in each region's central city and the downtown area. In the Indianapolis region, elected leaders from the counties that adjoin the consolidated city and county of Indianapolis and Marion raised taxes to pay for Lucas Oil Stadium (home of the Indianapolis Colts). Suburban governments and their taxpayers may not be willing to share revenues to help central cities pay for basic urban services. There are examples, however, when suburban taxpayers and governments will help central cities pay for sports facilities for professional teams. That possibility creates an opportunity for central cities to improve their financial condition if the venue built is an anchor for a broad-based real estate development plan that produces a new neighborhood. When that occurs, the central city can receive new tax revenues and the region also benefits, as an urban living experience is created that can support the region's economic development strategy. Downtown neighborhoods are attractive amenities to certain segments of a workforce. Having that amenity makes a region more competitive in its efforts to attract and retain a well-educated workforce.

The most important lesson from each of the case studies is that regardless of circumstance, each central city was able to secure some level of real estate development anchored by the sports facility. In some settings, more development occurred, but there is sufficient information or data to underscore the point that no city, county, or state should enter into a partnership to build a venue without a robust commitment for related real estate development. Achieving what took place in Columbus, Los Angeles, and San Diego—central cities of different sizes and at the center of markets of different sizes—is a realistic benchmark that underscores for every city what it is that taxpayers should receive if their dollars are to be invested in a facility.

## 10.2 Subsidies to Investments in the Aftermath of the Credit Crisis

Discussing these strategies as recommendations to avoid or minimize subsidies in the aftermath of the 2008–2009 credit crisis and the collapse of real estate values might appear to be tainted with some irony. For some people, the collapse of real estate values and the credit crisis might be seen as synonymous with an overreliance on revitalization strategies that included or even catered to the building of sports, entertainment, and cultural facilities with adjoining residences, hotels, and commercial space. The fiscal tools used in the revitalization strategies, the assembly of land for real estate redevelopment, and the resulting construction linked teams, governments, cultural organizations, and entertainment firms with some of the financial organizations and banks that were at the center of the 2008 collapse of the credit markets. Does that association mean the revitalization of downtown areas through the creation of new neighborhoods and an emphasis on entertainment, sports, and culture to attract human capital and bring people back to cities is wrong-headed? Should community leaders be worried that another real estate bubble is just around the corner?

The collapse of real estate values and the depth of the recession delayed some revitalization projects while also reducing the value of properties. In some instances, those reduced property values also meant less revenue for the local governments that had made prudent investments in facilities that were to anchor new neighborhoods. For example, in the New York metropolitan area the Atlantic Yards project in Brooklyn was delayed, and the iconic nature of the venue had to be redesigned to reduce costs. The real estate development was initiated years later than anticipated. The mixed-use project adjoining MetLife Stadium built by the New York Giants and New York Jets in New Jersey's Meadowlands has also been delayed. Yet, today, real estate development surrounding the extraordinary, and considered by many to be quite iconic, venue known as the Barclays Center is underway. New residential properties, apartments, and condominiums will be available by the end of 2015. MetLife Stadium in New Jersey hosted the 2014 Super Bowl. While real estate development has still not been realized, the facility was privately financed. New Jersey will likely see substantial nearby redevelopment within the decade ahead. Furthermore, the real estate development surrounding Citi Field in Queens was also delayed, but infrastructure work on that large-scale project began in 2014. It will take more than a decade to complete the redevelopment of the more than 75 acres adjoining Citi Field, but that project will lead to an entirely new neighborhood for New York City.

The private sector investments in downtown Cleveland have not yet fulfilled the promise or hope that drove the funding for the new ballpark and arena, but the initiatives now underway will likely lead to far more downtown revitalization than even the project's initial proponents claimed was possible. Lastly, toward the end of 2013 Cobb County and the Atlanta Braves announced a new partnership for a ballpark district that includes a commitment by the team to build a mixed-use community on a 60+-acre site. Cobb County's financial model indicates that the property and sales taxes from the expected development will support the public sector's investment in the ballpark and generate additional revenue to provide enhanced services to residents. The City of Calgary, Alberta, and the Calgary Flames are each evaluating a project that could include a new neighborhood and a new set of sports facilities. These initiatives suggest that even in the aftermath of the real estate bubble, opportunities exist for teams and the public sector to satisfy their financial interests. Moreover, as was discussed in the San Diego case study, the real estate developed in the Ballpark District was able to sustain values throughout the market's contraction. A well-planned new neighborhood anchored by sports and entertainment venues can be sustained when real estate markets contract.

The success elsewhere does not mean that every project and city will succeed. Reading and Fort Wayne *have not* enjoyed the levels of real estate development success that were envisioned. Two large residential developments in Reading's downtown area have been postponed, and it took several additional years before construction of a hotel was initiated. Do these disappointments imply that a focus on real estate development linked to sports, entertainment, and culture for revitalization is the latest example of a search for fool's gold or an elixir to cure the ills in many core urban areas? Some important trends suggest that building new neighborhoods anchored by sports venues should be part of any city's revitalization effort. Before proceeding to the lessons learned from the case studies, it is useful to summarize those trends and their linkage to the conceptual framework that is at the core of this book's focus. Ignoring the success that turned subsidies into investments for revitalization would be to reject these more permanent societal changes as guides for prudent policies and approaches to redevelopment and revitalization.

## 10.2.1 The Value of Amenities for Economic Development and Revitalization

Businesses are increasingly dependent on human capital for their growth and expansion. Successful firms locate in regions with the largest concentrations of the most talented and skilled workers. This means firms locate where people want to live, changing older business-labor linkages where workers moved to those locations where businesses capitalized on comparative advantages. Today it is talented human capital that is the most important factor of production for a business. If a business is to be successful, it must be located in a region or area where people want to live. There are many facets or elements that comprise the amenity package that is valued by workers. Sports, however, are an important element or part of any region's amenity package, and they can be used to enhance the location of economic activity. If a central city can build new neighborhoods anchored by sports facilities, regional economic activity can be transferred back to downtown areas. These new or revitalized areas also offer to the region's residents a unique urban environment close to entertainment venues. That residential experience is valued by some segments of every region's workforce. In that sense, a new downtown area helps regional economic development by making this amenity package (entertainment, sports, and an urban living environment) available to interested households.

This shift in the relationship between businesses and labor is a result of the importance and value of highly skilled and educated workers for innovation and the changing structure of the American economy. Within this new structure, research, services, health care, computing, information technology, robotics, and advanced manufacturing assume larger roles than do the manufacturing processes involving assembly lines that produced millions of jobs in the 20th century. The expanding sectors of today's economy are less dependent on the traditional factors that affected the location chosen by businesses and patterns of economic development that dominated America's growth in the past.

Highly skilled workers place a great deal of value on the mix and availability of amenities when choosing a place to live. Areas with fewer amenities are seen as less desirable. One important amenity is a lively downtown area that capitalizes on the potential to be a residential neighborhood for the increasing numbers of people enjoying long and active periods of their lives after fulfilling their child-rearing responsibilities. The desire of young professionals for cities with dynamic downtown areas is also part of the attraction that propels the growth of Boston, Charlotte, Chicago, and New York. In addition, as more and more professionals work well after their children are independent and until they are 70 years of age or older, this growing segment of the labor force and real estate market also has interest in urban living environments that offer condominium homes and easy access to entertainment options. As these proportions of the population increase, the popularity of safe downtown and urban neighborhoods located in close proximity to a large number of amenities will continue to increase. Lastly, as more professional women enter the labor force and postpone family formation, there is additional demand for urban lifestyles in downtown areas.

## 10.2.2 Urban Tourism

Temporary contractions of the economy do not lead to a devaluation of tourism and entertainment. There is as much demand for entertainment and sports in the postrecession period as there was before the collapse of the credit markets. The demand for and interest in entertainment, tourism, and travel overcame the substantial contractions that took place in the aftermath of the 9/11 attacks and terrorist incidents in Spain, England, and Israel. While there is debate over the relative value of different amenity packages for economic development and their causal connection to economic development and revitalization, there is little disagreement that areas lacking in amenities will increasingly find themselves less likely locations for growth, expansion, and the attraction and retention of younger and high-value workers.[1] Add to all of these factors the changes in technology that accelerate the declining period of time that comparative advantages can be sustained, and the emphasis on amenities is easier to understand as communities strive to achieve a competitive advantage based on human capital.[2] As a result, the lessons learned from the case studies can help communities include amenities as part of a revitalization and economic development strategy.

## 10.3  Lessons Learned: Similarities within Differences

Before focusing on recommended strategies for communities to consider based on the case studies, it is useful to point out similarities among the challenges confronting the cities studied regardless of differences in population size, economic size, and regional growth patterns. For example, each city had a declining area that was increasingly avoided by people and was being bypassed by investors. In some instances these depressed areas constituted part of a downtown area, the entire downtown area, or an entire city. What is important to note is that the challenges that Los Angeles faced in revitalizing its downtown area were more similar rather than different from the challenges set before Fort Wayne (or Reading) as each city's leaders tackled a problem that encompassed its entire downtown area as well as numerous neighborhoods. Columbus' leadership was also frustrated by a deteriorating section of its downtown area, and Indianapolis' leadership watched as people and economic activity moved to more outlying areas within its boundaries after consolidation. In response to the consolidation of Indianapolis with Marion County and its focus on revitalizing a deteriorating downtown area, communities in counties adjacent to the merged city/county built their own new town centers. These new centers combined retail, commercial, and residential space to create competing urban lifestyle settings within economically segregated suburban towns and smaller cities. As a result, downtown Indianapolis needed to compete with its surrounding suburbs even though it was a consolidated government.

In Cleveland, Los Angeles, and Reading there was a perception that parts or all of the downtown areas were dangerous and crime-ridden places that should be avoided. All three cities needed strategies to change their images and attract crowds back to areas that were once the center of their region's retail and entertainment activity. Indianapolis' and Columbus' downtown areas might have been seen as less dangerous, but businesses and people had been relocating to more suburban areas for decades. There was also no reason or need to be downtown after business hours.

Three of the case studies involved cities that were state capitols. As a result, Columbus, Denver, and Indianapolis benefitted from a concentration of state workers as a result of the presence of their state's legislatures. Despite this labor pool, each had downtown areas that were also avoided after business hours as entertainment amenities were available in suburban areas. When the legislatures were in session, there was additional activity in and around the state government's buildings. When the legislatures were not in session or after the business day ended, the downtown areas were increasingly deserted. Each city had to focus on building new downtown neighborhoods to ensure that a 365-day-a-year urban center existed and that private companies still wanted to be located downtown. Each city also wanted its downtown area to become a new neighborhood where people wanted to live.

Only in San Diego did some believe that the area targeted for development could or might have revived or become vital without a new large-scale development plan. But even there, residential development was languishing and suburban growth was accelerating as people preferred to live away from the downtown area. San Diego's leaders wanted to avoid the sense of sprawl that characterized Los Angeles. In each of the other cities, trends indicated the downtown areas were either deteriorating, declining, or stagnant, with little private sector investment in new properties or projects. There was little or no evidence of development taking place or imminent in most of the downtown areas before the revitalization efforts linked to sports, entertainment, and culture were launched. Columbus had made a large investment in a new downtown mall, but it failed and was eventually razed. The area that was designated as the Arena District had languished for decades. At the time of Cleveland's big-ticket investments, there was a substantial shift of the region's population away from the city, a trend also evident in Indianapolis. While it would take decades before there was a substantial level of new real estate development (in Cleveland after 2010), the development that occurred from the opening of the ballpark and arena would likely not have taken place without the presence of the sports facilities. Reading was able to avoid a loss of residents, but similar to Cleveland, its residents had incomes substantially lower than those of people living outside its boundaries. Population growth was also concentrated in suburban Columbus and adjacent counties. Those residents who remained in downtown Los Angeles also had incomes far below those earned by people living elsewhere in the region. Fort Wayne has not enjoyed the population changes anticipated, but its downtown development strategy has stabilized employment patterns. Denver, on the other hand, achieved its goals of creating stable downtown neighborhoods and enhancing parts of its employment base. Denver also established a growth rate in residential development that matched that of its suburban areas.

A lack of confidence in a city's future was probably most evident or pressing in Cleveland and Reading, but there were serious reservations about what was possible relative to new development in downtown Los Angeles, Indianapolis, and

Columbus. In these three areas, as revitalization plans were put forward, most people were looking to the suburban areas for their region's future, and there was considerable skepticism that redevelopment efforts would have any impact or change longer-term trends. Cleveland and Reading, because of their small sizes, were becoming economically and racially segregated within their respective counties and metropolitan regions. In Columbus, Indianapolis, and Los Angeles there was confidence in the future for other parts of the city and certainly in the region, but not in the core or central parts of the downtown area. It is important to underscore these similarities and to keep them in mind as community leaders from other cities and regions seek to benefit from the lessons learned in efforts to rely on amenities to anchor revitalization and economic development strategies. Denver was losing its sense of centrality, and before its revitalization plan was put forward, people and businesses were relocating to suburban communities. **In summary, each city had to take aggressive action to change economic and demographic patterns that were undermining the financial base of the central city.**

This commonality of issues combined with the rapid pace of economic decentralization away from central cities and older downtown areas draws direct attention to a major issue for all community leaders. There has been some concern and opposition to a perspective that master-planned neighborhoods would subvert vital principles of urban planning and design. The most successful examples of new neighborhoods, however, were those that adhered to principles of urban design often articulated by Jane Jacobs and others. The most important ideas for making a neighborhood successful have each been integrated into the new areas developed in Columbus, Denver, Indianapolis, and San Diego. Each area was also anchored by at least one sports facility and each was part of a master plan to build a new downtown area. In some cases the new neighborhoods were developed in a relatively short period of time. In other instances, build-out took decades. But in these cities there was no rejection of the idea that pedestrian pathways, green space, and parks had to be included. *Each city ensured that the development plans and strategies included public spaces, parks, or green spaces.* Fort Wayne, for example, keeps the new minor league ballpark opened each day, creating a setting for exercise for nearby residents and employees of firms that regularly use its concourses and steps for individual exercise programs. Community planning principles were incorporated into "uber planned areas."

Each redevelopment plan argued for and reused existing buildings, and in Columbus, discarded artifacts from other areas were incorporated into the new neighborhood. Denver also reused existing infrastructure, such as bridges and buildings to insulate new neighborhoods from busy thoroughfares reserved for vehicular traffic. PETCO Park incorporated older buildings into the new ballpark, and the surrounding development includes projects that converted existing buildings into new offices or residential properties. In short, there was no discarding of the old in favor of newer buildings; rather, there was a mix of buildings and building styles that created a distinct urban texture that encouraged people to live in areas that had been losing residents for decades.

There is sometimes concern that new urban neighborhoods built in relatively short time periods and anchored to sports facilities would become economically segregated and inhibit housing options for lower- or more moderate-income households. Evidence from Los Angeles and San Diego suggests that economically integrated neighborhoods were in fact created. It is possible to produce new neighborhoods in relatively brief time periods to counter rapid decentralization trends that are economically integrated and offer below-market-rate housing for middle- and lower-income households.

Finally, the inclusion of a growth machine or regime that supports an investment by a government in a sports facility does not necessarily mean that other community development initiatives are thwarted or ignored. Cleveland's Greater Cleveland Partnership (GCP) has led the effort to expand public funding for inner city education, and in almost every other city a focus on big-ticket items never meant there was an absence of support for other forms of community development. Some will argue that any support for big-ticket items means there is less money for other community initiatives. While that is certainly possible given the number of sports initiatives financed by suburban cities, counties, and state governments, there is also the possibility that investment in sports facilities were the only investment in central cities those governments would support. Hence, it then falls to central cities to utilize the funds secured from other governments for the big-ticket items, to generate new revenue streams to fund community development projects.

## 10.4 Lessons Learned: The Advice for Other Cities Looking to Sports, Entertainment, and Cultural Amenities for Revitalization

How can cities use sports to build desirable and economically integrated neighborhoods that are also profitable locations for professional sports teams? Several important lessons emerge from the experiences of the cases that will help other cities as they consider public–private partnerships to minimize and avoid subsidies. There is no priority or ordering for these recommendations. Each is a tool that can help revitalize a downtown area.

### 10.4.1 Recommendation 1: The Value of Advertising

Communities sometimes overlook the value of advertising and how particular locations, because of commuting patterns or the attraction of crowds at events, can generate advertising revenue that can support the public sector's investment in a facility. These locations, if appropriately marketed and then leased to businesses that can sell opportunities for advertising to other firms, can generate substantial revenues for the public sector. Those funds—or the revenue streams given to the firms that lease the advertising space—can reduce the need for tax dollars in a revitalization effort. In exchange for Los Angeles' decision to allow AEG (and its partner) to build two advertising pylons visible to motorists on both freeways (and retain all advertising revenues) the firms agreed to pay for the cost of building and maintaining the arena. In addition, AEG also went forward with its plan to build a new hotel as part of the entertainment and commercial development in L.A. LIVE. The total private sector investment exceeded $2.5 billion. Some might counter that the size of the Los Angeles market makes its experience in using advertising opportunities an unlikely option for other cities. Cleveland, Reading, and Fort Wayne, however, were each able to use advertising and naming rights deals to generate funds from the private sector for the building of sports venues in their communities.

Cleveland also capitalized on expanded advertising options for the Indians and Cavaliers at the ballpark and arena to renegotiate leases with both teams. In exchange for the teams receiving broader support from Gateway to lease space for advertising inside and on the outside of both facilities, the franchises agreed to assume responsibility for annual maintenance expenses and to make additional improvements in the arena and ballpark. In terms of the annual maintenance costs, the public sector saved more than $40 million,[3] and each team has also made other substantial investments to upgrade each facility. In this manner, the additional advertising permitted by Cleveland can be thought of as generating a revenue stream of more than $60 million across a 15-year period that will extend to at least 2020. That revenue reduces the need for any additional tax money to maintain certain elements of the arena and ballpark and fund the Gateway Development Authority's expenses.

Some might object to expanding advertising in public spaces, considering such practices to be too commercially oriented and inappropriate for a city. Others could object to the additional advertisement's contribution to a form of pollution of the visual aesthetics or vistas in a city. Across the last several years, transportation systems have sold advertising on buses and trains, and other governments have leased advertising space at venues that attract large crowds (bus and train stations, transit stops, airport terminals, publicly owned sports facilities, etc.). There are legitimate reasons to object to this level of commercial activity and to government policies that embrace market-oriented approaches to finance revitalization or community development activities. Those concerns can be amplified if inappropriate advertising is permitted. Los Angeles has set guidelines to ensure that some businesses viewed as inappropriate relative to the public interest (e.g., businesses selling tobacco products, firearms, or some forms of alcohol) are not able to advertise in public spaces. But Los Angeles did agree to permit Budweiser's name to appear on the pylons. While focusing on these concerns, it is also important to underscore that one way to avoid public subsidies and higher taxes for amenities, community development, and revitalization strategies is to take advantage of the marketing value created when large numbers of people are attracted to and use the facilities built by the public sector. Cleveland, Los Angeles, Fort Wayne, and Reading reduced the public sector's fiscal responsibilities for the building of amenities by permitting advertising on the buildings funded with public dollars. The value of this option should be considered by other communities to reduce the costs of their investments in revitalization efforts. Cities interested in building new amenities need to analyze the value of the public space they control, and then consider if that revenue would be helpful in securing revitalization or community development goals. As the evidence illustrates, this option exists for both the largest cities and smaller ones and reduces the fiscal cost to taxpayers while ensuring an amenity is built and maintained.

## 10.4.2 Recommendation 2: Concentrate Amenities and Make Detailed Plans

Indianapolis, San Diego, Los Angeles, and Columbus concentrated their revitalization efforts in a tightly defined geographic space. Denver used different amenities to create four distinct neighborhoods located close to each other, linked together by pedestrian and bicycle paths and convenient public transport. Cleveland's revitalization effort, in comparison, is spread across a very large downtown area and the different parts are not conveniently linked. A new public transit system connects some areas to each other, but other revitalized areas are really quite distinct or separated from each other in Cleveland. Reading's redevelopment projects are also diffused across a much smaller core area, but are still too disjointed, especially when compared to what was accomplished in Indianapolis. One clear advantage from a concentrated revitalization approach is that it is far easier to successfully complete a renewal plan in a tightly designed area and ensure that all of the buildings or lands within the districts are redeveloped.

When this is achieved, an image of success and vitality is created, contrasted with the previous period of decline and deterioration. Placing a number of amenities in a small and defined space also concentrates people and their activities, making it easier to create the presence of crowds that are essential to enhance impressions of safety. The absence (or far smaller presence) of abandoned, dilapidated, or vacant buildings or properties also creates an image of vitality and feelings of safety for visitors and pedestrians. If amenities are dispersed across a broad area, it requires far more resources to redevelop all properties within the revitalized district to create the image of the successful rebuilding of a portion of the downtown area. Dispersed amenities risk the impression that each is an isolated island of activity in a larger sea of deteriorating properties.

Cleveland's extraordinary assets anchoring its revitalization strategy are located in different parts across the footprint of a large downtown area. In the 1950s, the dominance of Cleveland made the size of that downtown area sensible. For the

Cleveland that exists in the 21st century, that large footprint is likely to never again be needed. As a result, Cleveland's future downtown needs to be smaller than the one that existed in the mid-20th century, and the revitalization efforts planned need to be set to realistic boundaries. The large number of buildings and properties between these amenities that need to be redeveloped would require a level of investment that is unlikely to occur. The failure of that level of investment to occur means there are blighted or abandoned properties that will remain dispersed between extraordinary amenities and assets. The presence of these properties creates an image of an unfinished and an unlikely to be finished downtown. Development levels in Cleveland are now poised to accelerate. But this new level of activity that is taking place in the second and third decades after the sports venues and museums opened and four decades after the renovation of Playhouse Square raise another issue. Even when a development strategy is created and financially supported by the public sector, it may take decades before market forces are adjusted to the point where private investments are sustainable. Even if all of the planned development now possible takes place, the surge of activity might not be sufficient to eliminate all of the vacant or abandoned properties between Cleveland's sports, entertainment, and arts and cultural amenities. This is particularly important to note as each of the three sports venues also need to be renovated as they have existed for almost 20 years. As markets change, venues need to adjust to what fans need; in addition, portions of the sports venues are simply in need of enhancements or restoration after two decades of use. It is unfortunate that the final emergence of large-scale private sector investments is taking place at the same point that the public sector has to financially support another round of investments to meet the terms of the renegotiated leases.

This confluence of outcomes in Cleveland underscores a basic principle for any redevelopment strategy given decentralizing market forces and the development of suburban and exurban cities. Redevelopment activities have to be concentrated in small geographic areas or parts of downtown areas. Further, the scale of the downtown area that is to be redeveloped has to match the future likely shape or scale of the core area of the central city. Simply put, Cleveland (and cities like Detroit) will never have a downtown area that matches the size of those that existed in decades past. Shrinking the footprint of downtown areas has to be a central theme of any revitalization strategy. If that difficult task is not undertaken, no single core area will have a fully developed appearance. What will result are "bubbles" of developed space with amenities that are surrounded by deteriorating properties and abandoned buildings. While Indianapolis' leadership may be frustrated that more development has not taken place to the north of its revitalized (and properly sized) new downtown area, within the 4 square miles (plus Lucas Oil Stadium and the White River Park) that has been redeveloped, there is a successful convention center, two new sports facilities, a relatively successful retail mall, two theatres for the performing arts, an elevated arts garden connecting buildings and serving as an archway for the downtown area, a new multiplex movie theatre as part of the mall, several hotels, several museums, two park areas, and dozens of restaurants. Across three decades, all evidence of deterioration has been erased in the new right-sized downtown core. Visitors from the region or from other cities, when in the midst of Indianapolis' appropriately sized downtown area, find themselves able to walk in a vibrant urban core that is also the location of several thousand residential units. The image of success and vitality that Indianapolis' revitalized core area projects stands in sharp contrast to the abandoned buildings and storefronts that are interlaced between the extraordinary amenities built in Cleveland. What should Cleveland and Detroit do with land that will likely not be needed in the future? Greening the downtown with new parks is the best tactic as those green spaces make the downtown area a more desirable urban neighborhood. New parks in Indianapolis and San Diego were quite important in both cities' plans and strategies.

The investments by AEG that became L.A. LIVE adjacent to the Staples Center created an extraordinary entertainment zone. The Ballpark District in San Diego and the Arena District in Columbus are far smaller than the entertainment district in Indianapolis, but they too are complete and create an image of vibrancy, excitement, and safety. Denver's redevelopment strategy was also guided by a detailed plan that included extensive linkages between each of the separate areas where new neighborhoods were created. Reading, having also dispersed its new assets within a relatively small downtown area, will be challenged to refine its strategy to eliminate vacant and dilapidated buildings adjacent to or near its vibrant new assets. Its arena is several blocks from the performing arts center, and both of those facilities are at opposite ends of the small downtown area from goggleWorks and the entertainment center. Efforts to fill in development to connect these areas—a central component of the Penn Corridor Development Plan developed for the city—will require substantial investment and a long-term commitment; that commitment has yet to be realized.[4] Fort Wayne has two event centers, and it is hard to imagine how, in an area that is highly decentralized and where automobile usage is preferred, there will ever be a fully redeveloped downtown area.

Revitalization strategies amidst the economic forces that are leading to a greater decentralization of business activity have a greater potential to achieve their objectives and goals if there is commitment to concentrate assets in close proximity to one another. Some of the success that Denver, Indianapolis, Los Angeles, San Diego, and Columbus have realized is a function of their planning decisions not to diffuse the location of strategic assets. That concentration helps to create an atmosphere that includes crowds and high levels of pedestrian traffic. When assets are close to one another or conveniently linked by pedestrian thoroughfares, an image of vitality and safety results. All communities considering the use of sports and cultural amenities to revitalize a downtown area would be well served to follow in the footsteps of Denver, Indianapolis, Los Angeles, San Diego, and Columbus and concentrate all of the new assets in a zone or in separately well-supported areas, and then build out from the center. Trying to connect separated nodes of activities as economies continue to decentralize seems to make revitalizing a central city's core area a harder task to complete.

Circumstances pushed Cleveland, Fort Wayne, and Reading to more diffused strategies, and leaders were not willing to force other actors to compromise or confront the reality of the challenges these cities faced to restore vitality to the downtown areas of shrinking cities. I.M. Pei wanted a majestic vista to match his iconic design for the Rock and Roll Hall of Fame and Museum. In order to meet the NFL's schedule, the new home for the Cleveland Browns could only be built in one location and not near the new arena and ballpark. Reading capitalized on the availability of abandoned factory space for googleWorks despite its more distant location from the legacy locations where the arena and the performing arts center are located. The performing arts center, similar to Cleveland's Playhouse Square District, is a renovated older theatre. The arena is located on the former site of the city's grand Astor Theatre, and no land assembly was needed to facilitate its construction. Allen County chose the location for the Memorial Coliseum decades before decentralization pressures were reshaping Fort Wayne. Once built, leadership might have made the wrong choice when renovations were contemplated (in the 21st century) if restoring downtown Fort Wayne was the priority for the city and county.

While it may not be possible to have as clear a plan and vision as Columbus, Indianapolis, Los Angeles, or San Diego did, documents that allow the public and private investors to clearly understand a city's redevelopment goals and what the completed projects will produce help create confidence that the dream of a new downtown area can become a reality. The presentation of a vision and plan enables private investors to determine how a related project that they create would complement and benefit from the overall strategy and interconnections among all of the planned assets. Indianapolis' plans and vision were probably deemed unrealistic, but doubts also existed whether downtown Los Angeles or Reading could attract crowds to events. Columbus relied on architects hired by Nationwide Insurance, but the vision for the Arena District was subsequently approved by the city and helped people understand the direction that was being taken on behalf of the community. In that sense, the city had control over what was to be built and the plan for the area and its fit with the master plan for Columbus. Los Angeles succeeded without a plan and relied on AEG for a vision, and things were still successful. Other private developers understood what AEG envisioned, and their subsequent investments in residential and other properties helped to substantially improve the image of the area and achieve the city's goal of an attractive and dynamic area surrounding the convention center. There is a great benefit to a widely circulated and clear plan, and no revitalization effort should move forward without an easily understood vision.

## 10.4.3 Recommendation 3: Build Neighborhoods and the Value of Iconic Architecture

The success of revitalization efforts in Columbus, Denver, Los Angeles, and San Diego was related to the fit of anchor facilities in and with new neighborhoods.

The scale of the large amenities was carefully crafted, and their exteriors designed to ensure that even with their required size, these capital assets would still fit as anchor tenants for the new neighborhoods. The resulting designs, whether inspired by Wrigley Field or Fenway Park or not, accomplished a similar purpose. The new facilities made the new neighborhoods built around them instantly popular places to live and work. Denver's Coors Field, Indianapolis' Bankers Life Fieldhouse, Columbus' Nationwide Arena, Los Angeles' Staples Center, and San Diego's PETCO Field have been great assets for the revitalization of downtown areas. Some of the design elements that facilitate neighborhood integration include street-level entrances and open-air vistas or glass walls that allow people both inside and outside of the facility to observe what is taking place on the street and inside the venue. The construction materials and the scale (height) of the facilities also need to fit into the neighborhood's design, so that neither an arena nor a ballpark is the tallest structure. Indianapolis' Bankers Life Fieldhouse and Lucas Oil Stadium each have a wall of glass that allows people inside to gaze at downtown Indianapolis. PETCO Park has open space that allows people enjoying a public park outside the right field fence to peer into the ballpark. Cleveland's Progressive Field has a similar vista with a public street and pedestrian promenade passing behind its left field home run porch. The neighborhood design framework has been a success for several communities, and that framework for revitalization to encourage pedestrian traffic and the development of residential and neighborhood amenities around a facility can be a very successful revitalization tool.

Los Angeles, while including street-level access for the Staples Center and a large public square for L.A. LIVE, was attracted to an alternative perspective, one also incorporated into the Barclays Center in Brooklyn. Described by *New York Times* writer Charles Bagli as "STARchectiture," numerous cities have favored the use of renowned architects or spectacular facilities to create iconic and controversial exteriors that both excite and create instant celebrity status for an arena. The new facilities planned for the Minnesota Vikings and Atlanta Falcons will be among the most extraordinary sport venues ever built. Each will have the potential to anchor revitalization efforts in their respective downtown areas.

L.A. LIVE and the Staples Center are anchors for a new downtown neighborhood, but there is nothing neighborhood-like in their design. Instead, bathed in pastel lighting and larger-than-life video boards and advertisements, these facilities are designed to create the impression of instant celebrity status. That status appeals to a certain segment of the residential and commercial markets in Los Angeles. The decision to focus on star architecture has clearly been successful for Los Angeles and for Brooklyn. Edmonton, Atlanta, and Minneapolis are among the cities that are now embarking on the use of iconic sports venues for urban revitalization.

The value from building facilities that fit comfortably into the design of new or emerging downtown neighborhoods is obvious when a city and developer agree on plans and then integrate the amenity to create areas similar to what exists around Wrigley Field in Chicago and adjacent to Fenway Park in Boston. San Diego and

There are then two strategies or sets of guidelines to be used when thinking about the design of facilities and urban revitalization. Any venue built should fit into a neighborhood design that sustains substantial real estate development and the creation of a new neighborhood. If a venue is to be iconic, it must create a visual statement for the downtown area and offer "viewscapes" that make it valuable for adjoining real estate. Iconic structures have to support the elevation of property values, or they do not help improve a central city's finances. Revitalization efforts have to always be focused on enhancing the financial stability of central cities.

Columbus have realized that goal. The alternative approach, the building of an iconic structure, is the best strategy when a new facility must stand out against its competition with other regional venues, or when a decidedly different image for a city is desired. The location of Cleveland's Rock and Roll Hall of Fame and Museum was not ideal relative to a revitalization program that concentrated new assets in a designated area. Its iconic design by I.M. Pei, however, assured that the building would not be simply an efficient structure that would be seen as just another in a series of hall of fames. The building itself became an attraction as a result of its effects on visitors. The building was as much of a tourist attraction as was the Rock and Roll Hall of Fame and Museum. Cleveland also placed value on the possible impact an iconic design would have on its civic image. Pei's design was a "game changer" in terms of its impact on people and the city.

The recommendation from these two different approaches to the design and integration of assets into a revitalization strategy is to choose one framework or another, but remain committed to building a new neighborhood and enhancing revenue streams to a central city. If a community's interest lies in the development of a new neighborhood, a facility has to be designed to complement and anchor a neighborhood and be part of the daily life of the area. Avoiding functional designs is critical if an iconic structure is needed to make an amenity the chosen place for events or to create an entirely new image for a community. When iconic structures are built, the site chosen must permit the special nature of the architecture to be clearly visible. Iconic facilities can lose their ability to have an effect on people when the special or different aspects of their design are difficult for people to appreciate. As one developer observed, a truly iconic structure creates its reputation and image from the effect it has on people. If the location works against its ability to affect people's image of a city or community, an innovative design will have a far less dramatic impact.

Iconic facilities can also create their own neighborhoods. L.A. LIVE and the Staples Center made an area that was once avoided into one that attracts visitors from the region and tourists alike. Its star architectural elements have attracted people who want to live near the celebrity status created by the facilities.

Columbus, Denver, Indianapolis, and San Diego created new neighborhoods, and the demand for housing in these areas attests to the success of a design for a sports venue that makes it a natural complement to a neighborhood. The failure to either pursue a neighborhood design or focus on iconic architecture wastes the opportunities available when amenities are built. Clear direction and a distinct choice of the framework—neighborhood or "star power"—should be made and then followed.

### 10.4.4 Recommendation 4: Link Private Sector Investments to a Commitment of Tax Money

Columbus, Los Angeles, and San Diego created models that provide substantial guidance and benchmarks for other communities that want to link big-ticket items to revitalization strategies. Each of these cities secured commitments from private sector partners for new investments that supported the revitalization program and generated new tax revenues. The new taxes produced by the related real estate development were sufficient to repay the investments made by the public sector in a new facility or the needed infrastructure. Nationwide Insurance Company agreed to pay for most of the shortfalls if new taxes were insufficient to repay the bonds issued by Columbus for the Arena District. Los Angeles had similar protections for its investments that made the Staples Center possible, and the revenues the city received created a positive financial return. The investment from Los Angeles to ensure that L.A. LIVE was built was also offset by new taxes generated by the facility and the nearby residential development. Los Angeles' investment is classified as cash positive in that its returns exceeded the costs tp repay the bonds it sold to finance its investment. Columbus' investment was also cash positive by 2010.

San Diego also received guarantees regarding real estate investment that turned the plan for the Ballpark District into a reality. JMI Realty has built more than three times the promised amount (assessed value) of new real estate in the Ballpark District. While a single large headquarters hotel was not constructed, the number of new hotel rooms that JMI built satisfied its commitment to San Diego.

Two lessons are learned from the experiences of these three cities. First, both a large (Los Angeles) and a medium-sized (Columbus) city were able to avoid the provision of large subsidies for the building of facilities used by professional sports teams. Each made an investment, but both received guarantees from their private sector partner that the financial exposure of taxpayers would be minimized, if not eliminated. By providing developers with site control and by using their power of eminent domain to assemble the land needed for the venues and related amenities, residences, and commercial space, the public sector was able to have the venue and a new neighborhood built without the provision of a subsidy. Some people criticize the use of eminent domain to transfer land from one set of private owners to another that promises to build what the city prefers. To be fair, use of eminent domain to transfer land to private developers can lead to political abuse and unfair favoritism by elected officials. Second, in bargaining with teams or others to avoid subsidies, the offer of public commitment to land assembly and the provision of site control to firms designed as master developers are valuable assets. Cities have to weigh the ability to secure benefits against the possible abuse of their power to seize land and then transfer it to other owners (or lease it to the other developers for their use). As Columbus and Los Angeles learned, agreeing to assemble land and providing site control to a single developer led to the building of new amenities without public subsidies. San Diego's use of eminent domain and its investment permitted it to have PETCO Park and a new neighborhood built even though it accepted more risk. San Diego also supported the designation of master developer status while the overall plan was approved and conceived with the participation of the city and its professional staff.

## 10.4.5 Recommendation 5: The Organizations Needed to Succeed as a Broker City

Securing guaranteed investments is not always possible. Indianapolis provides a model for cities that must use their own tax revenues to leverage investments from others to ensure that subsidies for big-ticket amenities become strategic investments. Without any advanced agreements from developers, Indianapolis actually secured more investments from private, nonprofit, and state government sources for new facilities and buildings (residential, commercial, and public) than any other city. The total private sector investments in Columbus, Los Angeles, and San Diego as part of the Arena District, L.A. LIVE, and Ballpark District were smaller in value than those made in downtown Indianapolis. Indianapolis accomplished its creation of a new and vibrant downtown area by following a detailed and focused strategy across 40 years. In addition, Indianapolis was able to partner with the state and surrounding counties to replace the original arena and football stadium when each became economically obsolete. Bankers Life Fieldhouse and Lucas Oil Stadium where paid for by partnerships between Indianapolis and Indiana (for the field house) and residents of adjacent counties (for Lucas Oil Stadium). To leverage its public investments, Indianapolis became the "broker city," aggressively negotiating for events and investments from the private, public (other governments), and nonprofit sectors, as well as the State of Indiana, to ensure that subsidies became strategic investments.

Two organizations assumed important roles in helping Indianapolis leverage its investments. The Indiana Sports Corporation was created to attract events (athletic competitions) and sports organizations (headquarters of associations and other groups) to the downtown area. Indianapolis Downtown, Inc. was responsible for recruiting and then advocating for businesses located in the downtown area. These organizations were part advocate, part deal maker, and part business recruiter for the downtown revitalization strategy. The consolidated city-county's Department of

Metropolitan Development also provided needed assistance. In 1985 Indianapolis created the Indianapolis Local Improvement Bond Bank to be the financing conduit for critical downtown redevelopment projects. The lesson to be learned from Indianapolis' effort was that a coordinated focus on downtown revitalization by numerous organizations made invaluable contributions to the efforts to secure investments by others in the downtown area. Revitalizing downtown was not a part-time activity of the mayor's office or even the responsibility of a regime of private leaders. The revitalization program was also not part of a "build it and they will come" process. Indianapolis did not just hope other investments would be made. Instead, a group of organizations and departments focused their staff on downtown's revitalization. The lesson from Indianapolis' success is that if there are not guaranteed commitments for development linked to the building of a sport, arts, culture, or entertainment amenity, then a focused effort by an array of organizations is required to increase the likelihood that subsidies become strategic investments.

If a city directs so much attention to its downtown area, does it run the risk of ignoring the needs of other communities? A criticism directed toward the administration of William Hudnut, Indianapolis' mayor for 16 years, was that he put too much focus on downtown and did not pay sufficient attention to other communities and their needs.[5] While the pattern of private sector investment in Indianapolis suggests there never was a deflection of attention from the other parts of the city, it is possible that some inner city neighborhoods did not receive the attention needed to achieve their development goals. Communities that follow Indianapolis' model need to simultaneously provide focused leadership for efforts in other inner city areas.

The organizations created to bolster and support Indianapolis' revitalization strategy raise important questions regarding Reading's efforts. Community leaders who have limited staff to support their efforts are leading Reading's revitalization program. As a result, they have very few resources available to focus on successfully leveraging the commitments to secure investments by others. The Berks County Economic Partnership, as well as city and county agencies, is assuming some or all of the responsibilities performed by organizations such as the Indiana Sports Commission and Indianapolis Downtown, Inc.; however, none are as large, and they seem to lack the needed resources and expertise to be as successful. If Reading is to capitalize on the investments made by its community leaders, elected officials will need to be sure the work associated with attracting events and businesses to the downtown area is performed. The elected leaders must also be sure sufficient staff resources are available to advocate for and ensure that businesses that relocate to the downtown area receive the services and attention they need to thrive and advance in the region's economy. Any city that follows Indianapolis' model must ensure that appropriate investments are made to create and staff the supporting institutions. Without that investment, it is likely there will be fewer events and lower levels of private, nonprofit, and public investments.

## 10.4.6 Recommendation 6: Prudent Risk Taking for Confidence Building

Cleveland's public sector and a growth coalition embarked on a revitalization strategy to restore confidence in the city's future. It committed approximately three-quarters of a billion dollars to the effort, and there was a subsequent and pronounced uptick in private sector investment in the years after the building of several big-ticket amenities. In that regard, Cleveland's risk taking was rewarded, but the largest benefit or reward would take at least 20 years before it would be realized. In a sense, Cleveland's achievement through its investments was to stabilize the downtown area until the private sector had confidence that market conditions had sufficiently changed so that its investments would be profitable. It is still unclear as to whether or not Cleveland's population will grow. Despite recent and extensive investments from private sector developers and an improved image, the region's economy has still faltered, and population losses for the city and county continue. Cleveland took needed risks, but two or three decades into its efforts, the city still cannot "win for losing" people and economic vitality.

What lesson does this offer?

Changes in the larger economy can swamp or thwart successful revitalization efforts. No community can simply rely on new buildings and amenities or a completely revitalized section of its downtown to restructure economic outcomes. The public sector, through big-ticket items and other investments in amenities, can establish a framework for private sector activity, but economic development is inexorably related to business innovation and entrepreneurship. Those innovations and advancements can be supported by the public sector, but leadership for economic advancement comes from the private sector. Successful revitalization efforts that lead to economic advancement require the existence of attractive amenities, the elimination of blight, and a focus on entrepreneurial activity and innovation by the private sector. But it is the private sector that drives the creation of jobs. For that to occur, confidence has to exist in a city's future.

These observations are particularly important for smaller cities like Fort Wayne and Reading. Reading's revitalization effort has been financed by a group of people committing their personal wealth to a dream of what the city could be while using their political capital to secure assistance from Pennsylvania and federal agencies. Their extraordinary success and the impressive nature of their commitment will not change the city's or region's future without new business development. Creating jobs will require a strong partnership that must be led by the public sector, these committed community leaders, and the region's private sector. So far the private sector is not involved. Fort Wayne has sustained its regional position with regard to the location of jobs. Its population growth, as in Reading, is comprised of lower-income households, as wealthier families and individuals choose to live in suburban areas.

A sobering lesson is that even when there are large-scale private investments and a commitment to build amenities, success measured by population and job growth is not assured. Cleveland's efforts united a small group of business leaders (Cleveland Tomorrow), local governments, and the broader business and university communities in a revitalization effort, with each making a substantial commitment to advance the region through programs to aid business formation and entrepreneurship. Yet, Cleveland and Cuyahoga County continue to lose residents. The enhancement of the physical infrastructure, the availability of amenities, and the attraction of people to downtown locations are foundational elements for longer-term changes and economic development. In Cleveland's case, while the city and county are still losing residents, there is now an unprecedented level of venture capital committed to the health and advanced manufacturing sectors that took place 20 years after its focus on amenity enhancement. Rewards, however, may not be evident for another decade. Reading has taken the steps to build a secure foundation for its future that has involved a great deal of risk. More risk and investment must be taken to advance the work of corporations and entrepreneurs if successful economic revitalization is to lead to new jobs and higher incomes for residents.

## 10.4.7 Recommendation 7: Uber Plans Unifying Public and Private Capital

All of the cities studied shared two elements in their revitalization strategies. Each emphasized amenities for their role in the attraction of human capital, and each rejected an evolutionary approach to urban change in favor of large-scale plans. In every instance, years of stagnation or decline turned into decades filled with a loss of confidence in the perspectives that emphasized Jane Jacobs' approach to the life-death-life cycle of urban space and neighborhoods. Most community leaders by their actions believed that revitalization had to be jump-started, and that there would only be more decline if substantial resources were not injected into downtown areas. Each city had seen its downtown centers decline. Rising crime levels and economic and social segregation separated the downtown areas (and in some instances the entire city itself) from suburban areas or other parts of the region. These conditions suggested that without focused and concentrated actions, stagnation and decline would continue. In large and small cities, leaders were convinced that in the absence of coordinated action, there were simply other more attractive locations where investors would prefer to place their capital.

Revitalization in each of these cities involved the hyperinjection of coordinated public and private capital, a sort of "uber planning" view for the management and oversight of redevelopment. This does not mean that the ideas put forward by Jane Jacobs and others are wrong. What it does imply is that a spatial component has been added to Joseph Schumpeter's theory of creative destruction. Public and private leaders agree that innovation replaces shop-worn technologies and creates more jobs. But in an era when those new jobs can be located distant from the ones eliminated, cities must compete to ensure that new opportunities occur within their boundaries. To create an inviting environment for the new jobs, cities are rushing to revitalize deteriorating core areas as quickly as possible while also providing the amenities thought to appeal to entrepreneurs and talented workers. The focus on amenity theory is a progressive effort to create viable spaces within which the new technologies will develop and flourish. The uber planning approaches that led to the Arena or Ballpark Districts are efforts that spatially direct the life cycle of innovation into the area where jobs, businesses, and technologies have been displaced. Rather than rejecting ideas related to those of Jane Jacobs, the activities of leaders from Columbus and Indianapolis to Denver, Los Angeles, and San Diego could be seen as efforts to capture the positive outcomes from creative destruction.

The recommendation that emerges from each of the case studies is that revitalization efforts involving a large-scale infusion of public and private money can revitalize downtown areas that for decades have been declining. Some critics will argue that before such a conclusion can be sustained, comparisons need to be made with areas that pursued revitalization strategies that focused on existing neighborhoods and the improvement of urban services to match those available in suburban areas. An issue, of course, is the source of revenues for those initiatives. Despite the absence of appropriate comparisons with alternative strategies in cities similar to those studied, the evidence from each of the case studies shows that deteriorating downtown areas were restored. In the absence of uber plans, it seems reasonable to conclude that substantial or significant change was unlikely and development would continue to be attracted to other parts of a region or other regions. Further, a road map has been created that, if followed, can protect the finances of central cities and provide new revenues to support other community and neighborhood development initiatives.

## 10.4.8 Recommendation 8: Constructively Involve Business Leaders in Downtown and Community Development

A number of analysts viewed with dismay the roles played by business leaders in championing an emphasis on big-ticket items as anchors for revitalization strategies. Many correctly identified the benefits that big-ticket items typically produced for the corporations represented by the involved business leaders. The extraordinary profits earned by team owners, as a result of the public sector's use of tax dollars to pay for facilities, provided additional evidence of the substantial gains realized by already wealthy individuals when sport facilities were built with public money. Public subsidies for arts and cultural facilities also created benefits for those patrons who enjoy the new venues and who are typically wealthier than the residents of many inner city communities. Those subsidies lower the cost of enjoying the arts and performances in these new museums and theatres. In the absence of a public subsidy, the cost of amenities would require higher ticket prices to ensure that facilities and events occur. This underscores the possibility that public subsidies for big-ticket items advanced the self-interest of business leaders or of higher-income residents of regions.

It is impossible to study the role of amenities in revitalization efforts and not address the role of local corporations and their leaders. Special attention was directed toward this issue in Cleveland, Indianapolis, and Reading. Evidence there illustrates the complexity in putting forward a single set of observations regarding elite behavior with regard to redevelopment efforts. Cleveland's business leaders initially focused on advancing the region's economy through a focus on job and business creation and expanding the supply of venture capital in the region. These activities were initiated in response to the loss of thousands of manufacturing positions and a desire to create new jobs and foster growth for the region. Certainly the region's corporations would have benefitted from these activities, but job creation was the number one concern for all residents of the area. Additionally, small groups of business leaders were focused on providing leadership for economic development that was beneficial for the region. It would be hard to argue those activities were only or largely self-serving advancements for limited pecuniary interests.

At the same time that Cleveland and Cleveland Tomorrow (and then the GCP) were making investments in big-ticket items, professional staff working for the organizations argued for and secured resources to make a series of investments to rebuild inner city communities. Their work began with the funding of several neighborhood retail centers. With the population losses in Cleveland, most retailers had moved to suburban locations. Cleveland Tomorrow's investments helped to build several neighborhood shopping centers and attract stores to these projects. Cleveland Tomorrow and then GCP also took the lead in establishing organizations to advance the building of residential properties in the city's neighborhoods while organizing corporate support for public education. The corporate leaders provided all of the financial support for the campaigns to raise taxes to increase support for the Cleveland public schools. The corporations located in downtown Cleveland pay more than 60 percent of the local taxes assessed by the Cleveland public schools. Campaigning for school tax increases was tantamount to campaigning for higher corporate taxes. Other community development initiatives put forward included an annual discretionary fund for the head of the Cleveland public schools and the provision of volunteers for tutoring in numerous schools. Neighborhood Progress, Inc. (NPI) was created by the business community and continues to assist numerous community development corporations involved in building new affordable homes in neighborhoods across the city. Corporate leaders still serve on its board and provide needed capital for new residential projects.

It could be argued that the value of those investments was far less than the public's expenditures for the big-ticket items. Following that line of thought, had the public sector assumed responsibility for the corporate community's investment portfolio and the private sector made the investments in the big-ticket items, overall tax levels would be far less. That logic cannot be refuted even if its political efficacy is unrealistic. In Cleveland, financial responsibility for the big-ticket items was assumed by the county, meaning that at least two-thirds, if not three-quarters, of the fiscal burden was assumed by the wealthier residents of suburban areas and not residents of Cleveland. The direct tax revenue gains from the sports, entertainment, and arts facilities all accrue to Cleveland. While suburbanites voted for this arrangement, a willingness to support countywide responsibility for issues related to Cleveland's public schools or neighborhood-level retail and residential development would be harder to imagine. It is also unlikely that residents in other cities who were supporting tax abatements to advance housing in their own cities would have agreed to help support housing projects in Cleveland. They were, however, willing to help pay for venues for professional sports teams.

These issues could be endlessly debated. What is clear, however, was that the corporate leaders in Cleveland had a large focus on community development, suggesting the role of economic elites is not limited to self-serving activities. The review of revitalization efforts in Reading adds another layer of complexity. There a group of volunteers led the revitalization effort and are investing a substantial amount of their personal wealth with no clear path visible for them to recoup or directly benefit from the investments in amenities. The evidence in Reading suggests that in the absence of the leadership from business leaders (or retired executives and entrepreneurs), revitalization plans for the downtown area might never have been launched. The existence of googleWorks and Entertainment Square is a result of the efforts of a small group of volunteers. At this time, this group is also responsible for ensuring that goggleWorks has sufficient revenue to meet its operating expenses.

This suggests that any community looking at a revitalization plan would be well served by involving business leaders in the effort. Elected officials and community organizers must be vigilant in protecting the public interests and ensuring that the activities are not designed to only advance a corporate agenda. The evidence from Cleveland and Reading suggests this will be a far easier task than may have been previously recognized. The evidence also indicates that the view that corporate leaders are focused only on advancing their limited self-interest is not supported by a careful review of the complete range of their activities. It is still possible to suggest that the private sector should assume more responsibility for the cost of big-ticket items. At the same time, however, it must be recognized that corporations are often involved in community development activities and programs to advance a region's overall economic development.

## 10.4.9 Recommendation 9: Level the Negotiating Table

Including sports facilities and other amenities in revitalization strategies was presented as one approach to offset the advantages the sports cartels may have accrued. Several of the case studies illustrate that large and medium-sized markets have been able to offset some of the control exercised by teams through required real estate investments. The playing field, however, has not been made completely level. San Diego did break new ground with its Ballpark District by getting the owner of the San Diego Padres to guarantee new real estate development would occur if the ballpark were built. More than three times that guaranteed level of new development was built. San Diego also got a new neighborhood built where it wanted, and the extra hotel rooms it deemed necessary for its convention center. Columbus was able to level the negotiating table and did not subsidize the building of an arena for a new hockey franchise. Nationwide Insurance paid for the arena, helped ensure that a new neighborhood would be built, and guaranteed that if new property taxes were not sufficient to repay the bonds sold to build the needed infrastructure it would be responsible for a substantial proportion of any shortfalls. Indianapolis has a new image and a new downtown. Its acceptance of a role as a broker city has leveraged more money for revitalization than was ever imagined while it still has ensured that large subsidies to retain two professional sports teams would exist.

The negotiating table between cities and the interests that control amenities is not level. Yet, through their incorporation of sports, culture, the arts, and entertainment in revitalization efforts, several cities achieved important goals in creating benefits, excitement, and new images, while teams and other interests were enriched at the same time. Subsidies can be avoided or the effects minimized by including teams, the arts, and entertainment amenities into revitalization strategies. Indianapolis was only able to avoid losses from the excessive subsidies through its activities as a broker city, and its activities have produced extraordinary outcomes and an entirely new image. Columbus, Denver, Los Angeles, and San Diego received the benefits they wanted in exchange for their investments. Cleveland advanced its image and enjoyed substantial private sector investments in the aftermath of its provision of subsidies. Cities can win in negotiations with a team if plans and real estate development takes place. Achieving that goal is the responsibility of public officials.

# 10.5 Concluding Note

Sports, the arts, culture, and entertainment underscore the centrality of downtown areas. These amenities also contribute to the attractiveness of a region, and in an era where businesses locate where people prefer to live, those communities with fewer amenities will likely enjoy less economic development. The cities studied have applied these ideas to create jobs and underscore their centrality. Each city turned subsidies into strategic investments and created a level of success for themselves and their regions. Not all goals were achieved, and some areas are still frustrated by their inability to reach the desired levels of economic development and population growth. But each city still has a safer downtown and attracts crowds to areas where once few would venture.

There has been an appropriate and substantial level of concern with the possible regressive nature of the sources of tax revenues used by state and local governments for their investments in sports venues. The use of gaming taxes in some instances and any form of a sales tax should raise concerns with the regressive nature of those taxing instruments and the benefits produced by the investments. The case studies also illustrate an interesting addition to the issues of the best taxing instruments to use for the public sector's investments in sports or cultural amenities and venues. Cuyahoga County relied on its general revenue fund. The county collects property taxes and fees that are deposited in the general revenue fund. The vast majority of those funds are collected from businesses and residents of the county who live outside of Cleveland. While it is still possible for those taxes and fees to have regressive elements, the investments made by the county took place in Cleveland and generated new revenues for the city. In that sense, Cleveland's residents paid a smaller proportion of the cost of the venues but received far more, if not all, of the tax revenue generated. As noted, some of the amusement taxes collected by Cleveland were reinvested in the arena; yet the amusement taxes collected from ticket sales at the ballpark and from tickets sold to other for-profit forms of entertainment accrued to Cleveland. The parking taxes collected by Cleveland were also new revenues. While a complete financial assessment was not part of this book, it is appropriate to identify the possibility that Cleveland's net financial position (revenues received minus taxes collected from its residents) could have been positive.

Similarly, the taxes for the ballpark and stadium in Denver and Indianapolis had a regional and statewide component, which reduces the burden for city residents. Yet the venues were built in the downtown areas, and any resulting revenues or tax increases were not shared with the surrounding counties. It is possible, as a result, that both central cities enjoyed a net return.

These are cited as examples of the issues related to the location of economic activity that must be considered when analyzing the effects of sports and culture on revitalization efforts. Sports and culture might not change overall economic development for a region, but their location does change net tax flows. If that net increases the fiscal stability of central cities, then sports and culture could well create more major league winners than once thought.

# Endnotes

1. Clark, T.N., ed., *The city as an entertainment machine* (Amsterdam, The Netherlands: Elsevier-JAI Press, 2004).
2. Berks County Economic Partnership, Sasaki Architects PC, and the Brookings Institution, *Penn Corridor development plan* (Reading, PA: Berks County Economic Partnership, 2006); Hill, E.W., and J.F. Brennan, Methodology for identifying the drivers of industrial clusters: The founding of regional competitive advantage, *Economic Development Quarterly* 14(1): 65–96, 2000; Markusen, A., and G. Schrock, Placing

labor center stage in industrial city revitalization, in *Retooling for growth: Building a 21st century economy in America's older industrial areas*, ed. R.M. McGahey and J.S. Vey, 179–210 (Washington, DC: Brookings Institution, 2008).

3. Gateway Economic Development Corporation, Board of directors meeting agenda, November 12, 2008.

4. Berks County Economic Partnership, Sasaki Architects PC, and the Brookings Institution, *Penn Corridor development plan* (Reading, PA: Berks County Economic Partnership, 2006).

5. Hudnut, W., *The Hudnut years in Indianapolis, 1976–1991* (Indianapolis: Indiana University Press, 1995).

# Bibliography

American Craft. 2006. goggleWorks, Reading, PA. *American Craft*, October/November 6.

Andrews, D. 2004. Sports in the late capitalist movement. In *The commercialization of sport*, ed. T. Slack, 3–28. London: Routledge.

Austrian, Z. 2008. *Manufacturing brief.* Cleveland, OH: Center for Economic Development, Maxine Goodman Levin College of Urban Policy and Public Administration, Cleveland State University.

Austrian, Z., and M.S. Rosentraub. 2002. Cities, sports and economic change: A retrospective assessment. *Journal of Urban Affairs* 24(5): 549–565.

Baade, R.A. 1996. Professional sports as catalysts for metropolitan economic development. *Journal of Urban Affairs* 18(1): 1–17.

Baade, R.A. 2003. *Los Angeles city controller's report on economic impact: Staples Center.* Los Angeles: City of Los Angeles, Office of the Controller.

Baade, R.A., and R. Dye. 1988. Sports stadiums and area development: Assessing the reality. *Heartland Policy Study* 68.

Bach, A. 2007. Arena District. *Urban Land*, January–March, Case C037003.

Barnes, B. 2008. A film year full of escapism, flat in attendance. *New York Times*, January 2. http://www.nytimes.com/2008/01/02/movies/02year.html (accessed July 6, 2008).

Berks County Economic Partnership, Sasaki Architects PC, and the Brookings Institution. 2006. *Penn Corridor development plan.* Reading, PA: Berks County Economic Partnership.

Birch, E. 2005. *Who lives downtown?* Washington, DC: Brookings Institution, Metropolitan Policy Program.

Broderick, P. 2005. Eminent domain: A new tool for business? *San Diego Business Journal* 26(27): 1.

Broderick, P. 2006. It takes a baseball park to raise a village. *San Diego Business Journal* 27(43): 40.

Brown, G., and M. Morrison, eds. 2008. *ESPN sports almanac 2008.* Lake Worth, FL: Sports Almanac.

Burns, M. 2007. Nationwide, schools settle arena valuation dispute. *Columbus Business First*, December 5. http://columbus.bizjournals.com/columbus/stories/2007/12/03/daily22.html (accessed April 3, 2008).

Bush, B. 2008. Rivals to this day: As Ohio State's Schottenstein Center turns 10, its bumpy history with Nationwide Arena hasn't been forgotten. *Columbus Dispatch*. http://www.crainscleveland.com/apps/pbcs.dll/section?category = fram…es_2008_11_17_arena_anniv.ART_ART_11-17-08_A1_KOBTM3E.html_sid = 101 (accessed November 17, 2008).

Cagan, J., and N. deMause. 1998. *Field of schemes: How the great stadium swindle turns public money into private profit.* Monroe, ME: Common Courage Press.

Cantor, M., and M.S. Rosentraub. 2012. A ballpark and neighborhood change: Economic integration, a recession, and the altered demography of San Diego's Ballpark District. *City, Culture and Society* 3(3): 219–226.

Chalip, L. 2002. *Using the Olympics to optimise tourism benefits: University lecture on the Olympics.* Barcelona: Centre d'Estudies Olympics. http://olympicstudies.uab.es/lectures/web/pdf/chalip.pdf (accessed December 21, 2008).

Chapin, T. 2002. Beyond the entrepreneurial city: Municipal capitalism in San Diego. *Journal of Urban Affairs* 24(5): 565–581.

Chema, T. 1996. When professional sports justify the subsidy: A reply to Robert A. Baade. *Journal of Urban Affairs* 18(1): 19–22.

Children's Museum of Indianapolis. 2005. *The economic impact and value of the Children's Museum to the central Indiana economy.* Indianapolis: Children's Museum.

City of Columbus. 1998. Capital improvements project development and reimbursement agreement for Nationwide Arena District, September 15. City of Columbus: Office of the Mayor.

City of Los Angeles. 1998. *Analysis of violent crimes in the city of Los Angeles (February 24).* Los Angeles: City of Los Angeles, Management Services Department.

City of San Diego. 1998. Memorandum of understanding between the City of San Diego, the Redevelopment Agency of the City of San Diego, the Centre City Development Corporation, and Padres, L.P. concerning a ballpark district, construction of a baseball park, and a redevelopment project. City of San Diego: Resolution R-291450, Attachment A.

City of San Diego. 1999. *Manager's report.* Report 99-64. City of San Diego.

Clark, T.N, ed. 2004. *The city as an entertainment machine.* Amsterdam, The Netherlands: Elsevier-JAI Press.

Coates, D., and B.R. Humphreys. 1999. The growth effects of sports franchises, stadia, and arenas. *Journal of Policy Analysis and Management* 14(4): 601–624.

Curry, T.J., K. Schwirian, and R.A. Woldoff. 2004. *High stakes: Big time sports and downtown redevelopment.* Columbus: Ohio State University Press.

Dahl, R.A. 1961. *Who governs? Democracy and power in an American city.* New Haven, CT: Yale University Press.

Danielson, M.N. 1997. *Home team: Professional sports and the American metropolis.* Princeton, NJ: Princeton University Press.

Davies, J.S. 2002. Urban regime theory: A normative-empirical critique. *Journal of Urban Affairs* 24(1): 1–17.

Deady, T. 1994. L.A. County hotel room occupancy shows a significant increase in 1993. *Los Angeles Business Journal*, March 7. As cited in *High-Beam Encyclopedia.* http://www.encyclopedia.com/doc/1G1-15277102.html (accessed April 1, 2008).

Deka, D. 1998. Job decentralization and central city well-being: An empirical study with sectoral data, *Urban Affairs Review*, 34: 263–290.

Delaney, K.J., and R. Eckstein. 2003. *Public dollars, private stadiums: The battle over building sports stadiums.* New Brunswick, NJ: Rutgers University Press.

Duke, V., and L. Crolley. 1996. *Football, nationality, and the state.* London: Addison Wesley Longman.

Eisinger, P. 2000. The politics of bread and circuses. *Urban Affairs Review* 35(3): 316–333.

Elkin, S.L. 1987. *City and regime in the American republic.* Chicago: University of Chicago Press.

Elkins, D.R. 1995. The structure and context of the urban growth coalition: The view from the chamber of commerce. *Policy Studies Journal* 23(4): 583–601.

Erie, S.P., V. Kogan, and S.A. Mackenzie. 2011. *Paradise plundered: Fiscal crisis and failures in San Diego*, Stanford, CA.: Stanford University Press.

Euchner, C.C. 1994. *Playing the field: Why sports teams move and cities fight to keep them.* Baltimore: Johns Hopkins University Press.

Farmer, S. 2007. SC, Coliseum Commission still trying to find solution. *Los Angeles Times*, December 14. http://articles.latimes.com/2007/dec/14/sports/sp-newswire14 (accessed March 10, 2008).

Fels Institute of Government. 2008. *Vacancy inventory and reinvestment strategies for Reading, PA*. Philadelphia: University of Pennsylvania. http://www.readingpa.gov/documents/fels_report.pdf (accessed November 1, 2008).

Fidler, J. 2006. Reading: It's not just outlet malls anymore. *Washington Post*, July 19, C2.

Florida, R. 2002. *The rise of the creative class.* New York: Basic Books.

Fogarty, M.S., G.S. Garofalo, and D.C. Hammack, C. 2002. *Cleveland from startup to the present: Innovation and entrepreneurship in the 19th and early 20th centuries.* Cleveland: Center for Regional Economic Issues, Weatherhead School of Business, Case Western Reserve University. http://generationfoundation.org/pubs/ClevelandFromStartupToPresent.pdf.

Forbes. 2008a. NFL team valuations. http://www.forbes.com/lists/2008/30/sportsmoney_nfl08_NFL-Team-Valuations_Rank.html (accessed December 1, 2008).

Forbes. 2008b. NBA team valuations. http://www.forbes.com/lists/2008/32/nba08_NBA-Team-Valuations_MetroArea.html (accessed December 4, 2008).

Garmise, S. 2006. *People and the competitive advantage of place: Building a workplace for the 21st century.* Armonk, NY: M.E. Sharpe.

Gateway Economic Development Corporation of Greater Cleveland. 2008. *Resolution no. 2008-5 regarding authorization and approval of annual operating budget for 2009.* Cleveland: Gateway Economic Development Corporation of Greater Cleveland.

Glaeser, E. 2011. *Triumph of the city: How our greatest invention makes us richer, smarter, greener, healthier, and happier.* New York: Penguin Press.

Glaeser, E L. and Kahn, M.E. 2001. *Decentralized employment and the transformation of the American city.* Cambridge, MA.: National Bureau of Economic Research.

Glaeser, E., M. Kahn, and C. Chu. 2001. *Job sprawl: Employment locations in U.S. metropolitan areas.* Washington, DC: Brookings Institution.

Gottdiener, M. 2001. *The theming of America: American dreams, media fantasies, and themed Environments.* Boulder, CO: Westview Press.

Gronbjerg, K.A., and R. Clerkin. 2003. Indianapolis nonprofit sector: Management capacities and challenges. Unpublished paper, Center on Philanthropy and the School of Public and Environmental Affairs, Indiana University, Indianapolis.

Hamashige, H. 1994. Downtown L.A. office rents tumble more than 30%: But high-rise towers ride out quake with little damage—Los Angeles, California—Special report: Quarterly real estate. *Los Angeles Business Journal*, January 31. http://findarticles.com/p/articles/mi_m5072/is_n4_v16/ai_15125486 (accessed March 8, 2008).

Hannigan, J. 1998. *Fantasy city: Pleasure and profit in the postmodern metropolis.* London: Routledge Press.

Hanson, R.H., H. Wolman, and D. Connolly. 2006. *Finding a new voice for corporate leaders in a changed urban world: The Greater Cleveland Partnership.* Washington, DC: Brookings Institution Metropolitan Policy Program.

Harrison, B., and B. Bluestone. 1988. *The great U-turn: Corporate restructuring and the polarizing of America*. New York: Basic Books.

Harvard Business School. 1996a. *The Cleveland turnaround (A): Responding to the crisis, 1978–1988*. N9-796-151. Cambridge, MA: Harvard University.

Harvard Business School. 1996b. *The Cleveland turnaround (B): Building on progress, 1989–1996*. N9-796-152. Cambridge, MA: Harvard University.

Haughwout, A.F., and R.P. Inman, 2002. Should suburbs help their central cities? Brookings-Wharton Papers on Urban Affairs, http://papers.ssrn.com/sol3/papers.cfm?abstract_id=348980.

Heister, M. 2008. *Public secondary school dropouts, 2006–2007*. Harrisburg: Pennsylvania Department of Education.

Hill, E.W., and J.F. Brennan. 2000. Methodology for indentifying the drivers of industrial clusters: The founding of regional competitive advantage. *Economic Development Quarterly* 14(1): 65–96.

Hirschman, A.O. 1958. *The strategy of economic development*. New Haven, CT: Yale University Press.

Hobbs, F., and N. Stoops. 2002. *Demographic trends in the 20th century: Census 2000 special reports*. Washington, DC: U.S. Department of Commerce, Bureau of the Census.

Hoffman, L., S.S. Fainstein, and D.R. Judd, eds. 2003. *Cities and visitors: Regulating people, markets, and city space*. New York: John Wiley & Sons.

Home Box Office (HBO). 2008. *Nine innings from ground zero: The healing of a nation began with the swing of a bat*. http://www.hbo.com/sports/nineinnings/ (accessed October 8, 2008).

Hoyman, M., and C. Faricy. 2009. It takes a village: A test of the creative class, social capital, and human capital theories. *Urban Affairs Review* 44(3): 311–333.

Hudnut, W. 1995. *The Hudnut years in Indianapolis, 1976–1991*. Indianapolis: Indiana University Press.

Humphrey, B., and D.R. Howard, eds. 2008. *The business of sports: Economic perspectives*. New York: Praeger Publishers.

Hunter, F. 1953. *Community power structure: A study of decision makers*. Chapel Hill: University of North Carolina Press.

Iarns, A., P. Kaplan, A. Bauerfeind, J. Huestis, and K. Quilliman. 2006. *Economic development and smart growth: 8 case studies on the connections between smart growth development and jobs, wealth, and quality of life in communities*. Washington, DC: International Economic Development Council.

Imbroscio, D.L. 1998. Reformulating urban regime theory: The division of labor between state and market reconsidered. *Journal of Urban Affairs* 20(3): 233–248.

Indianapolis Downtown, Inc. 2006. *Annual report*. Indianapolis: Indianapolis Downtown, Inc.

Jacobs, J. 1969. *The economy of cities*. New York: Penguin Books.

Jacobs, J. 1993. *The death and life of great American cities*. New York: Modern Library.

Jennings, M.K. 1964. *Community influentials: The elites of Atlanta*. New York: Free Press.

Joassart-Marcelli, P., J. Wolch, and J. Musso. 2005. Fiscal consequences of concentrated poverty in a metropolitan region, *The Annals of the Association of American Geographers* 95: 2, 336–356.

Johnson, A. 2000. Minor league baseball: Risks and potential benefits for communities large and small. In *The economics and politics of sports facilities*, ed. W.C. Rich, 141–151. Westport, CT: Quorum Books.

Judd, D., ed. 2002. *Infrastructure of play: Building the tourist city*. Armonk, NY: M.E. Sharpe.

Judd, D.R., and S.S. Fainstein, eds. 1999. *The tourist city*. New Haven, CT: Yale University Press.

Kang, Y.S., and R. Perdue. 1994. Long-term impact of a mega-event on international tourism to the host country: A conceptual model and the case of the 1988 Seoul Olympics. In *Global tourist behavior*, ed. M. Uysal, 205–226. New York: Haworth Press.

Kennedy, S., and M.S. Rosentraub. 2000. Public–private partnerships, professional sports teams, and the protection of the public's interests. *American Review of Public Administration* 30(4): 436–459.

Kneebone, E. 2009. *Job sprawl revisited: The changing geography of metropolitan employment.* Washington, D.C.: The Brookings Institution.

Kotler, P.D., H. Haider, and I. Rein. 1993. *Marketing places: Attracting investment, industry, and tourism to cities, states, and nations.* New York: Free Press.

Kurtzman, J. 2005. Economic impact: Sport tourism and the city. *Journal of Sport Tourism* 10(1): 47–71.

L.A. Arena Company, LLC. *Proposal for L.A. Arena Company LLC to Los Angeles City Council, Mayor Richard Riordan, Los Angeles Convention and Exhibition Center, and the Los Angeles Community Redevelopment Agency.* Los Angeles: Office of City Council, 1996.

Lackritz, M.E. 1968. *The Hough riots of 1966.* Cleveland: Regional Church Planning Office, Louis M. Brereton, Chairman.

Larkin, B. 2008. How Cleveland fumbled away Eaton corporation. *Cleveland Plain Dealer*, October 5, D1, 3.

Lefebvre, H. 1991. *The production of space.* Maiden, MA: Blackwell Publishers.

Lefebvre, H. 1996. *Writings on cities.* Maiden, MA: Blackwell Publishers.

Leland, S., and M.S. Rosentraub. 2009. Consolidated and fragmented governments and regional cooperation: Surprising lessons from Charlotte, Cleveland, Indianapolis, and Kansas City. In *Who will govern metropolitan regions in the 21st century?* ed. D. Phares, 143–163, Armonk, NY: M.E. Sharpe.

Levine, M. 2000. A third world city in the first world: Social exclusion, racial inequality, and sustainable development in Baltimore, Maryland. In *The social sustainability of cities*, ed. M. Polese and R. Stren, 123–156. Toronto: University of Toronto Press.

Levine, P. 1993. *From Ellis Island to Ebbets Field: Sport and the American Jewish experience.* Cary, NC: Oxford University Press.

Logan, J.R., and H.L. Molotch. 1987. *Urban fortunes: The political economy of place.* Berkeley: University of California Press.

Longworth, R.C. 2007. *Caught in the middle: America's heartland in the age of globalism.* New York: Bloomsbury USA.

Los Angeles. 1997a. *Proposed arena at the Los Angeles Convention Center—Memorandum to the Ad Hoc Committee on the Sports Arena from Keith Comrie, City Administrative Officer and Ronald Deaton, Chief Legislative Analyst.* Los Angeles: Office of the City Council.

Los Angeles. 1997b. *Los Angeles Convention Center Arena: Proposal summary. Internal Memorandum, City Council.* Los Angeles: Office of the City Council.

Los Angeles. 1998. *Gap funding agreement between city of Los Angeles and L.A. Arena Company, LLC (Los Angeles Arena Project).* March 26. Los Angeles: Office of the City Council.

Malanga, S. 2004. The curse of the creative class. *City Journal*, Winter, 36–45.

Markusen, A., and G. Schrock. 2008. Placing labor center stage in industrial city revitalization. In *Retooling for growth: Building a 21st century economy in America's older industrial areas*, ed. R.M. McGahey and J.S. Vey, 179–210. Washington, DC: Brookings Institution.

Marshall, A. 1920. *Principles of economics.* 8th ed. London: Macmillan and Company.

Mason, D.S. 2008. Synecdochic images and city branding. Presented at the Role of Sports and Entertainment Facilities in Urban Development Conference, Edmonton, Alberta, February 12.

McGahey, R., and J.S. Vey, eds. 2008. *Retooling for growth: Building a 21st century economy in America's older industrial areas*. Washington, DC: Brookings Institution.

McGovern, S.J. 2003. Ideology, consciousness, and inner city redevelopment: The case of Stephen Goldsmith's Indianapolis. *Journal of Urban Affairs* 25(1): 1–26.

Mikelbank, B., M. Rosentraub, and C. Post. 2010. Residential property tax abatements and rebuilding in Cleveland, Ohio. State and Local Government Review, 42(2): 104–117.

Misener, L., and D.S. Mason. 2006. Creating community networks: Can sporting events offer meaningful sources of social capital? *Managing Leisure* 11: 39–56.

Molotch, H. 1976. *The city as a growth machine: Toward a political economy of place*. American *Journal of Sociology* 82: 2, 309–332.

Molotch, H. 1979. Capital and neighborhood in the United States: Some conceptual links. *Urban Affairs Quarterly* 14: 289–312.

Molotch, H. 1993. The political economy of growth machines. *Journal of Urban Affairs* 15(1): 29–53.

Montgomery, D. 2008. The engine of change: Reading, Pa. has proven it's deft at switching tracks. As residents head to the polls, the question is: Where to next? *Washington Post*, April 22, C01.

Moret, S., M. Fleming, and P.O. Hovey. 2008. Effective chambers of commerce: A key to regional economic prosperity. In *Retooling for growth: Building a 21st century economy in America's older industrial areas*, ed. R.M. McGahey and J.S. Vey, 119–148. Washington, DC: Brookings Institution.

Money Magazine. 2008. 100 best places to live and launch. http://money.cnn.com/galleries/2008/fsb/0803/gallery.best_places_to_launch.fsb/index.html (accessed September 9, 2008).

Moss, M. and H. O'Neill, 2014. A port authority that works. New York: Rudin Center for Transportation Policy and Management, New York University.

Nelson, A.C. 2002. Locating major league stadiums where they can make a difference. *Public Works Management and Policy* 7(2): 98–114.

Newman, M. 2006. The neighborhood that the ballpark built. *New York Times*, April 26, 10.

Nicholson, M., and R. Hoye, eds. 2008. *Sport and social capital*. London: Elsevier.

Noll, R.G., and A. Zimbalist. 1997. Build the stadium—Create the jobs! In *Sports, jobs, and taxes: The economic impact of sports teams and stadiums*, ed. R.G. Noll and A. Zimbalist, 1–54. Washington, DC: Brookings Institution.

Nowak, J. 2008. The market-building potential of development finance in older industrial cities. In *Retooling for growth: Building a 21st century economy in America's older industrial areas*, ed. R.C. McGahey and J.S. Vey, 373–410. Washington, DC: Brookings Institution.

Paynter, B., and M. Pledger. 2001. Comeback city fights old-shoe image. *Cleveland Plain Dealer*, October 14. http://www.cleveland.com/quietcrisis/index.ssf?/quietcrisis/more/1003059000242700.html (accessed September 10, 2008).

Peck, J. 2005. Struggling with the creative class. *International Journal of Urban and Regional Research* 29(4): 74–770.

Perroux, F. 1955. Note sur la notion de pole de croissance. *Économique Appliquée* 1–2: 307–322.

Pierce, N.R. 2000. Ohio looks hard at what's lost through business subsidies. In *Readings in urban economic issues and public policy*, ed. R.W. Wassner, 151–153. Malden, MA: Blackwell Publishers.

Pine, J., and J.H. Gilmore. 1999. *The experience economy: Work is theatre and every business a stage.* Cambridge, MA: Harvard Business Press.

Porter, M.E. 1985. *Competitive advantage: Creating and sustaining superior performance.* New York: Free Press.

Porter, M.E. 1990. *The competitive advantage of nations.* New York: Free Press.

Porter, P.R., and D. Sweet. 1984. *Rebuilding America's cities: Roads to recovery.* New Brunswick, NJ: Rutgers University, Center for Urban Policy Research.

Potter, D. 2012. *The victor's crown: A history of ancient sport from Homer to Byzantium.* New York: Oxford University Press.

Pramik, M. 2007. City Center might close once Macy's leaves. *Columbus Dispatch*, September 27. http://www.dispatch.com/live/content/local_news/stories/2007/09/27/city_center.html (accessed April 5, 2008).

Reese, L.A., and D. Fasenfest. 2004. *Critical evaluations of economic development policies.* Detroit: Wayne State University Press.

Riley-Katz, A. 2007. Nokia Theatre ready for its close-up: Construction of AEG's $120 million project down-to-wire. *Los Angeles Business Journal*, October 15. http://findarticles.com/p/articles/mi_m5072/is_42_29/ai_n21080011 (accessed March 9, 2008).

Rose, M.M. 2008. Forlorn downtown mall waits. *Columbus Dispatch*, August 1, 1.

Rose, M.M., and M. Pramik. 2009. Goodbye, City Center. *Columbus Dispatch*, February 4, 1.

Rosentraub, M.S. 1997a. *Major league losers: The real cost of sports and who's paying for it.* New York: Basic Books.

Rosentraub, M.S. 1997b. Stadiums and urban space. In *Sports, jobs, and taxes: The economic impact of sports teams and stadiums*, ed. R.G. Noll and A. Zimbalist, 178–207. Washington, DC: Brookings Institution.

Rosentraub, M.S. 1998. *The San Diego Padres and the proposed ballpark and redevelopment plan: An assessment of business, economic, and spatial issues.* San Diego: San Diego Padres Baseball Club.

Rosentraub, M.S. 1999a. Are public policies needed to level the playing field between cities and teams? *Journal of Urban Affairs* 21(4): 377–395.

Rosentraub, M.S. 1999b. *Major league losers: The real cost of sports and who's paying for it.* Rev. ed. New York: Basic Books.

Rosentraub, M.S. 2000. Sports facilities, redevelopment, and the centrality of downtown areas: Observations and lessons from experiences in a rustbelt and sunbelt city. *Marquette University Sports Law Journal* 10(2): 219–236.

Rosentraub, M.S. 2006. The local context of a sports strategy for economic development. *Economic Development Quarterly* 20(3): 278–291.

Rosentraub, M.S., and W. Al-Habil. 2009. Why metropolitan governance is growing as is the need for flexible governments. In *Who will govern metropolitan regions in the 21st century?* ed. D. Phares. Armonk, NY: M.E. Sharpe.

Rosentraub, M.S., and P. Helmke. 1996. Location theory, a growth coalition, and a regime in a medium-sized city. *Urban Affairs Review* 31(4): 482–507.

Rosentraub, M.S., and M. Joo. 2009. Tourism and economic development: Which investments produce gains for regions? *Tourism Management* 30: 759–770.

Rosentraub, M.S., D. Swindell, M. Przybylski, and D. Mullins. 1994. Sports and a downtown development strategy: If you build it, will jobs come? *Journal of Urban Affairs*, 16(3): 221–239.

Rosentraub, M.S., D. Swindell, and S. Tsvetkova. 2009. Justifying public investments in sports: Measuring the intangibles. *Journal of Tourism* 9(2): 133–159.

Rother, C. 2002. Chargers offered to explore dropping ticket guarantee. *San Diego Union Tribune*. www.sandiego.gov/chargerissues/documents/explore.shtml (accessed March 30, 2008).

Rubenstein, H.M. 1992. *Pedestrian malls, streetscapes, and spaces*. New York: John Wiley & Sons.

Saito, L.T. 2007. *Economic revitalization and the community benefits program: A case study of the L.A. Live project, a Los Angeles sports and entertainment district*. Los Angeles: Department of Sociology, University of Southern California.

Sanders, H. 2002. Convention myths and markets: A critical review of convent center feasibility studies. *Economic Development Quarterly* 16(3): 195–210.

Sanders, H. 2005. *Space available: The realities of convention centers as economic development strategy*. Washington, DC: Brookings Institution.

San Diego Union-Tribune. 2004. Change the mix: A vibrant downtown now needs more offices. *San Diego Union-Tribune*, March 31, B8.

Sandy, R.P.J. Sloane, and M.S. Rosentraub, 2004. *The economics of sports: An international perspective*. New York: Palgrave McMillan.

Schneider, K. 2008. A waterfront revival in the Midwest: Home and businesses enliven an old industrial district in Columbus, Ohio. *New York Times*, December 3, B4.

Schoettle, A. 2009. Fieldhouse flop? Pacers: We've lost money 9 of last 10 years. *Indianapolis Business Journal*, February 7. https://www.ibj.com (accessed February 7, 2009).

Schweitzer, M., and B. Rudick. 2007. A closer look at Cleveland's latest poverty ranking. Federal Reserve Bank of Cleveland, Economic Commentary, February 15. http://www.clevelandfed.org/research/commentary/2007/021507.cfm (accessed August 8, 2008).

Scully, G. 1995. *The market structure of sports*. Chicago: University of Chicago Press.

Searle, G. 2002. Uncertain legacy: Sydney's Olympic stadiums. *European Planning Studies* 10(7): 845–860.

Sheban, J. 2004. Rise in urban housing cheered. *Columbus Dispatch*, June 3, 1E.

Sloane, P.J. 1971. The economics of professional football: The football club as a utility maximiser. *Scottish Journal of Political Economy* 18(2): 121–146.

Snider, M. 2008. DVD feels first sting of slipping sales. *USA Today*, January 7. http://www.usatoday.com/life/movies/news/2008-01-07-dvd-sales-slippage_N.htm (accessed January 5, 2008).

Spatz, D. 2008. Reading's two civic centers combine for $164,000 profit. *Reading Eagle*, August 21. https://www.readingeagle.com (accessed September 6, 2008).

Squires, G., ed. 1989. *Unequal partnerships: Political economy of urban redevelopment in postwar America*. New Brunswick, NJ: Rutgers University Press.

Stoffel, J. 1990. New sports complex for Cleveland. *New York Times*, June 13. http://query.nytimes.com/gst/fullpage.html?res=9C0CE2DC1F31F930A25755C0A966958260 (accessed September 9, 2008).

Stolarick, K., and R. Florida. 2006. Creativity, connections and innovation: A study of linkages in the Montreal region. *Environment and Planning A* 38: 1799–1817.

Stone, C. 1989. *Regime politics: Governing Atlanta, 1946–1988*. Lawrence: University of Kansas Press.

Swiatek, J. 2008. A work in progress: Even before designs are finalized, massive JW Marriott project is forging ahead. *Indianapolis Star*, October 5, D1, 4.

Swindell, D. 2000. Issue representation in neighborhood organizations: Questing for democracy at the grassroots. *Journal of Urban Affairs* 22(2): 123–137.

Swindell, D., and M.S. Rosentraub. 2009. Doing better: Sports, economic impact analysis, and schools of public policy and administration. *Journal of Public Administration Education* 15(2): 219–242.

Tiger, C. 2008. See for yourself: A former eyeglass factory brings a Pennsylvania city's vision to life. *American Style*, August, 70–75.

Timmons, A. 2006. Winning on the field and at the ballot box: The effect of the fan base on stadium subsidies. Unpublished public policy thesis, Stanford University, Department of Economics.

Trumpbour, R. 2007. *The new cathedrals: Politics and the media in the history of stadium construction.* Syracuse, NY: Syracuse University Press.

Turner, D. 1995. Police crackdown causes crime rate to plummet in downtown LA. *Los Angeles Business Journal*, April 3. Contained at BNET, http://findarticles.com/p/articles/mi_m5072/is_n14_v17/ai_17015000 (accessed March 10, 2008).

US Airways. 2006. The man with a plan. *US Airways Magazine*, November 2006, 136.

Viles, P. 2008. L.A. land: Downtown blues. *Los Angeles Times*. https://latimesblogs.latimes.com/laland/2008/03/downtown-blues.html.

Vincent, R. 2007. Vacancy rates are falling and rents are rising, giving cause for continued optimism among landlords. *Los Angeles Times*, October 29. www.latimes.com/business/la-fi-office29oct29,0,3718293.story?coll=la-home-business (accessed March 6, 2008).

Vogelsang-Coombs, V. 2007. Mayoral leadership and facilitative governance. *American Review of Public Administration* 37(2): 198–225.

Warren, S. 1994. Disneyfication of the metropolis: Popular resistance in Seattle. *Journal of Urban Affairs* 16(2): 89–108.

Weiner, E. 2004. Sports owners profit from taxpayer deals. *Newsday*, August 3. http://www.commondreams.org/views04/0803–03.htm (accessed June 8, 2008).

Winfree, J., and M.S. Rosentraub. 2012. *Sports finance and management: Real estate, entertainment, and the remaking of the business.* Boca Raton, FL: CRC Press/Taylor & Francis Group.

Williams, J. 2004. Warehouse rejuvenation transformed East Village. *San Diego Union-Tribune*, December 12. http://www.signonsandiego.com/uniontrib/20041212/news_mz1j12buss.html (accessed March 28, 2008).

Wilson, D. 1996. Metaphors, growth coalition discourses, and black poverty neighborhoods in a US city. *Antipode* 28(1): 72–96.

Wilson, J. 1994. *Playing by the rules: Sport, society, and the state.* Detroit: Wayne State University Press.

Wojan, T.R., D.M. Lambert, and A. McGranahan. 2007. Emoting with their feet: Bohemian attraction to creative milieu. *Journal of Economic Geography* 31: 711–736.

Zahniser, D. L.A. LIVE promoters tout Times Square West. *Daily Breeze*, September 18, 2005. http://www.joelkotkin.com/Commentary/DB%20LA%20Live%20promoters%20tout%20Times%20Square%20West.htm.

Zimbalist, A. 2006. *The bottom line: Observations and arguments on the sports business.* Philadelphia: Temple University Press.

Zimbalist, A., and J.G. Long. 2006. Facility finance: Measurement, trends and analysis. *International Journal of Sport Finance* 1: 201–211.

# Index